THE CAMBRIDGE ILLUSTRATED HISTORY OF

China

THE CAMBRIDGE ILLUSTRATED HISTORY OF

China

PATRICIA BUCKLEY EBREY

CAMBRIDGE
UNIVERSITY PRESS

To the memory of

Lloyd Eastman

and

Howard Wechsler

Published by the Press Syndicate of the University of Cambridge
The Pitt Building, Trumpington Street, Cambridge CB2 1RP
40 West 20th Street, New York, NY 10011-4211, USA
10 Stamford Road, Oakleigh, Melbourne 3166, Australia

First published 1996

This book was produced by
CALMANN & KING LTD
71 Great Russell Street,
London WC1B 3BN

Project editor: Damian Thompson
Picture research: Merilyn Thorold, Zhang Shuicheng, Wang Lu, Qiu Xi
Layout: Andrew Shoolbred
Cartography by Hardlines, Charlbury, Oxford

Printed in Italy

A catalogue record for this book is available from the British Library

Library of Congress cataloguing in publication data
Ebrey, Patricia Buckley, 1947–
The Cambridge illustrated history of China / Patricia Buckley Ebrey.
p. cm. — (Cambridge illustrated history)
Includes index.
ISBN 0-521-43519-6
1. China — History. 2.. China — Civilization.
I. Title. II. Series.
DS706.E37 1996
951 — dc20
95-38548
CIP

ISBN 0 521 43519 6 hardback

Contents

Foreword
by Kwang-Ching Liu

Chinese history has often been seen as a mirror image of the history of the West. After the unification of China under the Qin (221–206 BC) and the Han (202 BC–AD 220), successor regimes were overwhelmed, like Rome, by nomadic people of the northern frontiers and by the infusion of a foreign religion. But China, unlike Rome, was to rise again, into a centralized, universal empire under the Tang (618–906). Many of the Han imperial institutions were revived. The aristocracy, powerful since the late Han, still retained its influence, but it recognized a universal sovereign with real authority. Unlike the feudal lords of Europe, the aristocrats in Tang China needed the ranks and titles dispensed by the imperial court to give them prestige required for the protection of their vast landed estates.

From Tang to Song (960–1279) came greater centralization of imperial power and transformation of the aristocracy into a social-bureaucratic elite, of whom an increasing number were products of a mature examination system. The Chinese gentry, a term often used to refer to retired officials in the context of their home communities, essentially identified with the imperial state. With the spread of lineage organizations during the Ming and Qing, Confucian social ethics grew to be recognized as norms on which the government of China depended.

The history of imperial China, a subject of intrinsic interest, gains further fascination with the rise of China as a world power, especially in the 1990s. What can be learned, for example, about Chinese attitudes towards the Muslim world west and northwest of China, especially since the Yuan (Mongol) dynasty (1260–1368)? What lessons are there in the non-existence of a politically active business class despite the growth in long-distance trade and the significant urbanization from the Song through to the twentieth century?

Patricia Buckley Ebrey is our foremost scholar of Chinese family and kinship from the Han to the Song, and has meticulously analysed the cultural and social outlook of the social-bureaucratic elite, both men and women, as well as the capping (coming of age), wedding and funeral rituals prescribed by Song monarchs and philosophers. Editor of a widely used source book, *Chinese Civilization and Society*, she has extended her analysis through the Ming (1368–1644) and Qing (1644–1911) to twentieth-century developments. In calm and refined prose, she brings her vast learning regarding earlier history to bear on China's present, in the belief that continuity in history is inevitable.

The splendid collection of pictures in the following pages displays the results of a painstaking search; the features on aspects of Chinese life (from ceramics to cuisine)and on the lives of distinguished writers add to the volume's appeal. But it is the author's careful and clear synthesis of China's long history that is most remarkable. This book will, in time, I believe, be regarded as a classic.

Preface

A westerner who visits China for the first time is likely to find much that intrigues, surprises, confuses, inspires, or dismays. The sheer number of Chinese is staggering. There are more than a billion Han Chinese – more than the entire population of Eastern and Western Europe and North America put together. How can so many people see themselves as sharing a common culture? Why haven't differences in dialect, religion, or way of life led them to divide up into mutually suspicious groups the way so much of the rest of the world's population has? How can a single government cope with ruling so many people?

Besides being staggered by their numbers, a visitor will also wonder about Chinese as individuals. Men and women observed working in the fields, buying or selling in the markets, doting on their children in parks, enjoying their meals at restaurants: What are their lives like? How has the tumult of the last century affected them and their families? What do they think of China's future?

The Chinese countryside is likely to make a deep impression as well. Throughout China proper (the region historically settled by the people speaking Chinese), land that can be used to grow crops has been treated as too precious to waste on less productive purposes like pasturing animals. Even forested hills that might have provided lumber and firewood have often been cleared and terraced to grow grain. Why have the Chinese turned their earth into a vast garden? What connection is there between Chinese techniques of agriculture and Chinese modes of social organization?

Urban spaces in China also have an unexpected look for a country with such a long history. In Chinese cities, the past does not loom before one in the physical presence of statues of famous generals and statesmen, nor can one search out many old houses, churches, and palaces where great events of the past occurred. Even famous ancient capitals like Xi'an, Luoyang, Nanjing, and Beijing lack visible monuments on the order of those found in Rome, Athens, London, or Paris. Do the Chinese have no heroes of the sorts we are familiar with, or are heroes celebrated a different way?

Within museums, it is true, relics of an older China can be found, but these artefacts raise questions of their own. Ancient masterpieces – bronze ritual vessels, landscape paintings, calligraphy, and porcelains – often seem silent indictments of the visual dreariness of much of contemporary China, raising troubling questions: Has the high point of Chinese culture already passed? Has the cultural link between the past and the present become so attenuated that the two might as well be viewed as different cultures? Those who discover themselves asking these questions may well begin to wonder whether they are being fair: Am I judging the aesthetic attainments of Chinese culture by western, not Chinese, aesthetic standards?

Am I comparing the elite culture of the past to a mass culture of the present? This book was written for those who enjoy pondering these sorts of questions.

China is an extraordinarily complex society that has been in the making for several thousand years, and its present is not comprehensible without an understanding of its past. Contrary to the old western view of China as stagnant or unchanging, as almost without history, the story of how China came to be the huge country we know today is one full of drama. In each period Chinese have made use of what they inherited, but also have come up with new ideas and practices as they have struggled to find meaning or peace, to impose their will or contend with opponents, to survive and thrive, to care for their families and fulfil their duties, in the process creating the society we call China. The present thus is rooted in a complex, multi-layered, dynamic past that always had the potential to develop in ways it did not, meaning that every stage provides an essential part of the story.

One could write a general history of 'greater China', the region of east Asia in which China was the dominant power, much of which is now included within the political borders of the People's Republic of China. Here, however, I have set myself a somewhat smaller task, the history of Chinese civilization, a civilization never confined within well-demarcated borders, but loosely associated with China proper. When neighbours imposed their rule on Chinese populations, my point of reference is the impact of the encounter on the Chinese people and Chinese culture, not the other way around. Although I have narrowed the meaning I give 'China', I have not narrowed it to the Chinese state or the Chinese educated elite. My focus is on the Chinese people and the culture they have created.

Patricia Ebrey

Acknowledgements

This book owes most of its ideas to others. Everything I have learned during nearly thirty years studying Chinese history has had some influence on the shape and content of this book. Still, I did not write it with my desk clear, trying to distil from memory what I knew of the course of Chinese history, but with a desk continually overflowing with books and articles. I re-read many pieces I vaguely recalled as trenchant or stimulating. I looked through – and sometimes became totally engrossed in – books I had purchased over the years but never before found enough time actually to read. Many of the books I drew from have been included in the 'Suggestions for Further Reading', but that list by no means exhausts my intellectual debts, because I also relied on specialized studies not written for a general audience. I hope that authors who recognize places where I have adopted their interpretations will feel pleased that I was persuaded by their evidence and arguments rather than annoyed that they receive no credit. Certainly my debt to them is very great.

Part of the pleasure of preparing this book was getting to pore over a great many wonderful art and archaeology publications in search of good illustrations. As I tried to narrow down my choices, I showed my preliminary selections to other China specialists, and often received excellent advice in return. I would particularly like to acknowledge the advice of Wu Hong, Ellen Laing, Joseph McDermott, and Jessica Rawson, each of whom had many suggestions to make. I am equally indebted to colleagues who have generously read and commented on one or more chapters, including Roger Ames, Alan Baumler, Zong-qi Cai, Kai-wing Chow, John Dardess, Peter Gregory, Emily Hill, and David Keightley. For assistance with the mechanics of preparing this book, I would like to thank three graduate research assistants, supported at different times by funds from the University of Illinois's Research Board. Yao Ping helped bring order to the selection of illustrations; and Kathy Battles and Samantha Blum both helped with the preparation of reference materials and related chores. Finally I am also grateful to Professor K. C. Liu for reading through the entire manuscript as advisory editor and for contributing a foreword.

I have dedicated this book to two historians of China who formerly were my colleagues at the University of Illinois. Writing this book made me miss them all the more, for often I stopped to think how they would have treated an issue.

CHAPTER 1

The Origins of Chinese Civilization:
Neolithic Period to the Western Zhou Dynasty (to 771 BC)

Most peoples have myths about their origins, and the Chinese are no exception. Through most of the imperial period, literate Chinese had a 'great man' theory of how their civilization developed. Unlike other peoples who pointed to gods as their creators or progenitors, the Chinese attributed to a series of extraordinarily brilliant human beings the inventions that step by step transformed the Chinese from a primitive people to a highly civilized one. Fu Xi, the Ox-tamer, domesticated animals and invented the family. Shen Nong, the Divine Farmer, invented the plough and hoe. Huang Di, the Yellow Lord, invented the bow and arrow, boats, carts, ceramics, writing, and silk. He also fought a great battle against alien tribes, thus securing the Yellow River plain for his people. In China's earliest history, he was labelled the first of the five great pre-dynastic rulers, the last two of whom were Yao and Shun. Yao was credited with devising the calendar and rituals. Rather than hand over power to his own less worthy son, he selected Shun as his successor, a poor peasant whose filial piety had been demonstrated by his devoted service to his blind father and evil stepmother. Shun not only became the next ruler but also married two of Yao's daughters. Despite their virtue, even Yao and Shun were unable to prevent floods, so Shun appointed an official, Yu, to tackle this problem. For over a decade Yu travelled through the land, dredging the channels that became the rivers of north China. So zealous was he that he passed his own home several times without pausing to greet his wife and children. Shun named Yu to succeed him. Yu divided the realm into nine regions, and had bronze vessels cast to represent each one. When Yu died, the people ignored the successor he had chosen and turned to Yu's son to lead them, establishing the precedent of hereditary, dynastic rule. Yu and his son thus were the first two kings of the Xia dynasty, a dynasty which lasted through fourteen rulers. It was overthrown when King Jie, a tyrant, was deposed by a subordinate who founded his own dynasty, the Shang. This dynasty in turn lasted through thirty rulers until a self-indulgent and obstinate king lost the support of his nobles and people, making it easy for the armies of Zhou to come from the west to overthrow the Shang. The Zhou became the last of the three ancient dynasties (Xia, Shang, and Zhou).

These legends reveal how educated Chinese from the time of Confucius (c.500 BC) onwards constructed 'China'. To them China was defined by technology and statecraft – agriculture, writing, flood control, monarchy combining virtue and

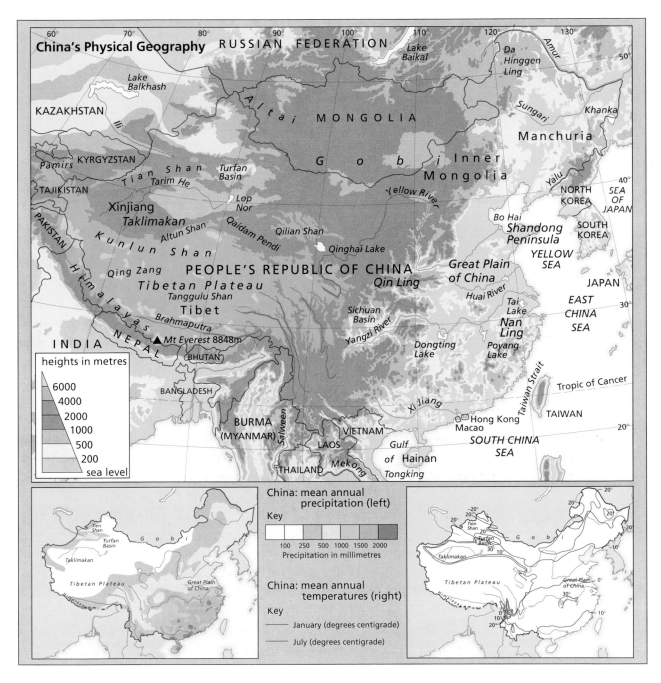

China's Physical Geography

China: mean annual precipitation (left)

Key

100 250 500 1000 1500 2000
Precipitation in millimetres

China: mean annual temperatures (right)

Key

— January (degrees centigrade)
— July (degrees centigrade)

heights in metres

6000
4000
2000
1000
500
200
sea level

Chinese civilization has throughout history had a strong association with agriculture. The earliest stages of Chinese culture developed in river valleys in which crops could be cultivated even with primitive techniques. Over time these early settlements spread broadly within the more temperate regions of eastern Eurasia.

hereditary succession, and so on. They recorded the story of China as a single-stranded narrative or genealogy, centred on a succession of rulers; China's past was thus much like the past of a family that could be traced back through a single line of ancestors one before the other.

Modern scholars, drawing on knowledge of geology, paleoanthropology, and archaeology, not surprisingly construct very different stories of the origins of Chinese civilization. Their accounts do not slight agriculture, writing, bronze technology, and state formation, but usually differ from the traditional story in giving more weight to the role of ritual and religion in shaping the significant characteristics of Chinese culture. Equally important, they do not see Chinese history as a single-stranded story, centred on a royal line, but a many-stranded one in which a great many distinguishable cultures interacted, some of which would undoubtedly have been labelled alien by the Shang or Zhou rulers. By influencing each others' development, these cultures all participated in the evolution of Chinese civilization.

THE GEOGRAPHY OF THE CHINESE SUBCONTINENT

Chinese civilization developed in a particular geographical setting, the more temperate zones of eastern Eurasia, an area large and diverse enough to open many possibilities to early occupants but not without imposing some constraints as well. China proper extends over 1,000 miles north to south and east to west; the distance from Beijing in the north to Guangzhou in the south is about that from Bangor to Miami, or Oslo to Barcelona; the distance from Chengdu in the west to Shanghai in the east is almost as great as that from Paris to Warsaw or Des Moines to New York. This huge expanse of land is interlaced with mountain ranges, which separate the more habitable river valleys from each other. It was in these river valleys that the first human settlements were established.

Two great river systems flow east through China proper, the Yellow River in the north and the Yangzi River in the centre. The Yellow River rises in the far western highlands, makes sharp turns through the northern deserts, then flows swiftly from north to south through a hilly area of loess – fine, wind-driven yellow earth that is fertile and easy to work even with primitive tools. At the southern end of the loess highlands, the Yellow River turns abruptly eastward and spreads out, yellow with silt, between banks a mile or more apart. Finally it traverses the whole of the alluvial plain and empties into the sea. The other great river, the Yangzi, takes in the water of many tributaries and carries a much greater volume of water. It rises in Tibetan highlands, crosses the mountains encircling the Sichuan basin, moves through magnificent gorges with sheer cliffs a thousand or more feet in height, then flows eastward a thousand miles to the sea, each day delivering an average of half a cubic mile of water into the Pacific Ocean.

The regions drained by these two rivers differ in soil, topography, temperature, and rainfall. The north is colder, flatter, and more arid; its growing season is shorter and its soil more alkaline, making it best suited to crops like wheat and millet. North of the Yellow River, rainfall is frequently too light for unirrigated agriculture; in many areas it averages less than 20 inches a year. Flood and drought recur with much greater frequency than in the south. The Yellow River is prone to flooding because as it flows though the loess regions of the northwest, it collects silt which is gradually dropped as the river makes its way east and the current slows. Because the silt builds up the height of the river bed, over the centuries, farmers and government forces constructed dykes to keep the river in its course, a practice that made floods, when they occurred, that much more destructive, inundating huge regions.

The region drained by the Yangzi River is warmer and wetter than the north. Most of it stays green all year and receives more than 60 inches of rainfall annually, making it well suited to rice cultivation and to double-cropping. The Yangzi and many of the numerous small rivers crisscrossing the south are navigable, making the south a land suited to boat travel. In the north, by contrast, until modern times people travelled by land, on foot, on the backs of horses or donkeys, or in carts drawn by animals.

Large stretches of land ill-suited to crop agriculture separated the Chinese subcontinent from Mesopotamia and the Indus Valley, the nearest sites of other early civilizations. Beyond China proper to the north is the steppe or grasslands of Inner Asia, a region even colder and more arid than north China, where animal husbandry is a more productive use of land than planting crops. Inner Asia was never populated primarily by Chinese; instead it was the home of nomadic pastoralists, such as the Xiongnu and Mongols, China's traditional enemies. These steppes extend across Eurasia to the Ukraine, but China proper is cut off from these steppe lands on the northwest by vast deserts where nothing grows except in rare oases. South of these deserts and directly west of south and central China is Tibet, the 'roof of the world', whose high mountains were as unsuited to Chinese farming life as the deserts and grasslands to the north. The mountainous regions southeast of Tibet (modern Yunnan and Guizhou provinces) were not quite so impassable, but by the time there was much reason to cross through them into south and southeast Asia, travelling by sea had become the more practical option.

To see the Chinese subcontinent as early Chinese saw it, we must erase from our minds all the maps we have seen showing it to occupy only a small fraction of the landmass of Eurasia, and far to one side at that. The Chinese subcontinent is so vast that by the first millennium BC the Chinese thought of it as All-Under-Heaven (*tianxia*), the entire earthly stage on which human beings acted out the drama of civilization. Surrounding it were vast oceans, wild deserts, steep mountains – regions much less central to the project of civilization. How far they extended, no one knew for sure. But the location of the centre of civilization was not in doubt.

The Yellow River, shown here, acquired its name because the silt it carries gives it a muddy look. The earth of the north China plain is predominantly wind-borne and river-borne loess soil, which led early Chinese also to think of the earth as yellow.

The well-watered hills and valleys of south China offer a much lusher landscape than the colder, drier north.

The geometric designs on the pots of the Yangshao culture (c. 3200–2500 BC) often evolved from images of birds, fish, frogs, and other animals that may originally have had totemic significance. The assemblage of painted pottery depicted here captures the variety of the geometric designs that resulted, but does not show how the pots were used, since no grave had so many pots placed together.

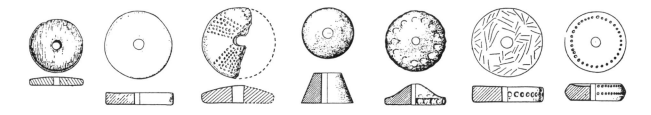

The first sign of textile production is the appearance of spindle whorls like these ones found at Hemudu, near Shanghai, which date from about 5000 BC. These wooden and ceramic whorls were used to put a twist in hemp yarn, making it strong enough to use in weaving.

PREHISTORY

Early human beings, called *Homo erectus*, appeared on the Chinese subcontinent over a million years ago, having gradually spread from Africa and west Asia during the Pleistocene geological era (the Ice Age). Even though no major glaciers extended into China, the average temperature was colder than in subsequent ages, and mammoth, elk, and moose roamed north China. Peking Man, discovered in the 1920s, is one of the best-documented examples of *Homo erectus*. He could stand erect, hunt, make fire, and use chipped stones as tools.

Modern human beings (*Homo sapiens*) appeared in East Asia around 100,000 years ago, probably also spreading from somewhere in Africa. During the long paleolithic period (Old Stone Age, c.100,000 to 10,000 BC) of predatory hunters and gatherers that followed, humans began to speak. Language expanded symbolic capabilities, allowing the development of notions of gods and kinship, for instance. Over the course of these thousands of years, we can reasonably assume that many bands of people migrated across the Chinese subcontinent, fighting with each other when threatened, splitting up or merging when survival dictated. Some early bands moved on to the Pacific islands or the Americas. In what sense

This finely made stone grinder, about 20 by 8 inches, was unearthed at the site of a neolithic village in Cishan, Hebei province, and dates from no later than 5000 BC. Stone tools were used in food processing even before crops were cultivated; this one was probably used to crush the stalks of uncultivated vegetables to make them more digestible.

any of those that spent time in the Chinese subcontinent should be considered ancestral to the historic Chinese is largely a matter of speculation.

Distinctly Chinese history, therefore, begins much later, after the end of the last ice age in about 10,000 BC. By 5000 BC neolithic cultures with agriculture, pottery, villages, and textiles had emerged in many of the river valleys of today's China. Agriculture was undoubtedly the key change, facilitated by climatic change towards warmer and wetter weather (warmer and wetter even than today). Cultivating crops allows denser and more permanent settlements. Pottery and textiles make life much more comfortable: pottery jars are excellent for transporting water and storing grain; cloth made into clothing and bedding provide protection against cold. Tending crops, weaving textiles, and fashioning pots require different sorts of technical and social skills than hunting, so warriors probably had to share leadership with skilled and experienced elders. At the same time permanent settlements brought new forms of social organization; a territorial unit, the village supplemented kinship-based forms of organization.

Ignoring later historical legends and examining only material remains, these neolithic cultures can be divided by latitude into the southern rice zone and the northern millet zone. In the Yangzi valley rice was cultivated as early as 5000 BC, supplemented with fish and aquatic plants such as lotus, water chestnut, and caltrop. At Hemudu, a site south of Shanghai, neolithic villagers built wooden houses on stilts and made lacquered bowls and blackish pottery with incised geometric designs. Basketry and weaving were highly developed; residents left behind spindle whorls used to twist yarns and shuttles used in weaving. Other wooden tools included hoes, spears, mallets, and paddles. The technological level of the Hemudu villagers, in other words, was already higher than that of most North American Indian tribes in the seventeenth century.

North China was too cold and dry for rice; the cereal that became the foundation of agriculture there was instead millet. In Cishan, a site in Hebei dating to before 5000 BC, millet was cut with stone sickles and stored in crude pottery bowls, jars, and tripods (three-legged pots), often decorated with cord or comb impressions. The loess soil common in north China made cultivation relatively easy for primitive farmers as it was easily worked and its loose structure allowed fresh nutrients to rise to the surface. In both north and south, the domestication of animals accompanied the domestication of plants. Dogs and pigs were found in both areas as early as 5000 BC, and by 3000 BC sheep and cattle had become important in the north, water buffalo and cattle in the south.

In addition to this north–south division on the basis of subsistence technology, Chinese neolithic cultures can be roughly divided east–west on the basis of artistic styles and burial practices. In the west, in the Yangshao culture area (primarily Shaanxi and Gansu provinces from about 5000 to 3000 BC) burials were generally simple and pottery was often decorated with painted geometrical designs. Grain jars decorated in the fully developed Yangshao style were exuberantly painted in

This stemmed cup excavated from Taian, Shandong province, has extremely thin walls, as thin as an eggshell. Such finely made black pottery is a distinctive feature of Dawenkou culture (c. 2300 BC).

red and black with spirals, diamonds, and other geometric patterns. The range of shapes, however, was relatively limited, confined mostly to utilitarian jars and urns. By contrast, in the east, over an area extending from Liaoning province to Shanghai, pottery was rarely painted, but more elaborate forms appeared very early, including tripods and pedestalled bowls and cups. The finest wares, formed on the potter's wheel, were thin-walled with a burnished surface almost metallic in appearance. Many forms were constructed by combining parts, adding legs, spouts, handles, or lids. The frequent appearance of ewers and goblets in this region suggests rituals of feasting or sacrifice. Also in the east burials gradually became more elaborate. At one site, Dawenkou in Shandong province, some of the dead were buried in coffins and occasionally a wooden chamber was built to line the burial pit, giving a further layer of protection. The richest graves at this site contained fifty, sixty, or even well over a hundred objects, including, for instance, necklaces and bracelets made of jade, stone, or pottery beads. One unusual feature of the Dawenkou culture is that many people had their upper lateral incisors extracted, a practice Chinese authors in much later times considered barbarian.

Even more distinctive of the eastern cultures is their investment in the production of finely worked jade. Jade is a very hard stone, formed when the crystals of

Jade object with a snake- or dragon-like body and pig-like snout, 6 $\frac{1}{2}$ inches long, excavated at Sanguan Dianzi in Liaoning province (Hongshan culture, c. 3500 BC). Neolithic villagers, using sand or other abrasives, would have had to devote many days to fashioning this small ornament or talisman.

Left. The most spectacular neolithic jade discoveries are from the Liangzhu culture (c. 3300–2250 BC). This grave excavated at Sidun in Jiangsu province contained long rows of twenty-five *cong* (tubes with cylindrical bores and squared sides) and thirty-three *bi* (discs). Archaeologists speculate that the individual buried there was a priest interred with the treasures he used in ceremonies.

Below. Skill at precise measurement and planning was needed to achieve the highly regular motifs on the jade *cong* found at Liangzhu. The prominent eyes and symmetrical design on this 2¾-inch-tall *cong* tube, excavated at Sidun, Jiangsu province, suggest connections with the famous *taotie* design found on bronzes a thousand years later.

rocks have been crushed over millions of years to make a matted configuration of molecules. As jade does not split or fracture easily, to shape it requires grinding with abrasive sand in a slow, labour-intensive process. The most spectacular discoveries of neolithic jades are from the Hongshan culture of Liaoning province (c.3500 BC) and the Liangzhu culture of Jiangsu province (c.2500 BC) – areas that even two thousand years later were not considered fully 'Chinese'. In the Hongshan area, jade was made into ornaments and small figurines of turtles, birds, and strange coiled 'pig dragons'. Some of these figurines were found at sites of stone ritual structures, suggesting that they had symbolic or religious meanings. In the Liangzhu area as well, jade was fashioned into ritual objects, and hundreds of *bi* (disks) and *cong* (columns) have been excavated. A couple thousand years later *bi* and *cong* were still used in rituals and were considered to have cosmological significance, the circles and squares representing heaven and earth respectively. Elsewhere in the eastern half of China jade objects were not so distinctive, but jade axes, presumably used for ritual purposes, have been widely found.

The late neolithic period (c.3000–2000 BC) was a time of increased contact between these regional cultures. Pottery shapes and designs spread into new areas; cooking tripods, for instance, spread west, while geometric decoration spread east. It was also a time of increased conflict between communities. Metal began to be used on a small scale for weapons, and in the north China plain walled settlements appeared. The wall at Chengziyai in Shandong province is estimated to have been 20 feet high and 29 feet thick. Enclosing a settlement with such a wall of rammed earth no doubt required the ability to coordinate labour and thus also indicates advances in social organization – by this time there must have been chiefs capable of commanding men and resources in considerable quantity. Another sign of the power of religious or military elites was the appearance of human sacrifice. By 2000 BC, human remains were being buried under the foundations of major buildings in the north China plain. Sacrificing captives may have been seen as a way of pleasing ancestors or gods; it probably also strengthened the political power of the elites who wielded the power of life and death so dramatically. Social differentiation also was expressed in burials. In one large cemetery in southern Shanxi province with over a thousand graves, nine individuals were given elaborate burials, with wooden coffins and over a hundred grave goods each, including musical instruments, jades, and jugs. Some eighty medium-sized graves had similar objects in smaller numbers. More than 600 graves were simple burials with neither coffins nor grave goods.

Even as late as 2000 BC, neolithic communities in the Chinese subcontinent were probably as varied as they were in North America before Europeans arrived: a great many languages were undoubtedly spoken, some related and some not; shamans were probably powerful in some tribes, unknown in others; it seems likely that warfare dominated life in some times and in some places but not so much in others. Although archaeologists have identified features of these cultures

Ancestors

The practice of burying the dead with containers of food and drink or other objects needed by the living was in historical times associated with beliefs about the mutual dependency of the living and their dead ancestors. The dead needed the living to supply them with offerings in the tomb and also through sacrifices after burial, while the living needed to please their ancestors so that they would protect them or at least not do them harm. Neolithic burials incorporating both utilitarian containers for food and drink and precious objects like jade and cowry shells suggest that such beliefs go back to prehistory. The earliest definite evidence of these beliefs can be found on the oracle bone inscriptions of the late Shang period.

Shang kings communicated with their ancestors through sacrificial rituals and through divination. The most common technique of divination involved the diviner applying a glowing metal poker or other heat source to turtle shell or cattle shinbone. The resulting heat-stress crack was interpreted as an auspicious, inauspicious, or neutral response to a question or statement that the diviner had posed. Inscriptions on these oracle bones show that ancestors were often asked about sacrificial offerings, for instance whether an offering of a cow would be appropriate. Ancestors could be asked other questions as well, such as whether they were causing the king's toothache or dream. There were spiritual forces separate from ancestors – especially Di, the Lord on High, who could grant bountiful harvests, lend divine assistance in battle, send rain, thunder, wind, drought, or epidemics. But to communicate with these forces, the king regularly called on his ancestors to act as intermediaries.

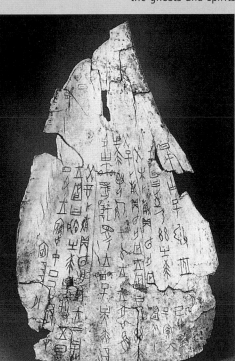

Inscribed cattle scapula excavated at Anyang. The king Wu Ding (c. 1250 BC) had this bone used several times to make predictions (such as 'in the next ten days there will be no disasters') and to record what actually happened after the divinations had been made. Among the events recorded were a death and a hunting accident.

Ancestors were no less central to the religious imagination in Western Zhou times. Bronzes were often inscribed with reports to ancestors detailing the achievements of their descendants. The *Book of Documents* portrays the Duke of Zhou as having a deep belief in the power of the Zhou royal ancestors to affect the welfare of both their descendants and the whole country. When his brother the king was ill, the duke performed an open-air ceremony, addressing his ancestors and offering to give up his own life to serve his ancestors in the netherworld if they would spare the king: 'Take me as a substitute for the king. I was kind and obedient to my father. I have many talents and skills and can serve the ghosts and spirits.' If this text accurately reflects early Zhou belief, family ethics and the ancestral cult were already merged: ancestral rites had a moral cast, reflecting notions of filial piety of sons towards fathers, and patterns of authority within the family had a religious cast, as parent–child relations would in time become ancestor–descendant ones.

Sacrificial odes in the *Book of Songs* portray ancestral rites in early Zhou aristocratic circles as emotionally charged rituals of great symbolic power. The ancestor was represented by a human impersonator, often a grandson, who acted as a medium so that the ancestral spirit could be present among those sacrificing to him. The impersonator was offered many glasses of wine, presented the best available food, and entertained with singing and dancing. The descendants, by joining the feast, were in communion with the ancestor present in the body of the impersonator. The odes often imply reciprocity: because the rites are performed meticulously and without mistake, the ancestors confer long life and many descendants.

that persisted into later times, it would be misleading to think of them all simply as proto-Chinese.

THE SHANG DYNASTY

Some time soon after 2000 BC there emerged out of the diverse neolithic cultures in the north China plain a more complex bronze-age civilization marked by writing, metal-working, domestication of the horse, class stratification, and a stable political-religious hierarchy administering a large territory from a cult center. The earliest stages of this transition are traditionally associated with the Xia dynasty. Since no site that might possibly be Xia has yielded written documents, it is still

The abrupt appearance of the light, spoke-wheeled war chariot in about 1200 BC suggests contact with bearers of Indo-European culture – similar chariots with large, many-spoked wheels had been in use in the Caucasus for several centuries. Chariots came to play such an important role as symbols of rulership in late Shang and Zhou warfare that they were sometimes buried with their owners in their graves. This burial pit, unearthed at Liulihe in Hebei province and dating from the Western Zhou period, contains the remains of horses and chariots.

uncertain whether or not there was a fully fledged Xia dynasty before the Shang (c. 1600–c. 1050), but there was, without doubt, a major transition in this period of Chinese history. From this point on, organized political entities become crucial elements in the story of China. And a literate elite associated with the polity begins to give us their version of what is important by producing the documents that colour how we see all beyond them – not only other peoples they considered to be alien, but also other elements in their own society, ranging from slaves to rival elites.

The Shang state did not control a very large part of China proper – their domain probably did not even encompass all of Henan, Anhui, Shandong, Hebei, and Shanxi provinces. The influence of Shang culture, however, extended far beyond its territorial limits, with its technology and decorative motifs adapted by peoples throughout the Yangzi valley. The Shang was said to have had five successive capitals, and several large settlements of Shang date have been discovered, including Zhengzhou, possibly an early cult centre, and Anyang, from which the Shang kings ruled for more than two centuries. Shang civilization was not as densely urban as that of Mesopotamia, but these cult centres were large and com-

This tomb (number 1001) of a Shang king is one of eleven large tombs and over a thousand small graves excavated at Anyang, all of which are oriented north–south. Although this tomb was robbed in ancient times, perhaps even by the Zhou invaders, when excavated it contained numerous stone, jade, shell, bone, antler, tooth, bronze, and pottery artefacts. As the pit is more than 300 feet long and 60 feet deep, moving the earth to create the tomb must have required a huge mobilization of labour.

Headless skeletons of human sacrificial victims in tomb 1001 at Anyang. Textual evidence of the practice of human sacrifice has been confirmed by discoveries of clearly aligned headless skeletons like these. The heads were found elsewhere in the same tomb.

plex. At their core were large palaces, temples, and altars constructed on rammed-earth foundations, in one case 26 by 92 feet in size. Surrounding the central core were industrial areas occupied by bronze workers, potters, stone carvers, and other artisans. Further out were small houses built partly below ground level and, beyond them, burial grounds.

The inscribed oracle bones found at Anyang present a picture of an embattled central power, allied with some local powers and at war with others. The king sent out armies of 3,000 to 5,000 men on campaigns. Over time vassals became enemies and enemies became allies. War booty provided the king with resources: captives could be made into slaves or slaughtered as sacrificial victims. Even though agricultural technology had not advanced much since pre-Shang times, military technology had. Bronze-tipped spears and halberds, composite bows, and horse-drawn chariots provided significant advantages in warfare to the warrior elite who possessed them. Chariots came into use around 1200 BC, probably as a result of diffusion from western Asia. Pulled by two or four horses, the chariot allowed commanders to supervise their troops and gave archers and soldiers armed with long halberds more mobility. Chariots were also used in royal hunts, grand outings *cum* military exercises that might last months. Deer, bears, tigers, wild boars, elephants, and rhinoceroses were plentiful, indicating that there was considerable forest cover in the north China plain.

Shang kingship, however, was not based simply on military supremacy, but was firmly grounded in religion and ritual. The Shang king played a priestly role in the worship of the high god Di and the royal ancestors, a role that justified his political powers. To put this another way, it was because among the dead his ancestors were best able to communicate with Di and because among the living he was best able to communicate with his ancestors that the king was fitted to rule. Given the importance of the royal ancestral cult, it is not surprising that patrilineal principles also governed succession to the throne: kingship passed from elder to younger brother and father to son, but never to or through sisters or daughters.

To discover his ancestors' wishes, the king employed professional diviners to prepare the bones used in divinations, but he himself interpreted the meaning of the heat-induced cracks. Many of the predictions the king made sound almost like magical incantation or prayers – 'It will rain', or 'During the next ten days there will be no disasters.' The king also played a priestly role during his frequent travels through the realm, for he often stopped to make sacrifices to local spirits.

As in many other societies, both animals and human beings were sacrificed to royal ancestors and to various nature gods. The principles underlying sacrifice, in China and elsewhere, are reciprocity and feeding: one makes offerings to those from whom one wants help, and one feeds rich foods to the god or ancestor to keep him strong. Shang kings frequently offered sacrifices of human beings, sometimes dozens at a time. Subordinates would also voluntarily 'accompany' a superior in death, showing that they felt obligations tantamount to servitude to those above them. At the early or middle Shang royal burials at Zhengzhou, one, two, or three sacrificial victims were often buried between the inner and outer coffin chambers or on the roof of the outer chamber. By the late Shang, many more people accompanied the rulers into their graves. Tomb 1001 at Anyang, which may be for the king who reigned about 1200 BC, has yielded the remains of ninety followers who accompanied him in death, seventy-four human sacrifices, twelve horses, and eleven dogs. These victims were placed in the shaft, ledges, and ramps. Some followers were provided with coffins and bronze ritual vessels or weapons of their own, some (generally female) with no coffins but with personal ornaments; others were provided with no furnishings and were beheaded, cut in two, or put to death in other mutilating ways.

The vast tombs of the royal family are one sign of the ability of the Shang rulers to mobilize human and material resources. Thousands of labourers had to be assembled to dig huge holes up to 40 feet deep, construct massive wooden burial chambers, and then fill in the site with layers of rammed earth. This ability to mobilize labour clearly predated the move to Anyang; the enormous city walls of Zhengzhou, which were 60 feet wide, 30 feet high, and 2,385 feet long, would have taken ten to twenty years to complete, even with 10,000 labourers working to move and ram the earth.

WRITING

The modern Chinese writing system evolved from the script employed by diviners in the Shang period.

The organizational capabilities of the Shang government probably should be credited in part to the perfection of a system of writing. In China, as elsewhere, writing, once adopted, has profound effects on social and cultural processes. Exactly when writing was first used in China is not known since most writing would have been done on perishable materials like wood, bamboo, or silk. Symbols or

ox	goat, sheep	tree	moon	earth	water	tripot vessel (ring)	To show, declare	field (showing divisions)	then (men and bowl)	ancestor (phallus)	to go against, towards	heaven	to pray
屮	𦍋	朿	𝟚	𝟙	巛	鼎	示	田	就	祖	屰	大	祝
牛	羊	木	月	土	水	鼎	示	田	就	祖	逆	天	祝

Lady Hao's tomb

The ancient Chinese did not invest in the construction of stone monuments; there are no Chinese equivalents of the pyramids, the Palace of Minos, or the Parthenon to make later visitors ponder their greatness. What comes closest in terms of expenditure and desire for permanence are the vast tombs of the Shang royal family, the splendours of which were carefully hidden from public view underground.

The only royal Shang tomb never to have been robbed before it was excavated is tomb 5 at Anyang for Lady Hao (c.1250 BC). One of the smaller tombs (about 13 by 18 feet at the mouth and about 25 feet deep), and not in the main royal cemetery, it was nonetheless filled with an extraordinary array of sacrificial goods.

Human sacrifice is evident (the sixteen human skeletons include both males and females, children and adults), but not on as great a scale as some of the larger tombs. Rather it is the burial of a profusion of valuable objects that is the most striking feature of this burial, suggesting almost potlatch-like conspicuous destruction. In this tomb were 460 bronze objects (including more than 130 weapons, 23 bells, 27 knives, 4 mirrors, and 4 tigers or tiger heads), nearly 750 jade objects, some 70 stone sculptures, nearly 500 bone hairpins, over 20 bone arrowheads, and 3 ivory carvings. In addition, there were nearly 6,900 cowry shells, possibly evi-

dence that these shells were used for money. Most of these items are distinctly metropolitan in style; others may have been sent from distant places as tribute.

The 200-odd bronze vessels constitute the largest and most complete set of ritual vessels unearthed from a Shang

emblems inscribed on late neolithic pots may be early forms of Chinese graphs. Early Shang bronzes sometimes have similar symbols cast into them. The earliest evidence of full sentences is found on the oracle bones of the late Shang. From these divinatory inscriptions, there can be no doubt that the Shang used a language directly ancestral to modern Chinese and moreover used a written script that evolved into the standard Chinese logographic writing system still in use today. Of the thousand-odd characters that have been deciphered, some are pictographs that visually represent a thing or an idea, some are borrowed for their sounds, and others were created by combining two characters, one giving meaning, the other sound. In China, as elsewhere, with writing comes list-making and efforts to organize thoughts that facilitate higher-order mental processes of abstraction and theorizing. In Shang times, one sign of such complex cognitive organization is the use of two sequencing systems, one based on ten and the other on twelve. The cycle of ten was used to label days in the ten-day week, and a combination of the two was used to produce a sixty-day cycle.

grave. More then twenty types are represented, including goblets, tripods, and basins. Vessels for holding wine predominate, suggesting that as a last step at the funeral ceremonies mourners made a libation of wine and tossed in the wine cup as well as the wine. Some sixty bronze vessels have Lady Hao's name inscribed on them. Striking among them are ones in the form of real animals, possibly reflecting influence from the south where similar forms had been produced earlier.

The artefacts in this tomb do not provide much evidence of what Lady Hao was like as a person. Probably she is the same Lady Hao mentioned in many oracle bone inscriptions as one of the many wives of the king Wu Ding (c.1200 BC). The king made divinations concerning her illnesses and pregnancies. From these inscriptions we also know that she took charge of certain rituals and had a landed estate outside the capital. She even led military campaigns, once with 13,000 troops against the Qiang to the west, at other times against the Fu Fang in the northwest, the Ba Fang in the southwest, and the Yi in the east.

The 2¾-inch jade figure (*left*) and the nearly foot-tall ivory wine cup inlaid with torquoise (*right*) were both among the goods in Lady Hao's tomb. The figure kneels in the formal posture adopted in China before the chair came into common use more than 2,000 years later.

It is essentially accidental that the Shang developed a logographic script rather than a phonetic script like most of those that became dominant elsewhere in Eurasia. This accident, however, had momentous consequences for the way Chinese civilization developed. It shaped the nature of the elite: the difficulty of mastering this script made those expert in it an elite possessed of rare but essential skills. Because the Chinese logographic script did not change to reflect differences in pronunciation, the literate elite easily identified with others whose writings they could read, including predecessors who lived many centuries earlier and contemporaries whose spoken languages they could not comprehend. Just as crucially, this script also affected the processes of cultural expansion and assimilation. People on the fringes of Chinese culture who learned to read Chinese for pragmatic reasons of advancing or defending their interests were more effectively drawn into Chinese culture than they would have been if China had had a phonetic script. Reading and writing for them could not be easily detached from the body of Chinese texts imbued with Chinese values, making it difficult for them to use their literacy to articulate the vision of a local population defined in opposition to China.

BRONZES

As in other parts of the world, the development of more complex forms of social organization in Shang China was tied to perfecting metal-working techniques. Ways to smelt metal ores were probably discovered in China as a by-product of the use of high-temperature kilns for ceramic production. The earliest-known bronze vessels date from about 1700–1600 BC, and were found at Erlitou, in

Cultural spheres. The cultural influence of the two great states of Bronze Age China, the Shang (c.1600–1050 BC) and the Western Zhou (c. 1050–771 BC) extended from the Yellow River valley into the Yangzi River valley. In neolithic times distinct cultures had emerged in many regions of the Chinese subcontinent, but by the third millennium BC borrowing had become so extensive that this central China region had already become a sphere of interacting cultures.

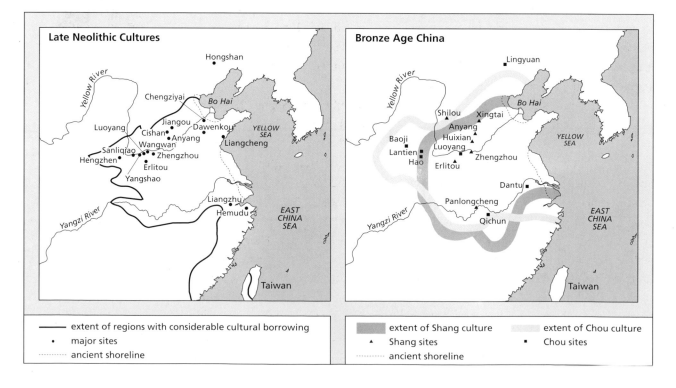

Henan province, a region associated with the Xia dynasty. The extreme thinness of some of the vessels found there (in one case only 1 mm thick), coupled with features of their shapes, such as sharp angles and crimped edges, suggest the possibility of imitation of sheet-metal prototypes. But bronzes steadily got larger and heavier, and by late Shang times huge bronze vessels were produced, some weighing more than 200 pounds.

The great bulk of the surviving bronze objects are cups, goblets, steamers, and cauldrons, beautifully shaped and decorated, in a great variety of shapes and sizes, presumably made for use in sacrificial rituals. Some distinctive neolithic pottery forms, such as tripods, were reproduced in Shang bronzes, showing links between the artistic tradition of the Shang and the previous cultures of the area. The complexity of design of Shang bronzes was achieved through mould casting and prefabrication. Thus legs, handles, and other protruding members were cast first and then the body was cast on to them.

The bronze vessels produced in Shang China reveal much about Shang culture and society. Thousands of Shang bronzes survive today, and we know from excavations that as many as 200 vessels could be interred in a single grave. Their numbers testify to the willingness of the Shang elite to devote huge quantities of a valued resource to ritual uses. The production of such quantities of bronzes also provides further evidence of the organizational capacity of the Shang rulers, for they had to mobilize men and material to mine, transport, and refine the ores, to manufacture and tool the clay models, cores, and moulds used in the casting process and to run the foundries. Additionally, the history of the decoration on Shang bronzes provides evidence of the dynamics of cultural change during Shang times. The animal mask or *taotie* was the predominant decoration throughout, but its appearance changed markedly over time (see pages 36–37). Moreover, in some periods patrons were more open to borrowing new forms from their neighbours; at other times they turned back to old forms and motifs, reworking them, presumably finding something admirable in their antiquity.

Bronze technology spread beyond the area controlled by the Shang, probably even into areas the Shang would have considered entirely alien. In 1986 archaeologists discovered at Sanxingdui in Sichuan province a bronze-producing culture apparently contemporary with the late Shang that did not share either the basic Shang artistic repertoire, nor, it would seem, Shang religious beliefs. At this site were rammed earthen city walls of the familiar sort, but also outside the wall two sacrificial pits entirely unlike anything found earlier. One contained about 300 gold, bronze, jade, and stone objects along with thirteen elephant trunks and nearly 100 cubic feet of burnt and broken animal bones. The most astonishing finds were life-sized bronze heads with angular facial features and enormous eyes. In the second pit, about 100 feet away, there was a life-sized statue and forty-one bronze heads of varying size, some with gold masks. As most objects had been burnt and broken, archaeologists infer that these two pits are the remains of large-

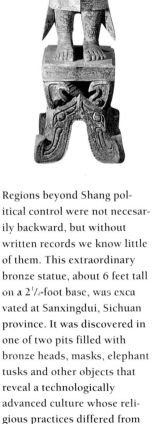

Regions beyond Shang political control were not necesarily backward, but without written records we know little of them. This extraordinary bronze statue, about 6 feet tall on a 2¹⁄₂-foot base, was excavated at Sanxingdui, Sichuan province. It was discovered in one of two pits filled with bronze heads, masks, elephant tusks and other objects that reveal a technologically advanced culture whose religious practices differed from those of the Shang and early Zhou.

scale sacrificial ceremonies held about a generation apart. There is no evidence of human remains in these pits, which has led to speculation that the bronze heads and the statue stood in for the sacrifice of human beings.

Bronzes did not, of course, constitute all of Shang art, even if they have survived the best. Finely worked jade objects, many perpetuating neolithic forms, such as *cong, bi,* knives, and axes, continued to be included among the objects in opulent burials. Silk was already being woven, and traces of elaborate silk weaves have been found. Carved wood and ivory, sometimes inlaid with turquoise, have been discovered, as have traces of lacquer decoration. All this suggests that the Shang kings and probably other noble families lived surrounded by objects of great beauty.

THE ZHOU CONQUEST

How directly or tightly the Shang controlled its territories can only be dimly discerned from oracle bones and archaeological excavations. Certainly the Shang campaigned constantly against enemies. To the west were the fierce Qiang, considered barbarian tribesmen, and perhaps speaking a proto-Tibetan language. Between the Shang capital and the Qiang was a frontier state called Zhou, which seems both to have inherited cultural traditions from the neolithic cultures of the northwest and to have absorbed most of the material culture of the Shang. In about 1050 BC, the Zhou rose against the Shang and defeated it in battle.

The early Zhou is the first period from which texts have been transmitted. The *Book of Documents (Shujing),* one of the Confucian classics, purports to contain texts from the beginning of the Zhou, giving us the Zhou version of their history. These documents describe the Zhou conquest of the Shang as the victory of just

Remains of rammed-earth foundations at Fengchu in Shaanxi province have allowed archaeologists to reconstruct the design of this early Zhou palace or temple. The compound was 145 by 105 feet, the main hall in the centre 56 by 20 feet and the whole was built around courtyards in the fashion typical of later Chinese architecture.

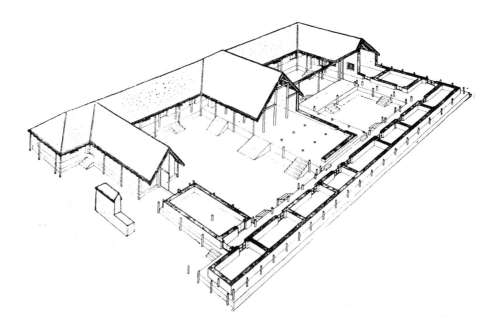

and noble warriors over decadent courtiers led by a dissolute, sadistic king. At the same time, they show that the Zhou recognized the Shang as occupying the centre of the world, were eager to succeed to that role rather than dispute it, and saw history as a major way to legitimate power. Besides these transmitted texts, hundreds of inscriptions on ritual bronzes have survived. Particularly useful are inscriptions that record benefactions from the king and mention the services that had earned the king's favour.

The founding of the Zhou was associated with a series of important religious changes. The scale of human sacrifice at burials declined, suggesting that ideas about death and the afterlife were changing. The practice of voluntary accompanying in death continued, but on a considerably smaller scale. The practice of divining with oracle bones declined and the new divination system laid out in the *Classic of Changes* (*Yijing*) gained ground, involving interpretations of randomly selected sets of broken and unbroken lines. Another key development was the introduction of the concept of heaven, conceived as something like the sacred moral power of the cosmos. In transmitted texts and bronze inscriptions alike, the rule of the Zhou kings was linked to heaven. A king and a dynasty could rule only so long as they retained heaven's favour. If a king neglected his sacred duties and acted tyrannically, heaven would display its displeasure by sending down ominous portents and natural disasters. If the king failed to heed such warnings, heaven would withdraw its mandate, disorder would increase, the political and social order would fall into chaos, and heaven would eventually select someone else upon whom to bestow a new mandate to rule. Moral values were thus built into the way the cosmos worked, and history was read as a mirror of heaven's will. The ruler mediated between heaven and the realm of human beings, and his virtue ensured the proper harmony of the two sides. Because these ideas do not seem to have any place in Shang cosmology, it may be that they were elaborated by the early Zhou rulers as a kind of propaganda to win over the conquered subjects of the Shang. Whatever their origin, the ideas proved compelling and remained a central tenet of Chinese political cosmology until modern times.

In early texts, three Zhou rulers have been given great credit for establishing a stable state. King Wen (the 'Cultured King') formed alliances with neighbouring states and tribes in preparation for attacking the Shang. His son King Wu (the 'Martial King') built a new capital further east and launched the expedition that succeeded in defeating the Shang army and taking its capital. Rather than kill all members of the Shang royal house, he left a son of the last king as nominal ruler of the city to continue sacrifices to his powerful ancestors. King Wu died young, only six years after the conquest, and his brother, the Duke of Zhou, acted as

Bronze was used not only for ritual objects, but also for more practical things such as weapons and armour. This early Zhou helmet was probably actually used in warfare, as it was unearthed alongside weapons in the Beijing area.

Inscribed bronze ritual vessel, unearthed from a storage pit in Fufeng, Shaanxi province. The 284-character inscription on this bronze, composed shortly before 900 BC by Historian Qiang, relates the major events under the six kings from Wen to Mu, such as campaigns against various 'barbarians', as well as the deeds of Qiang's own ancestors in the service of these kings.

regent for King Wu's young son. The Duke of Zhou extended and consolidated the new territories, conducting a series of expeditions eastward to bring the whole Yellow River plain under Zhou control, destroying in the process, it is said, fifty states. He built a new city at modern Luoyang in Henang province from which to govern the eastern territories and moved former Shang nobles to his new city. When the young king came of age, the Duke of Zhou relinquished his powers and became at once the most reverent of subjects. These three early Zhou rulers thus became emblematic figures, representing the leadership qualities required for the establishment of enduring states: military prowess, the morally based civil arts, and loyalty.

The process of absorbing the tribes and states on the periphery of the Zhou realm was slow and not always successful (the fourth Zhou king disappeared with his armies on a campaign into modern Hubei province and was not heard from again). Rather than attempt to rule all of their territories directly, the early Zhou rulers sent out relatives and trusted subordinates with troops to establish walled garrisons in the conquered territories. Where that was not possible, they recognized local chiefs as their representatives. These lords were given titles that became hereditary and were obliged to render military service and send tribute. But all power was not parcelled out; the kings also set up a central proto-bureaucratic administration that made extensive use of written records. Moreover, the kings maintained a royal army that fought alongside warriors contributed by the feudal lords.

Kinship and the cults associated with it tied the lords to the king and to each other. The king bore the title 'Son of Heaven' and had the unique right to make sacrifices to heaven at the capital. He also presided at rites to royal ancestors, in much the way the Shang kings had. Lords conducted similar sacrifices to the first holder of their fiefs as well as their more recent ancestors. Marriage among patrilineal relatives was not practised, so the king and lords of his surname had to marry with the families of lords of other surnames, linking virtually all of the upper ranks of the nobility through either patrilineal or affinal kinship. Loyalty and military valour were much esteemed among these nobles, but familial ethics of obedience, respect, and kinship solidarity were just as prized.

By 800 BC there were around two hundred lords with domains large and small, of which only about twenty-five were large enough to matter much. Each lord appointed various officers under him, men with ritual, administrative, or military responsibilities, and these posts and the associated titles tended to become hereditary as well. In this way each domain came to have aristocratic families with patrimonies in offices and associated lands. Society was conceived in strongly hierarchical terms, ranging from the Son of Heaven, through the lords, to the great ministers, other officers, the knights and court attendants, and finally the ordinary farmers who generally seem to have been attached to domains in a serflike manner.

Along the Zhou borders and interspersed among the Zhou domains were non-Chinese peoples who resisted Zhou hegemony. Chinese writers of the time classified them into four ethnic groups: the Yi centring on modern Shandong, the Man in the Yangzi valley, the Di along the northern border, and the Rong centring in Shaanxi. These outsiders were not necessarily primitive tribesmen. In the south, along the Yangzi, several political entities had come into existence independently of the Zhou – the states of Chu, Wu, and Yue. Their chiefs called themselves kings, but by the end of the eighth century BC were allowing the Zhou kings to consider them peripheral parts of the Zhou feudal order.

Zhou art shows important shifts from Shang tradition. Large bronze ritual vessels continued to be produced in great abundance in early Zhou times, probably often by the same craftsmen who had served under the Shang rulers. Nevertheless, within a couple of generations of the conquest of the Shang, the dominant motif on Shang bronzes, the animal mask or *taotie*, all but disappeared. Birdlike imagery became more important, along with purely ornamental decorations, such as spikes and ribs. The use of bold ribs and spikes suggests that vessels were being viewed from greater distances, during rituals performed in front of audiences. At the same time, ritual vessels came to be frequently treated as vehicles for texts, which grew longer and longer, suggesting that the vessels were seen as family heirlooms in the making, with thoughts to their effects on descendants as much as on ancestors.

The earliest Chinese poetry originates from the early Zhou period. Many of the 305 poems in the *Book of Songs* (*Shijing*) would have been sung at court during important ceremonies. Some celebrate the exploits of the early Zhou rulers; others praise the solemnity with which the living provide food offerings to their ancestors during sacrifices. One court ode expresses a profound distrust of women's involvement in politics and the affairs of government:

> Clever men build cities,
> Clever women topple them.
> Beautiful, these clever women may be
> But they are owls and kites.
> Women have long tongues
> That lead to ruin.
> Disorder does not come down from heaven;
> It is produced by women.

Other poems in the *Book of Songs* appear to have begun as folk songs. These include love songs and songs depicting ordinary people at work clearing fields, ploughing and planting, gathering mulberry leaves for silkworms, spinning and weaving. There are even complaints about tax collectors and the hardships of military service. One stanza of a love poem reads:

> Please, Zhongzi,
> Do not leap over our wall,
> Do not break our mulberry trees.
> It's not that I begrudge the mulberries,
> But I fear my brothers.
> You I would embrace,
> But my brother's words – those I dread.

A stanza of a poem of complaint reads:

> Which plant is not brown?
> Which man is not sad?
> Have pity on us soldiers,
> Treated as though we were not men!

Poems like these remind us that ancient China was populated by more than kings, warriors, diviners, and bronzesmiths. The vast majority of the population, then and later, were farmers, toiling in their fields, trying to fashion satisfying lives and to limit the exactions of those with power over them.

Most of the basic elements of ancient Chinese civilization were not unique to China. All over the world, people discovered that animals and plants could be domesticated; there is little reason to think agriculture was invented in one place and then carried to all parts of the world through migration of peoples or communication of ideas. Very basic ideas about kinship and religion – such as tracing descent solely through the male line, or making sacrifices of animals or humans to gods or ancestors – and very basic ideas about social order – such as enslaving those defeated in war and passing kingship from one man to his son or brother –

are also extremely common cross-culturally. These phenomena are more plausibly attributed to shared human psychology than to cultural contact.

Much less common in world history is the leap to complex civilization, to the ideas and technology that allow co-ordination of large populations. Writing, metallurgy, and strong priestly kings appeared together in several ancient civilizations: Mesopotamia, Egypt, the Indus Valley, China, and Mexico. It is generally accepted that the American civilizations must have been independent in origin from those of Asia and that those of the ancient Near East were influenced by each other. But what about China? Did it make the leap entirely on its own? Or did knowledge of some of the advances of the ancient Near East cross the Eurasian steppe and stimulate or spark similar developments in China? Are similarities all the result of a common logic of socio-political-technological development, or are some the result of diffusion? Most Chinese historians and archaeologists seem to think that it is more to China's credit the less their ancestors learned from others and the more they discovered or invented themselves. They point to marks on neolithic pots as possible early stages in a writing system to refute the notion that the idea behind writing (that marks can represent words) might have been transmitted by illiterate peoples across the steppe. They demonstrate how distinctive Chinese bronze mould-casting was in order to cast doubt on the notion that the idea behind metallurgy (that rocks can be smelted into a strong and malleable substance) could have been transmitted in a similar way. Nor do they like to draw attention to the strong probability that wheat, the chariot, the domesticated horse, and the compound bow spread from west Asia.

Questionable assumptions about the worth of civilizations lie behind these patriotic efforts to make China as independent a civilization as possible. Surely the ancient Chinese would not somehow be more worthy of admiration if they had refused to adopt useful ideas they learned about second or third hand for fear of cultural contamination. Chinese civilization is obviously not an off-shoot of any of the ancient civilizations of the Middle East in any meaningful sense, since its language, script, cosmology, and art are too distinctive. Still what made China one of the great civilizations of the world was not its isolation or purity, but the way the complex of ideas, social forms, skills, and techniques which coalesced in ancient times gave China the capacity to grow, adapt, and expand

In the art of the ancient Middle East, including Egypt, Assyria, and Babylonia, representations of agriculture (domesticated plants and animals) and of social hierarchy (kings, priests, scribes, and slaves) are very common, matching our understandings of the social, political, and economic development of those societies. Thus it is somewhat puzzling that images of wild animals predominate in Shang art.

The zoomorphic images on Shang bronzes range from clearly mimetic low- or high-relief images of birds, snakes, crocodiles, and deer, to imaginary animals like dragons, and to highly stylized *taotie* designs that allude to animals but do not directly represent them. It is much less common for bronze implements to have images of human beings, and these rare human images are generally associated with images of animals. Since bronze vessels were used in sacrificial rituals as containers for food or drink, most observers assume the decoration on them symbolized something important in Shang political and religious cosmology. Unfortunately, texts that discuss the meaning of images exist only from much later periods.

Some animal images readily suggest possible meanings. Jade cicadas were sometimes found in the mouths of the dead, and images of cicadas on bronzes are easy to interpret as images evocative of rebirth in the realm of ancestral spirits, as cicadas spend years underground before emerging. Birds, similarly, suggest to many the idea of messengers that can communicate with other realms, especially ones in the sky.

More problematic is the most common image, the *taotie*. To some it is a monster – a fearsome image that would scare away evil forces. Others imagine a dragon – an animal whose vast powers had more positive associations. Some hypothesize that it reflects masks used in rituals, others that it carries over the face-like imagery on neolithic jades from the Liangzhu area. Still others see these images as hardly more than designs. By tracing the evolution of the *taotie* over the course of the Shang, it is possible to show how the vivid, highly animal-like images of late Shang evolved from thin line and dot designs of early Shang. Perhaps the *taotie* came simply to be associated with the Shang kings and the order they presided over, respected and admired because it was an emblem of power and focus for identity more than for any association with real or imagined animals.

Those who wish to find significance in the fact that Shang imagery made so much use of animals (much more than plants, for instance) have tended to associate it with animal sacrifices, totemism, or shamanism. Since animals were slaughtered to be offered in sacrificial ceremonies, the argument goes, the decoration on the vessels used in the ceremonies probably alludes

This bronze axe blade (13 by 14 inches), found in the entrance ramp of a late Shang tomb at Sufutun in Shandong, may have been used for the execution of some of the forty-eight sacrificial victims found there. The face, depicted by perforation, bears some resemblance to more standard *taotie* forms yet seems at the same time distinctly human.

to eating, killing, and the transformation brought on by death. Others point to signs that ancient tribes or clans saw themselves as descended from particular animals (totemism) and may have worshipped particular animals or birds. Shamanism is brought in because men and animals are sometimes associated on Shang bronzes. As practised elsewhere in north Asia or in south China in later times, shamans commonly relied on animals to help them communicate with the spirit world. In this interpretation, images on bronzes of men in the mouths of animals depict shamans submitting to the powers of the animals who aid them in their trances.

China in ancient times was undoubtedly no less diverse a place than China in more recent times, and these explanations need not be mutually exclusive. There are enough regional differences in design to suggest that animal and human imagery may have had different meanings in different times and places. Even in the late Shang period the *taotie* did not have the same absorbing interest to the southern artist that it had in Anyang. But images of distinguishable birds and animals proliferate in the south, suggesting that they carried meanings there not commonly given to them in the Anyang area.

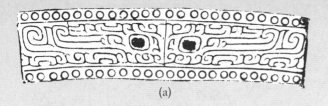

(a)

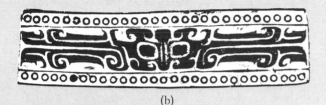

(b)

Rubbings of *taotie* decoration on Shang bronzes. Examples *a* to *d* are from central Shang sites, in chronological order; *e* is from further west in Sichuan province. Over time, as can be seen in *a* to *d*, *taotie* designs evolved from simple lines and dots to high relief and more prominent eyes, horns, and claws, rather than developing from more animal-like to more abstract. The treatment in the last example from the Sichuan area is in marked contrast, suggesting considerable cultural differences between the regions.

(c)

(d)

(e)

Man and animal are fused in an unusual way in this Shang bronze ritual vessel, 13 inches tall. The vessel takes the shape of a bear or tiger with mouth open and poised to swallow a man. The man seems not at all concerned, but rather to be holding on to the animal as a child would hold on to its mother. Other animals, including a deer, serpents, cattle, and dragons, are incorporated into the decoration of the sides.

CHAPTER 2   # Philosophical Foundations:
The Eastern Zhou Period 770–256 BC

The intellectual foundations of Chinese civilization were established during the Eastern Zhou dynasty (770–256 BC), a period of political fragmentation and moral crisis. The first half of this era is commonly called the Spring and Autumn period, after the name of a chronicle covering the years 722 to 481 BC. During these centuries the Zhou kings continued to reign by default while their putative vassals competed against each other, making and breaking alliances, exchanging hostages, and sporadically taking up arms. Over time military conflict became more frequent and more deadly, and the second half of this period is conventionally called the Warring States period (403–221 BC). By then the Zhou king was no longer a major player and one by one the smaller states were conquered and absorbed by the half-dozen largest ones.

The ruthlessness of the competition among the regional powers, although uniformly lamented, nevertheless served to foster social, technological, and economic advances. These included the introduction of iron casting, infantry armies, coinage, private ownership of land, and social mobility. New ideas also emerged in profusion. Those engaged in advising rulers about state affairs began analysing basic principles of human society and the natural order. Soon the most reflective officials were questioning established assumptions and values. Their ideas began to be written down, and the circulation of these treatises further stimulated intellectual debate.

RIVAL STATES

The decentralized rule of the Western Zhou had from the beginning carried within it the danger that the regional lords would become so powerful that they would no longer respond to the commands of the king. As generations passed and ties of loyalty and kinship grew more distant, this indeed happened. In 771 BC the Zhou king was killed by an alliance of Rong tribesmen and Zhou vassals. One of his sons was put on the throne, and then for safety's sake the capital was moved east out of the Wei River valley to modern Luoyang, located just south of the Yellow River in the heart of the central plains. The revived Zhou never fully regained control over its vassals, and China entered a prolonged period without a strong central authority. The Zhou kings still had ritual functions as intermediaries with heaven, but militarily they were inferior to many of their supposed vassals. In 335 BC regional lords began calling themselves kings, in essence refusing to recognize the sovereignty of the Zhou king, who was finally deposed in 256 BC.

The Eastern Zhou was a violent age, a time when victors presented the cut-off ears of enemies at their ancestral temples, when the blood of captives was spread on ceremonial drums, when thieves had their feet cut off, and when rulers ran the considerable risk of assassination. At the same time it was a period when diplomacy was studied earnestly and practised with finesse. During the Spring and Autumn period a code of chivalrous or sportsmanlike conduct still regulated warfare between the states. For instance, one state would not attack another while it was in mourning for its ruler, and during battle one side would not attack before the other side had time to line up. Perhaps out of fear of the wrath of the ancestors of defeated rulers, efforts were made not to wipe out ruling houses, but to leave at least one successor to continue the sacrifices.

In the Spring and Autumn period the head of one state was sometimes able to get the others to recognize him as hegemon or overlord, chief of an alliance of states. The most notable of these was Duke Huan of Qi (r. 685–643 BC). With the help of his able minister Guan Zhong, he built up the economic power of Qi state, casting coins, controlling prices, and regulating the production of salt and iron tools. He organized the states in the central plains to resist the expansion of the semi-barbarian state of Chu in the central Yangzi valley. With a mutual-defence pact in place, he also organized defence against tribesmen to the north and even got Chu to sign a peace treaty agreeing to send tribute to the Zhou kings.

Because of the need to form alliances, rulers regularly married their sons and daughters into the ruling families of other states. These marriages then gave them stakes in other states' succession disputes, which were extremely common because of the practice of concubinage. Rulers regularly demonstrated their power and wealth by accumulating large numbers of concubines and thus would have children by several women. In theory, succession went to the eldest son of the wife, then younger sons by her, and only in their absence to sons of concubines. In actual practice, however, the ruler of a state or head of a powerful ministerial family could select the son of a concubine to be his heir if he wished, leading to much scheming for favour among the various sons and their mothers and the common perception that women were incapable of taking a disinterested view of the greater good. Succession disputes of this sort provide much of the narrative interest in the fullest history of this period, the *Zuo zhuan*. Sons not designated as heir were frequently assigned fiefs or posts in outlying regions where they had the opportunity to build up a local power base and challenge the succession by recourse to arms. Even those unswervingly loyal to the legitimate successor might face trumped up treason charges and have to flee to another state to avoid execution, picking when possible a ruler related through a mother, wife, or sister. Such hosts were often happy to help them, unafraid of stirring up trouble in nearby states.

The seats of power for each ruler were cities protected by thick earthen walls of the sort that had been built in north China since before the Shang dynasty. Within the walls were the palaces and ancestral temples of the ruler and other aristocrats. Sometimes there was an outer wall as well that protected the artisans, merchants,

Late Zhou iron moulds for casting iron knives. In Europe wrought iron preceded cast iron, but in China iron was cast from the beginning. In Shang times bronze ritual vessels had been cast one at a time, as major works of art. The casting of iron tools, by contrast, constituted a form of mass production.

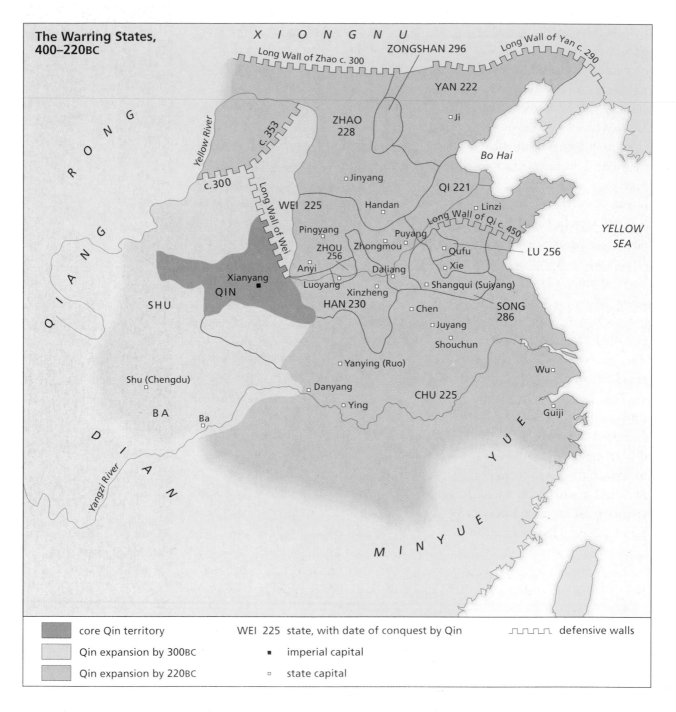

The Warring States, 400–220BC

X I O N G N U

ZONGSHAN 296

Long Wall of Zhao c. 300

Long Wall of Yan c. 290

YAN 222

Yellow River

ZHAO 228

Ji

c. 353

Bo Hai

QIANG RONG

c. 300

Jinyang

QI 221

Linzi

Long Wall of Wei

WEI 225

Handan

Long Wall of Qi c. 450

YELLOW SEA

Pingyang

Puyang

ZHOU 256

Zhongmou

Qufu

LU 256

Anyi

Daliang

Xie

Xianyang

Luoyang

QIN

Xinzheng

Shangqiu (Suiyang)

SHU

HAN 230

Chen

SONG 286

Juyang

Shouchun

Shu (Chengdu)

Yanying (Ruo)

Wu

B A

Danyang

Guiji

Ba

Ying

CHU 225

Y U E

Yangzi River

D I A N

M I N Y U E

	core Qin territory	WEI 225	state, with date of conquest by Qin	⌐⌐⌐⌐⌐ defensive walls
	Qin expansion by 300BC	■	imperial capital	
	Qin expansion by 220BC	□	state capital	

During the Warring States period, the feudal domains of the early Zhou came to function as independent states. Over time the number of states rapidly declined as the more powerful ones conquered and absorbed their neighbours. In the north, Jin broke up into Zhao, Wei, and Han in 453 BC, leaving Qi in the east, Chu in the south, and Qin in the west as the strongest powers. Chu exterminated Yue in 334 BC and Confucius's home state of Lu in 249 BC, but it was Qin that was eventually victorious over all the other states in 221 BC.

and farmers who lived outside the inner wall. Descriptions of military confrontations in this period are filled with accounts of sieges launched against these walled citadels, with scenes of the scaling of walls and storming of gates. The technology of building walls had to be steadily improved because techniques of attacking and laying siege to city walls were steadily perfected. Treatises were written describing siegecraft and other facets of military art and strategy, and many classical texts devoted lengthy sections to these topics.

Constant warfare stimulated advances in military techniques and technology that altered the social relations of warfare and rendered it increasingly deadly. The need for a chariot-riding aristocracy declined with the mastery of cavalry and infantry armies. Cavalry techniques were first perfected by non-Chinese peoples to the north of China proper, who at that time were making the transition to full nomadism. In self-defence, the northern state of Jin developed its own cavalry armies, which it soon used against other Chinese states. Acquiring and pasturing horses became a key component of military preparedness, as it would remain for many centuries. Well-drilled infantry armies, introduced in this period, also proved potent against chariot-led forces. By 300 BC states were sending out armies of hundreds of thousands of drafted foot-soldiers, often accompanied by mounted warriors. When armed with the powerful newly introduced crossbow, farmers could be made into effective soldiers, able to shoot further than horsemen carrying light bows. The trigger of a crossbow is an intricate bronze mechanism that could only be produced by skilled craftsmen.

Since victory went to the ruler who could raise and outfit the largest armies and deploy the largest workforces to build defence walls, ambitious rulers began to worry about ways to increase their populations and revenues. To bring new land into cultivation, marshes were drained and irrigation works established. Serfdom gradually declined, as rulers wanted to reward farmers for their efforts and to have direct access to their labour power. Rulers looked on trade favourably and began casting coins, which quickly supplemented the use of bolts of silk as units of exchange. Economic expansion was also aided by the introduction of iron technology. By the seventh century BC iron deposits were being exploited, and within a couple of centuries iron was being widely used for both farm tools and weapons. By the late Warring States period, great smelters might employ more than 200 workmen, and ironmongers were prominent among the rich entrepreneurs making their appearance in this period.

To expand their control over people and land, rulers also tried new techniques of governing. More and more they sent out their own officials rather than delegate authority to hereditary lesser lords. This trend towards centralized bureaucratic control created opportunities for social advancement for those on the lower end of the old aristocracy. Competition among such men guaranteed rulers a ready supply of able and willing subordinates, and competition among rulers for talent meant that ambitious men could be selective in offering their services.

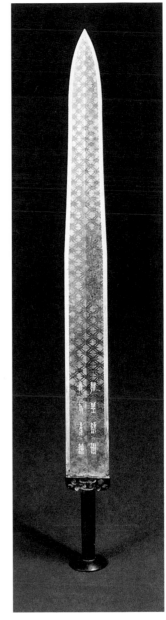

Double-edged swords are not mentioned in Chinese sources until the seventh century BC. The inscription on this specimen, unearthed at Wangshan in Hubei province, states that it is owned by Gou Jian, the king of Yue (r. 496–465 BC), a famous connoisseur of fine swords.

States on the periphery – Jin in the north, Qi in the east, Chu in the south, and Qin in the west – had the advantage in these struggles for supremacy because they could expand outward. After they had expanded, they turned inward and soon they were conquering the small states of the central plain between them, each lord aspiring to be the great unifier. By 300 BC, only seven major states survived and it was apparent that strife would end only when one state eliminated all its rivals.

Rulers searching for ways to survive or prevail were more than willing to patronize men of ideas. As states were destroyed and their former nobles had to look for employment elsewhere, ambitious rulers and even high officials were able to gather around them numerous advisors, assistants, teachers, strategists, and clerks. These men made proposals about what the rulers should do and rebutted each other's ideas, in the process advancing the art of oratory, the science of strategy, and the study of logic. Books recording the teachings of various masters came to be compiled and circulated, a development that fostered the appearance of schools of thought, since the existence of a text tended both to freeze a viewpoint among followers and to elicit refutations from other masters. The traditional label for this period as the time when 'a hundred schools of thought contended' aptly captures the spirit of exuberant intellectual creativity that proved the most important legacy of the late Zhou.

CONFUCIUS AND HIS FOLLOWERS

The earliest important would-be advisor was Confucius (traditional dates, 551–479 BC). Born in Lu, a small state in Shandong province that had been the fief of the Duke of Zhou, Confucius spent some years at the Lu court without gaining much influence. He then wandered through neighbouring states with his disciples, in search of a ruler more receptive to his advice. Finding much that dismayed him – greed, insincerity, irresponsibility, callous disregard for others' needs and interests – he committed himself to trying to inspire people to do good, becoming China's first moral philosopher. He linked moral behaviour to traditional roles and hierarchies and thus became a great defender of the Zhou order, by then already in decay. He identified with the 'learned men', the court experts who assisted rulers in the performance of rituals and ceremonies, such as sacrifices to ancestors and reception of envoys. These learned men knew about the heavens and could advise on setting the calendar; they performed divinations and interpreted the results; and they kept records and advised on precedents. In Confucius' vision of the early Zhou, these learned men and all others – rulers and subjects, nobles and commoners, parents and children, men and women – wholeheartedly accepted the parts assigned to them and devoted themselves to their responsibilities to others. His ideal world thus was one where conventions governed actions and hierarchical differentiation resulted in harmonious co-ordination.

In Confucius' moral vision, intentions and acts towards other men are at least as important as those toward gods or ancestors. He extolled filial piety – the rev-

Early coins, like these bronze examples of the Zhou period, were made in the shape of knives and spades; circular coins with square central holes for stringing them together later became predominant.

erent respect of children toward their parents. Filial piety was to him both ritual and attitude; conventional actions needed to be animated by sincere feelings. Moreover, filial piety could be extended outward beyond the family, since society could be seen as the family writ large. Still, the highest virtue in Confucius' vocabulary was *ren*, variously translated as perfect goodness, benevolence, humanity, co-humanity, human-heartedness, and nobility. It entailed deep concern for the well-being of others, an orientation that makes right action almost effortless. *Ren* extended to everyone and thus was a virtue without the hierarchical dimension of filial piety.

Confucius was apparently an extraordinary teacher. As he gained a reputation as a learned man, people came to consult him, and many stayed on to study the ancient traditions with him. Nevertheless, he continually hoped to play a greater role in government and he prepared his students for careers in government service. Towards that end he encouraged them to master the venerated traditions, especially the *Book of Songs, Book of Documents*, and ritual texts; indeed Confucius is traditionally credited with having compiled several of these texts himself.

Confucius' students – and their students – deserve much of the credit for the eventual success of Confucian ideas. The first important successor remembered

Line drawing of the decor on an inlaid bronze wine vessel from the Warring States period. Depictions of people engaged in such activities as warfare, hunting, boating, rituals, music-making, and food preparation were a new feature of the art of the late Zhou period.

The decline in human sacrifice and 'accompanying in death' led to substitute representations of attendants being placed in graves, a practice Confucius mentioned approvingly. This painted wooden figure of a woman was unearthed from a fourth- to fifth-century BC tomb at Changtaiguan, Henan province.

by history was Mencius (c.370–c.300 BC), who had studied with Confucius' grandson. In imitation of Confucius, Mencius travelled around offering advice to rulers of nearby states. He reminded rulers of the Mandate of Heaven, telling them to their faces that if they did not rule well, heaven would bring it about that their people would rebel and oust them. He made it the responsibility of rulers to see to it that their people had enough to eat at every meal in good years and could avoid starvation in bad years.

The opening chapter of the *Mencius* records that during an audience with King Hui of Liang (370–319 BC) Mencius responded to the king's question about ways to profit his state by asking, 'Why must Your Majesty use the word "profit"? All I am concerned with are the good and the right. If Your Majesty says, "How can I profit my state?" your officials will say, "How can I profit my family?" and officers and common people will say, "How can I profit myself?" Once superiors and inferiors are competing for profit, the state will be in danger.' In a subsequent conversation, Mencius told this king that if he treated his people well by reducing taxes and lightening punishments, they would be so eager to fight for him that even if armed only with sharpened sticks they could defeat the well-equipped soldiers of the powerful and aggressive states of Qin and Chu.

Mencius' concern with the common people was coupled with a comparable concern for officials who, he felt, should be treated respectfully by the ruler and be given incomes in proportion to their rank. He argued for the superiority of hereditary ministers over ones chosen by the ruler for their merit, wanting ministers to have some independence from the ruler.

In conversations with his disciples and fellow philosophers, Mencius showed interests beyond government. He debated abstract issues in moral philosophy, such as the incipient nature of human beings, their inborn potential and tendencies. Mencius came out strongly on the positive side, stressing human potential for goodness. Proof, he asserted, could be found in people's spontaneous responses to the sufferings of others: 'Anyone today who suddenly sees a baby about to fall into a well feels alarmed and concerned' and automatically reaches out to help, without thought of personal gain. Gaozi, Mencius' philosophical opponent, had argued that 'Human nature is like whirling water. When an outlet is opened to the east, it flows east; when an outlet is opened to the west, it flows west.' To this Mencius countered, 'Water, it is true, is not inclined to either east or west, but does it have no preference for high or low? Goodness is to human nature like flowing downward is to water.' Just as water can be forced up, people can be led to be bad, but this is not their natural inclinations. In another conversation Mencius used another analogy from nature. Ox Mountain, he said, had once been covered by vegetation, but farmers had denuded it with their animals and wood-cutting, until anyone looking at it would think that it was barren by nature. By implication, the lamentable way most men act is no more natural to them than barrenness is to a mountain.

The book recording Mencius' thought, the *Mencius*, is, like the *Analects*, a collection of the philosopher's conversations, presented in no particular order. Inconsistencies among his ideas are left for readers to resolve. The ideas of the next most influential Confucian thinker, Xunzi, or 'Master Xun' (c.310–c.220 BC), survive in much more coherent and orderly form because the *Xunzi* is a set of essays that Xunzi wrote by and large himself.

Xunzi had much more political and administrative experience than either Confucius or Mencius and showed consideration for the difficulties rulers might face in trying to rule through ritual and virtue. At the same time he was a rigorous thinker who extended the philosophical foundations of many ideas merely outlined by Confucius or Mencius. For instance, whereas Confucius had declined to discuss gods, portents, and anomalies, Xunzi explicitly argued for a humanistic and rationalistic view of the cosmos. He argued that heaven is impartial and human affairs result from human efforts. Praying to heaven or to gods does not get them to intervene. 'Why does it rain after a prayer for rain? In my opinion, for no reason. It is the same as raining when you had not prayed.'

Xunzi still took great interest in ritual, for he saw both beauty and social benefits in its practice. He believed educated men should continue traditional ritual practices, such as divining before major decisions and praying during droughts, even when they know their actions do not bring about the ostensible goal. He held that rites are valuable because they provide an orderly way to express feelings and satisfy desires while maintaining distinctions of rank, title, and honour. Just as music shapes people's emotions and creates feelings of solidarity, so ritual and etiquette shape people's understanding of duty and create social differentiation. In defending ritual, Xunzi was probably responding to the attacks of the Daoists and Mohists, discussed below.

Xunzi directly attacked Mencius' argument that human nature tends toward goodness, claiming to the contrary that men's inborn tendencies are wayward and require curbing through education. He distinguished between what is inborn in people and what is learnt only with effort. 'It is human nature to want to eat one's fill when hungry, to want to warm up when cold, to want to rest when tired.' Much of what is desirable does not come naturally and must be taught. 'When a son yields to his father, or a younger brother yields to his elder brother, or when a son takes on the work for his father or a younger brother for his elder brother, their actions go against their natures and run counter to their feelings. And yet these are the way of the filial son and the principles of ritual and morality.'

Mencius and Xunzi were the two best-known of the hundreds of late Zhou followers of Confucius. Some followers became experts in ritual, others masters of

The *Analects*

Confucius' ideas are known to us primarily through the sayings recorded by his disciples in the *Analects (Lunyu)*. In this short, loosely organized text, Confucius discussed the human world of families and states rather than the world of gods or spirits. The thrust of his thought was thus ethical rather than theoretical or metaphysical. He tried to verify his ideas by discussing concrete situations, not general principles, and did not employ logic of the sorts the ancient Greeks developed, with formulas like the syllogism for measuring the validity of statements.

The *Analects* provided the foundation for much of Chinese social, political, and ethical thought. In later centuries it became a sacred book, memorized by students, and as a consequence many of its passages became proverbial sayings, unknowingly cited even by illiterate peasants.

The selections below preserve the original order.

The Master said, 'When your father is alive observe his intentions. After he passes away, model yourself on the memory of his behavior. If in three years after his death you have not deviated from your father's ways, then you may be considered a filial child.' (1.11)

The Master said, 'Lead the people by means of government policies and regulate them through punishments, and they will be evasive and have no sense of shame. Lead them by means of virtue and regulate them through rituals and they will have a sense of shame and moreover have standards.' (2.3)

The Master said, 'By fifteen I was intent on learning; by thirty I was standing straight; by forty I was no longer confused; by fifty I knew heaven's commands; by sixty I was attuned; and at seventy I could follow my heart's desires without transgressing what is right.' (2.4)

The Master said, 'The gentleman is not a tool.' (2.12)

Zigong wished to get rid of the sacrifice of a sheep at the new moon rite. The Master said, 'Si, you love the lamb. I love the rite.' (3.17)

The Master said, 'The gentleman understands moral duty; the petty person knows about profit.' (4.16)

The Master said, 'When you meet someone wise, think about becoming his equal. When you see someone inferior, reflect on yourself.' (4.17)

The Master said, 'You can be of service to your father and mother by remonstrating with them tactfully. If you perceive that they do not wish to follow your advice, then continue to be reverent towards them without offending or disobeying them; work hard and do not murmur against them.' (4.18)

The Master said, 'I am way past my prime. I have not seen the Duke of Zhou in a dream for a long time.' (7.5)

The Master said, 'I am not someone who was born wise. I am someone who loves the ancients and tries to learn from them.' (7.19)

Zhonggong asked about humanity. The Master said, 'When you go out, treat everyone as if you were welcoming a great guest. Employ people as though you were

---

the ancient texts. Historically, the strand emphasizing moral self-improvement is worth particular note. Two short treatises, of unknown authorship, the *Great Learning* (*Daxue*) and *Doctrine of the Mean* (*Zhongyong*), expressed these ideas concisely and compellingly. Peace in the realm cannot be achieved without first transforming people. A ruler must perfect his own virtue before he can regulate his family; not until his family is in order can he hope to govern his state effectively; and only on the basis of a well-governed state can he bring peace to the entire realm. In other words, one must change oneself before one can change other people or improve the world.

DAOISM

Confucius and his followers were activists. They believed that government benefited the people and felt called on to do what they could to make the government

conducting a great sacrifice. Do not do unto others what you would not have them do unto you. Then neither in your country nor in your family will there be complaints against you.' (12.2)

Zigong inquired about governing. The Master said, 'Make food supplies sufficient, provide an adequate army, and give the people reason to have faith.'

Zigong asked, 'If one had no choice but to dispense with one of these three, which should it be?'

'Eliminate the army.'

Zigong continued, 'If one had no choice but to get rid of one of the two remaining, which should it be?'

'Dispense with food,' the Master said. 'Since ancient times, death has always occurred, but people without faith cannot stand.' (12.7)

When Zhonggong was serving as chief minister to the Ji family, he asked for advice on governing. The Master said, 'Put priority on your subordinate officials. Pardon their minor mistakes and promote those who are worthy and talented.'

'How can I recognize those who are talented and worthy to promote them?'

Confucius replied, 'Promote those you know. Will others neglect those you do not know?' (13.2)

The governor of She said to Confucius, 'In my land there is an upright man. His father stole a sheep, and the man turned him in to the authorities.'

The Master responded, 'The upright men of my land are different. The father will shelter the son and the son will shelter the father. Righteousness lies precisely in this.' (13.18)

Duke Ling of Wei asked the Master about the marshalling of troops. The Master replied, 'The ordering of ritual vessels is something I can comment on, but military matters are a topic I have never studied.' (15.1)

Zigong asked about the virtue of humanity. The Master said, 'The artisan who wants to do his work well must first of all sharpen his tools. When you reside in a given state, enter the service of the best of the officials and make friends with the most humane of the scholars.' (15.9)

The Master said, 'The gentleman feels bad when his capabilities fall short of the task. He does not feel bad when people fail to recognize him.' (15.18)

The Master said, 'I once spent a whole day without eating and a whole night without sleeping in order to think. It was of no use. It is better to study.' (15.30)

The Master said, 'The gentleman must exert caution in three areas. When he is a youth and his blood and spirit have not yet settled down, he must be on his guard lest he fall into lusting. When he reaches the full vigour of his manhood in his thirties and his blood and spirit are strong, he must guard against getting into quarrels. When he reaches old age and his blood and spirit have begun to weaken, he must guard against envy.' (16.7)

work well. Those who came to be labelled Daoists did not accept this basic premise. They defended private life and wanted the rulers to leave people alone. Seeking to go beyond everyday concerns, they let their minds wander in the more fanciful aspects of life. They did not place human beings at the centre of the cosmos and were concerned that human contrivance upsets the natural order of things. Rather they affirmed the Way or Dao, the indivisible, indescribable, immaterial force or energy that is the source of all that exists or happens.

Our knowledge of early Daoism is based mostly on two surviving books, the *Laozi* and *Zhuangzi*. The *Laozi*, also called the *Classic of the Way and Its Power* (*Daodejing*), is traditionally ascribed to Lao Dan (sixth century BC) but was probably compiled in the third century BC. Poetic and elliptical, this masterpiece can be interpreted and translated in many ways. A recurrent theme in it is the mystical preference for the yielding over the assertive and silence over words. The highest good is like water: 'Water benefits all creatures but does not compete. It occupies the places people disdain and thus comes near to the Way.' The interdependence and mutual transformation of all opposites is another common refrain: 'When everyone in the world sees beauty in the beautiful, ugliness is already there. When everyone sees good in the good, bad is already there.' One implication of these ideas is that almost any purposeful action is counterproductive, and the ruler should allow a return to a natural state in which the people are ignorant and content:

> Do not honour the worthy,
> And the people will not compete.
> Do not value rare treasures,
> And the people will not steal.
> Do not display what others want,
> And the people will not have their hearts confused.
> A sage governs this way:
> He empties people's minds and fills their bellies.
> He weakens their wills and strengthens their bones.
> Keep the people always without knowledge and without desires,
> For then the clever will not dare act.
> Engage in no action and order will prevail.

It would be better, the *Laozi* asserts, if people knew less, if they gave up tools and abandoned writing, if they lost their desire to travel or engage in war. They would be satisfied with their own lives and not envy their neighbours.

The other key text of Daoism is the *Zhuangzi*, a good portion of which was probably written by the philosopher Zhuang Zhou or Zhuangzi (369–286 BC). Zhuangzi shared much of the philosophy found in the *Laozi*, seeing the usefulness of the useless and the relativity of ordinary distinctions. Uninterested in politics, he celebrated spiritual freedom. He told of receiving an envoy from the King of Chu who offered to give him charge of the entire realm. In response he asked the envoy whether a tortoise that had been held as sacred for 3,000 years would prefer to be dead with its bones venerated, or alive with its tail dragging in the mud. On getting the expected response he told the envoy to go away; he wished to drag his tail in the mud.

A masterful writer, Zhuangzi filled his book with flights of fancy, parables, and fictional encounters between historical figures, including delightfully malicious parodies of Confucius and his disciples. Whereas Laozi was concerned with protecting each person's life, Zhuangzi searched for a conception of man's place in the cosmos that would reconcile him to death. How can we be sure life is better than death? People fear what they do not know, but like a captive girl forced to become a king's concubine, they may learn to love what had terrified them. When a friend expressed surprise that Zhuangzi was singing rather than weeping after his wife died, Zhuangzi explained:

When she first died, how could I have escaped feeling the loss? Then I looked back to the beginning before she had life. Not only before she had life, but before she had form. Not only before she had form, but before she had vital energy. In this confused amorphous realm, something changed and vital energy appeared; when the vital energy was changed, form appeared; with changes in form, life began. Now there is another change bringing death. This is like the progression of the four seasons of spring and autumn, winter and summer. Here she was lying down to sleep in a huge room and I followed her, sobbing and wailing. When I realized my actions showed I hadn't understood destiny, I stopped.

Zhuangzi's views of life and death coloured his views on politics. In one parable he had a wheelwright insolently tell a duke that books were useless since all they contained were the dregs of men long gone. When the duke demanded either an explanation or his life, the wheelwright replied:

I see things in terms of my own work. When I chisel at a wheel, if I go slow, the chisel slides and does not stay put; if I hurry, it jams and doesn't move properly. When it is neither too slow nor too fast, I can feel it in my hand and respond to it from my heart. My mouth cannot describe it in words, but there is something there. I cannot teach it to my son, and my son cannot learn it from me. So I have gone on for seventy years, growing old chiselling wheels. The men of old died in possession of what they could not transmit. So it follows that what you are reading are their dregs.

Truly skilled craftsmen do not analyse or reason or even keep in mind the rules they once learned; they respond to situations spontaneously, a course others should try. In other words, rational discrimination between alternative courses of action did not appeal to Zhuangzi as much as simply knowing, a form of understanding that exists beyond the need to make choices.

Both Laozi and Zhuangzi treat the Dao or Way as a key concept. In contrast to the Confucians who used this word to refer to the ethically correct way for humankind, the way of the sages and the true kings, the Daoists used it to refer to the way of nature, a way beyond the full comprehension of human beings but a way with which they must seek to accord. Confucianism, with its focus on human affairs, is properly labelled a humanistic philosophy. In Daoism human society is seen as only a small part of the total reality, and to gain freedom and power people must come to see their continuity with the natural world.

LEGALISM

During the fourth and third centuries BC, as small states one after another were conquered by large ones and the number of surviving states dwindled, those rulers still in contention were receptive to political theorists who claimed to

Music

Music played a central role in court life in ancient China. Visitors to the courts of kings and lords could expect to be entertained by troops of dancers and accompanying musicians. Many of the poems in the classic *Book of Songs* were odes or hymns meant to be performed on ritual occasions.

Music was believed by early thinkers to have great moral powers. Confucius distinguished between different sorts of music; the ancient Shao dance, for instance, was considered a positive force, bringing people into harmony, whereas the music of the state of Zheng was dangerous, leading to wanton thoughts. The word 'music' was written with the same character as 'enjoyment', a fact that led Xunzi to posit a connection between the two: 'Music is joy, an emotion which human beings cannot help but feel at times. Unable to resist feeling joy, they must find an outlet through voice and movement.' Xunzi also stressed that music affects people of all social levels and thus the performance of moderate and tranquil or stern and majestic music are excellent ways for a ruler to encourage a sense of harmony and restraint in common people. The more quantifiable aspects of music attracted the attention of cosmological theorists who speculated on the significance of pitch measurement and its relationship to other numerical relationships. Sound as a natural phenomenon was perceived to be paradigmatic of many natural processes, especially those that involved remote and imperceptible influence between entities at a distance. In fact, where visual 'geometric' vocabulary is employed in classical western philosophy, in the classical Chinese tradition aural 'communicative' vocabulary is much more dominant.

Archaeologists have unearthed quite a few sets of instruments used in court performances in Zhou times. Key instruments were stone chimes, bronze drums, stringed lute-like instruments, bamboo flutes, and sets of bells, struck from the outside. The biggest cache of instruments was discovered in the tomb (c.433 BC) of Marquis Yi of Zeng, ruler of a petty state in modern Hubei just north of the great state of Chu. In the tomb were 124 instruments, including drums, flutes, mouth organs, pan pipes, zithers, a 32-chime lithophone, and a 64-piece bell set (*above*). The zithers have from five to twenty-five strings and vary in details of their construction; they may have come from different regions and been used for performances of regional music. The bells bear inscriptions that indicate their pitches and reveal that they were gifts from the king of Chu. The precision with which the bells were cast indicates that the art of bell-making had reached a very advanced state.

understand power and the techniques that would allow rulers to enhance their control over officials and subjects. These advisors argued that strong government depended not on the moral qualities of the ruler and his officials, as Confucians claimed, but on establishing effective institutional structures. Their starting point was not what society should be but what it is. These statist thinkers are usually labelled the Legalists because of their emphasis on laws. Uninterested in cosmology, epistemology, or personal ethics, these strategists concentrated on proposing political solutions to disorder and techniques for the accumulation of power.

The first of the two lengthy Legalist treatises that survive has traditionally been ascribed to Lord Shang (Gongsun Yang, d. 338 BC), chief minister of the state of Qin, the state that adopted Legalist policies most fully. During the late Warring States period, Qin took a series of steps to make itself a more efficient and powerful state. It abolished the aristocracy, substituting a hierarchy of military titles awarded on the objective criterion of the number of enemy heads cut off in battle. Thus the state alone determined rank and the privileges attached to it. With fiefs rescinded, Qin divided the country into counties governed by appointed officials. To attract migrants from other states, new settlers were offered lands and houses. Private serfdom was abolished and farmers were free to buy and sell land. Ordinary farmers were thus freed from the domination of the local nobility, but in exchange they had the Qin state, with all its power, directly controlling them. The state organized all families into mutual responsibility groups, making each person liable for any crime committed by any other member of their group. Ordinary residents also had heavy obligations to the state for taxes and labour service and could not travel without permits; vagrants and criminals were forced into penal labour service.

In the book ascribed to him, Lord Shang heaped scorn on respect for tradition and urged the ruler not to hesitate to institute changes in his efforts to strengthen his state. The founders of the Xia, Shang, and Zhou had not been afraid to make changes, because 'wise people create laws while ignorant ones are controlled by them; the worthy alter the rites while the unworthy are held fast by them.' Law to him was the sovereign's will, carefully codified and impartially applied. The monarch regulates those under him through rules but he himself remains above the law.

The fullest exposition of Legalist thought was written by Han Feizi (d. 233 BC), who had begun as a student of the Confucian master Xunzi. In his writings, Han Feizi analysed situations from the perspective of the ruler. Knowing whom to trust was a major problem for 'when the ruler trusts someone, he falls under that person's control'. This includes not only ministers but also wives and concubines, who think of the interests of their sons. 'A man of fifty has not lost his interest in women, but a woman begins to lose her looks before thirty. When a woman whose looks are deteriorating serves a man who still loves sex, she will be despised and her son is not likely to be made heir. This is the reason queens, consorts, and concubines plot the death of the ruler.' Given the propensity of subordinates to pursue their own selfish interests, the ruler can not afford to be candid or warm towards any of them. Rather, he should keep them in awed ignorance of his intentions and control them by manipulating competition among them.

The Confucian notion that government should be based on virtue and ritual Han Feizi viewed as unworkable in his day. Hierarchical relations had to be based on the power to reward and punish; affection or example were not adequate.

> Think of parents' relations to their children. They congratulate each other when a son is born, but complain to each other when a daughter is born. Why do parents have these divergent responses when both are equally their offspring? It is because they calculate their long-term advantage. Since even parents deal with their children in this calculating way, what can one expect where there is no parent-child bond? When present-day scholars counsel rulers, they all tell them to rid themselves of thoughts of profit and follow the path of mutual love. This is expecting rulers to go further than parents.

Han Feizi urged rulers to be firm but consistent, to make the laws and prohibitions clear and the rewards and punishments automatic. This would make the officials and common people tractable, with the result that 'the state will get rich and the army will be strong. Then it will be possible to succeed in establishing hegemony over other states.'

Confucians often likened the state to the family and the good ruler to a good parent. Han Feizi drew different conclusions from his observations of family life: 'A mother loves her son twice as much as a father does, but a father's orders are ten times more effective than a mother's.' Moreover, he thought the common people had about as much understanding of what is good for them as infants.

> If an infant's head is not shaved, his sores will not heal; if his boils are not lanced, his illness will worsen. Even when someone holds him and his loving mother does the shaving or lancing, he will howl without stop, for a baby cannot see that a small discomfort will result in a major improvement. Now the ruler wants people to till land and maintain pastures to increase their production, but they think he is cruel. He imposes heavy penalties to prevent wickedness, but they think he is harsh. He levies taxes in cash and grain to fill the storehouses and thus relieve them in time of famine and have funds for the army, but they consider him greedy. He imposes military training on everyone in the land and makes his forces fight hard in order to capture the enemy, but they consider him violent. In all four cases, he uses means that will lead to peace, but the people are not happy.

Han Feizi and other Legalists had a highly authoritarian vision of order. There was no room for private conceptions of right and wrong because diversity leads to weakness and disorder. Law is something rulers decree for the interests of the state. If well publicized and enforced unwaveringly, it gets people to do things they would not otherwise be inclined to do, such as work hard and fight wars. Order and predictability result, bringing benefit to all. The opinions of people other than the rulers thus had no place in this system, any more than ancient privileges or traditional customs. In Legalist thought, there was no law above and independent of the wishes of the rulers, no law that might set limits on their actions in the way that natural or divine law did in Greek thought.

OTHER SCHOOLS OF THOUGHT

Singling out Confucians, Daoists, and Legalists for more extended discussion can be justified in terms of their long-term impact on Chinese civilization. It does not, however, fully capture the intellectual vitality of the late Zhou. In addition to the masters discussed so far, there were sophists fascinated by logical puzzles, utopians and hermits who developed rationales for withdrawal from public life, agriculturalists who argued that no one should eat who does not plough, and cosmologists who propounded theories concerning the forces of nature. Military affairs, not surprisingly, also attracted theorists. The *Art of War*, attributed to Confucius' contemporary Master Sun, not only discussed battle tactics but also the gathering of intelligence and other ways to deceive the enemy and win wars without combat.

Special mention should also be made of theorists of yin and yang. Yin is associated with feminine, dark, receptive, yielding, negative, and weak; yang with opposite qualities and forces: masculine, bright, assertive, creative, positive, and strong. The interaction of these complementary poles was viewed as integral to the processes that generate the natural order. The rhythmic movement from day to night and from summer to winter result from the interaction of yin and yang. Disturbances and imbalances can disrupt this order, in the way that improper food or inadequate rest disturb the health of the body.

Of the masters who cannot be classed as Confucian, Daoist, or Legalist, Mozi (active c.420 BC) is particularly interesting. Only slightly later than Confucius, Mozi came from a lower social level. There is some evidence that he may have been an expert in the construction of scaling ladders and other weapons used for both war and defence. Mozi loved to debate, and the style of argument found in the *Mozi* is different from that in other early texts. He laid out his criteria for judging practices and institutions. Did they work well? Were they beneficial to people? Was there authority for them in the teachings of the sages? Did they correspond to common experience? In calculating utility, Mozi used the entire population as the yardstick. He argued against aggressive war, saying that territorial gain was not worth loss of life. To do away with war, he advocated mutual concern for all, with no favouritism for relatives and neighbours. In place of contention, he advocated adherence to the views of superiors, up to the ruler, who follows the will of heaven: 'What the superior considers wrong, all shall consider wrong.'

Silk

Silk has a special association with China. By the late Zhou period, to those beyond China's borders, China was the land that produced silk, the most valued of all textiles, a soft, sheer, lightweight, long-lasting fabric that could be dyed brilliant colours. Silk was used for writing in a culture where the written word retained a sacred quality. Silk also symbolized wealth: not only was it worn by the wealthy, but bolts of silk were used as currency from Zhou times through the Tang dynasty a millennium later.

Archaeological remains reveal that already in Shang times Chinese were making fine silk damasks (single colour fabrics with woven-in designs) and elaborate silk embroideries. Substantial pieces of silk fabrics have been unearthed from late Zhou tombs in central China (the Chu area), showing that an extremely high level of technical skill had been reached by this time. Finds include multi-coloured brocades, beautifully designed embroideries, and open-work gauzes. Designs include human figures, animals, dragons, phoenixes, and geometric patterns.

The production of silk requires the cultivation of mulberry trees and the tending of silkworms (a kind of caterpillar), which feed on the leaves of these trees. Silkworms do not spin cocoons on demand; timing and temperature have to be handled carefully, and during the month between hatching and spinning the cocoons they have to be fed every few hours, day and night. If properly coddled, the worms eventually spin cocoons for several days, each cocoon made up of a strand of silk several thousand feet long. Still over 2,000 silkworms are needed to produce one pound of silk. In order to make textiles from these cocoons, they have to be boiled, then the separate strands reeled off, then a number of strands twisted together to make stronger threads. Only then come dyeing and weaving.

Women were traditionally associated with all stages of sericulture from the tending of silkworms to the reeling, spinning, and weaving needed to transform the cocoons into silk fabric. The division of labour summarized by the phrase, 'Men plough and women weave', dates back to the Zhou period and probably earlier.

Above
Detail of a three-colour patterned silk found in a fourth-century-BC tomb at Mashan, Hubei province. The material is densely woven with about 330 warp and 100 weft threads per inch.

Left
Detail of an embroidered silk gauze ritual garment from the same tomb. The flowing, curvilinear design incorporates dragons, phoenixes, and tigers. Rows of even, round chain-stitches are used both for outline and to fill in colour.

Mozi questioned the utility of traditional ritual practices, such as mourning austerities. He said both advocates and opponents of prolonged mourning claimed to be handing down the ways of the ancient sages, so the only way to choose between them was to analyse the consequences of the practices. His conclusion was that mourning interrupts work and injures health, thus it impoverishes the people and weakens the state's defences. In contrast to Confucians like Mencius who favoured hereditary office, Mozi came out strongly in favour of promoting the able and worthy, even if they were peasants, craftsmen, or traders.

STATES AND ETHNIC IDENTITIES

Perhaps because the late Zhou was a time of division into separate states, it was also a key period in the development of ideas about cultural and ethnic identity. In other words, the weakness of the Zhou dynasty as a political force unifying the known civilized world encouraged people to give more thought to issues of who belonged together, who could be considered one of 'us'.

Each of the major states came to have a distinct identity, tied to its own history and to distinctive features of its culture. People's identification with separate states was strong, and in most late Zhou literature, individuals are regularly identified by the state from which they came. Still, loyalties were not narrowly focused on states. People moved from one state to another frequently, and technological innovations and art motifs spread readily from one region to another. To advance diplomatic alliances the ruling houses of the various states intermarried, so rulers regularly had grandmothers, mothers, and wives from other states.

The idea of a broader realm on one central axis counterbalanced identification with home states. This broader realm could be referred to as 'All-Under-Heaven' (*tianxia*) or 'the Central States' (*zhongguo*). The Zhou king, as Son of Heaven, properly ruled over All-Under-Heaven. In late Zhou, when it was apparent to all that the Zhou king did not actually rule, the term 'All-Under-Heaven' continued to be used to refer to the civilized world, the collection of states and people that belonged together. Mencius, for instance, spoke of how a ruler who instituted good policies would please the farmers, merchants, and gentlemen of All-Under-Heaven; thus the people of neighbouring states would migrate to him, he would have no enemies in All-Under-Heaven, and could reign as a true king. But All-Under-Heaven was not an undifferentiated space or population; it was focused on the true king – the Son of Heaven.

Painted decoration on a coffin in the tomb of the marquis of Zeng in Hubei province (c. 433 BC). These hybrid, part-human creatures undoubtedly have something to do with early religious beliefs in the Chu area, perhaps representing otherworldly guards, weapons in their hands, ready to fend off evil forces.

Bronze oil lamp, almost 32 inches tall, excavated from the fourth-century-BC tomb of a Zhongshan king at Pingshan, Hebei province. Although the state of Zhongshan was established by the Di people, by the fourth century BC its elite had absorbed much of Chinese material and literary culture. This lamp with fifteen oil cups shows both superb casting technique and distinctive motifs, such as monkeys hanging from the branches of a tree.

A notion of centrality, this time geographical, is also apparent in the term 'the Central States', which referred to the states along the Yellow River, a region that had been central to the Xia and Shang and continued through the Eastern Zhou to set the standard against which outsiders could be judged deficient.

The degree to which outsiders were held to be deficient varied along a continuum. At one end were those totally outside the Zhou sphere, who did not recognize even the nominal sovereignty of the Zhou kings. The distinction between Zhou subjects and those who did not submit to the Zhou tended to be merged with the distinction between Hua or Xia people (which by this period can be taken as ethnic terms for Chinese) and barbarians, of whom there were several broad categories (Yi, Man, Di, Rong) and a great many particular names for specific tribes or cultures. A Rong lord allied with the state of Jin was reported to have said in 599 BC, 'Our Rong drink, our food, our clothes are all different from those of the Hua. We do not exchange presents with them. Our languages are mutually incomprehensible.'

The concept of 'barbarian' was not invested with what we would call racial characteristics. People's physical endowments were not seen as what makes them different. Rather, there seems to have been a rather sophisticated understanding of the variability of customs. Mozi, for instance, to prove that people think that whatever has been done in the past is right, gave some examples of strange beliefs and practices. 'Formerly east of Yue there was the country of Shaishu whose residents would dismember and eat the first-born son, saying they did so out of obligation toward the younger sons. After a grandfather died, they would carry off the grandmother and abandon her, saying one could not live with the wife of a ghost.' Mozi saw these customs as strange, but did not suggest or imply that the people themselves were beastly. Mencius had a similar sense of the relativity of culture. 'The northern tribes do not grow all the five grains, only millet. They have no cities, houses, or ritual sacrifices. They do not provide gifts or banquets for feudal lords, and do not have a full array of officials. Therefore, for them, [a tax of] one part in twenty is enough. But we live in the Central States. How could we abolish social roles and do without gentlemen?' Xunzi said, 'Children born among the Yue in the south or among the Mo barbarians of the north sound the same when they cry at birth, but as they get older they follow different customs.' If culture is a by-product of environment as Mencius implied, or an accretion of custom as Mozi and Xunzi implied, it follows that people can acquire cultures, and in Confucian teachings there are in fact many statements that reveal a conviction that people can be transformed from barbarians to civilized beings. When someone asked Confucius how he could consider moving to live among uncouth barbarians, he responded, 'If a gentleman lived among them, what uncouthness would there be?'

For the late Zhou, there is considerable evidence, both textual and archaeological, of the process by which the Chinese world was extended and groups that had once been considered barbarian or quasi-barbarian came to participate in the Chinese world as full members. In early Zhou the southern half of modern China was considered barbarian or semi-barbarian. In the Yangzi valley the state of Chu expanded rapidly, defeating and absorbing fifty or more small states as it extended its reach north to the heartland of Zhou and east to absorb the old states of Wu and Yue. By this point it controlled a territory as extensive as the Shang or Western Zhou dynasties at their heights. The tremendous material wealth of Chu can be gauged by the large number of late Zhou tombs found within its sphere. In art it borrowed and elaborated styles from further north and added distinctive elements not present elsewhere, such as antlered cranes, motifs which may have connections to distinctive religious ideas.

The Chu ruling elite was certainly conversant with both the material and intellectual culture of the Central States, and by late Zhou was contributing to that culture in a major way. Chu, for example, proved an innovator both in bureaucratic methods of government and in the use of infantry armies. Zhuangzi spent some time in Chu, and many scholars associate Daoism with Chu. The fantastical poems in the *Songs of Chu* (*Chuci*) are worlds apart from the earth-bound poems of the *Books of Songs* of the early Zhou. The principal poem is presented as the lament of Qu Yuan, a minister whose loyalty to his ruler is not appreciated and who ends up throwing himself into a river. In the poem Qu Yuan imagines himself wandering on the clouds and looking down on the earth. There are also poems in which shamans and shamanesses court elusive deities or fly through the spirit world.

The history of Chu can be compared to that of a much more minor state in the northeast, Zhongshan. The rulers of this state were recognized to be White Di, non-Chinese nomads who in the sixth century BC had been driven by other tribes from Shaanxi into Hebei, where the local Chinese states were unable to expel them. By the early fifth century BC, these Di had gained the help of the state of Wei and had established a city, from which they ruled for about a century before being defeated by the state of Yan, further north. Excavations of two tombs of kings of Zhongshan show acculturation to the taste and values of the Chinese amongst whom they lived. The figurines found in the graves are dressed in clothes more typically Chinese than northern. The ninety-odd inscribed bronzes buried there give detailed accounts of historical events in typically Confucian language. At the same time the royal tombs also contained artefacts needed for life on the steppe, such as hardware for tents. Shortly before the downfall of the state of Zhongshan, the king of a neighbouring state sent someone to assess Zhongshan, and this spy reported on his return that the king of Zhongshan loved learning, his people sought fame, but his soldiers were cowardly.

The ideas expounded in the late Zhou originated in specific geographical and temporal circumstances. The preference of the Daoists for private life and the earnest wish of the Confucians and Mohists for a moral transformation of humankind can be seen as responses to the brutality of the era. Moreover, late Zhou schools of thought had strong ties to particular regions of the country where they were first propounded and where followers found adherents.

Still, because the ideas of these thinkers were recorded in 'books' – actually, rolls of bamboo strips or silk – in time the ideas expressed in them were detached from their historical and geographical context. In this detached form, they came to play an enormous role in shaping the development of Chinese culture. Chinese education until modern times involved deep immersion in texts from this period. Chinese who read these texts were not prevented from learning of very different ways of looking at the world (the success of Buddhism is proof enough of that), and certainly they always were capable of disagreeing with each other on how to interpret and apply what they learned from ancient books, but it would be difficult to exaggerate the importance of these books in providing a common set of understandings about the world and the people who live in it. This influence was of course greatest on the educated, but over time as education spread and the educated interacted in more varied ways with the ordinary illiterate farmer, the most basic elements in these cultural orientations came to be widely shared and thus to constitute a large part of what is meant by 'Chinese' culture.

China was not the only place where key philosophical ideas were elaborated in the first millennium BC. In India of the Upanishads and the Buddha, in Greece of Socrates, Plato, and Aristotle, as in China of the Hundred Schools of Thought, intellectual breakthroughs occurred as cultural or religious experts ceased to limit themselves to expounding the rules of their culture and began to stand back and look beyond, to question and reflect on established conventions. In all these places creative individuals began to propose new visions and perspectives. But the visions thinkers of each region offered were rather different, with the result that the outpouring of reflective thought in this era marks a major step in the divergence of civilizations. When late Zhou philosophers are compared to Indian or Greek thinkers, their disagreements fade a bit and what all Chinese thinkers had in common becomes more striking.

At the cosmological level all the major philosophical schools in China shared ideas related to ancestors and heaven discussed in the last chapter. They also shared an underlying assumption that the cosmos came into being on its own, without a creator of the sort so important in most western thinking. Instead of focusing on mechanisms that set things into motion, which are important where there is an assumption of a creator, these thinkers emphasized the organismic interconnections among all the constituent parts, stressing relationships and concurrences much more than causes. Seeing the cosmos as an integrated whole, Chinese thinkers were not inclined to organize their world in terms of opposites that exclude the other, such as natural and supernatural, life and death, or mind and body. Rather, they saw all oppositions as complementary polarities, on the order of night and day, yin and yang, and knowledge and action. Moreover, they thought in terms of processes and phases more than discrete things.

At the level of social and political order, differences between Chinese assumptions or basic cultural orientations and those of other major civilizations are also telling. Particularly important here is the unchallenged conviction that the family is both natural and good. Unlike Greece, for instance, where the 'private' realm of the family was not given the positive evaluation of the public realm of the polis, in China devotion to family was taken as an obvious good. Laozi's utopia is not one that liberates the individual from the family, but one that lets families operate with little or no pressure from social or political units much larger than the village. Not only did Chinese thinkers assume that the family is essential to society, they also did not question that it is patrilineal and patriarchal. The family thus also provided for many a model for the ideal political order, one centred on an authoritarian ruler who would make hierarchical co-operation as natural as it seemed to them in the family.

Political visions also show considerable agreement. Among all Chinese thinkers of the period, order was viewed as inextricably connected to rulers, indeed to cosmically based universal kings. It is the universal king who embodies political order and possesses the power to transform the society below him for good or ill. Law, by contrast, was not granted comparable power by any Chinese thinker. Whether from a Confucian, a Legalist, or even a Daoist perspective, law was viewed as an expedient, not as something noble or inviolable, or something that exists above and beyond the ruler.

Another widespread conviction in Chinese thought, one that contrasts especially with early Indian thought, is the belief that life in this world can be improved. Most major schools of thought, with the important exception of the Legalists, looked to the early Zhou or even earlier to ancient rulers like Yao, Shun, and Yu for a better world. This belief in a golden age also meant that Chinese thinkers, lamenting the failings of their own age, did not conclude that reality or goodness lay in some other, unworldly realm. Achieving a golden age in this world was possible.

CHAPTER 3

The Creation of the Bureaucratic Empire:
The Qin and Han Dynasties 256 BC–AD 220

With Qin's victories over all of its rivals, China became a great agrarian empire. The centralized bureaucratic monarchy, the form of government that was to characterize most of the rest of Chinese history, was created by the Qin (ruled in all of China 221–206 BC) and entrenched during the much longer Han dynasty (202 BC–AD 220). It was in this period too that the geographic scope of China proper – the region in which Chinese were to become the dominant ethnic group – was staked out as the government extended overlordship across vast regions as far south as Vietnam. The ideology of the new state incorporated elements of Legalist, Daoist, and Confucian origin, but the officials who administered the state came to be identified more and more with Confucian learning, giving them a degree of independence from the throne. Over time local elites were drawn both to Confucian learning and to government service, and the Han government came very much to depend on co-operation between local officials and the local elites.

UNIFICATION BY QIN

Qin, the westernmost of the Zhou states, had begun as a royal domain assigned the task of raising horses and defending against the barbarians. After the Zhou royal house fled the Wei River valley to resettle at Luoyang in 770 BC, Qin was able to expand its territory and become the main power in the west. Not as urban or as culturally advanced as the eastern states, Qin seemed in early and mid Zhou times a rough and crude place, not that far removed from the Rong, Qiang, and Di tribes along its frontiers with which it regularly fought.

To help them strengthen their state, the Qin rulers of late Zhou times recruited advisors, strategists, and diplomats from the territories of their rivals. Lord Shang arrived in Qin in 361 BC and soon launched a series of Legalist measures intended to strengthen the power of the ruler (see pages 49–53, Chapter 2). By the third century BC, the people of Qin had become exceptionally law-abiding, agricultural production had been increased, and direct taxation was bringing substantial revenues to the king's coffers. On visiting Qin in about 264 BC, the Confucian philosopher Xunzi reported that the people stood in deep awe of their officials and the officials were serious and sincere, free from the tendency to form cliques.

The man who was to preside over the unification of China, King Zheng, came to the throne in 247 as a boy of nine. With the aid of two key ministers, Lü Buwei and Li Si, he led Qin to one military victory after another. In the final decade, from 230 to 221 BC, Qin conquered the states of Han, Zhao, Wei, Chu, Yan, and Qi.

Bronze weight, 6 ¾ inches high, excavated from the ruins of the Qin palace in Xianyang, Shaanxi province. Cast on to it are the name of the workman who made it and the unit of weight, bearing testimony to the Qin standardization of measurement.

Finally ruling 'All-Under-Heaven', King Zheng took a new title for himself, First Emperor (*Shi huangdi*). 'Emperor' (*huangdi*) was a term he coined by combining two words for 'august' and 'lord', words that until then had been used for the legendary sage rulers of China's remote past.

Later Chinese historians did not celebrate the First Emperor as one of the greatest conquerors of all time (as one suspects Greek or Roman historians would have), but rather castigated him as a cruel, arbitrary, impetuous, suspicious, and superstitious megalomaniac. The First Emperor was determined not only to amalgamate China into a single state, but to impose uniformity on it. Maintaining local forms of currency, weights and measures, or writing scripts was made an act of treason. The old states and their noble houses were abolished; the country was divided into thirty-six commanderies, each in turn divided into counties. The government dispatched officials to administer these new units and controlled them by a mass of regulations, reporting requirements, and penalties for inadequate performance. To guard against the possibility of local leaders organizing rebellions, private possession of arms was made illegal and hundreds of thousands of prominent or wealthy families from the conquered states were ordered to move to the capital, Xianyang (near Xi'an in Shaanxi province). As a result of the First Emperor's thoroughness, China lost much of its heritage, including local traditions of all sorts.

Criticism of the government was not tolerated by the First Emperor, who wanted the government to control knowledge. Education was to be provided only by officials and solely for the purpose of training future officials. After his advisor Li Si complained that scholars used records of the past to denigrate the emperor's

policies and undermine popular support, all writings other than useful manuals on topics like agriculture, medicine, or divination were ordered to be collected for burning. Recalcitrant scholars were also suppressed – tradition holds that 460 were buried alive in a common grave as a warning against defiance of the emperor's orders.

Ordinary people also suffered harsh treatment. Reporting crimes was rewarded, and the lawbreakers, once convicted, were punished severely by execution, hard labour, or mutilation (ranging from cutting off the whiskers to the nose or the left foot). Even perfectly law-abiding people were subject to onerous labour service, and both conscripted and penal labour were used for the building of palaces, roads, canals, imperial tombs, and fortifications. Several hundred thousand subjects were conscripted to build a huge new palace complex in 212 BC. Even more were drafted to construct the Great Wall. Earlier states had built ramparts of rammed earth along their borders. Qin knocked down those that separated the old states and connected those along the northern frontier to make a vast defensive system to protect against incursions from the nomads to the north.

The First Emperor's successes were due in no small measure to his determination to manage every detail of his government himself. He set quotas for the weight of documents he would read and dispose of each day, not resting until he had finished his paperwork. He made several tours of the country to inspect his new realm and awe his subjects. At sacred places he erected stone tablets inscribed with accounts of his exploits; his empire, he declared in one, extended in all directions, so that 'Wherever human life is found, all acknowledge its sovereignty.'

After surviving three assassination attempts the First Emperor became obsessed with avoiding death and devoted his energies to discovering the secrets of immortality. He sent a delegation of young men and women out to sea to search for Peng Lai, a mythical land of immortality. Historical accounts of the vast sums and huge labour contingents he expended on the secret construction of his tomb have been verified by archaeological excavations. Three pits discovered about half a mile from the emperor's tomb (not itself yet excavated) contain thousands of life-size terracotta figures of armed soldiers and horses, lined up to protect the emperor.

THE HAN GOVERNMENT

The institutions Qin had fashioned to concentrate power in the hands of the monarch made the stability of the government dependent on the strength and character of the occupant of the throne. When the First Emperor died in 210 BC, the Qin imperial structure fell apart. The legitimate heir was promptly murdered by his younger brother and uprisings soon followed. In 209 BC a group of conscripted peasants delayed by rain decided to become outlaws rather than face death for arriving late for their frontier service. To their surprise they soon found thousands of malcontents eager to join them. Similar revolts of people eager to

Opposite
The vast size of the terracotta army buried about a half mile from the tomb of the First Emperor of Qin near Xi'an in Shaanxi province points to both the might of the Qin military machine and the concern of the First Emperor with the afterlife. Originally painted in twelve or thirteen bright colours, these life-sized figures were made from moulded interchangeable parts but were hand finished, so that no two are identical. To add to the sense of verisimilitude, they were equipped with real chariots and bronze weapons.

escape the burden of Qin labour and military service broke out elsewhere. In 208 BC the Second Emperor killed his minister Li Si; in 207 BC he was assassinated by the new chief minister, who was in turn murdered by the successor he placed on the throne. Meanwhile, Qin generals were defecting and former nobles of the late Zhou states took to raising armies. The eventual victor was Liu Bang, known in history as Gaozu (r. 202–195 BC), a man of modest background who had served the Qin as a minor local functionary, in charge of a postal relay station. In 206 BC he took the title King of Han and in 202 BC defeated his main rival, the brilliant aristocratic general Xiang Yu. Gaozu made his capital at Chang'an, only a few miles from the site of the Qin capital, which had been burnt to the ground during the rebellion.

At the time Qin was overthrown, most people apparently associated centralization with tyranny and believed the Han government should parcel out domains as the early Zhou had. Gaozu thus began by rewarding his old comrades with large territories to govern as vassal states, an action he soon recognized as a mistake, since dispersed power proved a danger to the emperor. Thus the challenge for the early Han government was to develop a form of centralized power that could secure order and dynastic stability without undue harshness, one that, in more Chinese terms, combined military strength (*wu*) with the morally centred civil arts (*wen*).

The Han dynasty retained Qin's principal weapon against the old aristocracy, namely direct administration of localities by officials appointed by the court for their merit, not their birth, and subject to dismissal, transfer, and discipline. Han prefects and magistrates had broad responsibilities and powers: they judged lawsuits, collected and dispatched taxes, performed ceremonies of the state-sponsored religion, commanded troops, decided when and how to undertake public works like flood control, kept an eye on the local economy and local education, and selected subordinates from the local population. Those successful as local administrators could be promoted to serve at court as the head of a ministry or as a counsellor to the emperor.

The key figure in the strengthening of the Han governmental apparatus was Wudi (r. 141–87 BC), emperor for over fifty years. After coming to the throne as a vigorous young man of fifteen, Wudi set about curbing the power of princes and other lords; he confiscated the domains of over half of them on whatever pretext he could find. Moreover he decreed that domains would have to be divided among all the lord's heirs, thus guaranteeing that they would diminish in size with each passing generation. He curbed the power of great merchants as well, in the

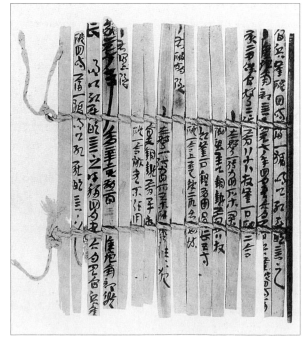

The bureaucratic government of Han times produced huge quantities of documents on wooden and bamboo strips, and great caches of such documents have been found among the ruins of the garrisons established along the north-western frontier. The one shown here was excavated at Juyan in Gansu province; dated AD 95, it is an inventory of the equipment of two infantry units.

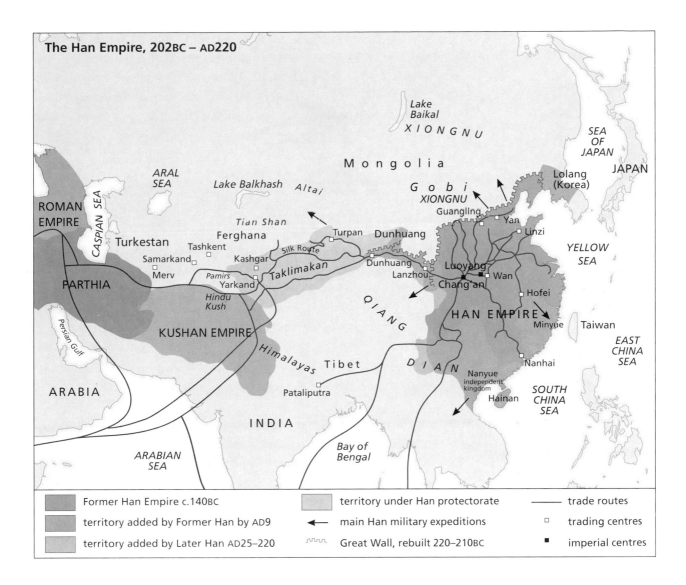

The Han Empire, 202BC – AD220

Legend:
- Former Han Empire c.140BC
- territory added by Former Han by AD9
- territory added by Later Han AD25–220
- territory under Han protectorate
- main Han military expeditions
- Great Wall, rebuilt 220–210BC
- trade routes
- trading centres
- imperial centres

process gaining new sources of revenue through his state monopolies and commercial taxes. In foreign relations he was especially aggressive, reversing earlier conciliatory policies (see below). In the cultural realm he imposed his authority as well. He instituted imperial rituals as grand as the empire he ruled. He lured the finest writers and scholars to his court and at the same time suppressed rival cultural centres, including some princely courts.

Wudi and other Han emperors, like the Qin emperors before them, were essentially above the law, autocrats of theoretically unlimited powers. But rather than try to control officials through Legalist means such as exhaustive specification of rules and procedures, Wudi and other Han rulers made use of Confucian notions of the moral basis of superior–subordinate relations, appreciating that in the long run the ruler would achieve his goals more easily and economically when his subordinates viewed their relationship with the ruler in moral terms of loyalty and

The Han dynasty asserted sovereignty over vast regions from Korea in the east to Central Asia in the west and Vietnam in the south. Once garrisons were established, traders were quick to follow, leading to considerable spread of Chinese material culture.

Gilt bronze figure of a maid-servant holding an oil-lamp, almost 19 inches tall, excavated from the tomb of Dou Wan, wife of one of Emperor Wu's brothers, at Mancheng in Hebei province. This elegant gilded bronze lamp was cleverly designed to allow adjustments in the directness and brightness of the light and to trap smoke in the body. It was one of the nearly 3,000 objects of bronze, iron, gold, silver, jade, pottery, lacquer, and silk from this huge tomb that testify to the luxury and refinement of palace life.

responsibility. To cultivate such attitudes in his officials, Wudi became a patron of Confucian education (see below).

One problem Wudi did not solve was the vulnerability of the imperial institution when a young or weak-willed emperor succeeded to the throne. Men of the imperial lineage – brothers and sons of emperors – were regularly sent out of the capital to their domains and were thus effectively kept out of court politics. The same was not true of the male relatives of emperors' wives and mothers, who thus often became influential figures at court. After Gaozu died, his strong-willed widow, Empress Lü, took control and promoted the interests of her family. On her death fifteen years later, her relatives were executed. Over a century later Wang Mang came to power as a relative of Empress Wang (d. AD 13), a woman of importance at court for more than forty years as the widow of one emperor, mother of another, and grandmother of a third. In AD 9, after serving as regent during the reigns of two child emperors, Wang Mang acceded to the requests that he take the throne himself and founded the Xin or 'New' dynasty.

Although condemned by later historians as a usurper, Wang Mang was a learned Confucian scholar who sincerely wished to implement political programmes described in the classics. He renamed offices, asserted state ownership of forests and swamps, built ritual halls, revived public granaries, and cut court expenses. Yet Wang Mang's policies, particularly the repeated issuing of new coins and nationalization of gold, led to economic turmoil. Added to this, in AD 11 the Yellow River changed course to exit south rather than north of the Shandong peninsula, flooding enormous tracts of land and driving millions of peasants from their homes. Opponents of Wang Mang soon came to include displaced and hungry peasants, landlords who had suffered under his fiscal policies, Confucian scholars who regarded Wang Mang as a usurper, and members of the Liu imperial family. The eventual victor was Liu Xiu (reigned as Guangwu, AD 25–57), a member of the imperial clan whose family for generations had lived not as nobles but as substantial local landlords. From the beginning, he made Luoyang on the eastern plain his capital. The period after Wang Mang is conventionally called the Later or Eastern Han (25–220), the period before him the Former or Western Han (206 BC–AD 9), east and west referring to the location of the capitals.

THE STEPPE AND THE SILK ROAD

The success of the unified bureaucratic form of government owes a great deal to military necessity: beginning in the third century BC, in order to fend off incursions from the steppe, north China needed a government capable of deploying huge, well-trained fighting forces.

Sima Qian and the *Historical Records*

The way the Chinese have conceived of their past – and thus of themselves – was profoundly shaped by a book written in Han times, the *Historical Records (Shiji)* of Sima Qian 145–c.85 BC). Before Sima Qian was able to complete his history, he made the political mistake of defending a general who had surrendered to the Xiongnu. Given a choice between death and becoming a palace eunuch, he chose the humiliation of castration and servitude rather than leave his history unfinished. He wrote to a friend that he had chosen to live in disgrace 'because I have things in my heart that I have not been able to express fully'.

The resulting monumental work in 130 chapters presents the past from several perspectives: a chronological narrative of political events; topical accounts of key institutions; and biographies of important individuals. The political narrative begins with the Yellow Lord and continues through the Xia, Shang, and Zhou dynasties, down to Wudi of Sima Qian's day. Chronological charts with genealogical data and information on government posts come next, followed by topical treatises on matters of interest to the government, such as state ritual, the calendar, the construction of waterworks, and government finance. Thirty chapters are devoted to the ruling houses of the states of the Zhou period, recounting the reigns of successive rulers. These are supplemented by seventy chapters on other important individuals, including not only great officials and generals, but also personalities not associated with the government, the famous and the infamous – philosophers, poets, merchants, magicians, rebels, and assassins. Even non-Han peoples along the frontiers were described in narrative accounts.

The punishment Sima Qian suffered did not incline him to flatter those in power; in fact he gave ample evidence of Wudi's credulity and policy errors. If he was biased in anyone's favour, it was towards those whose courage, chivalry, and loyalty had gone unrecognized in their day. Sima Qian saw himself as writing fact-based, objective history and attempted to separate his personal judgments from his basic narrative. He quoted directly from documents when they were available. In their absence he invented speeches and dialogues that he felt fitted the characters and situations, thus bringing events to life. For example, he reported a conversation between the first emperor of the Han, Gaozu (or Liu Bang), and his chief minister Xiao He in the eighth year of his reign:

Chief Minister Xiao was in charge of the construction of the Eternal Palace and was working on the eastern and western gate towers, the front hall, the arsenal, and the storehouse. When Gaozu arrived and saw the magnificence of the buildings, he was outraged. 'Warfare has kept the empire in turmoil for years, and victory is not yet assured. What is the idea of building palaces on such an excessive scale?'

'It is precisely because the fate of the empire is not yet settled', Xiao He responded, 'that we need to build palaces and halls like these. The true Son of Heaven treats the four quarters as his family estate. If he does not dwell in magnificent quarters, he will have no way to display his authority, nor will he establish the foundation for his heirs to build on.'

On hearing this, Gaozu's anger turned into delight.

The *Historical Records* was such an extraordinary achievement that it set the pattern for the government-sponsored histories compiled by later dynasties. The composite style – with political narratives, treatises, and biographies – became standard. Equally important, Sima Qian, by writing so well on so much, had a profound impact on Chinese thinking about government, personal achievement, and even the nature of China. Government, for instance, was too complex to be narrated around rulers alone: institutional practices had their own complex histories that had to be told in their own terms. The way Sima Qian constructed biographies similarly reflected and shaped understandings of the individual. He selected incidents that showed consistency in a person's character and how well the person performed a role rather than turning points in personal development.

Sima Qian's descriptions of barbarians indirectly helped to shape ideas about the Chinese. The group that provided the key 'other' to Sima Qian was clearly the Xiongnu. Everything about them seemed to be the opposite of the Chinese: they had no written language, family names, or respect for the elderly; they had no cities, permanent dwellings, or agriculture. Where the Xiongnu excelled was in warfare, for their men could all ride and shoot and would raid without hesitation: 'When they see the enemy, eager for booty, they swoop down like a flock of birds.'

The metal ornaments of the Xiongnu provide convincing evidence that they were in contact with nomadic pastoralists further west in Asia, such as the Scythians, who also fashioned metal plaques and buckles in animal designs. This gold buckle or ornament, about 3 inches long, probably dates from the third century BC.

From long before Han times, China's contacts with the outside world had involved a combination of trade and military conflict. Chinese products like silk and lacquerware were superior to those of its neighbours, creating a demand for Chinese goods. Some neighbours had goods they could offer in exchange, such as timber, horses, sheep and cattle. But raiding was a common alternative to trade; non-Chinese groups who found that they could acquire the goods they wanted by force had less incentive to trade. Moreover, those normally willing to trade might turn to raiding when previously established trade relations were disrupted or when drought drove them to desperate measures. Defending against the raids of non-Chinese peoples had been a problem since Shang times, but with the rise of nomadism in the arid steppe north of China proper in mid Zhou, the severity of the problem was greatly exacerbated.

The Inner Asian steppe is a vast region of grasslands, mountains, and deserts, capable of supporting only a sparse population. In the best grasslands, such as those of modern Mongolia, rainfall is too light for grain to grow but animals can be pastured. Nomads of the steppe near China raised sheep, goats, camels, and horses, moving their camps north in summer and south in winter. Their skill as horsemen and hunters, especially their ability to shoot arrows while riding horseback, made them a potent military striking force. The typical social structure of the steppe nomads was tribal, with family and clan units held together through loyalty to chiefs selected for their military prowess. This structure could be exploited for efficient military mobilization when enough tribal units coalesced. The differences in the modes of living of farmers and herders led to sharp contrasts in their social values. For most of the imperial period, Chinese farmers looked on horse-riding pastoralists as a scourge, as pitiless gangs of bullies who preferred robbing to working for their living. The nomads, for their part, gloried in their military might and looked with scorn on farmers as weaklings incapable of defending themselves.

The first great confederation of nomadic tribes in Inner Asia was formed by the Xiongnu in the late third century BC. The First Emperor of Qin sent 100,000 troops against them in 213 BC, and his Great Wall was intended for defence against them. The early Han emperors tried conciliatory policies, wooing the Xiongnu leaders with generous gifts, including silk, rice, cash, and even imperial princesses as brides. Critics of these policies feared that they merely strengthened the enemy; and indeed, in 166 BC 140,000 horseman raided deep into China, reaching a point less than 100 miles from the capital.

Wudi took the offensive. He sent 300,000 troops far into Xiongnu territory in 133 BC. Subsequent expeditions, like those in 124, 123, and 119, often involved over 100,000 men. These campaigns were enormously expensive, requiring long supply lines and entailing great losses of men and horses. The gain was territory: regions north and west of the capital were acquired, cutting off the Xiongnu from the proto-Tibetan Qiang, whom they had subjugated. Four commanderies were established in Gansu, and more than a million people were dispatched to colonize this northwest region. At the same time Wudi sent troops into northern Korea to establish commanderies that would flank the Xiongnu on their eastern border.

Wudi turned his attention to Central Asia as well, in part to find allies, in part to improve the supply of horses for the army. In 139 BC he sent one of his officials, Zhang Qian, west in search of allies to fight against the Xiongnu. Captured and kept prisoner for ten years, Zhang eventually escaped and made his way to Bactria and Ferghana, returning in 126 BC. In 115 BC he set out on a second journey west. From his reports, the Chinese learned for the first time of other civilized states comparable to China that had developed independently of China. Ferghana, for instance, he described as 10,000 *li* (about 3,000 miles) due west of China, a land of fortified cities and dense population, that grew wheat and grapes for wine and had fine horses that sweated blood. He described Parthia in similar terms, but drew particular attention to its merchants and to its coins, made of silver and bearing the image of the king's face. Zhang Qian discovered that these regions were already importing Chinese products, especially silk. In 101 BC, after three years' effort, a Chinese army made its way beyond the Pamir Mountains to defeat Ferghana, seize large numbers of its excellent horses, and gain recognition of Chinese overlordship, thus obtaining control over the trade routes across Central Asia. The territorial reach of the Han state had been vastly extended.

Soon the threat of the Xiongnu began to recede. In 55 BC the Xiongnu confederation broke up into five contending groups. Not long afterwards the chief of the

Retinues of soldiers and attendants that accompanied officials when they travelled were an important symbol of official rank, and many Later Han tombs had paintings of them on their walls. More spectacular is this set of bronze figures excavated from a second-century-AD tomb at Leitai in Gansu. Altogether this procession included seventeen soldiers, twenty-eight attendants, thirty-nine horses, and fourteen carriages, each roughly a foot tall.

southern Xiongnu acceded to tributary status like that of the tribes and states along China's western and southern borders. Vassal states had to send a prince as a hostage to the Chinese capital where he would be given a Chinese education. Vassals also had to send periodic missions with tributary gifts, a practice that appealed to them because it allowed opportunities for trade. To the Chinese the tribute system was costly but it avoided war and confirmed that China was the centre of the civilized world. Over the course of the dynasty the Han government gave enormous quantities of silk to the states and tribes that accepted tributary status; in 25 BC, for instance, it gave out 20,000 rolls of silk and about 20,000 pounds of silk floss. It has been estimated that nearly 10 per cent of state revenues went on gifts of this sort.

Much of the silk acquired by the Xiongnu and other northern tributaries eventually ended up in lands far to the west. Chinese silk was already popular in Rome by the time Julius Caesar died in 44 BC, and was imported in even larger quantities in subsequent decades. This silk reached Rome after passing though many hands; the middlemen included Sogdian, Parthian, and Indian merchants. The silk arrived both as skeins of silk thread and as woven silk cloth produced in China itself or in Syrian workshops. Caravans returning to China brought gold, horses, and occasionally luxury goods of west Asian origin such as glass beads and cups.

When the power of the Han government waned under Wang Mang and the civil war that accompanied his fall, many of the distant territories broke away from China, but during the Later Han period, Chinese authority was reasserted. The generals Ban Chao and his son Ban Yong re-established Han supremacy in Central Asia, Ban Chao marching an army past the Pamir Mountains in AD 97. The city-states along the Silk Road did not necessarily resist the Chinese presence; they could carry out the trade upon which they depended more conveniently with Chinese garrisons to protect them than with rival tribes raiding them.

The danger for the Han government was over-extension; supplying such distant frontiers could bankrupt the government. Maintaining the supply of horses, for instance, was a constant problem, even after the government set up vast horse farms. The Han government vigorously pursued cost-cutting ways to defend its far-flung borders. It set up military colonies along the frontiers where soldiers could be self-supporting and recruited non-Chinese nomads to serve as auxiliary forces. In the Later Han, the Southern Xiongnu, who had been offered land and other inducements to ally with the Han, were frequently used as the main forces to fight the common enemy, the Northern Xiongnu. But defence remained costly, and the need to support a huge military establishment kept pressure on the government to maintain its efficiency in extracting revenue and to improve transport facilities by building roads, bridges, and canals.

MYTH, MAGIC, AND THE MARVELLOUS

Perhaps because of the influence of the culture of the Chu region – the home of the Han founder and most of his early followers – Han art and literature are rich in references to spirits, portents, myths, the strange and powerful, the death-defying and the dazzling. The *Huainanzi,* a Daoist-tinged compilation of texts sponsored by the prince of Huainan during the mid second century BC, contains lore of mountain gods, some with human faces and dragons' bodies, and describes the magic realm of the Kunlun Mountains in the far west where immortality could be attained. Han emperors attempted to make contact with the world of gods and immortals through elaborate sacrifices, often designed by Daoist magicians. Wudi, in particular, welcomed to his court astrologers, alchemists, seers, and shamans; he listened to stories of how Huangdi, the Yellow Emperor, had ascended to the realm of the immortals with his whole court and all his consorts. Both at court and among the general population the desire to understand the workings of cosmic forces and predict the future led to intense interest in omens and portents. In the years leading up to and following Wang Mang's accession, portents of coming change were repeatedly discovered, including rocks and other objects with messages inscribed on them. Although both Wang Mang's allies and opponents may well have manipulated much of this, they were building on an abiding belief in messages from heaven.

The fate of the dead was similarly a subject of intense concern in Han times. The soul was conceived to have two aspects. The lighter, more heavenly part would ascend to the clouds and might possibly enter the realm of the immortals. The more earthly part of the soul stayed in or near the grave and benefited from the food and other goods placed in the grave. Constructing and furnishing a grave was thus not simply an act of good will toward the dead, but also a way for the living to protect themselves from the anger of dissatisfied ghosts. Notions of post-mortem judgement – so important in later Chinese religion – began to appear in Han times. Soon after the establishment of the centralized bureaucratic empire, it seems, the otherworld became bureaucratized as well. Han tombs contain itemized lists of their contents addressed to the Lord Master of the Dead. Other texts mention the tribunal on Mount Tai, a sacred mountain in Shandong, where the records of the living and the dead were judged and appropriate rewards and punishments meted out.

During the Han period, the hope for deathlessness or immortality found expression in the cult of a goddess called the Queen Mother of the West. Her paradise was portrayed as a land of marvels where trees of deathlessness grew and rivers of immortality flowed. Mythical birds and beasts were her constant companions, including the three-legged crow, the dancing toad, the nine-tailed fox, and the elixir-producing rabbit. People of all social levels expressed their devotion to her, and shrines were erected under government sponsorship throughout the country. At times worship of her reached frenzied proportions. As an illustration,

Left

Bronze 'money tree' of Eastern Han date excavated at Guanghan in Sichuan province. The common coin of Han times (round with a square hole) magically grows on this nearly five-foot-tall tree. The Queen Mother of the West is shown perching like a bird, seated on her dragon-and-tiger throne. Money trees of this sort have been found only in Sichuan.

Below

Inscribed on this small Han bronze mirror are the words: 'The blue dragon made this mirror of unsurpassed quality. May you attain the highest political rank like the King Father of the East. May you attain longevity like the Queen Mother of the West.' The Queen Mother, with wings, has two seated attendants at her side, while the King Father is attended by a standing man. Probably because the dominant yin-yang cosmology called for complementary pairing, by Later Han times the Queen Mother of the West was often paired with the King Father of the East.

the *History of the Han* provided the following vivid account from 3 BC:

> People were running about in a state of alarm, holding stalks of hemp that
> they passed from one to another, saying they were delivering the wand of
> the edict of the Queen Mother of the West. Thousands of people converged
> on the roads, some with dishevelled hair or barefoot... . They passed
> through twenty-six commanderies and principalities on their way to the
> capital... [Even those who stayed home in their villages] became caught up
> in the enthusiasm, holding services, setting up gaming boards for lucky
> throws, and singing and dancing in worship of the Queen Mother. They
> also passed around texts reading 'The Mother tells the people that those
> who wear this talisman will not die.'

This movement was the first recorded messianic, millenarian movement in
Chinese history. It coincided with prophecies foretelling the end of the dynasty,
fulfilled when Wang Mang took the throne.

THE AGRARIAN ECONOMY

Han civilization was built on an agrarian base. At the technical level, agriculture
certainly advanced during the Han. Improved methods included planting two
crops in alternate rows and planting a succession of carefully timed crops. Han
ploughs were notable for such advanced features as struts that could be adjusted
to control the depth of furrows and curved metal mould-boards that reduced friction. Use of oxen to draw ploughs became common, allowing farmers to cultivate
larger fields. Better irrigation was achieved not only through large state-sponsored
canal projects, but also through the spread of improved techniques like brick-
faced wells to ordinary farmers. The donkey, an animal of western origin introduced into north China by the Xiongnu, came to be widely used as a pack animal.
Probably equally useful was the wheelbarrow, first seen in Han times.

As a result of advances of these sorts, as well as relative peace and the extension
of frontiers, the Chinese population grew rapidly in the Former Han period; the
census of AD 2 recorded a population of fifty-eight million, making the Han
empire somewhat larger than the contemporaneous Roman empire. Nevertheless,
in most texts written in the Han period, the fragility of the economy seems to have
been much more on people's minds than its underlying strengths. This sense of
insecurity was aggravated by key features of the political economy that were to
characterize much of the rest of Chinese history. Land tenure, inheritance practices, and government fiscal policies all fostered the simultaneous presence of
both very small family farms and large landed estates, with rapid mobility
between wealth and poverty as some families lost their land and others were able
to build up substantial holdings.

The economic insecurity of smallholders was described by Chao Cuo in 178 BC
in terms that could well have been repeated in most later dynasties:

This 6¼-foot-long painting on
silk was found draped over the
coffin in the grave of Lady Dai
(c. 168 BC) at Mawangdui near
Changsha in Hunan province.
The scenes depicted on it
seem to illustrate the journey
of the woman's soul. The top
section shows the heavenly
realm, complete with dragons,
leopards, and hybrid creatures. At the corners are the
crow that symbolizes the sun
and the toad that symbolizes
the moon, the pairing of sun
and moon representing the
cosmic forces of yin and yang.

They labour at ploughing in the spring and hoeing in the summer, harvesting in the autumn and storing foodstuff in winter, cutting wood, performing labour service for the local government, all the while exposed to the dust of spring, the heat of summer, the storms of autumn, and the chill of winter. Through all four seasons they never get a day off. They need funds to cover such obligations as entertaining guests, burying the dead, visiting the sick, caring for orphans, and bringing up the young. No matter how hard they work they can be ruined by floods or droughts, or cruel and arbitrary officials who impose taxes at the wrong times or keep changing their orders. When taxes fall due, those with produce have to sell it at half price [to raise the needed cash], and those without [anything to sell] have to borrow [at such high rates] they will have to pay back twice what they borrowed. Some as a consequence sell their lands and houses, even their children and grandchildren.

The expansion of the area of cultivated land under the Han probably owes something to the development of the animal-drawn plough, depicted here on a stone relief found at Mizhi, Shaanxi province.

One fundamental reason farmers often had barely enough to survive was the equal division of family property among all sons, a custom fully established by Han times. In the Zhou period, aristocratic titles and offices as well as the responsibility to maintain ancestral rites had been passed to a single heir, generally the eldest son. With the decline of feudal tenures and the spread of free buying and selling of land, the division of family property became customary. Partible inheritance in turn had profound consequences for both the structure of the family and the dynamics of the rural economy. The Chinese family remained patrilineal, patrilocal, and patriarchal, but it no longer favoured oldest sons in the transmission of property. Ownership of land changed hands frequently as those with wealth (perhaps from office or commerce) purchased it and those who inherited land had to sell parts of it to meet expenses. To a family head, the survival of his family depended not merely on the survival of a male heir to continue the ancestral sacrifices, but also on preserving or securing enough family property to allow all the sons to marry and support a family.

Hard-pressed small farmers were driven to cultivate marginal land and to farm intensively whatever they had. When that was not enough, they could search out patrons, becoming tenants or dependants of local magnates, whose land and power accordingly swelled. Sometimes, undoubtedly, the decision was not voluntary; poor peasants could not always count on government officials to protect them from the demands of local bullies. As critics already pointed out in the first century BC, the greater the number of peasants who escaped the tax rolls, the harder tax-collectors pressed those who remained. When demands became too great, the poor were left to choose between migration to areas where new lands could be cleared or quasi-servile status as the dependant of a magnate.

The Han government, like most of its successors, was unhappy with the shrinkage of its tax base and tried to stem the loss of independent, land-owning peasants. It promoted irrigation works to enhance production. It issued limits on the size of landholdings. It responded to bad harvests with tax reductions and direct relief. For those who had fled in time of famine, it offered tax remissions and loans of seed to induce them to return. Its most basic policy, however, was to try to keep land taxes light. The Han drew revenues both from a poll tax and a tax on agricultural production which for most of the Han period was only one-thirtieth of the autumn harvest. Large landowners, of course, benefited at least as much as small ones from the light taxation on land.

Because the Han government did not want to burden farmers, it had to find other ways to increase its revenues. To pay for his military campaigns, Wudi took over the minting of coins, confiscated the lands of nobles, sold offices and titles, and increased taxes on private businesses. A widespread suspicion of commerce – from both moral and political perspectives – made it easy to levy especially heavy assessments on merchants. Boats, carts, shops, and other facilities were made subject to property taxes. The worst blow to businessmen, however, was the government's decision to enter into competition with them by selling the commodities that had been collected as taxes. In 119 BC government monopolies were established in the production of iron, salt, and liquor, enterprises that had previously been sources of great profit for private entrepreneurs. Large-scale grain dealing had also been a profitable business, which the government now took over under the name of the system of equable marketing. Grain was to be bought in areas where it was plentiful and cheap and either stored in granaries or transported to areas of scarcity. This procedure was supposed to eliminate speculation in grain, provide more constant prices, and bring profit to the government.

The long-term result of these fiscal policies was a disruption of the development of the private commercial sector of the economy. During the first century of the Han, the prosperity of this sector had led to the growth of towns and cities and increased specialization in trade and manufacture. After the government took over the iron foundries and salt works and became deeply involved in the grain trade, the vitality of the business sector suffered. Even though the Later Han government abandoned these ventures, its laissez-faire policies tended to benefit large landowners more than merchants. The Chinese economy thus became firmly agrarian, a pattern that was to continue through Chinese history.

CONFUCIANISM, THE STATE, AND THE EDUCATED ELITE

The Han period is, for good reason, associated with the victory of Confucianism. Where the Qin had given political support to Legalism, the Han gave it to Confucianism. As seen above, the special status of Confucianism did not keep all sorts

Houses

Because the Chinese used timber as the primary building material, there are no remains of the palaces of the Qin or Han, much less more ordinary buildings. Nonetheless, basic features of house construction can be discerned from ceramic models of houses placed in tombs and sketches of the layout of houses drawn, carved, or impressed on the walls of tombs. Much can also be learned from tombs themselves, which were built like underground houses.

Wood, tile, plaster, brick, and stone were the standard materials used to construct houses. Medium-sized houses were usually built around one or more courtyards, with rooms, set a few steps above ground level, on some sides and covered walkways or galleys on others. Multi-storey buildings were also constructed, either as main buildings within courtyard structures or as watch towers outside.

The basic structure of any residential building was a timber frame with wooden pillars to support the thatched or tiled roof. The walls built up around the wooden frame were not load-bearing, and were commonly made of brick, stamped earth, or mud. Projecting eaves, which served to protect the walls from rain, were supported by wooden brackets that were sometimes elaborated for decorative effect. The ends of the roof tiles also were commonly decorated with moulded designs.

Left
Ceramic models of multi-storey houses or watch towers were often placed in Han tombs.

Corners
Ceramic roof tiles from the ruins of the Qin palace.

Below
Laying out a house around a courtyard creates a series of inner and outer spaces. Outdoor activities such as washing dishes or processing grain could still be done within the confines of the home. This scene of a courtyard house was impressed on a brick used to face a second-century-AD tomb in Sichuan province.

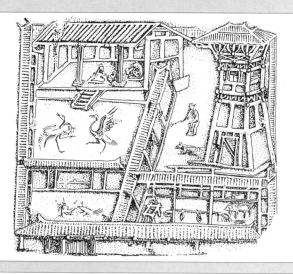

Lacquer cups, bowls, chopsticks, and trays unearthed from tomb 1 at Mawangdui near Changsha in Hunan province. Lacquer, made from the sap of a tree indigenous to China, was used from neolithic times to waterproof bamboo and wooden objects. In Han times well-made lacquer objects were so highly valued they could cost more than bronze pieces.

of non-Confucian ideas about spirits, portents, or the marvellous from gaining a hold on the Han imagination. Moreover, Han Confucianism itself was eclectic, fortifying itself with precepts and philosophical concerns drawn from what had been competing philosophical schools in the pre-Qin period. The Han 'victory' of Confucianism thus did not entail the eradication of other ways of thinking. Its historical importance lies rather in the ways it coloured the connections between the elite, the society, and the state.

The first Han emperors, although prudently avoiding the harsh policies of the repudiated Qin government, were not partial to Confucianism. Gaozu found the Confucian scholars of his day useful primarily as formulators of court rituals that would elevate him above his erstwhile companions and keep them from getting rowdy in court. Wendi (r. 179–157 BC) favoured Daoism, finding much of value in its laissez-faire message. Ironically it was under his grandson Wudi, who was often accused of Legalist tendencies, that Confucianism gained a privileged position at court. Wudi recognized the advantages to the throne of employing men who had learned Confucian self-restraint, concern for others, love of ritual, devotion to principle, and loyalty to superiors, and he developed a state educational system to train potential officials in the Confucian classics. The imperial academy he founded was staffed with professors for each of the Five Classics (*Book of Changes, Book of Documents, Book of Songs, Book of Rites*, and *Spring and Autumn Annals*). His successors maintained these policies and by the first century BC, it became widely accepted that officials should be men trained in the Confucian classics and respected for their character. Officials could nominate their sons or other close relatives for government posts, but a man did not have to come from an official family to enter the civil service. The prestige and influence of government posts steadily rose, and men of wealth and local standing throughout the

The pre-Han texts that had survived the Qin burning of the books came to be greatly revered, especially the Five Classics. In AD 175 the government had them carved in stone in the calligraphy of the eminent man of letters Cai Yong and erected the stone slabs at the Imperial Academy. Scholars could come there to copy or take rubbings of them, fostering the establishment of definitive versions of these classics. This surviving fragment is from the *Spring and Autumn Annals* and measures 19 square inches.

country began to compete to gain recognition for their learning and filial piety so that they could become government officials. Since the criteria for selecting and advancing candidates for government office laid stress on Confucian learning and virtues, it was in the interest of ambitious young men to engage in study, for learning could lead to power and prestige. All over the country teachers attracted large numbers of students and disciples, and enrolment at the Imperial Academy increased from a few dozen students to more than thirty thousand in the mid second century AD.

Credit for the political success of Confucianism should also be given to scholars who developed Confucianism in ways that matched the mood of the time and met the needs of the state. It was as though the unification of the country called out for a synthesis of ideas of diverse origin. Han Confucians sought ways to comprehend the world around them as a self-generating and self-sustaining organism governed by cyclical yet never replicating flows of yin and yang and the five phases (fire, water, earth, metal, and wood). These cosmological theories were incorporated into explanations of historical cycles and dynastic succession. Confucian scholars propounded correspondences between the qualities of the successive phases and other sets of categories (the seasons, cardinal points, tastes, smells, colours, musical notes, numbers, planets, bodily organs, feelings, and so on), theorizing that disturbance in any one category would resonate with corresponding alterations in every other category, in much the way that a note played on one musical instrument resonates on a similarly tuned instrument.

This correlative and relational cosmology was used to legitimate the imperial state and to elevate the role of emperor. Among human beings, the ruler was deemed unique in his capacity to link the realms of heaven, earth, and humanity. The philosopher Dong Zhongshu (c.179–104 BC) spoke of the ruler in terms that echo Daoist and Legalist conceptions, describing him as ruling through non-action and keeping away from everyday affairs to maintain his exalted status. Confucian moral conceptions of the ruler nonetheless pervade his thinking. A ruler who did not fulfil his role properly, Dong wrote, would directly disturb the balance of heaven and earth, causing floods, earthquakes, and other natural calamities. As a revived and expanded theory of the Mandate of Heaven, these ideas became intrinsic to imperial ideology, never publicly questioned even in later dynasties.

Besides cosmological theorizing, Confucian scholars in the Han devoted enormous energy to the reconstruction of the books destroyed by the Qin government and the revival of the traditions of interpretation that had grown up around them. A handful of recovered books came to be regarded as classics, canonical scriptures containing the wisdom of the past, to be studied with piety and rendered more useful for moral guidance through written and oral exegesis. Confucian scholars often specialized in a single classic, with teachers passing on to their disciples their understanding of each sentence in the work. Two separate sets of texts of the classics gained currency – the 'new texts', recorded in Han period script from the oral recitation of elderly scholars who had memorized the classic before the Qin destroyed all copies, and the 'old texts', based on books in Zhou-period script discovered hidden in a wall in the home of descendants of Confucius. Two great Confucian scholars of the Later Han, Ma Rong and Zheng Xuan, fused these two traditions; they mastered all of the classics and wrote important commentaries to them, usually favouring the old text versions. Nevertheless, disputes about which set of texts truly contained the wisdom of the ancients persisted into the twentieth century.

Because Confucian officials were trained to view their relationship with the ruler in moral terms, they were not bureaucrats in the modern sense of functionaries, controlled primarily by a code of procedures and laws. Committed to a principled loyalty, they retained their stance as critics of government and resisted automatic compliance with the policies of their superiors, even the ruler. During the Han period, many Confucian scholars and officials opposed activist policies such as government monopolies, questioning their morality and their effect on people's livelihoods. Aggressive foreign policies were similarly criticized on the grounds that military campaigns took a great toll on the people and might not be as effective as conciliatory policies in securing peace. Scholars also regularly objected to imperial extravagance, urging emperors to reduce their spending on palace ladies, entertainment, hunting parks, stables, and rituals. In the Later Han, especially after 150, Confucian scholars were active in opposing the eunuchs then influential at court, often risking their careers or even their lives to stand up to those in power (see below). Thus, the coupling of Confucianism and the Chinese bureaucracy created a sort of balance of power between the 'inner court' of the emperor and those who relied directly on him (the consort families and eunuchs) and the 'outer court' of the Confucian-educated officials.

A common set of ideas, values, and historical references contributed to the cohesion of the bureaucracy and the ties between officials and the educated local elite, which was expanding in this period. Local officials often promoted education, sending promising young men to the capital for advanced study. The spread of education was undoubtedly aided as well by the invention of paper in Han times, allowing an increase in the supply of books. The expansion of Confucian education among the local elite was in the interest of the government, since it helped to keep down the cost of government, as this elite tended to act in ways compatible with the needs of the government. By the end of the Han, educated men throughout the country, despite their geographic separation and the local focus of most of their activities, came to see themselves not just as leaders of their communities but also as participants, however marginally, in national literary, scholarly, and political affairs. In the succeeding centuries, the strength and

In the art of the Han, representation of famous figures from history played a larger role than in any earlier period. The lacquer panels on the sides of this covered basket shows a series of men identified by name, each about 3 inches tall. The basket was unearthed from a second century AD grave in northern Korea, the site of the Lelang colony established after the region was conquered by Wudi's forces in 109–8 BC.

Filial sons and devoted women

Confucius had praised filial piety, which to him meant loving, respectful, and dutiful attention to the needs and wishes of family elders, especially parents and grandparents. In the Han dynasty, the exaltation of filial piety was carried considerably further. Men could get appointments as officials on the basis of reputations for exemplary filial piety, and in order to gain such a reputation some would perform exaggerated acts, such as refusing to end their mourning for their parents. Tales circulated about filial sons whose devoted service to the whims of peculiar parents brought natural or supernatural reward. The text of the *Classic of Filial Piety* (*Xiaojing*) came to be a common primer, used to inculcate generations of students with such dicta as 'He who really loves his parents will not be proud in high position, insubordinate in a low position, or quarrelsome among his peers.'

Exemplary women were similarly celebrated. Pre-Han philosophers directed little of their writing to women, even women of the nobility. In the Han period, however, the eminent scholar and bibliographer Liu Xiang (79–8 BC) wrote the *Biographies of Heroic Women* (*Lienü zhuan*), a collection of accounts of the gallant deeds and unselfish behaviour of 125 women of antiquity, who were notable for their loyalty to the ruler, wise counsel to their husband or father, or preservation of chastity under duress. An equally influential text on women's virtues was written by a woman, Ban Zhao (c. 45–116), who after being widowed took a post in the palace as instructress to the girls there. Her *Admonitions for Girls* (*Nü jie*) preached the cultivation of virtues appropriate to women, such as humility, subservience, obedience, cleanliness, and industry. She assumed men's and women's social places were quite distinct and argued that women should therefore cultivate the virtues suited to their role:

> Humility means yielding and acting respectful, putting others first and oneself last, never mentioning one's own good deeds or denying one's own faults, enduring insults and bearing with mistreatment, all with due trepidation. Industriousness means going to bed late, getting up early, never shirking work morning or night, never refusing to take on domestic work, and completing everything that needs to be done neatly and carefully. Continuing the sacrifices means serving one's husband-master with appropriate demeanour, keeping oneself clean and pure, never joking or laughing, and preparing pure wine and food to offer to the ancestors. There has never been a woman who had these three traits and yet ruined her reputation or fell into disgrace. On the other hand, if a woman lacks these three traits, she will have no name to preserve and will not be able to avoid shame.

Rubbing of an engraved stone slab depicting the filial son Laizi, from the Wu Liang shrine, erected in AD 151 at Jiaxiang in Shandong province. Laizi was renowned because even when he was over seventy himself he tried to make his parents think they were not yet old by pretending to be a boy playing with toys.

The wooden and ceramic figures unearthed from Han
period tombs offer many
glimpses of everyday life,
including games and entertainment. This pair of wooden
figures, about 11 inches tall,
were excavated from a first-
century-BC tomb at Mozuizi in
Wuwei, Gansu province.

Below
Seals inscribed with names or
titles were a potent symbols of
authority; the Han emperor
conferred this dragon-embell-
ished one on Zhao Mei, Zhao
Cuo's successor as king of
Nanyue. Gold, 1¼ inches long,
unearthed at Guangzhou,
Guangdong province, first
century BC.

coherence of this elite of educated gentlemen proved as important as political centralization or economic integration as a basis for the unity of Chinese civilization.

COLONIZING THE SOUTH

The Qin–Han period was one of great territorial expansion southwards encouraged by the state. Throughout these four centuries settlers kept advancing along
the river valleys, pushing the indigenous population further south or into more
marginal upland areas. The pace was particularly fast in the first and second centuries AD, as peasants fled the economic confusion, natural disasters, and
upheaval of Wang Mang's reign, and then the incursions of the Xiongnu and other
non-Han peoples to the north and northwest. When the censuses of AD 2 and 140
are compared, it appears that between roughly five to ten million people migrated
from the north to the Yangzi valley and further south during the first and early
second centuries.

Armies played a role in this vast expansion. The Qin had sent
expeditions into Fujian and Guangxi provinces, and even
into what is now Vietnam. The Han re-established these garrisons, protecting merchants, settlers, and adventurers and
thus aiding the commercial penetration of Chinese products. Once a sizable population of settlers was established,
the government would assign officials to govern and tax them,
resulting in a steady increase in the numbers of counties in the
south. As the Chinese presence increased, local officials could switch
their tactics for controlling the indigenous population, for instance

encouraging full assimilation for those already partly assimilated by opening schools to train them in Chinese texts. Those who resisted the Chinese government presence, however, were dealt with through military force.

The life and career of Chao Tuo offers a good example of how adventurers contributed to Chinese expansion. Born in north China, Chao went south as a member of the Qin expeditionary force and soon took a wife from among the local Yue clans. With the death of his superior and the collapse of the Qin, he took control of the Guangdong region, allying himself to the leaders of the Yue. By the time the Han was established, he had amalgamated the three most southerly commanderies and declared himself King of Southern Yue. When an envoy of the new Han emperor approached him, Chao Tuo consented to being enrolled as a vassal king. He nevertheless continued to act on his own, conquering and annexing territory in the northern part of present-day Vietnam. When Empress Lü came to power, she tried to curb him by prohibiting the export of useful products to his territory, such as iron

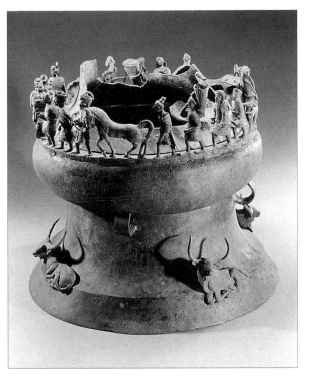

The expansion of the Han empire to the south brought China into contact with many distinctive cultures. The vivid, realistic depictions of people and animals on this 15-inch-tall drum-shaped cowrie container are quite unlike anything from the heartland of China but typical of Dian artefacts of the period before extensive Han influence. Bronze drums were also found in southeast Asia, suggesting contact between the Dian and cultures further south. Excavated at Shizhaishan, Yunnan province; about 100 BC.

implements and horses. He responded by attacking Changsha in Hunan and taking the title emperor. Wendi took a more conciliatory approach toward Chao Tuo, bestowing honours on his brothers still in the north and offering to renew friendly relations if he would just stop calling himself emperor. Chao Tuo's strength was based on gaining the support of the local population; he called himself Great Chief of the Southern Barbarians, used local warriors as generals and officers, and encouraged intermarriage. At the same time, he strove to promote the absorption of Chinese material culture by the local population. After Chao Tuo's death in 137 BC at the age of ninety-three, Wudi was able to gain relatively effective control over his successors.

More often, of course, strongmen in the frontier zones were not Han Chinese in origin. The Dian state, which held the region of modern Yunnan, was dominated by horse-riding aristocrats who made captured enemies into slaves and drew considerable wealth from trade conducted both in Chinese coins and in cowry shells. Dian religious life centred on bronze drums that symbolized both political power and fertility. Although the Dian had no system of writing, their material culture was advanced; archaeological excavations have unearthed bronze weapons, tools, and ritual implements. In 109 BC Wudi attacked and defeated the Dian and incorporated them into the Han realm as a tributary state. The Dian rebelled several times (in 86 and 83 BC, AD 14 and 42–5), but each time the Han government was able to maintain or regain its presence.

THE FALL OF THE HAN

The first seventy years of the Later Han dynasty was a time of recovery and reassertion of imperial power. During the second century AD, however, Han court politics turned nasty as the eunuchs who served as palace servants vied with relatives of the empresses for control of the court. Rulers had long used eunuchs for more than tending to the needs of their women's quarters, since eunuchs, recruited from insignificant families, had no outside power base and could therefore be depended on to do their master's bidding; moreover, emperors raised in the palace often trusted them. Weak emperors, however, ran the danger of becoming the captives rather than the masters of the eunuchs. In AD 124 a group of eunuchs staged a coup and put on the throne a child that they could manipulate. In 159, an emperor turned to the eunuchs to help him oust a consort family faction, and from then on the eunuchs were in command. 'Outer court' officials who protested were persecuted; hundreds were jailed, killed, or barred from office and exiled from the capital in the purges that took place in 166 and 169.

With the central government in disarray, little was done to stem the shrinkage of the tax base brought on by the steady decline in smallholdings and rise of local magnates. With the fiscal resources of the Han government steadily deteriorating it became more and more difficult for the government to provide relief during bad harvests. In 143 government revenue was so depleted that official salaries were cut and the government made the kings and nobles pay their land tax a year in advance. In 153 swarms of locusts and a flood of the Yellow River resulted in several hundred thousand people taking to the roads in search of food, but all the central government could do was give local authorities permission to requisition 30 per cent of private stores of grain.

The Han imperial institution never recovered from the outbreak in 184 of a large-scale rebellion staged by followers of the Way of Great Peace, a religious cult inspired by Daoist ideas that offered mystical faith healing and social welfare programmes. Hundreds of thousands of zealots attacked local government offices simultaneously in several parts of the country, killing magistrates and prefects wherever they could. Although this uprising was suppressed within a year, other rebels, some preaching similar doctrines and using similar principles of organization, appeared throughout the country and proved difficult for the government to defeat or contain. The generals sent to put down the rebellions used the armies they amassed to gain power for themselves, and this resulted in several decades of civil war as they fought each other. In 189 the warlord who gained control of the capital slaughtered more than 2,000 eunuchs and made the emperor his own pawn. Luoyang was sacked and burned, the government libraries and archives almost totally destroyed. The Han dynasty had effectively come to an end.

One of the aims of Qin Legalism was direct rule by the emperor of everyone in society. Even though the Han government moderated many Qin policies, it did not abandon the goal of uniform administration reaching down to each household. The Han imposed its taxes directly on each subject according to age, sex, and imperially granted ranks. Periodically, rich and influential families were forcibly relocated; in 198 BC, for instance, 100,000 were moved to the new capital at Chang'an. Public works projects similarly continued to involve drafting of huge labour armies, including convict labour, albeit at a less onerous pace than under Qin; over the course of the Han these projects included extensions of the Great Wall, repairs on the dykes of the Yellow River, and great road-building projects.

Nevertheless, in Han times, the state and the capital did not totally dominate life in local communities. Only the exceptional official (labelled a 'harsh official' in the terminology of the time) ignored the reality of the local power structure and attempted to enforce in the local context all of the theoretical powers of the state. More typical was a conciliatory approach, with officials sent from the centre offering subordinate posts to members of locally prominent families and leaving many matters in the hands of the local elite in return for their support. This sort of balancing act between the central government and the locality was as much a part of the heritage of the Han imperial system as it was the assertion of unlimited imperial authority.

The Han dynasty was contemporaneous with the Roman Empire and has often been compared to it. Han and Rome both had strong governments that expanded geographically, promoted assimilation, and brought centuries of stability to the central regions. Both managed to deal with enormous problems of scale, ruling roughly similar numbers of people over roughly similar expanses of land. Both developed bureaucratic institutions, staffing them with educated landowners. Both invested in the construction of roads, defensive walls, and waterworks. Both were threatened by barbarians at their frontiers and often used barbarian tribal units as military auxiliaries.

The contrasts between the Han and Roman empires are equally instructive. China was a civilization based much more profoundly on crop agriculture. Not only did animal husbandry play less of a role in agriculture, but cities and commerce played a lesser role in the overall economy. Cultural cohesion was also of a different order in Han China than in Rome. Perhaps because of the Chinese script, it is much easier to talk about a common culture among the elite in Han China than in the Roman Empire. As the influence of Chinese culture increased in frontier areas with the presence of Chinese garrisons and magistrates, members of the local population learned to read Chinese in a logographic script that fostered the acceptance of basic Chinese premises and hindered articulation of distinctly local values. Even if Latin became a lingua franca in the Roman Empire, other written languages continued to be used, including Greek, Hebrew, and Demotic Egyptian, which facilitated the survival of non-Roman ideas in a way unknown in China. What we know of the values of the Dian, Yue, and Xiongnu comes almost entirely from texts written in Chinese.

CHAPTER 4

Buddhism, Aristocracy, and Alien Rulers:
The Age of Division 220–589

The centuries that separated the fall of the Han dynasty in 220 and the reunification of China by the Sui dynasty in 589 were marked by political division and governments unable to gain firm control of their territories. After several decades of rivalry among three contenders (the Three Kingdoms, 220–265), China was briefly reunified by the Western Jin (265–316). After the Jin fell to internal squabbling, non-Chinese tribes entered the fray, and China entered a prolonged period when the north was controlled by alien rulers and the south by a transplanted court of emigré aristocrats. The weak governments of this period rarely tried to curb tendencies towards social inequality, and during these centuries aristocracy developed at the top of society and personal bondage expanded at the bottom. Confidence in the Confucian view of the social and political order declined and people in all walks of life found hope in religions promising salvation and transcendence, not only Daoist cults but also the newly introduced Buddhist religion, which vastly expanded China's intellectual and religious imagination.

THE THREE KINGDOMS AND JIN DYNASTY

During the period between the Han and Tang dynasties, short-lived courts were the norm, and even these courts never had the degree of control over society that the Han or Tang did at their heights. Tendencies of Chinese social organization and culture that strong governments usually curbed were able to develop with relative freedom – for better and for worse.

The political history of these three-and-a-half centuries is one of the most complex in Chinese history. It began when the generals assigned by the Han government to put down the rebellion of the Yellow Turbans became stronger than the throne and fought among themselves for supremacy. By 205 the poet–general Cao Cao had made himself dictator of north China. Instead of trying to curb the growth of hard-to-tax local magnates, Cao Cao developed alternative ways to supply his armies. He carved out huge state farms from land laid waste by war and settled landless poor and captured rebels to work them and thus made the state the greatest of all landlords. He also established military colonies for hereditary military households whose men would both farm and fight. For his cavalry, Cao Cao recruited Xiongnu tribesmen in large numbers, settling many in southern Shanxi. After his death in 220, his son Cao Pei formalized the family's dominance by forcing the abdication of the last Han emperor and founding the Wei dynasty at the old Han capital of Luoyang.

Two rival claimants to the throne had sufficient local power to thwart Cao Cao's and Cao Pei's efforts to build a government on the scale of the Han. In the central and lower Yangzi valley and further south, the brothers Sun Ce and Sun Quan established the state of Wu, supported by the great families that had settled in this frontier region, which was still heavily populated by indigenous peoples. West in Sichuan a distant member of the Han imperial family, Liu Pei, established a stronghold, aided by the brilliant strategist, Zhuge Liang. Because Wei had more than twice the population of either of the other states as well as the largest army, it is not surprising that it eventually prevailed, defeating the Han state in Sichuan in 263. Two years later, however, the son of the victorious general forced the Wei emperor to abdicate in his favour, founding the Jin dynasty (later called Western Jin, 265–316). In 280, after a major naval campaign, the southern state of Wu was defeated. The Jin dynasty had thus succeeded in reunifying China,

China was fragmented for most of the three and a half centuries after the fall of the Han, but no set of boundaries ever lasted very long. The states established in the south, while nominally holding huge territories, never had the military might of the strongest northern states, and before the end of the sixth century China was reunified by states originating in the northwest.

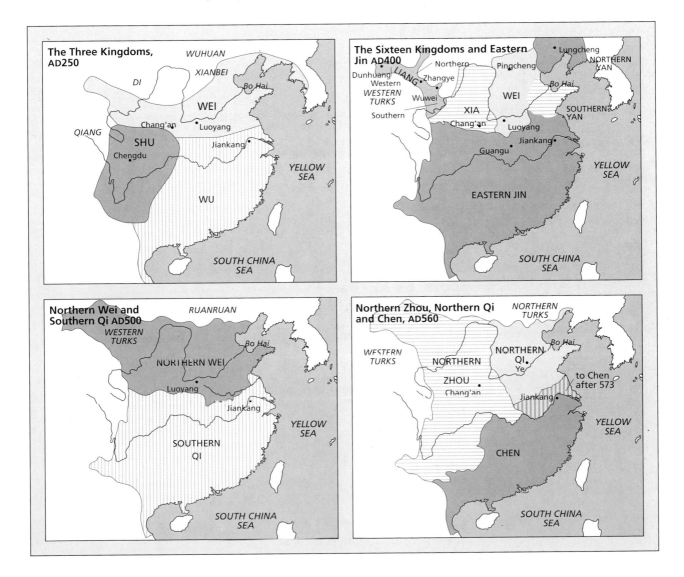

and for a brief interlude it seemed possible that the glories of the Han dynasty could be reattained.

During this century of military struggles, an atmosphere of alienation and personal indulgence pervaded elite circles. Confucian ideals of public service lost much of their hold, as the educated and well-off vied instead in extravagant and often unconventional living. 'Study of the Mysterious' captured the interests of the philosophically inclined. Books like the *Book of Changes*, the *Laozi*, and the *Zhuangzi* were reinterpreted, arguments swirling over metaphysical questions such as the meaning of 'nonbeing' and its relationship to 'being'. Clever repartee, called 'pure talk', was much in style, especially pithy characterizations of prominent personalities. Rather than participate in the often vicious clique struggles at court, many men expressed an abhorrence of political life with its elaborate conventions. A search for 'naturalness' and 'spontaneity' led to a burst of self-expression in the arts, especially poetry. Cao Cao, his successor Cao Pei, and Pei's younger brother Cao Zhi were all remarkable poets, important for developing the lyric potential of verse in lines of five syllables. Among the sophisticated aesthetes of this period were a group of gifted poets later immortalized as the Seven Sages of the Bamboo Grove. One of them, Ruan Ji, shocked his contemporaries by wailing in grief when an unmarried neighbour girl died, but eating meat and drinking wine on the day of his own mother's funeral. He summed up his attitude when someone rebuked him for talking to his sister-in-law: 'Surely you do not mean to suggest that the rules of propriety apply to me?' Such behaviour outraged conservative Confucians and autocratic rulers, and in 262 one of the Seven Sages, Xi Kang, was executed for perversion of public morals.

Although it had unified China, the Western Jin never succeeded in establishing an autocratic imperial institution, that is, one capable of preserving

ultimate power for the emperor and preventing dissension and power struggles. The imperial family's power was threatened by the families of empresses, especially the Jia family, who were suspected of arranging the assassination of the previous empress and her family as well as more than one heir to the throne. Nor was it possible for the emperors fully to control the civil service. The system of recruitment to government posts that had been instituted by the Wei – the 'Nine Rank System' – had degenerated from a system of local assessments of character and talent into a procedure for assigning places in the bureaucracy according to the standing of the candidate's family. The Jin dynasty allowed further erosion of centralized imperial control by their policy of parcelling out enormous tracts of land to imperial princes. Gaining such resources spurred the princes' fratricidal instincts and culminated in a series of bloody struggles over succession. Each prince sought out allies, including generals and non-Chinese chieftains with their troops, and full-scale civil war raged in and near the capital between 291 and 305.

THE NORTHERN AND SOUTHERN DYNASTIES

The dissolution of the Jin into internecine war invited non-Chinese chiefs to stage a rebellion. During the second and third centuries, hundreds of thousands of Xiongnu and other northern peoples had been settled within China's political frontiers as an alternative to defending against their raids. Often recruited as soldiers or used as auxiliary troops, these formerly nomadic peoples, now generally settled pastoralists, were not easy to govern or assimilate. In 304 the sinified Xiongnu chief Liu Yuan declared himself king of Han. His son went on to sack the Jin capital at Luoyang in 311, sending its inhabitants fleeing in terror. Another Xiongnu leader assaulted Chang'an in 316, and less sinified chiefs, such as Shi Le and Fu Jian, soon joined the fray. For a period of over a century (known as the

Within a century of their deaths, the 'Seven Sages of the Bamboo Grove' had come to be celebrated as prime exemplars of the individualistic and idiosyncratic artist. This rubbing of two sections of the bricks lining a fourth-century tomb excavated near Nanjing, Jiangsu province, depicts them engaged in conversation.

Opposite
The introduction of stirrups, at first used mainly to make mounting a horse easier, in time greatly enhanced the mobility of mounted warriors. This 9-inch-tall ceramic tomb figurine, unearthed at Shashi in Hunan province, shows a horseman not taking full advantage of the stirrup.

Armour was worn by infantry-men, cavalrymen, and war horses in the frequent battles that marked the Age of Division. Its use is illustrated in this sixth-century battle scene on a wall of cave 285 at Dunhuang in Gansu province.

Sixteen Kingdoms', 304–439), north China was a battleground and Chinese civilization seemed seriously threatened.

As warfare brought in its wake banditry and famine, rural communities all over north China built forts and organized self-defence forces, with power devolving to the local level even more than it had in the waning years of the Han. The commercial economy suffered and the circulation of money declined. A couple of million residents of north China packed up what movable property they had and fled southwards across the Yangzi. Even the wealthy and high-ranking, facing depredations and the unknown peril of alien rule, made the trek in huge numbers. At Jiankang (modern Nanjing) leading officials set a Jin prince on the throne, creating a government in exile. This Eastern Jin dynasty (317–420) was followed by four other dynasties that ruled from Nanjing – the Song, Qi, Liang, and Chen, collectively called the Southern Dynasties (420–589). These four short dynasties were all founded by generals who proved capable of holding the government together during their lifetime but not of assuring a successful transfer of power to their heirs. They possessed the desire to create imperial institutions but not the ability to concentrate power.

Part of the difficulty these rulers faced can be traced to the emergence of a hereditary aristocracy that entrenched itself in the higher reaches of officialdom. Much more so than in the Han period, these families judged themselves and others on the basis of their ancestors, and would only marry with other families of equivalent pedigree. They even compiled lists, complete with genealogies, of the most eminent families. By securing near automatic access to higher government posts through the Nine Rank system, the aristocrats were assured of government salaries and exemptions from taxes and labour service. Many were also able to build up great landed estates worked by destitute refugees from the north who were settled as serf-like dependants. At court, the aristocrats often set themselves at odds with the 'upstart' rulers, doing what they could to frustrate these emperors' efforts to appoint or promote whom they wished. But the aristocrats should not be looked on as foes of Chinese civilization. The men in these families saw themselves as embodying Chinese civilization, maintaining the high cultural accomplishments of the Han dynasty and the tradition of the scholar-official. The solidarity of these cultivated families provided a centre around which Chinese culture could adhere during a period when no state could serve that function.

Constructing a capital south of the Yangzi had a beneficial effect on economic development of the south. When Luoyang fell in 311, the south probably had only about 10 per cent of the registered population of the Jin (which did not include non-Chinese, indigenous people of the south who paid no taxes). To pay for an army and to support the imperial court and aristocracy in a style that matched their pretensions, the government had to expand the area of taxable agricultural land, whether through settling migrants or converting the local inhabitants into tax-payers. The south, with its temperate climate and ample supply of water, offered nearly unlimited possibilities for such development.

The courts at Nanjing repeatedly had to deal with challenges to their authority. The most destructive uprising began in 548, initiated by a would-be warlord from the north, Hou Jing, who gathered a huge army of the disaffected and set siege to the capital. By the time the city fell four months later, many members of the great families had starved to death in their mansions. Although a general soon declared a new dynasty (Chen), his control over outlying areas amounted to little more than the privilege of confirming local strongmen as his governors.

Meanwhile, the north was following a different trajectory. In the fourth century, rival warlords of many different ethnic groups fought for control, ousting each other whenever they could. The first to secure their position by finding ways to draw on the wealth of China's settled agriculture was the Tuoba clan of the Xianbei who established the (Northern) Wei dynasty (439–534). Originally from southern Manchuria, by the early fourth century the Xianbei occupied land in northern Shanxi province, which they used as a base to raid other tribes and Chinese settlements, bringing back captives, horses, cattle, and sheep. As they expanded into Chinese territory, they forced massive relocations of population to bring deserted land back into cultivation and to supply the capital they built. In their desire to preside over the whole Chinese world, they turned to educated Chinese as experts in statecraft. It was expedient for them to employ Chinese officials and adopt the institutions they proposed, because the total number of Xianbei and other northern tribesman in their confederation could not have been more than a couple of million, but the Chinese, over whom they were trying to maintain military control, numbered twenty or thirty million or more.

It was on Chinese advice that in 486 the Northern Wei government undertook a major overhaul of its fiscal system, instituting an 'equal field' system reminiscent of Han efforts to tax individual cultivators and Cao Cao's military colonies and state lands. The Wei system was based on the premise that the state owned all land. Individual families were to be assigned 20 *mu* of permanent, inheritable land for growing mulberry and other trees plus lifetime allotments of crop land, the amount depending on their available labour; for instance 40 *mu* was allocated per able-bodied man (including slaves) and 30 per ox. Larger landholdings were only to be allowed for the families of officials. The memorial proposing this 'equal field' system argued that it would 'ensure that no land lies neglected, that no people wander off, that powerful families could not monopolize the fertile fields, and that humble people would also get their share of the land'. Even if the powerful were usually able to manoeuvre around the law, the government had asserted its power to assign and tax land, a key step towards building a fiscal base for a more intrusive form of government.

A few years later, Emperor Xiaowen (r.471–99) decided to transform his state into a true Chinese dynasty on the model of Han and Jin. In the 490s he moved the capital more than 300 miles south to the ruins of Luoyang and built a splendid new city there; he gave Chinese surnames to the Xianbei, taking the name Yuan ('origin') for the imperial house; he ordered the use of the Chinese language and Chinese dress at court, even by Xianbei; and he encouraged intermarriage between the Xianbei and Chinese elites. Within twenty-five years Luoyang had become a magnificent city with half a million people, vast palaces, elegant mansions, and over a thousand Buddhist monasteries. Many members of the Xianbei nobility became fully versed in Chinese cultural traditions, at home among the leading Chinese families.

The stability of this Luoyang-centred sino-foreign hybrid regime was brief. The Xianbei soldiers assigned to the northern frontier garrisons to fend off incursions by new occupants of the steppe such as the Ruanruan and Turks came to hate the sinified Xianbei aristocrats leading what seemed to them self-indulgent lives in the thoroughly Chinese atmosphere of Luoyang and in 524 they rebelled. Civil war ensued as those sent to suppress the rebels took to fighting each other. When Luoyang was sacked, some 2,000 officials were slaughtered.

After a decade of constant warfare, two principal rivals emerged, each controlling a claimant to the Wei throne. In 552 the fiction of Wei rule was abandoned in the east, and the (Northern) Qi dynasty (552–77) was established; in 557 the western powers followed suit and declared the (Northern) Zhou dynasty (557–81). Both courts suffered from ethnic tension between the sinified Xianbei, Chinese aristocrats, and unsinified warriors. In the northwestern court, not only was the law requiring Xianbei to take Chinese names rescinded, but Chinese officials were given Xianbei names. In 553 the northwestern court conquered Sichuan, until then held by the south. In 575 the Zhou court, through clever diplomacy, got the southern court of Chen to join in invading Qi. Qi was destroyed in 577, most of its territory going to Zhou, thus reunifying the north. The Zhou throne was in its turn usurped in 581 by one of its generals who declared the Sui dynasty. Before long he destroyed Chen to unify all of China proper (see Chapter 5).

Reunification was made possible by the introduction of a new military institution that allowed for expansion of the army without bankrupting the state. This was the divisional militia, an army of volunteer farmer-soldiers who served in rotation in armies at the capital or on the frontiers. By the 570s this divisional militia had been expanded to about 200,000 soldiers. Equipping soldiers had become quite expensive because cavalrymen needed not only horses but also armour for the men and horses to protect against arrows fired from powerful crossbows. Cavalrymen carried light crossbows that could shoot arrows 1,000 feet, and infantry used ones with a range of 1,500 feet. Those defending or attacking city walls used larger, more powerful crossbows with a range of over 3,000 feet. The cavalrymen of the divisional militia had to provide their own horses, and presumably came from families that had long served in the military, while foot soldiers were recruited from better-off peasant families who supplied them in exchange for exemption from taxes. The cost of this army was also kept down by letting the soldiers farm when not called up for training or campaigns. The divisional militia was also easier to co-ordinate and command than the military forces it replaced, most of which had been loyal only to their own officers.

CLIENTS, RETAINERS, SERFS, AND SLAVES

The Qin and Han dynasties had extracted the bulk of their revenue directly from agricultural producers. It followed that these governments continually had to strive to keep land and people from falling off the tax registers. The weaker governments that followed the Han were even less able to stop the poor from fleeing debt and tax collectors or the rich and powerful from amassing land and dependent labourers. The Age of Division thus witnessed an increase in the proportion of the population occupying servile statuses.

Demeaned status was not in itself new. By the late Zhou period a broad distinction was commonly made between ordinary 'good' people and base or ignoble people, the latter including those who had undergone mutilating punishments for crimes and those condemned to slavery as part of the punishment of a close rela-

Ox carts became a common means of transportation, an economical alternative to horse-drawn carriages. This ceramic model was excavated from a mid-sixth-century tomb in Taiyuan, Shanxi province.

tive condemned to death for a heinous crime. In addition, in late Zhou and Han times, those desperately impoverished might sell their wives and children to be household slaves or bondservants. The law codes, however, imposed severe penalties for kidnapping 'good' people and selling them as slaves. Perhaps few people thought the aborigines in the south counted as 'good' people, for in the Han and later they were a major source of slaves.

With the appearance of great landed estates and the creation of private armies from the Later Han period on, a whole variety of client statuses emerged. Many people voluntarily became dependants, despite the loss of status, because rich patrons could provide protection. Clients of local strongmen might till their land and turn out to help during battles; others were essentially private soldiers. Already in the third century the government gave some recognition to the widespread existence of such dependants by trying to limit acquisition of them to officials. The Jin government decreed that the highest-ranking officials could have a maximum of forty households of dependants free from taxation and labour service, and lower-ranking officials proportionally fewer, down to a minimum of ten households. These limits never seem to have been effectively enforced, however. During the Southern Dynasties, serf-like dependent households grew in number because many refugees accepted the status when they settled on estates.

The customs of the northern pastoral tribes reinforced the tendency towards increased incidence of serfdom and slavery. It was traditional for tribes to have both full members and slaves. When one tribe or confederation defeated another, the victors enslaved the losers, distributing them as favours, and requiring them to do most of the menial labour. In its battles against the Southern Dynasties, the Northern Wei armies would enslave captives, sometimes in the thousands. Generals who had been granted captured soldiers might incorporate them into their own armies, but high officials who received dozens or hundreds of captives made them into household servants or settled them to work on the land. The Wei government supported the use of slaves in agriculture through the provision in the equal-field system that slaves be counted in allotting land.

Captives made into slaves were sometimes freed or redeemed. In the mid fifth century a southern official offered 1,000 bolts of cloth to redeem his sexagenarian wife who had been captured and made into a palace slave. Once a northern officer was sent to the south to offer 1,000 horses in exchange for fifty men captured in a military campaign. When the Northern Zhou captured the city of Jiangling from the Liang in 554, more than 100,000 civilians were enslaved. The general Yu Jin was granted 1,000 slaves, and 200 were given to one of his sons. Some of the captives were redeemed by friends and relatives or freed by their new masters within a few years. In 577 those still in slavery were freed by an imperial rescript, with the provision that if they wished to remain with their master, they would be promoted to the less ignominious but still mean rank of bound retainer.

Much of what we know of the life of slaves and bondservants is found in casual references to them in accounts of their masters. Members of high-ranking families sometimes beat slaves to death on minor provocations, without any fear that they would be charged with a crime. Slaves could also be tattooed on the face to make it more difficult for them to flee. Female slaves were often used as concubines, and some of the stigma of their status attached itself to their children. The offspring of male slaves were unambiguously mean in status; their father's master could give them away, keep them on, or free them, as he pleased.

BUDDHISM

In this period when it was difficult to place much faith in civil governments, China encountered a religion whose reach extended way beyond any known government, a religion then spreading its teachings across Asia. As knowledge of Buddhism filtered into China during these centuries, Chinese learned a radically different way of conceiving of life and death, humanity and the cosmos.

Shakyamuni, the historical Buddha ('Buddha' means enlightened one), lived in India at about the time of Confucius. He naturally took for granted the basic concepts of Indian cosmology, such as karma and reincarnation. In this world view, men, women, animals, heavenly beings, hell dwellers, and other sentient beings pass through an endless series of lives, moving up or down according to the karma, or good and bad deeds, that they have accumulated. Shakyamuni's own spiritual journey led him to feel he had discovered basic truths about the human condition, and he began to teach people that their desires and attachments were the source of their suffering; because they became enmeshed in the web of their attachments, their lives were inevitably filled with disappointments and anxieties. The way to put a stop to this process, he preached, was to live an ethical life (abstaining from the taking of life, for instance) and engage in spiritual exercises that enhance concentration and insight. Those who progress along this path can eventually escape the cycle of rebirth and enter nirvana, though it may take many lifetimes to reach that ultimate goal. Shakyamuni's most committed early followers left their families and made the quest for salvation the prime activity in their lives. After Shakyamuni's death, his disciples passed down his sermons orally, though after a few centuries these sermons were recorded, forming the basis of a huge corpus of scriptures called sutras.

Buddhism arrived in China along with commercial goods, following trade routes from northern India through the Buddhist kingdoms of Central Asia such as Khotan and Kucha. At first the new faith was mostly a religion of foreigners. What Chinese encountered in the second, third, and fourth centuries was not a single creed, but an extraordinary array of ideas and practices, ranging from monastic discipline to magic, the worship of statues and relics, and techniques of meditation and ecstasy. Mahayana ('Great Vehicle') Buddhist philosophy was developing just as Buddhism was being introduced to China, and the Chinese learned of earlier and later theories at the same time. Mahayanists argued that pursuing the goal of nirvana was selfish compared to becoming a bodhisattva, a being of advanced spiritual standing who postponed entry into nirvana in order to help other beings.

By the end of the Western Jin, members of the upper levels of Chinese society had begun to be attracted to Buddhism. Those who decided to become monks had to give up their surname and take a vow of celibacy, thus cutting themselves off from the ancestral cult that tied the dead, the living, and the unborn. Yet many made this decision, and Buddhist philosophy came to be widely discussed in aristocratic circles. The alien rulers in the north also found Buddhism appealing. Devoted missionaries from Central Asia were quite willing to use feats of magic to convince these rulers that Buddhism was a more powerful religion than the shamanism they had traditionally practised. But Buddhism had other advantages to alien rulers; its universalistic claims did not put them at a disadvantage in relation to the Chinese in the way Confucian theories did, and thus offered a basis for unifying an ethnically mixed population.

To many Chinese, Buddhism seemed at first a variant of Daoism, which was understandable since Daoist terms were used by early translators to convey Buddhist ideas. For instance, the Mahayana concept of the fundamental emptiness of phenomena was identified with the Daoist notion of non-being. A more accurate understanding of Buddhism became possible after the eminent Central Asian monk Kumarajiva (350–413) settled in Chang'an and directed several thousand monks in the translation of thirty-eight texts. Chinese also began in this period to undertake the arduous journey to India to discover for themselves what might have been lost in translation. The first to leave a record of his trip was the intrepid Faxian, a monk who went to India overland in 399 via Kucha and Khotan, returning by the sea route via Sri Lanka and Sumatra in 414.

The steady adaptation of Buddhism to China can be illustrated through the career of the great teacher Huiyuan (334–417). Born in the north, in the period of greatest disorder, he still managed to get a basic education in Confucian and Daoist texts. It was hearing a sermon by a Chinese monk (himself a disciple of a Kuchan missionary) that led Huiyuan to decide to 'leave the family' himself. Eventually he moved to the south, founding a monastery on Mount Lu in Jiangxi province. He kept up a learned correspondence with Kumarajiva on points of doctrine but also interacted with lay followers whom he taught concentration techniques involving visualizing Buddhas. In 402 he assembled a group of both monks and lay people in front of an image of Pure Land, the western paradise of the buddha Amitabha. Buddhism thus was well on its way to becoming a religion of universal salvation with appeal to all the faithful. Two years later, in 404, Huiyuan wrote a treatise entitled *On Why Monks Do Not Bow Down Before Kings*, asserting the political independence of the Buddhist church. He also tried to assure the ruler that Buddhism was not subversive, arguing that lay Buddhists make good subjects because their belief in the retribution of karma and desire to be reborn in paradise make them act circumspectly. 'Those who rejoice in the Way of the Buddha invariably first serve their parents and obey their lords.'

Before the end of the Age of Division, Buddhism had gained a remarkable hold in China. It appealed to people in China above all because it addressed questions of suffering and death with a directness unmatched in native Chinese traditions. It offered a fully developed vision of the afterlife and the prospect of salvation, promising that all creatures might one day find blissful release from suffering. Its code of conduct, including the injunction against the taking of life, seemed to many to carry the principle of compassion to its logical extreme. Retreating to a monastery or nunnery offered a new alternative to the world-weary, one especially attractive to high-born widows. Indeed, Buddhism had particular appeal to women. Although incarnation as a female was considered lower than incarnation as a male, it was also viewed as temporary, and women were encouraged to

Bronze altarpiece, depicting the Buddha Amitabha seated on a lotus throne and accompanied by disciples and attendants. The inscription indicates that it was commissioned in 593 by a group of eight older women (who identify themselves as mothers of named men) as a way to earn merit for members of their families.

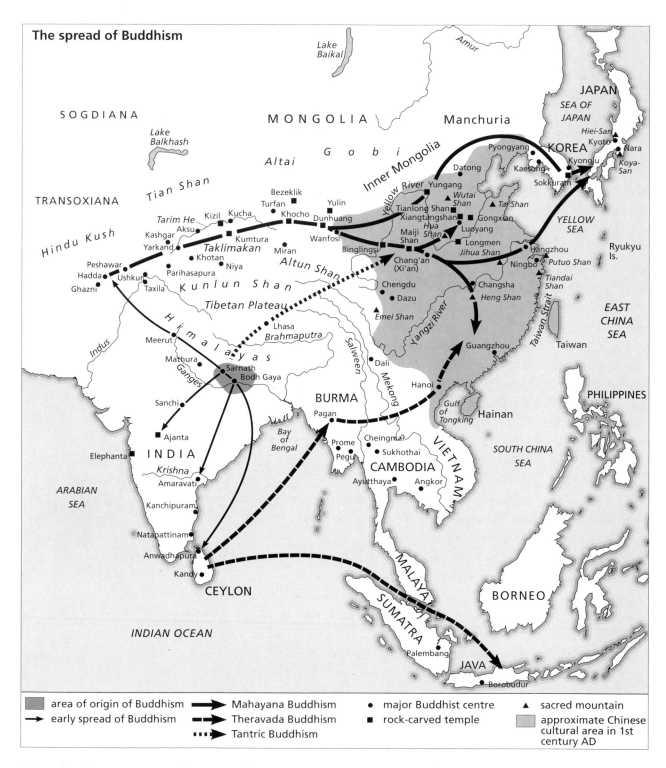

The spread of Buddhism

▨ area of origin of Buddhism	➡ Mahayana Buddhism	● major Buddhist centre	▲ sacred mountain
→ early spread of Buddhism	➡ Theravada Buddhism	■ rock-carved temple	▨ approximate Chinese cultural area in 1st century AD
	⋯▸ Tantric Buddhism		

In its transit from one country to the next, Buddhism absorbed local ideas and art styles and passed them on in transmuted forms. Thus Greek-influenced art forms reached China in the form of Buddhist artistic traditions developed in the region of Afghanistan. In a comparable way, Chinese understandings of filial piety and ancestors reached Japan as part and parcel of sinified Buddhism with its 'merit ceremonies' for the salvation of ancestors.

pursue salvation on nearly equal terms with men. Moreover, Buddhism held out for women some androgynous symbols unlike anything in native Chinese traditions; bodhisattvas were conceived as neither male nor female, transcending differences of gender in addition to differences of class and ethnicity.

The landscape of China, too, was transformed by Buddhism as temples and monasteries were built in towns and remote mountains. The Buddhist church in north China reportedly had 6,478 temples and 77,258 monks and nuns by 477; south China was said to have had 2,846 temples and 82,700 clerics some decades later. The beauty of Buddhist art and architecture (see pages 106–7) appealed to people of all levels of education. Buddhism helped transcend class differences; inscriptions on Buddhist statues and temples show that Chinese and non-Chinese officials, local notables, commoners, and Buddhist clergy often all contributed to a project, working together. The scale of contributions was enormous; pious lay believers donated tracts of land and serfs in the conviction that donation of worldly wealth to the monastic community was an especially effective way to gain merit and to fulfil filial obligations to fathers and mothers. The most generous imperial patron was Wudi of Liang (r. 502–549), who banned meat and wine from the imperial table, built temples, wrote commentaries on sutras, and held great assemblies of monks and laymen, one of which attracted 50,000 people. To raise money for Buddhist establishments, he had himself held 'hostage' until those at court raised huge sums to get him freed.

Not everyone, of course, was pleased by the many-faceted success of Buddhism. Resentful Daoists and Confucians denounced many Buddhist ideas and practices as immoral or unsuited to China. Monks' practices of shaving the head and cremating the dead they decried as violations of the body, not allowed in Confucianism. Even worse was celibacy, for Mencius had stated that the ultimate unfilial act was failure to provide one's ancestors with an heir. The refusal of monks to pay homage to the ruler, as well as their failure to contribute to the tax coffers, were depicted by critics as threats to the well-being of the state. Such critics argued that the great sums spent on construction of temples, statues, and ceremonies were a drain on the economy, impoverishing the people and thus indirectly the state. To rebut such criticisms, and to overcome resistance on the part of potential converts, Buddhist apologists argued that their religion was basically compatible with Chinese values. It was the utmost expression of filial piety, they argued, to free a parent from the suffering of purgatory by performing pious acts in his or her name. By praying for the welfare of the ruler and the population, they argued, monks were aiding the state, not injuring it.

Even rulers who accepted these arguments saw some need to set rules for the Buddhist establishment, since it took so much land off the tax registers. Rulers generally consented to making monastic lands inalienable and free from taxation and to exempting monks from labour service, but in return they wanted guarantees that monks were indeed pious and learned, not just tax-evaders. Twice

Tao Yuanming and the art of Chinese poetry

The classical Chinese language, with its tones and abundant rhymes, was well suited to rhymed verse. The Chinese script is similarly conducive to poetry-writing because it stimulates visual associations in ways that purely phonetic scripts do not. Perhaps for these reasons poetry was from early times the central literary art in China. During the age of Confucius, envoys and philosophers alike quoted the *Book of Songs* in their speeches and essays, not only to demonstrate their education but also to make their points more effectively. During Han times the scholarship surrounding this classic emphasized the connection between poetry and the expression of emotion. Poetry is what happens when emotions are stirred, commentators explained, and a sensitive reader of poetry can perceive through a poem the state of mind of the writer. The art of poetry reached great heights in the aesthetically inclined aristocratic society of the period of division, and poets came to play a distinctive cultural role as exemplars of the complex individual, moved by conflicting but powerful emotions.

Tao Qian, better known as Tao Yuanming (365–427), was one of the first poets to create such a persona. From the south (modern Jiangxi province), Tao had an inconsequential political career, never holding any post very long. Once, it is told, he quit his post rather than entertain a visiting inspector, objecting, 'How could I bend my waist to this village buffoon for five pecks of rice!' On some occasions he expressed fierce ambition, at other times a desire to be left alone to follow the dictates of his heart. By the age of forty he quit government service altogether and supported himself by farming.

Tao's extant corpus includes more than 100 pieces, many of which could be considered philosophical, tinged with such Daoist sentiments as 'excessive thinking harms life', 'nothing is better than to trust one's true self', or 'propriety and conventions, what folly to follow them too earnestly'. Although he celebrated the quiet life, Tao was not a hermit who withdrew from friends and family. In his poems he expressed his enjoyment of books, music, and wine. 'I try a cup and all my concerns become remote. / Another cup and suddenly I forget even heaven. / But is heaven really far from this state? / Nothing is better than to trust your true self' (from 'Drinking Alone in the Rainy Season'). Tao Yuanming

northern rulers were swayed by the more virulent anti-Buddhist rhetoric to initiate persecutions of Buddhism. In 446–52 and again in 574–79, orders were issued to close the monasteries and to force Buddhist monks and nuns to return to lay life. No attempt was made in these or subsequent persecutions to suppress private Buddhist beliefs, however; the state never sponsored any sort of inquiry into people's beliefs, nor did it ever insist that its officials renounce Buddhism. Moreover, both of these persecutions lasted only to the end of the reign, and the next occupant of the throne made generous amends.

DAOIST RELIGION

The development of Buddhism in China as a higher religion – a religion with a body of sacred texts and a clergy expert in them – coincided with and helped stimulate the emergence of Daoism as a higher religion. Daoist religion drew inspiration from the quietistic Daoist philosophy of the Zhou period, but was not simply an extension of it. It drew as well from folk religion (worship of local gods along with exorcistic and mediumistic techniques for dealing with them) and from elite traditions related to the pursuit of longevity and immortality. Daoism as an organized communal religious movement began in the second century AD, when the

also idealized the farming life, describing its pleasures as a genuine alternative to public service. In 'On Returning to My Garden and Fields', he portrayed himself as a contented rustic:

> Since youth I have not fit the common mould,
> Instinctively loving the mountains and hills.
> By mistake I fell into the dusty net
> And was gone from home for thirty years.
> A bird in a cage yearns for its native woods;
> A fish in a pond remembers its old mountain pool.
> Now I shall clear some land at the edge of the
>   southern wild
> And, clinging to the simple life, return to garden
>   and field,
> To my two-acre lot,
> My thatched cottage of eight or nine rooms

Chinese painters over the centuries frequently depicted Tao Yuanming, finding in his life a potent symbol of the individual able to withdraw from active political concerns and find satisfaction in simple pleasures. Painting on silk by Chen Hongshou (1599–1652).

Han order was losing its hold in the countryside. Two religious leaders, Zhang Jue, the leader of the Yellow Turbans, and Zhang Daoling, the first Celestial Master, were able to harness popular yearnings for a new and better age into major religious movements. Operating in different parts of the country, both built up followings as faith healers and set up organizations of subordinates to supervise their adherents. Zhang Jue and his followers were crushed soon after they revolted in 184, but Zhang Daoling and his sect survived in Sichuan.

The strand of Daoism related to the pursuit of immortality was already very old at the end of the Han. The First Emperor of Qin and the Han emperor Wudi had both consulted experts in the arts of extending lifespans. The Daoist pursuit of longevity was phrased in terms of enhancing the body's yang energy, thus reversing the natural flow towards death. Through special techniques (such as breath control, restricted diets, sexual techniques, and the use of elixirs, herbs, and talismans) a person could collect and refine the yang energies in the body, transforming a heavy mortal body into a light immortal one.

During the Age of Division, Daoism acquired a body of scriptures that rivalled the Buddhist sutras. During the years 364–70 two men, father and son, had a series of visions of a group of immortals from the heaven of Supreme Purity, a

Daoist religion continued to flourish in later dynasties, and Daoist priests frequently conducted grand ceremonies. This illustration from a 1618 edition of a novel shows a Daoist priest performing a ceremony before an altar with statues, candles, and incense burners. Musicians are in attendance, and the man who commissioned the ritual is kneeling in the centre.

realm loftier than any with which the Celestial Masters had communicated. They learned from these immortals that demonic forces would cleanse the earth of evildoers to prepare it for the descent from heaven of a new universal ruler. Some of the revealed texts show a thorough familiarity with Buddhist thought, including notions of predestination and reincarnation; they also contain much alchemical lore. Within a few decades, other revelations resulted in the Lingbao scriptures, these ones containing elaborate liturgies for rituals. Then in 415 in the north, Kou Qianzhi, a Daoist priest in the line of the Celestial Masters, received revelations from Laozi himself. Laozi charged him with the task of reforming Daoism, eliminating sexual rites and other practices offensive to the high gods. The huge canon of scriptures that Daoism acquired in these ways was generally kept secret from the uninitiated, unlike the widely circulated Buddhist sutras.

Over the course of the Southern dynasties, Daoism developed institutions similar to Buddhist monasteries. By the end of the Age of Division, Buddhism and Daoism were in competition with each other for the patronage of ordinary Chinese in the cities and the countryside. In this competition, Daoists claimed that they had better spells, more potent hygiene techniques for achieving immortality, and more control over malevolent local gods. Buddhists claimed that they had loftier principles and better techniques for attaining salvation and helping deceased loved ones achieve better rebirths. Both religions tried to accommodate popular belief and tended to accept local deities as lesser figures in their pantheons but rejected the practice of making offerings of meat to gods of any sort. In this period and for centuries to come, more Chinese would become Buddhist clergy than Daoist clergy, and more Buddhist temples were constructed than Daoist ones, but both religions developed through interaction with each other and with Chinese political authorities and lay society.

DIFFERENTIAL REGIONAL DEVELOPMENT

By the mid sixth century, China had been politically divided north and south for over two centuries, a situation that allowed society and culture in each region to go their own ways.

The aristocratic families in the north and the south developed distinctive styles. In the north, eminent Chinese families, generally well entrenched in the countryside in places they had lived for centuries, put emphasis on their preservation of Confucian learning and their embodiment of Confucian traditions of family ethics and rituals. They sought substantive posts in the government not only out of a Confucian sense of duty but also because such service offered prestige, power, and connections to elite families from other parts of the country. They spent much of their careers in the provinces, often starting near home where access to entry-level positions was nearly automatic, then rising to posts like prefect that required commanding troops. At court, however, northern aristocrats were expected to exhibit mastery of the classics and histories. Many were quite learned, like Wei Shou, the scion of an eminent northeastern family, whose 114-chapter history of the Wei dynasty provides full accounts of both the Xianbei and the Chinese leaders and even an astute history of Buddhism and Daoism.

The practical experience of these high-ranking Chinese families made them a real asset to the northern rulers intent on state-building. In the south, by contrast, the families of highest prestige were ones who had settled there as homesick refugees nostalgic for the cultural life of the Wei and Western Jin eras. With government salaries nearly guaranteed, they were free to cultivate the arts. Witty conversation, wine, and poetry were all characteristic of the cultural life of the aristocrats in Nanjing. The 'pure talk', which in its early stages had concentrated on the analysis of individuals' characters, had gradually been extended to include probing the essential features of literary, artistic, and philosophical works. Literary criticism flourished in an environment where taste was a matter of much importance. In about 530 a prince of the Liang dynasty compiled an anthology, the *Selections of Literature*, containing carefully selected examples of thirty-odd genres of prose and verse. Calligraphy and painting similarly benefited from the concern with individual expression and aesthetics. Wang Xizhi, taken by many to be the greatest calligrapher of all time, drew inspiration from Daoism with its emphasis on the natural and spontaneous. His younger contemporary, Gu Kaizhi, became a master of figure painting. Interest in mountains where immortals dwelled – as well as general Daoist interest in nature – led to the beginning of landscape painting. Xie He, in the early sixth century, enunciated standards by which paintings should be judged, such as the degree to which they are imbued with vital force and the strength of the brushwork employed. Thus painting and calligraphy came to be seen as carrying intellectual content in a way not true of the decoration on ceramics, lacquerware, or textiles.

To northerners, southern aesthetes seemed effete. And even some southerners saw how the pursuit of aesthetic values could deteriorate into an empty preoccupation with style. Yan Zhitui complained that many young men in aristocratic families knew how to perfume their garments and powder and rouge their faces, but could not compose a poem for a court feast. In his view their vacuity stemmed from too sheltered a life; they could live off official salaries and never know anything about how grain was grown. His portrayal of the Nanjing aristocracy makes it sound not unlike the aesthetically inclined aristocracy of medieval Japan depicted in the *Tale of Genji*.

The political separation of north and south, thus, was not inimical to cultural advance, and may even have helped foster the maturation of Buddhism. The centres of Buddhist learning in the north were in closer contact with Central Asia, and awareness of the foreign origins of Buddhism was kept alive through the active and earnest efforts at translation. In the south, which had no direct overland connection to Central Asia, effort was directed instead toward the sinification of Buddhism and the interpretation and elaboration of Buddhist ideas within the framework of traditional philosophy and religion. With the reunification of China under the Sui and Tang dynasties, these two strands were able to cross-fertilize each other and strengthen the hold of Buddhism in Chinese society.

In a comparable way, Chinese political theorizing was stimulated by political division, as supporters of one regime or another tried to construct convincing claims to the status of Son of Heaven and successor to the Han dynasty. In the north much was made of geography, of controlling the region of the Zhou and Han capitals, the land where all the places sacred or memorable in Chinese history were located, including the tombs of all earlier monarchs. Much also was made of preserving the political traditions of the Zhou and Han. One of the northern successor regimes took the name Zhou and evoked the heritage of the Zhou by renaming government offices according to the nomenclature listed in the ancient *Rituals of Zhou* (*Zhou li*). Chinese at the southern court could not make similar claims to geographical centrality, but they could point to the ethnicity of their rulers – indisputably Chinese. They also elaborated a theory based on the rituals of succession, on the abdications that linked one ruler to the next in an unbroken succession of Sons of Heaven. Thus, because the Han had turned over the imperial seal to the Wei, the Wei to the Jin, and the Jin to the Song, it was the rulers in exile in the south who were the legitimate Sons of Heaven.

North and south were not, of course, evolving independently of each other, but rather in contact and competition with each other. The Chinese elite in both areas were literate in the same language and read the same books. There was much travel back and forth, some of it coerced, some voluntary. Thus distinctive identities were fostered as much by contact as by isolation.

To Chinese historians in subsequent ages, none of the rulers of the Age of Division fulfilled the central role of Son of Heaven, namely to establish a cosmically correct and harmonious order for All-Under-Heaven. Thus this period was treated as significant primarily as a negative example: the disorder and dislocation, the ethnic hostility and bloody court struggles, the tyrannical rulers and enslaved captives all demonstrated why powerful, intrusive, unified, centralized, imperial governments were necessary. Yet much that enriched Chinese culture was given a chance to flourish in this period when the state was unable to penetrate very deeply into society, and both ordinary people and the elites absorbed themselves in less state-centred systems of meaning.

Westerners and modern Chinese familiar with the course of western history have often labelled the Age of Division 'medieval' because of its similarities to Europe in the period after the fall of Rome. In both instances, a great empire broke up, barbarian tribes who had been used as auxiliary military forces gained the upper hand, and the old urban economy suffered. In both places a foreign religion with claims to universality rapidly gained adherents and the intensity of religious fervour led to vast expenditure on monumental art. Intriguing as these correspondences are, they should not deflect our attention from the equally important differences between the experiences of China and Europe. Although north China was in great disarray for over a century after the collapse of the Western Jin, state-building efforts were well underway by the middle of the fifth century. Perhaps because Chinese statesmen all knew the history of the Zhou dynasty – when bonds of fealty between vassals and lords led eventually to the emergence of separate states – empire-builders sought a strongly centralized, bureaucratically administered political order, and not a decentralized, feudal one.

In China, moreover, the barbarian influx had much less impact on culture and consciousness. Chinese continued to be the spoken language of north China, Xianbei eventually disappearing. Charlemagne could not deny or obscure his Germanic heritage and was restrained by it from acting out the part of a Roman emperor. By contrast, neither the Sui nor the Tang emperors had any difficulty presenting themselves and their ancestors as descended from ancient Chinese stock. The sense of disjuncture, of moral and emotional separation from the classical past, thus, was not nearly so great in China as in the west.

Equally important, education and scholarship never went into eclipse in China. The aristocracies in both the north and south were fully literate, and the intellectual atmosphere in the south was as conducive to literary and artistic experimentation as any in Chinese history. Leading men of letters were in no sense less sophisticated than their Han counterparts centuries earlier. Indeed, the encounter with Indian civilization – a civilization much more on a par with China than any China had encountered before – stimulated intellectual inquiry and self-reflection. Struggling with ways to convey the sounds of the Sanskrit language, for instance, led to the first analysis of the tones in the Chinese language. Even the commercial economy was not hit as hard in China as it was in the West. Trade was certainly disrupted in the fourth century and the use of coinage, for instance, declined. Still, the commercial economy had begun to revive by the late fifth century and even trade between north and south grew to a considerable level.

Trade with Central Asia continued through the Age of Division, and aristocrats in north China in particular remained willing to import luxury items from distant lands. This necklace of gold, pearl, and lapis lazuli, dating from the late sixth century and possibly made in Persia or Afghanistan, was among the objects unearthed from the tomb of a nine-year-old girl from a noble family.

Buddhism had an enormous impact on the visual arts in China, especially sculpture and painting. The merchants and missionaries from Central Asia who brought Buddhism to China also brought ideas about the construction and decoration of temples and the depiction of Buddhas and bodhisattvas. In this way Greek and Indian artistic influence reached China, travelling via the Buddhist kingdom of Gandhara (in present-day Afghanistan and Pakistan) through the Buddhist centres along the Silk Road to Dunhuang and later to central China.

The most extensive surviving early Chinese Buddhist art is found in the cave temples at Dunhuang and Yungang, spared during the political persecutions which destroyed the temples in urban centres. The cave temples at Dunhuang in western Gansu province were probably begun by 400, initiated by local monks; work continued on them over a period of several centuries. A large proportion of the residents of Dunhuang in this period were probably not Chinese, and it is therefore not surprising that the decoration of the early caves at Dunhuang shows strong connections to the Buddhist art at other oasis towns further west, such as Kucha and Khotan.

In 460 the Northern Wei court commissioned the carving of cave temples at Yungang, near its early capital in northern Shanxi. Most of the fifty-three caves there were carved out before the Wei moved their capital south to Luoyang in 494. The five earliest caves contain huge Buddha figures in stone,

the tallest a standing Buddha about 70 feet high.

Pre-Buddhist Chinese shrines had not contained statues or paintings of deities, but Buddhists used images both to teach Buddhist doctrine and provide a focus for devotional activities. Much of the early cave sculpture and painting portrayed the events in the life of the historical Buddha, Shakyamuni. Buddhas were often shown in a state of meditation, with masklike faces that betray no emotion. Their faces bore distinctive marks derived from Indian tradition, notably elongated ear lobes and cranial bumps. By contrast, the accompanying bodhisattvas were mortals, adorned with armlets and earrings, standing in more varied poses. In the sixth century Chinese artists gradually refined the ways they portrayed Buddhas and bodhisattvas, making them more slender and less angular, reflecting stylistic preferences seen also in secular Chinese painting.

Although the cave temples of Dunhuang and Yungang, along with the slightly later ones at Longmen near Luoyang, contain the bulk of surviving fifth- and sixth-century Buddhist art, at the time they constituted just a small fraction of Buddhist sites. The many temples and monasteries in cities, towns,

This huge Buddha at Yungang (c. 490), about 45 feet tall, was probably inspired by the colossal Buddha images at Bamiyan in Afghanistan. It is the most massive of some 51,000 Buddhist images carved into the surface of a cliff, which extends for over half a mile.

The walls of cave 9 at Yungang are decorated with standing or seated Buddha images surrounded by bodhisattvas, adoring heavenly beings, musicians, and flying apsaras. The lowest register carries a series of reliefs illustrating the life of Shakyamuni.

Central altar in Cave 432 at Dunhuang, Western Wei period, with painted clay statues of a Buddha flanked by a pair of bodhisattvas, each about 4 feet tall.

and mountainsides provided sensual stimulation of many sorts: the fragrance of incense; the sound of chanting; and the visual beauty of huge halls and towering pagodas whose walls were covered with paintings of the heavens or the lives of the Buddha and his main disciples. Yang Xuanzhi was so dismayed by the destruction of the temples and monasteries in Luoyang in the civil war beginning in 524 that he wrote an account of their glories. According to him, Jingming monastery had been the most magnificent. On the seventh day of the fourth month, all the Buddhist statues in the city, over a thousand altogether, were brought to this monastery, and the emperor would come in person to scatter flowers on them as part of the Great Blessing ceremony. 'The gold and the flowers dazzled in the sun, and the jewelled canopies floated like clouds; there were forests of banners and a fog of incense, and the Buddhist music of India shook heaven and earth. All kinds of entertainers and trick riders performed shoulder to shoulder. Virtuous hosts of famous monks came, carrying their staves; there were crowds of the Buddhist faithful, holding flowers; horsemen and carriages were packed beside each other in an endless mass.'

The grief of the Buddha's disciples at his death is captured in this painting from the west wall of Cave 428 at Dunhuang, painted in the early sixth century.

CHAPTER 5

A Cosmopolitan Empire:
The Tang Dynasty 581–907

North and South China were reunited at the end of the sixth century under the short-lived Sui dynasty (581–617) and fashioned into an expansive, dynamic, cosmopolitan empire by its successor, the Tang dynasty (618–907). The reunification of the country, the opening of the Grand Canal linking north and south, the creation of two huge capitals, and the expansion of interregional and international trade all stimulated economic growth. The Tang capital, Chang'an, grew to be the largest city in the world, housing perhaps a million people and attracting traders, students, and pilgrims from all over Asia. At least until the massive Rebellion of An Lushan (755–63) brought to an end this era of expansion, the Chinese of the Tang showed themselves remarkably open to what other cultures had to offer. Music and art in particular absorbed considerable foreign influence, and Buddhism continued to be enriched by doctrines and rituals introduced from outside China proper.

EMPIRE-BUILDING

The recreation of a unified Chinese empire in the late sixth century was not inevitable. By then China proper had been divided into separate northern and southern states for over two centuries, each of which considered itself the true heir to the Zhou and Han dynasties. Given the geographical differences between north and south China, this situation might well have become a permanent one, like the division into eastern and western Roman empires in the west; the north and south could each have developed its own version of Chinese civilization.

But union of the north and south did occur, and the long-term consequences for Chinese civilization were profound. The centralized bureaucratic monarchy was refashioned on an even stronger basis than in the Han. This reunification and the resultant peace ushered in three centuries of cultural flowering. From then on those who thought about the history of China had two examples from 'modern' times (the Han and Tang) to add to the three ancient dynasties (Xia, Shang, and Zhou) to prove the rightness of the unity of the Chinese world. Permanent division into independent states seemed less and less a natural, reasonable, or desirable state of affairs.

Unification came about through force of arms. The successors of the Xianbei Northern Wei, whose names changed as a result of palace coups from Western Wei to Zhou to Sui, took Sichuan in 553, the northeast in 577, and the south in 589. The conquest of the south involved naval as well as land attacks, with thousands of ships on both sides contending for control of the Yangzi River. The Sui conquerors razed the southern capital at Nanjing and forced the nobles and officials living there to move to the new Sui capital at Chang'an, thus eliminating them as a possible separatist threat and bringing their cultural traditions to the north of the country.

The Northern Zhou rulers who built the army that reunified China were unambiguously Xianbei, but in 581 Yang Jian, a general with a Chinese surname, ousted the heir to the throne (his daughter's son), secured his position by killing fifty-nine princes of the Zhou royal house, and founded the Sui dynasty. Known as Emperor Wendi (r. 581–604), he sought to legitimate his actions by presenting himself as a Buddhist Cakravartin King, that is, a monarch who uses military force to defend the Buddhist faith. Both he and his successor had grandiose plans for rebuilding China but tried to do too much too soon. Levies for labour service and military campaigns were onerous – 1,132,800 men were called up for a campaign against Korea in 612, for instance. In less than four decades rebellion resulted in the overthrow of the Sui dynasty. Of the many contenders who emerged, the most formidable came from the same northwestern elite that had produced the Northern Zhou and Sui rulers. The victor, Li Yuan (who reigned as Gaozong, 618–26), was in fact a first cousin of the second Sui emperor (their mothers were sisters). He and his son Taizong (r. 626–49) not surprisingly largely continued Sui initiatives. Taizong ruled three times as long as his father and is generally treated as a co-founder of the Tang. He used as much force as Wendi to come to the throne, killing two brothers and seeing to the execution of all ten of their sons. Then he demanded that his father abdicate in his favour. Despite this ruthless beginning, Taizong proved a wise and conscientious ruler, able to select good advisors and willing to listen to them, even when they criticized his personal behaviour.

Modern historians often describe the Sui and early Tang as sino-foreign regimes to draw attention to the large contributions of the Northern Dynasties to their institutional base and also the large component of families with Xianbei or other northern ancestry among the political and military elite of the period. It is

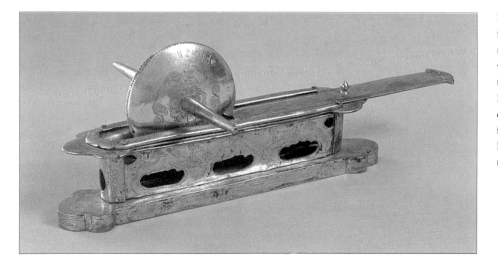

Drinking tea became popular in Tang times. The purpose of this gilded silver tea grinder was to pulverize powdered tea that had been made into cakes. Dated 869, it was among a set of objects donated by the imperial family to the Famensi Buddhist temple in Fufeng, near Xi'an, Shaanxi province.

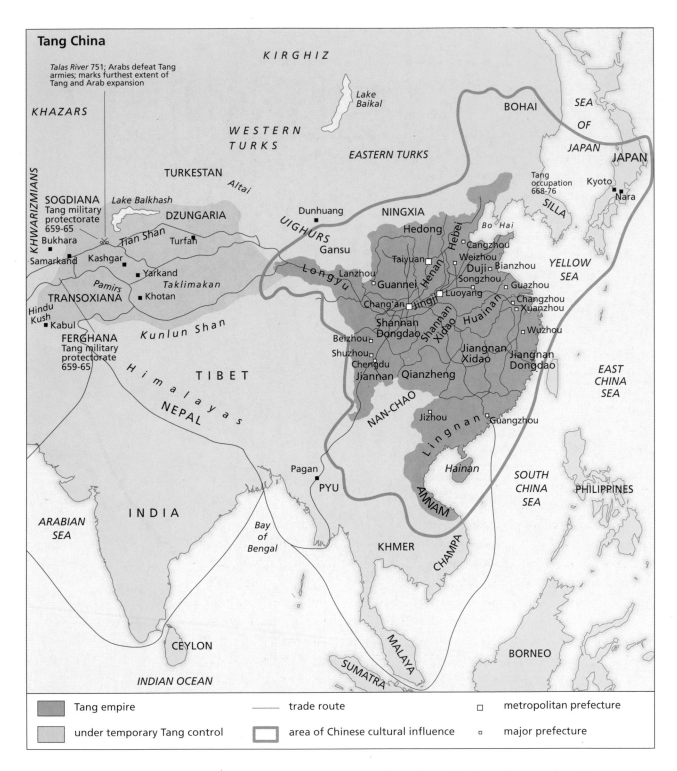

Tang China

Talas River 751; Arabs defeat Tang armies; marks furthest extent of Tang and Arab expansion

KIRGHIZ

KHAZARS

Lake Baikal

BOHAI

SEA OF JAPAN

WESTERN TURKS

EASTERN TURKS

JAPAN

KHWARIZMIANS

TURKESTAN

Altai

Tang occupation 668-76

Kyoto

SOGDIANA Tang military protectorate 659-65

Lake Balkhash

DZUNGARIA

Dunhuang

NINGXIA

SILLA

Nara

Bo Hai

Bukhara

Tian Shan

UIGHURS

Hedong

Hebei

Cangzhou

YELLOW SEA

Samarkand

Kashgar

Turfan

Gansu

Taiyuan

Weizhou

Duji

Henan

Bianzhou

Yarkand

Taklimakan

Lanzhou

Guannei

Songzhou

Guazhou

Pamirs

Khotan

Chang'an

Luoyang

Changzhou

Xuanzhou

TRANSOXIANA

Hindu Kush

Kunlun Shan

Shannan Dongdao

Shannan Xidao

Huainan

Kabul

Beizhou

Wuzhou

FERGHANA Tang military protectorate 659-65

Himalayas

TIBET

Shuzhou

Jiangnan Xidao

Jiangnan Dongdao

NEPAL

Chengdu

Qianzheng

Jiannan

EAST CHINA SEA

NAN-CHAO

Pagan

PYU

Jizhou

Guangzhou

Lingnan

Hainan

SOUTH CHINA SEA

PHILIPPINES

ARABIAN SEA

INDIA

Bay of Bengal

AMNAM

KHMER

CHAMPA

MALAYA

BORNEO

CEYLON

SUMATRA

INDIAN OCEAN

| | Tang empire | —— trade route | ☐ metropolitan prefecture |
| | under temporary Tang control | ▭ area of Chinese cultural influence | ▫ major prefecture |

Tang China's neighbours included states that had adopted many aspects of Chinese statecraft. These included the kingdoms of Silla and Bohai to the northeast, Nara Japan to the east, and Nanzhao and Tibet to the west. China also exerted political overlordship over large areas in central Asia where Chinese culture did not penetrate so deeply.

true that both founders came from families that had worked closely with the Xian-bei rulers and had intermarried with them. But none of these early rulers chose to present himself as synthesizing the best of Chinese and Xianbei traditions. Because both Yang and Li were Chinese names, they could present themselves as scions of old Chinese stock and emperors in the tradition of the Han. Certainly they did not think martial prowess or love of horses and hunting were un-Chinese. During this period the Xianbei presence rapidly faded as the Xianbei were assimilated and their language disappeared. Many men of Xianbei descent used the Chinese surnames they had been given at the end of the fifth century and served in civil rather than military offices. One of Taizong's chief experts in civil administration, for instance, was Zhangsun Wuji, a well-educated descendant of the Tuoba imperial clan.

Even if the Sui and Tang founders framed their state-building in entirely Chinese terms, they were heavily indebted to the groundwork laid during the Northern Dynasties. Both dynasties retained modified forms of the equal-field system started during the Northern Wei. By setting the uniform taxes in grain, cloth, and labour services relatively low, they were able to increase the numbers of households on the tax registers, and within a few years after reunification, the number of registered households had been doubled to about nine million (for a total population in the vicinity of fifty million). The Sui and early Tang also retained the Northern Zhou divisional militia, the army of volunteer farmer-soldiers who in return for their allocations of farmland served in rotation in armies at the capital or on the frontiers.

Using this army, the Sui and Tang rulers quickly extended their control beyond China proper. On the Inner Asian frontier, the powerful Turks had become a recurrent threat. To keep them in check, these rulers used the old strategies of strengthening fortifications, marriage diplomacy, investiture of their rulers, trade and tribute missions, and getting one tribe or contender to fight another. For instance, in 605, when the Khitan from the northeast made raids into China, a Chinese general was sent to lead 20,000 Turkish cavalrymen against them. When the Khitan were defeated, their women and livestock were given to the Turks as their reward. In 630, however, the Chinese turned against the Turks, wresting control of the Ordos and of southwestern Mongolia away from them, and winning for Taizong the title of great khan. This opened the way for joint Chinese-Turkish expeditions into the Silk Route cities of Central Asia in the 640s and 650s, which resulted in China regaining overlordship in the area.

The Sui and early Tang dynasties were also periods of empire building at home, of strengthening, standardizing, and codifying the institutions of political control. The Sui promulgated a code of law which combined elements of both northern and southern legal traditions, and the Tang built on it. The code of 653, the earliest to survive, has more than 500 articles specifying penalties to be imposed on those found guilty of a long list of crimes. The penalties ranged from a beating of

The calm, respectful, but determined demeanour of this stone statue was meant to capture the qualities desired in high officials. It was among a series of civil and military officials that lined the path to the grave of the first Tang emperor.

ten blows with the light stick, to a hundred blows with the heavy stick, to penal servitude lasting one to three years, to life exile to distant locations with penal servitude, to execution. Like earlier laws, these ones served to support social and political hierarchies by grading penalties according to the relationship of the parties; for example, it was more serious for a servant or a nephew to strike or kill a master or an uncle than vice versa. The legal principles articulated in this Tang code remained central to the Chinese legal system in all succeeding dynasties.

Imperial control over provincial administration was a critical issue in this period. During the Northern and Southern dynasties, the number of prefectures had proliferated, and staffing them had largely become the privilege of local elite families. To reassert central control over local government, the Sui reduced the numbers of prefectures and counties, gave the ministry of personnel the power to fill even the lower posts in them, and ruled that officials could no longer serve in their home prefecture or serve more than one tour in any prefecture. These new policies worked to limit the power of locally entrenched families and to keep centrally appointed officials from allying with them.

As in the Han period, appointing men imbued with Confucian values of loyalty to the ruler and duty to the people was another means of strengthening imperial power, since it was much less costly to appoint officials the government could trust than to supervise and monitor their every action. To identify true Confucians, the Sui introduced written examinations of candidates' literary abilities and knowledge of the classics. The Tang expanded this civil service examination system and took other measures to promote Confucian education, such as setting up state schools and issuing authorized versions of the Five Classics, complete with selected commentaries. Although in the Tang period on average only twenty to thirty men passed the civil service examinations per year, the exams gradually came to play an important role in identifying an elite within the bureaucracy, a group of men who would spend much of their careers in the central government, rapidly promoted from one post to the next. The new system moreover expanded opportunities for the highly talented from unconnected families; by mid Tang, a man from Guangdong province, far from any of the centres of aristocratic families, had risen through the examination system to hold some of the highest offices in the court. Still, members of the famous families were everywhere in the bureaucracy, especially at the highest reaches. Because men from old aristocratic families tended to do well in the examinations, this recruitment system did not put an end to their influence, but it did shape how they prepared themselves for government service.

Calligraphy as a fine art

In China, perhaps more than anywhere else, calligraphy came to be recognized as a fine art, practised by men of education and social eminence. Different scripts, such as 'seal', 'clerical', and 'draft' could be chosen to suit the calligrapher's mood or needs, and within each script a great number of styles evolved. Each piece of calligraphy was thought to reflect its writer's character and feelings. The strength, balance, and flow of the strokes made with a highly pliable hair brush were believed to convey the calligrapher's moral and psychological make-up as well as his momentary emotions. So indicative of character was calligraphy thought to be that in Tang times it was used as a criterion for assigning posts in the civil service. To attain a good hand took discipline and respect for tradition. Those aspiring to master the art of calligraphy would assiduously copy works by established masters before attempting to develop styles of their own. Thus the pieces of calligraphy by former masters were treasured, and the esteem accorded them had a profound influence on the development of the art.

The most famous piece of calligraphy in Chinese history is undoubtedly the *Record of the Orchid Pavilion Gathering*, written by Wang Xizhi in 353. Part of its fame is based on the story of how nearly three centuries later it got into the hands of the Tang emperor Taizong. Three times Taizong sent emissaries to request it from Biancai, an elderly monk living in a monastery in the south reputed to have possession of it, but each time Biancai claimed it had not survived the wars. Then Taizong sent Xiao Yi, a grandson of one of the last southern monarchs. Xiao Yi called on Biancai dressed as a Confucian scholar, and the two got along well, drinking, playing chess, and composing poetry. After several days of such visits, Xiao Yi brought out a painting to show Biancai and mentioned in passing that he possessed calligraphy by Wang Xizhi. Biancai asked him to bring the pieces the next day, and when he did, Biancai commented, 'These are authentic but not of the first rank. I happen to have a truly exceptional work, the original of the Orchid Pavilion manuscript.' Xiao Yi feigned disbelief, so the next day Biancai took his treasure out of hiding to show him. Xiao Yi pointed to flaws and declared it a copy, leading to a heated argument. When Biancai, flustered, failed to put it away before going off to participate in a monastic ritual, Xiao Yi grabbed the treasure and rode off. Overjoyed to get it, Taizong promoted

Xiao Yi to a rank five government post and rewarded him with precious objects of gold and silver, a town mansion, a country estate, and two fine horses from the imperial stable. At first Taizong wanted to punish Biancai for his miserliness but in the end instead sent him silk and grain which the monk used to have a pagoda built. Taizong had many copies of Wang Xizhi's calligraphy made, but the original, we are told, he treasured so much that he had it interred with him in his grave.

Whatever the truth of the details of this anecdote, it was recorded in Tang times, revealing that by that period the love of relics of the past had already reached the point where collecting and protecting them could become an obsession.

To make copies of Wang Xizhi's calligraphy, Taizong had them carefully traced, then carved on a stone from which copies could be rubbed. This impression dates from the Tang or Song dynasty.

Love stories

Undoubtedly the two most famous women of Tang times were Empress Wu and Yang Guifei, and popular understanding of the power that women could gain over men was very much shaped by the stories told about these two rather different palace women. Before the end of the dynasty, however, fictional women were coming to play nearly as important a role in shaping understandings of male–female relations. Well-crafted short stories written in the classical language by leading men of letters came to shape cultural expectations concerning what makes men and women attractive to each other, how they differ in the ways they express love, and their varying proclivities for devotion or callousness.

Tang love stories frequently concerned young literati who became enamoured of courtesans or prostitutes. Bai Xingjian wrote about a young examination candidate who fell for the beautiful courtesan Li Wa on first glance. She and her proprietrix gradually squeezed him of all his money and then disappeared. Totally impoverished, the young man was reduced to supporting himself as a singer of funeral dirges. When his father discovered him in that demeaned capacity, he beat him nearly to death. For a while the young man lived by begging, until by accident he again encountered Li Wa, who out of a sense of guilt and compassion first purchased her freedom from her proprietrix, then took him in. After nursing him back to health, she convinced him to resume his studies. In the end he passed the examinations with distinction, became an official, and was able to win over his father, who even accepted Li Wa as a daughter-in-law.

An even more famous love story concerns an examination candidate who fell in love with a girl of good family, a distant cousin. It was written by the eminent man of letters, Yuan Zhen. In this story, Zhang, the son of an official, falls in love with Yingying after her widowed mother introduced her to him to thank him for doing them a favour. On the advice of Yingying's maid, Zhang tried to win her over by writing poems to her. Both Zhang and Yingying were literate and sensitive. Yingying especially:

> She excelled in the arts but acted as if she knew nothing about them. She was quick and clever in speaking, but was not inclined toward repartee. She loved Zhang very much but never said so in words. She was subject to melancholy moods, but did not let her feelings show on her face. Once she was playing sad music on the zither alone at night. When Zhang, who had overheard her, appeared, he tried to get her to resume playing, but she refused. This made him all the more infatuated with her.

Without a formal engagement or the permission of either's parents, an affair began, interrupted when Zhang had to go to the capital to take the examinations. Yingying wrote him a long letter accusing him of faithlessness when he did not return, but he in the end broke with her, telling a friend that beautiful women spell disaster for men. Each married other partners chosen for them by their parents.

Opposite
Notions of what makes women attractive have changed over the course of Chinese history. The figurines found in Tang tombs reveal that active women, even ones playing polo on horseback, were viewed as appealing. So too were plump and full-faced women.

From Tang times on, the education of the upper class tended to become more bookish, and martial skills such as horsemanship, archery, and swordsmanship gradually came to play a lesser role in elite life.

The examinations system helped to standardize and overcome differences between the northwestern, northeastern, and southern elites. The economic and political integration of the empire was similarly aided by an engineering feat: the construction of the Grand Canal, dug between 605 and 609 by means of enormous levies of conscripted labour. Transport canals had been built since Qin times, but these had never been anything on this scale. The first stage linked the eastern capital of Luoyang to the Yangzi valley at modern Yangzhou. On its

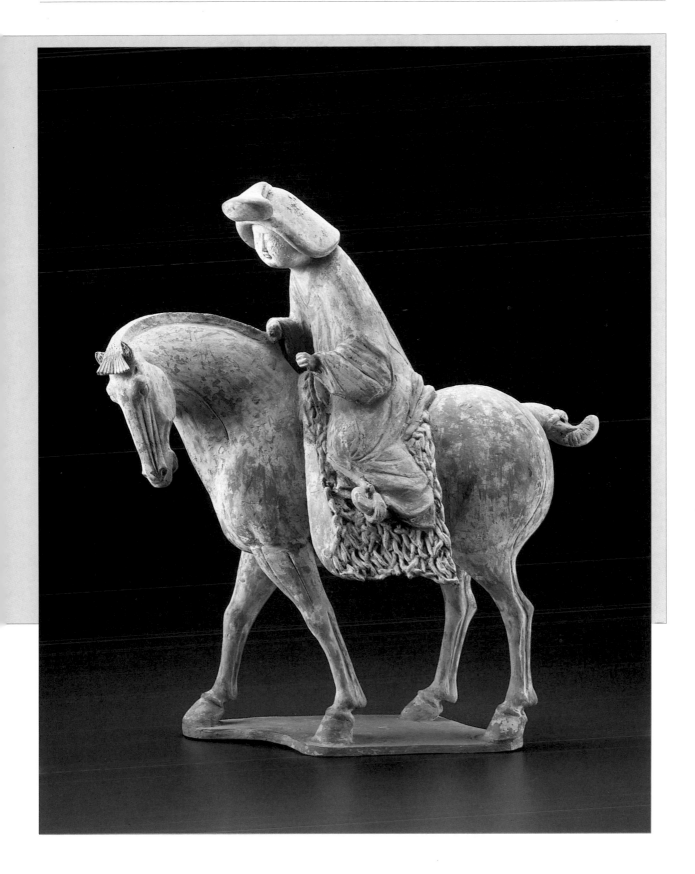

The Sui dynasty's contribution to the development of Chinese transportation was not limited to the construction of the Grand Canal. Roads were built in the north China plain to improve access to the northern frontier. This bridge in Zhouxian, Hebei province, was constructed between 605 and 616 using over a thousand stones weighing more than a ton each. It has a span of about 130 feet and a width of over 30 feet.

completion, the second Sui emperor led a 65-mile-long flotilla of boats down to his southern capital at Yangzhou. Soon the canal was extended south to Hangzhou and north to the Beijing area. An imperial road was built alongside the canal and relay post stations were provided. In total, the canal extended almost 1,200 miles, allowing the government to draw on the growing wealth of the Yangzi valley to support both the government in the capital area and the military garrisons along the northeastern frontier. This new long-distance supply system gradually obviated the need for the army to be self-supporting, as supplies could be brought from the south to the north.

Empire building continued apace during the late seventh century when the court was dominated by Empress Wu, a powerful personality, as ruthless and politically adroit as Wendi or Taizong. Her rise to power is that much more remarkable because she did not begin as an empress, but as Gaozong's concubine. Her influence on Gaozong (r.650–83) was such that within a few years of her entering the palace he was willing to oust his previous empress to install her instead, over the strenuous objections of his high officials. Once installed as empress, she moved quickly to eliminate her rivals and opponents. After Gaozong suffered a stroke in 660, Empress Wu took full charge. Even though he died in 683, she maintained her control during the reigns of her two sons, whom she summarily deposed, one after the other. In 690 she proclaimed herself emperor of a new dynasty, the Zhou, making her the only woman who took the title emperor in Chinese history. She circulated the *Great Cloud Sutra*, which predicted the imminent reincarnation of the Buddha Maitreya as a female monarch, under whom all the world would be free of illness, worry, and disaster, thus providing Buddhist legitimation for her ascent to the throne. During her reign the court fre-

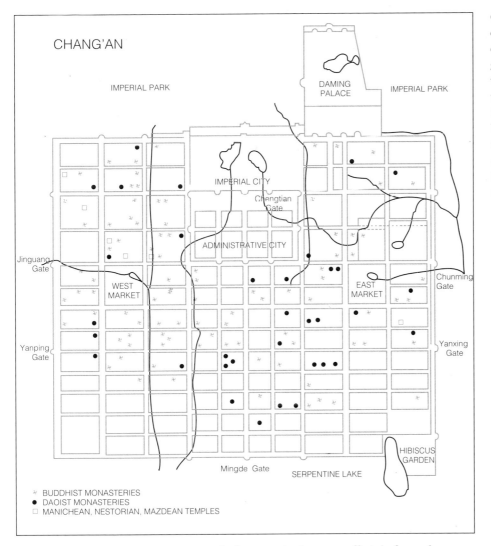

CHANG'AN

IMPERIAL PARK

DAMING PALACE

IMPERIAL PARK

IMPERIAL CITY

Chengtian Gate

ADMINISTRATIVE CITY

Jinguang Gate

WEST MARKET

EAST MARKET

Chunming Gate

Yanping Gate

Yanxing Gate

Mingde Gate   SERPENTINE LAKE

HIBISCUS GARDEN

⚏ BUDDHIST MONASTERIES
● DAOIST MONASTERIES
□ MANICHEAN, NESTORIAN, MAZDEAN TEMPLES

Chang'an was laid out in the early years of the Sui and developed in Tang times into a great city. It was divided into walled wards, the gates to which were closed at night. To facilitate state supervision, buying and selling was restricted to special market quarters, but religious establishments were to be found throughout the city.

quently moved east to Luoyang and she recruited many officials from the east, probably seeing in them a counterweight to the northwest aristocracy so closely connected to the Tang imperial family. Execrated by later historians as an evil usurper, Empress Wu was, without question, forceful. She suppressed rebellions of Tang princes and maintained an aggressive foreign policy. Her hold on the government was so strong that she was not deposed until 705 when she was over eighty and ailing.

LIFE AT THE CENTRE

A woman in the role of emperor, as the link between heaven and humankind, was certainly anomalous in Chinese history, but was not the only anomalous feature of the Tang period. More than in any other epoch in Chinese history before the twentieth century, Chinese in early and mid Tang had the self-confidence to be open to the new and different. Perhaps because a universal religion of foreign

Silk remained a major item of trade through Central Asia in Tang times. The most luxurious silks were generally used for women's clothes, as seen in this painted wooden figurine excavated from the tomb of a Chinese official posted to the far western frontier near Turfan in Xinjiang province.

origin gave China links to all the other countries of Asia east of Persia, perhaps because the elite included many families of non-Chinese descent, perhaps because China had the military might to garrison the Silk Road and keep it open for trade, Chinese in this period were more than happy to gather about them the best of what the rest of their world had to offer.

The magnificent capital at Chang'an exerted a powerfully attractive force on the outside world. Like earlier capital cities in the north, Chang'an was a planned city laid out on a square grid, but it was constructed on a much larger scale than any previous capital. Its outer walls, made of pounded earth about ten to fifteen feet thick and thirty-five feet tall, extended over five miles north to south and nearly six miles east to west. The palace was in the north, so the emperor could, in a sense, face south towards his subjects, whose homes were in the 108 wards, each enclosed by a wall. Certain blocks were set aside for markets, open at specified hours each day. The great southern gate of the city opened out on to an extremely broad avenue about 500 feet wide. Foreign envoys seeking to see the emperor all travelled along this thoroughfare directly to the palace. This and other main avenues were bordered by ditches planted with trees. When the city was first built in the Sui, officials and nobles were offered incentives to build residences and temples in the city, and many southern aristocrats were forced to move there after their capital was conquered in 589. But incentives and coercion were not needed for long; by the early Tang leading members of society sought to live in Chang'an or the secondary capital at Luoyang, also rebuilt in the Sui period.

The culture of Chang'an and Luoyang was enthusiastically cosmopolitan. Taizong was fascinated by the monk Xuanzang (602–64) who returned to China in 645 to tell about his fifteen years travelling across Central Asia and India. Knowledge of the outside world was also stimulated by the presence of envoys, merchants, and pilgrims who came from the tributary states in Central Asia as well as from neighbouring countries like Japan, Korea, and Tibet. Goods from these distant regions – horses, jewels, musical instruments, and textiles – were sources of endless fascination to both the court and the capital elite. Foreign fashions in hair and clothing were often copied, and foreign amusements like the game of polo became favourite pastimes of the well-to-do. The caravans that came from Central Asia were so appreciated that pottery representations of camels and their non-Han grooms were among the objects people commonly placed in tombs. Foreign religions, including Islam, Judaism, Manichaeism, Zoroastrianism, and Nestorian Christianity were practised among the thousands of foreign merchants resident there, though none of these religions spread into the Chinese population the way Buddhism had centuries earlier.

Foreign influence had longer-term impact in the arts. Silver-smithing was perfected, with cups, plates, ewers, and other small objects showing the influence of Persian designs and techniques. The introduction of new instruments and new tunes from India, Iran, and Central Asia brought about a major transformation of Chinese music. Interior furnishings were also transformed, as the practice of sitting on mats on the floor gradually gave way to the foreign practice of sitting on stools and chairs.

Prosperity undoubtedly aided the cultural vitality of the Tang period. The reunification of the country, the opening of the Grand Canal linking north and south, and the expansion of international trade via the Central Asian Silk Route

Ceramic model of a group of musicians seated on a camel, 26 inches tall, excavated in Xi'an (Chang'an) from a tomb dated 723. The dress of some of the musicians, along with their beards and facial features, indicate that they are from Central Asia. Tang tombs often contain ceramic models of Central Asian men, both musicians and grooms attending to horses or camels; the presence of these objects attests to the love of the Tang elite for Central Asian music and for the caravans that brought goods from the west.

and the higher-volume sea routes all stimulated the economy. Economic development of the south was particularly impressive, aided by convenient water transportation along rivers and streams. River traffic had grown so heavy that storms at Yangzhou in 721 and 751 were said to have led to the destruction of over 1,000 boats each time. Tea, native to the south, was no longer looked on as a medicinal herb, useful primarily to those trying to stay awake, but had come to be drunk all over the country, making it a major item in trade. The southern port cities of Canton, Quanzhou, and Fuzhou grew in size as maritime trade along the coast and throughout Southeast Asia expanded greatly, much of it in the hands of Arab merchants. By 742, when a census was taken, the proportion of the registered population living in the south had increased from only a quarter in the early seventh century to nearly a half.

Neither economic growth nor the development of thriving commercial cities brought about radical change in the composition of the social or political elite. Tang China was still an aristocratic society. In elite circles, genealogies continued to be much discussed and eminent forebears were looked on as a source of pride and admiration; the most prestigious families still largely married among themselves, giving coherence and visibility to the highest stratum of the elite. Early in the Tang dynasty the emperors sporadically made efforts to undermine the prestige of aristocratic pedigree and to assert that high office carries more honour than eminent ancestors. Once the families closest to the throne had become socially accepted as aristocratic families, however, the emperors largely gave up trying to challenge the aristocrats' pretensions.

Aristocrats and other educated men in Tang times engaged in a wide range of arts and learning. Confucian scholarship of many sorts flourished, especially the writings of histories and commentaries to the classics. In this period education in Confucian texts and commitment to Confucian principles of government service was not looked on as incompatible with faith in Buddhism or Daoism, and many men were learned in the texts of more than one tradition. The arts also attracted scholars, many of whom were esteemed for their calligraphy. Almost all educated men wrote an occasional poem, and poetic composition was tested on the most prestigious of the civil service examinations, the *jinshi*, or 'presented scholar' exam. Perhaps that contributed to the art of poetry, for the Tang produced many of China's greatest poets, including Wang Wei, Li Bai, Du Fu, Bai Juyi, and Li Shangyin. Over 48,900 poems by 2,200 Tang poets have survived. The parting of friends was a common theme of these poems, perhaps because officials were frequently transferred to the provinces. The immense distances of the empire, the dangers of travel, and the difficulty of keeping in touch once separated evidently made every parting seem momentous. Poets also frequented entertainment quarters of the cities where they could call on female musicians. In the late Tang period, courtesans played an important part in popularizing a new verse form by singing the lyrics written by famous men and by composing lyrics themselves.

The high point of Tang culture came in the first half of the eighth century, during the reign of Xuanzong (r.712–56), a grandson of Empress Wu whose court became the focal point of high culture. Xuanzong conducted state ceremonies on a grand scale and authorized a major codification of state ritual. Buddhist and Daoist clerics were also welcome at his court. Xuanzong invited teachers of the newly introduced Tantric school of Buddhism, in 726 calling on the Javanese monk Vajrabodhi to perform Tantric rites to avert drought and in 742 holding the incense burner while the Ceylonese Amoghavajra recited mystical incantations to aid the victory of Tang forces. To liven up the poetry written at his court and amuse him on his outings with his palace ladies, Xuanzong established a new academy for poets. The poet Li Bai served in this academy for a few years, writing light sensual poems celebrating the beauty of the imperial parks and the ladies in them. Xuanzong also enjoyed music and horses and even kept a troupe of dancing horses. Han Gan, a great horse painter, served at his court.

In his early years, Xuanzong's love of court life did not keep him from tending to affairs of state. He took prompt action to curb the power of imperial relatives and Buddhist monasteries, both of which had gained strength under Empress Wu. To deal with the declines in tax revenue caused by absconding peasants, he ordered a new census and reformed the equal-field system. Because of threats from the Turks, Uighurs, and Tibetans, he restructured the defence establishment, setting up a ring of military provinces along the frontier from Sichuan to Manchuria and giving their commanders great authority.

Xuanzong had many consorts and fathered thirty sons and twenty-nine daughters. But one woman had a special place in his life. In popular culture Xuanzong is remembered above all for falling in love, when nearly sixty, with the young imperial consort Yang Guifei, a beauty who shared his interest in music and dance but lacked sound political sense. She was amused by the company of An Lushan, one of the recently appointed military governors of non-Chinese origin. The doting Xuanzong showered An Lushan with favours and allowed him to amass 160,000 troops along the northern and northeastern frontiers. In 755 An Lushan rebelled and marched on Luoyang and Chang'an, compelling Xuanzong to flee west. The troops that accompanied him staged a mutiny and forced Xuanzong to have Yang Guifei strangled; Xuanzong, already over seventy and depressed by the turn of events, abdicated to his son and the most brilliant age of court culture came to an end.

THE PENETRATION OF BUDDHISM INTO CHINESE LIFE

The outwardly oriented, cosmopolitan mood of the Sui and Tang periods allowed Buddhist institutions to become an integral part of Chinese life. Buddhist monasteries ran schools for children; in remote areas they provided lodging for travellers; in towns they offered literati places to gather for social occasions like going-away parties. Monasteries also played a major role in the economy. Their huge tracts of land and large numbers of serfs gave them the financial resources to establish enterprises like mills and oil presses and to open up new land. With the income they earned from these ventures, they often expanded into money-lending and pawn-broking businesses, making monasteries an economic force in local communities and contributing to further monetization and commercialization of the economy.

Buddhism was also instrumental in transforming the Chinese imagination. Stories of Buddhist origin became in Tang times among the most widely known and popular tales. To spread the faith, monks would show pictures and tell stories to audiences of illiterate laymen. The story of Mulian, who journeyed to the netherworld to save his mother, suffering the most harrowing punishments there, gave rise to the ghost festival held on the fifteenth day of the seventh month, one of the most important festivals in Chinese popular culture. On this day Buddhists and non-Buddhists alike, from the most educated members of the clergy to ordinary illiterate villagers, would put out food in order to feed hungry ghosts suffering in the netherworld. The Japanese monk Ennin, who spent the years 838 to 847 in China, reported that on this day the forty-odd monasteries in Yangzhou would compete with each other to make unusual candles, cakes, and artificial flowers to offer in front of the Buddha halls. 'Everyone in the city

The Great Hall of Nanchansi at Mount Wutai, one of the oldest surviving buildings in China, was probably built shortly after the great suppression of Buddhism of 845 was relaxed.

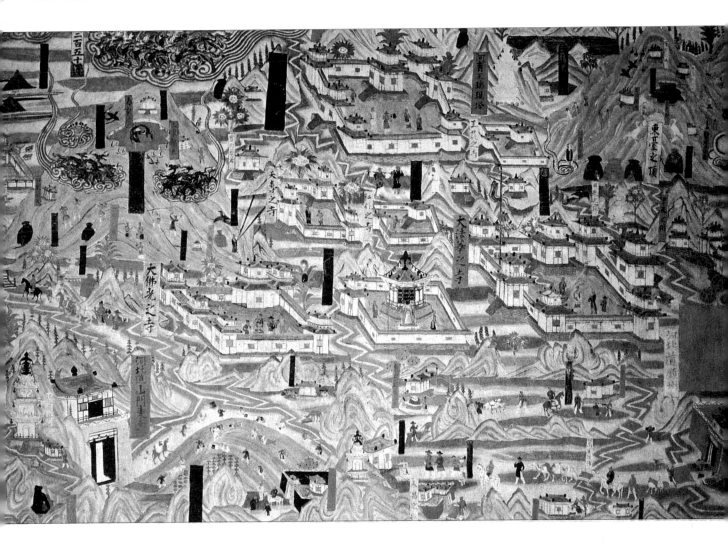

goes around to the monasteries and performs adoration during this most flourishing festival.'

By the mid-Tang period the most popular sects or schools of Buddhism were thoroughly sinified ones. Adherents of the Pure Land teaching devoutly paid homage to the Buddha Amitabha and his chief helper, the compassionate bodhisattva Guanyin, in order to be reborn in Amitabha's paradise, the Pure Land. Among the educated elite, the Chan school (known in Japan as Zen) was becoming just as popular. Chan teachings rejected the authority of the sutras and claimed the superiority of mind-to-mind transmission of Buddhist truth through a series of patriarchs, the most important of whom were the First Patriarch Bodhidharma, an Indian monk who came to China in the early sixth century, and the Sixth Patriarch Huineng, a Chinese monk who died in the early eighth century. The illiteracy of Huineng at the time of his enlightenment was taken as proof of the Chan claim that enlightenment could be achieved suddenly through insight into one's own true nature.

Of all the large monastic complexes built in mountains far from cities, probably none attracted more pilgrims than the great establishment at Mount Wutai in Shanxi province. Its fame was so great that hundreds of miles away at Dunhuang in Gansu province it was depicted on a mural in Cave 61.

In the *Lotus Sutra*, the bodhisattva Guanyin was said to have the power to grant children to any woman who prayed to her, an attribute that undoubtedly added to Guanyin's appeal and the Chinese tendency to conceive of this bodhisattva as female. These pages from a ninth- or tenth-century illustrated version show a couple praying to Guanyin for the birth of a child (on the right), followed by a midwife attending the woman giving birth (on the left).

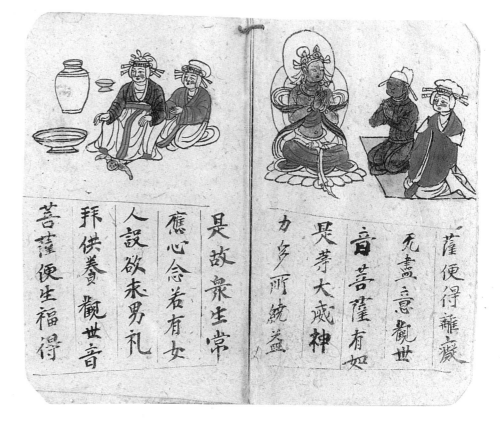

The history of Buddhism in Tang times was not solely one of expansion and penetration. In the late Tang period, opposition to Buddhism as foreign re-emerged as China's international position weakened, and the court's financial difficulties revived antagonism against Buddhism as an economic drain. In 841 the court initiated a massive suppression of Buddhism and other foreign religions. By 845, when the orders were rescinded, around a quarter of a million monks and nuns had been returned to lay life, 150,000 slaves had been confiscated, and some 4,600 monasteries and 40,000 chapels had been demolished or converted to other purposes. This blow came at an unfortunate time for Chinese Buddhism, for in this period it also lost the intellectual stimulation of contact with Buddhist centres in India and Central Asia due to the spread of Islam in Central Asia and the decline of Buddhism in India. As a result of these two blows, although Pure Land and Chan continued to flourish, the more philosophical and exegetical schools of Buddhist thought did not survive into later centuries.

LIFE FAR FROM THE CENTRE

A sense of what life was like for subjects of the Tang who lived far from the capital and well below the upper reaches of society can be glimpsed from a great cache of documents found sealed in a cave temple at Dunhuang, at the far northwestern edge of China proper where the Silk Road across the desert began. Surviving

Opposite
Printed calendar for the year 877 found at Dunhuang in the far northwest. It is perhaps not surprising that among the earliest surviving printed works are calendars giving the information needed to calculate what to do or avoid doing on particular days.

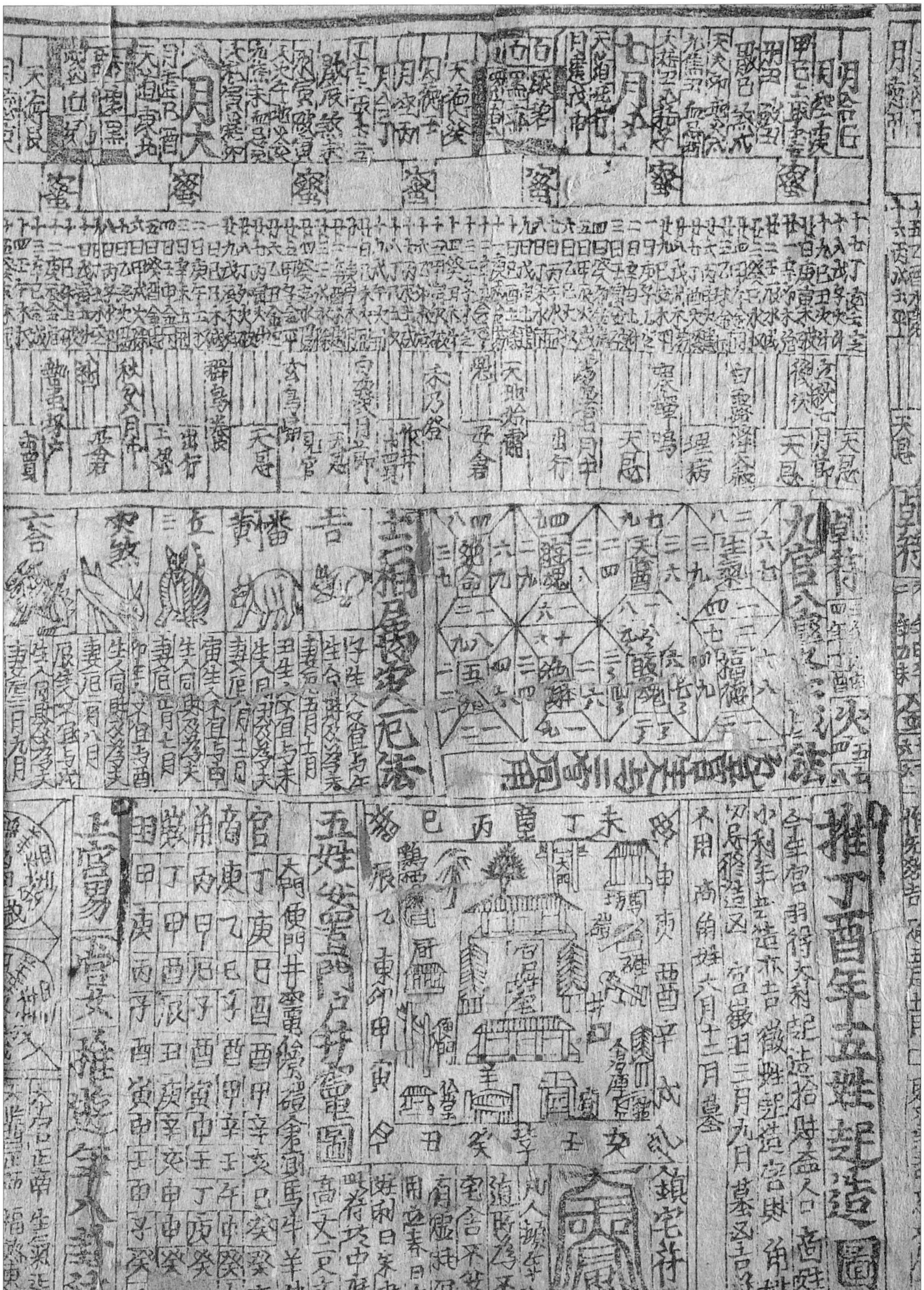
推丁酉年五姓起造圖

documents include contracts for the sale of land, houses, and slaves; household registration records used in the equal-field system; elementary education primers; forms for arranging divorce, adoption, or family division; sample or form letters for many occasions; circulars for lay religious societies; local histories and lists of local eminent families; and an enormous variety of government documents.

The farmers of Dunhuang may have lived far from the capital, but their daily lives were still profoundly affected by the policies established there, particularly the equal-field system. Documents found at Dunhuang prove that people did, in fact, receive allotments of land through this system, and this land did revert to the state after people died. But tenancy is also much in evidence. Not only were there government lands worked by various types of tenants, but also some people found it inconvenient to work the land allocated to them under the equal-field system and rented it to tenants while they worked as tenants themselves on other people's land. Monasteries were also large landlords, and their tenants were held on serf-like bondage, unfree to move elsewhere or marry outside their status group. Dunhuang documents show, nevertheless, that monastery dependants were free to own property of their own and to employ others to help them work it; some even had slaves of their own.

The state also had a large hand in the way goods were bought and sold. There are about ninety fragments of official price lists showing that every month the authorities established prices for three qualities of a wide range of commodities sold in government-supervised markets, including foodstuffs and textiles. In other matters, the role of the state was more indirect. Repair of irrigation ditches, for instance, appears to have largely been performed by small mutual-aid societies of those farmers most directly affected, supervised by men performing their labour-service duties.

This is not to say that there were no private or non-governmental collective activities in Dunhuang. The presence of Buddhist lay associations shows that even ordinary farmers could organize themselves, passing around circulars to call meetings. The expansion of education, largely outside government hands, can be seen from the great quantity and variety of educational texts that survived in Dunhuang. Confucian social ethics were taught in the primers used in schools run by monasteries. The *Family Instructions of the Grandfather*, which survived in forty-two copies in Dunhuang, employed simple verse to instruct young men in correct manners:

> When his father goes out to walk
> The son must follow behind.
> If on the road he meets a senior
> He puts his feet together and joins his hands.
> In front of a senior
> He does not spit on the ground.

The moral basis of women's manners was also expounded:

> A bride serves her husband
> Just as she served her father.
> Her voice should not be heard
> Nor her body or shadow seen.
> With her husband's father and elder brothers
> She has no conversation.

The Dunhuang documents also include many books for somewhat more advanced students, such as multiplication tables, arithmetic exercises, vocabulary lists and etiquette books with elaborate rules for how to vary polite language when addressing someone very superior, slightly superior, a peer, or an inferior; how to write a condolence letter or make a condolence visit; and how to conduct weddings and funerals.

The beginnings of printing can also be better understood in the context of the Dunhuang documents. There was clearly a large local demand for primers for children, calendars of lucky and unlucky days, manuals of charms for warding off evil, and guides for examination candidates. Another reason to make multiple copies was to earn religious merit by copying and distributing sacred Buddhist texts. It was perhaps not a large step to begin carving blocks to save time in reproducing texts, since the Chinese had long used seals made out of metal, stone, and clay to impress words on paper. They also knew how to make copies of texts by taking rubbings of inscribed stones. There is scattered evidence of the use of block printing as early as the eighth century, and by the ninth century the technique had been perfected. The oldest extant printed book is a copy of the *Diamond Sutra* preserved in Dunhuang, dated 868. Other Tang printed works preserved in Dunhuang include dictionaries and almanacs. At about this time the scroll format for long texts began to be superseded by flat books with folded pages, a format much more convenient for storage. Within a couple of centuries the invention of printed books would revolutionize the communications of ideas.

POLITICAL AND ECONOMIC REALIGNMENTS

The Tang government never completely recovered from the rebellion started by An Lushan. After eight years of fighting (755–63), Xuanzong's successor had little choice but to make a compromising peace. To restore order he

Metalwork in gold and silver reached a high point in Tang times. The shape of this gilded silver bottle, unearthed near Xi'an in Shaanxi province, recalls the leather bottles of nomadic horsemen, while the workmanship reflects Persian influence. The playful etching evokes the horses of Emperor Xuanzong, which were trained to dance with cups of wine in their mouths.

pardoned rebel leaders, often appointing them as military governors in the areas where they had surrendered. From then on in several vital areas military governors acted like rulers of independent states, paying no taxes, appointing their own subordinates, and passing their power to their own heirs. In these provinces, military men, often non-Han or semi-sinified, came to staff a large proportion of government posts. Even in provinces with civil governors, the provincial governors were enhancing their administrative powers at the expense of both the central government and the prefects and magistrates.

In these circumstances, the central government finally abolished the long outgrown equal-field system it had inherited from the Northern Dynasties and in 780 substituted a twice-yearly tax on actual landholding. From this time on, regions were given quotas of taxes to fill and allowed considerable leeway in how they raised the required funds. Government withdrawal from control of land ownership amounted to a return to an open market in land, facilitating the growth of large estates as those who fell into debt had to sell their land and those with money could amass more and more property.

The new land tax worked well, but the central government discovered it could raise revenue even more successfully through control of the production and distribution of salt. By adding a surcharge to the salt it sold to licensed merchant distributors, the government was able to collect taxes indirectly, through merchants, even from districts where its authority was minimal. By 779 over half the total revenue was being raised through the salt monopoly. Success with salt led the government to attempt similar policies with other commodities, including wine and tea. The Salt Commission became a very powerful organization, independent of the old organs of government and run by officials who specialized in finance.

Besides withdrawing from control of the market in land, the post-rebellion Tang government largely gave up supervision of the operation of urban markets. This retreat from management of the economy had the unintended effect of stimulating trade. The circulation of goods increased and markets were opened in more and more towns, facilitating regional trade centred on the new provincial capitals. Merchants, no longer supervised so closely, found ways to solve the perennial problems of a shortage of coins by circulating silver bullion and notes of exchange. By the ninth century a new economic hierarchy of markets and towns had begun to emerge alongside the state hierarchy of administrative centres. The entire south was also benefiting from yet another influx of migrants as Hebei province in particular and the north more generally were hard hit by the rebellion and its aftermath. Because agriculture was more productive in the south, every shift of the population in that direction aided the overall economic prosperity of the country. Cities of the lower Yangzi area, such as Yangzhou, Suzhou, and Hangzhou, flourished, inducing many elite families from the north to relocate permanently in the region.

Chang'an continued to thrive as an urban centre in the post-rebellion era, but the court based there did not fare so well. Capable and determined emperors and court officials took many measures to strengthen central control, but with limited success. To counter the threat posed by the regional commanders, the court created a Palace Army and put the emperor's personal servants, the palace eunuchs, in charge of it. It did not take long for the eunuchs to prove as much a bane as the mutinous provinces. They gained control of palace affairs, and high officials found themselves reduced to forming alliances with one group of eunuchs or another. Accounts of court politics after 820 revolve around plots and counter-plots, with the eunuchs and their allies enthroning, coercing, and murdering one emperor after another. In 835 the emperor and a group of officials tried to strike against the eunuchs but their plot was discovered. In retaliation, the eunuchs ordered the immediate slaughter of over 1,000 officials. As a public display of their power, the eunuchs had the three chief ministers and their families publicly executed in Chang'an's western market place.

External pressures coincided with these internal threats. Antagonistic states were consolidating themselves all along the Tang's borders – from Bohai on the northeast to Tibet and Nanzhao on the west and southwest. The Turkish Uighurs proved a burdensome ally. The An Lushan rebellion was put down in part through their help, but to keep them from plundering Luoyang after they helped retake it, they had to be paid off with huge quantities of silk. Thereafter, to keep them from raiding, they had to be allowed to trade horses for silk at extortionate terms. At the same time Tibet had formed a strong empire, and when Chinese troops were withdrawn from the western frontier to help defend the capital after An Lushan rebelled, it was easy for the Tibetans to step in, cutting off Central Asia from metropolitan China. When the Tibetan empire collapsed in 842 and the Uighur empire broke up soon after, the Chinese court decided not to attempt the recovery of their former dominions in Central Asia.

After 860, the decentralized government with so much of its power concentrated in the hands of regional commanders proved unable to maintain even a semblance of order. Bandit gangs, some as large as small armies, ravaged the countryside and even attacked walled cities. These gangs preyed on traders and tax convoys, smuggled illicit salt, and sometimes went on rampages that took them far from their original base. Huang Chao, the leader of the most successful band, was a salt merchant who had failed the civil service examinations. His army moved rapidly across the country, from north to south and then north again, in 879 taking Guangzhou where they slaughtered thousands of foreign merchants, and in 881 taking Chang'an, where they set up a government. At one point in 882, after a poem ridiculing this new regime was posted on a government building, orders were issued to kill all those capable of writing poetry, and some 3,000 people perished as a result. It was not for another twenty years, however, that all pretence of Tang rule was abandoned, and the (short-lived) Liang dynasty proclaimed, beginning the period conventionally called the Five Dynasties (907–960) when China was fragmented into as many as ten regional states.

REASSESSING CHINA'S CULTURE AND INSTITUTIONS

In ancient times, when Chinese notions of their place in the world were first formulated, it was quite possible for Chinese thinkers to see China as the sole locus of civilization, the only place with writing, cities, and advanced manufacturing techniques. In Tang times such a view was no longer sustainable. For centuries pilgrims and missionaries had been travelling back and forth from India, bringing knowledge of a land with a written tradition that was fully the match of China's. Moreover, China's near neighbours could no longer be dismissed as primitives: Korea, Bohai (in Manchuria), Nanzhao (in Yunnan), Tibet, and Japan all constructed states, adhered to universal religions, made use of writing (sometimes inventing their own scripts), built cities, and engaged in long-distance trade. China could view itself as the superior on any of a number of grounds, but could not view itself as the only place with culture. In the early Tang, China's political, institutional, and cultural excellence received affirmation from all quarters; rulers

At the same time that printing was introduced as a means to reproduce texts, it also began to be used to decorate textiles. This fragment of an eighth-to-ninth-century silk banner, from cave 17 at Dunhuang, contains motifs of Persian origin (the roundels come from Persian metalwork) mixed with other designs of Chinese origin, such as the pair of birds.

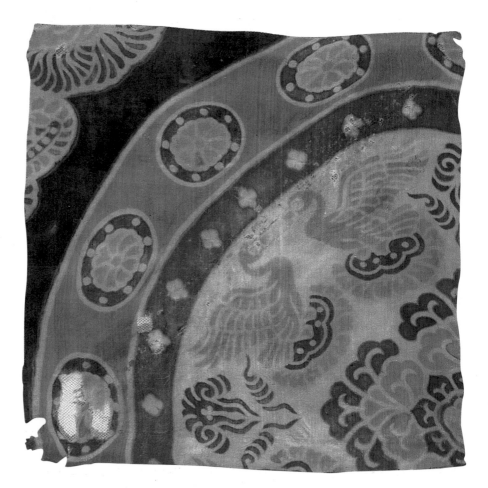

in Korea and Japan, in fact, copied much of Tang culture and institutions wholesale in their own efforts to create powerful political centres. In the late Tang dynasty, however, a profound sense of cultural crisis pervaded intellectual life. The sense that some sort of action had to be taken motivated many of the best minds to rethink basic issues concerning the Chinese state and Chinese culture, in the process reinvigorating Confucian thinking. The ideas of two leading writers, Du You (732–812) and Han Yu (768–824), can be taken to represent these intellectual trends.

Du You, from an eminent aristocratic family, served with distinction in a series of provincial and capital posts. In 801 he submitted to the throne his *Tongdian*, an enormous history of Chinese institutions, in 200 chapters (over 5,000 pages in a

In Tang times people began to sit on raised platforms, as depicted in this mural of a feast. The men seated are dressed in garb typical of scholars at their leisure, in gowns of blue or brown, black boots, and black hats. The mural, 70 by 92 inches, was painted on the wall of an eighth-century tomb near Chang'an.

modern edition). This work can be read as a plea for an activist approach to the problems of his day, for reforming the government in order to strengthen the centralized, interventionist aspect of imperial rule, then under threat from the autonomous provinces. Most officials, of course, believed in the primacy and centrality of the emperor, but in Du You's view too many of them had an antiquated view of the imperial institution, elevating the emperor's ritual and cosmological roles and ignoring the ways government actually sustained itself. In organizing his compendium, Du You did not begin with court ritual, in the traditional way, but with food and money, the people's livelihood and the government's source of revenue. In discussing taxation, he had great praise for Gao Jiong, the Sui official who had taken charge of enrolling additional households in the equal-field system. During the period when the northeastern and northwestern courts had been in a state of constant war, 'cruel rulers and dilatory officials, heavy taxes and frequent labour service drove the people to seek the protection of local strongmen'. When the Sui imposed order and people saw the government would take a much smaller share of their harvests than the magnates did, they were willing to be registered. Thus to Du You, 'It was all due to Gao Jiong's efforts that the Sui fiscal system was instituted throughout the land and the people thus able to enjoy prosperity.' With hindsight we can see that the late Tang withdrawal of the state from management of the economy had positive effects, but to Du You well-designed government control was much to be preferred to leaving people to their own devices.

Du You took particular issue with Confucian scholars of a literalist bent who thought the government should pattern itself on ancient institutions described in the classics. To refute them he argued that in distant antiquity the Chinese had been as backward as some of the barbarians on the borders in his day. He contended that the prefecture and county system of government perfected in the Han and Tang was superior to the feudal system of the Zhou on the grounds that it made possible long periods of peace and population growth. The author of a preface to the *Tongdian* described Du You as believing that 'for the superior man, realizing his purpose lies in ordering the state, ordering the state lies in accomplishing things, accomplishing things lies in learning from the past, and learning from the past lies in changing with the times'.

Du's younger contemporary Han Yu saw China's problems much more in cultural terms. A committed Confucian, he reaffirmed the Confucian classics as the basis of education and good writing and promoted simpler styles of prose based on the ancient ideals of clarity, concision, and utility. He was as concerned as Du You with the weakness of the central government, but believed a rejuvenation of Confucian learning would bolster the state. He submitted a memorial to the throne protesting against the emperor's veneration of a relic of the Buddha. In it he labelled Buddhism a barbarian cult and the relic a foul object, much too inauspicious to touch. He argued that the emperor, by showing respect for it, was encouraging the common people to give up their proper work and social obligations to pursue Buddhist goals, to the detriment of the state whose tax base was thereby reduced. In an almost equally famous essay on the origin of the Way, Han Yu argued that there was a single line of orthodox transmission of Confucian learning from the Duke of Zhou to Confucius and Mencius which had since been disrupted. Han Yu was, in a sense, proposing that to revive the 'Way of the Sages' it was necessary to go back to the *Analects* and *Mencius* to recover the authentic teachings. He provided a summary of Chinese civilization as broad in conception as Du You's but much more succinct: Chinese civilization began with the sages who saved people from peril, showed them how to secure food and clothing and defend against wild animals, taught them music and rituals, and created political institutions for defence and the suppression of crime; but it began to be perverted with the rise of Daoism and Buddhism. Han Yu ended his essay by advocating that Buddhist and Daoist clergy be layicized, their books burned, and their temples converted into homes.

Du You's and Han Yu's views are, of course, at odds with each other at many levels. Du You insisted on the need to grasp change and to know the details of concrete practices. Han Yu, by contrast, stressed what he saw as permanent and universal, and at the policy level stressed issues of moral character, arguing the need for leaders who had grasped the 'Way of the Sages'. Du You traced the successive stages of historical development, whereas Han Yu seemed to think it would be possible to leap back to a distant past as though the intervening centuries could be cancelled. Still, both men were in agreement on some matters. They both, for instance, had little interest in the sorts of cosmological theories about emperorship in vogue since the Han. Moreover, they shared a basic optimism about the possibility for men of good intention to take action in the world that would bring about change for the better. These attitudes were shared with many of their contemporaries and did a great deal to enliven intellectual debate in this period.

In Chinese historical consciousness, unity and expansion have been viewed as much more to the credit of the Chinese people than fragmentation and contraction. The first half of the Tang dynasty is thus viewed as one of the most splendid eras in Chinese history, the second half as its unfortunate aftermath. For a dynasty to decline in this way was not unexpected because traditional historians saw dynasties as progressing according to a predictable moral dynamic. Successful dynasties, like the Tang, were founded by men of vigour and purpose whose commitment to the larger good earned them the Mandate of Heaven. They built efficient governments on the basis of low but equitable taxes, having cleared away many of the local powers and corrupt practices that had accumulated before their rise. Their successors, however, would not all be supermen able to prevent power struggles at court, keep the cost of defence and local administration low, and

Instruments such as this three-foot-long, four-string pipa, a type of lute of Iranian origin, were given as gifts to envoys of Japan who visited China in the late seventh or early eighth centuries. The wooden marquetry on the reverse depicts flowers, birds, butterflies, and mountains.

preserve or enhance sources of revenue, all the while inspiring loyalty through their bearing and virtue. In this view of history, men of ability and integrity – both emperors and their counsellors – could arrest decline or even temporarily reverse it, but inevitably the dynasty would weaken and eventually fall.

To traditional Chinese historians, there was no comparable moral logic linking one dynasty to the next, and dynasties, presumably, could follow one after the other indefinitely. Thus, when Chinese historians in the late nineteenth and early twentieth centuries first came across European theories of linear progression from ancient, to classical, to medieval, and to modern civilization, they began to propose schemes for the larger periodization of Chinese history as well. As has already been mentioned in earlier chapters, they noted correspondences between Han and Rome, the Age of Division, and the Middle Ages. But the Sui–Tang reunification was an anomaly. In the west neither Justinian in Constantinople in the sixth century nor Charlemagne at Rome in 800 had been able to recreate an empire as large, centralized, or mighty as Rome. In China, the Tang more than matched the Han; it was able to contain more formidable external threats and manage a more diverse society with a more developed economy.

Few historians today accept either a cyclical view of Chinese history that downplays long-term change or a three- or four-stage periodization that assumes the normal pattern of historical development is the one that occurred in the West. In their search for China's own historical progression, it has become common for historians to focus on the late Tang as a key turning-point, elevating it from a period of lamentable decline to one of exciting growth. The distress that intellectuals felt as they witnessed the deterioration of central control sparked a major revitalization of Confucianism that continued into Song times. The inability of the central government to keep tight control over the economy may have hurt state coffers but it invigorated the underlying economy. Emerging from these confused and often distressing circumstances, China became a society less centred on the political and military structures of the state and therefore better able to weather political crises.

CHAPTER 6

Shifting South:
The Song Dynasty 907–1276

The pace of change in Chinese society began to increase in the late Tang period. By early Song times (960–1276) advances in agriculture and industry were contributing to dizzying economic growth. The pace of migration south accelerated and the Yangzi valley finally became as central to the Chinese economy and to Chinese culture as the Yellow River regions in the north. The civil service examination system came to dominate the lives of the elite, and Confucianism was reinvigorated. Despite these signs of vitality, the Song dynasty was never able to establish dominance of East Asia the way the Han and Tang dynasties had. Powerful neighbouring states had to be treated as equals, not vassals, and limiting their incursions became a major preoccupation of both the state and the intellectual elite.

THE EMBATTLED STATE

During the chaotic century from 860 to 960 following the disintegration of the Tang dynasty, political and military power devolved to the local level. Any strongman able to organize defence against rebels and bandits could become a local warlord and declare himself king, and many of the kings of this period rose from very lowly beginnings, one had even been a merchant's slave. In the south, no self-proclaimed king ever consolidated much more than the equivalent of a modern province or two, and historians generally refer to the regional states in the south as the 'Ten Kingdoms'. Political fragmentation in the south did not impair the economy there; on the contrary, rulers of the regional states, eager to expand their tax bases, successfully promoted trade.

The effects of fragmentation were less benign in the north. Many of the regional warlords there were not Chinese but Turks from the garrison armies. Both Chang'an and Luoyang had been ravaged by the wars of the late Tang period, and Kaifeng, located in Henan province at the mouth of the Grand Canal, came to be viewed as the central city in north China. The rapid succession of Five Dynasties (Later Liang, Later Tang, Later Jin, Later Han, and Later Zhou) reflects how little time any of the claimants of the throne was able to hold on to this capital before being ousted by rivals. In 937, one contender for the Chinese throne turned to the Khitans, the new power in Mongolia, to help him gain control of the city of Kaifeng; and in repayment, he recognized the Khitans as overlords and granted them the territory around modern Beijing. When his successor tried to renounce this arrangement, the Khitans attacked Kaifeng between 946 and 947.

The general finally able to bring about military unification was Zhao Kuangyin, who reigned as Taizu (r. 960–76), first emperor of the Song dynasty. Previously commander of the palace army, Taizu was elevated to emperor by his troops, who were unwilling to be led by the seven-year-old son of the former emperor. By the time Taizu died sixteen years later, most of the warlords in the south had submitted to the Song. Taizu's overwhelming accomplishment was putting an end to two centuries of independent regional armies. To solidify his control over all military forces, he got his own commanders to retire on generous pensions and gradually replaced the military governors with civil officials. The best units in the regional armies he transferred to the palace army, which he kept under his personal command, fashioning it into a large, mobile professional army charged with protecting the capital. To prevent the rise of new regional strongmen, Taizu put the army under civilian control and saw that its officers were regularly rotated. This reorganization of the military forces was completed by Taizu's younger brother (who succeeded to the throne in 976); he dismantled the military provinces and appointed intendants in charge of judicial, fiscal, military and transportation matters to supervise and co-ordinate overlapping sets of prefectures.

The reunification under the Song dynasty did not usher in an era of military expansion on the order of the Han or Tang. Not only was there no hope of regaining dominance in Central Asia, but it proved impossible under the Song to dislodge the Khitans from the area around Beijing. Moreover, the Tanguts, a people related to the Tibetans, had consolidated a state in the northwest, centred in modern Gansu. Like the Northern Dynasties in the fifth and sixth centuries, the Khitan's Liao state and the Tanguts' Xia state were ruled by non-Chinese who made use of Chinese officials and Chinese methods of government and ruled over mixed populations, including many Han Chinese peasants, merchants, and crafts-

Chinese civilization flourished within constricted borders in Song times – especially after 1127 when the Jurchen seized the north, dividing China proper between the Jin in the north and the (Southern) Song in the south.

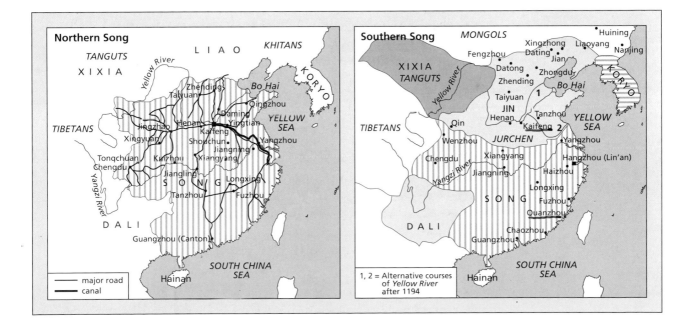

men (see Chapter 7). Under peace agreements reached in 1004 and 1044, the Song court agreed to make substantial annual payments to both Liao and Xia, in a sense buying peace. But defence remained a constant concern. The size of the Song army was more than tripled between 979 and 1041 to about 1,250,000 men, and the government manufactured armaments in huge quantities, arrowheads by the tens of millions per year, armour by the tens of thousands. Military expenses thus came to absorb over three-quarters of state revenue.

The need to defend against such powerful enemies stimulated improvements in military technology. In 1040, during the wars with the Tanguts, the emperor Renzong commissioned a forty-chapter manual on military matters, which includes instructions for the construction and use of a broad range of weapons and siege machines. It provides the first recipe for gunpowder, which at the time was used for incendiary grenades delivered by catapults. Not until later in the Song did military engineers discover that gunpowder could also be used as a pro-pellant, thus inventing true cannons. In its wars, however, the Song's technical superiority generally gave it only temporary advantages, because its enemies would capture craftsmen and engineers and set them to producing comparable weapons and tools.

Military crises also stimulated centralization of governmental power. Chinese imperial government had always involved balances between the central govern-ment and the local administrators, and between the emperors, who in theory held all power, and the civil and military officials charged by the emperor to carry out his orders. During the Song dynasty, these balances tipped in favour of central power and civil officials, and in many ways Chinese government came closer to matching the Confucian ideal in Song times than in any earlier or later period. There were no tyrants among Song emperors, no empresses suspected of anything but good intentions, and no coups staged by eunuchs.

Song emperors, moreover, rarely acted arbitrarily. They regularly listened to a range of opinion before making decisions and usually deferred to their leading officials. Taizu had vowed never to put anyone to death for disagreeing with him, and enjoined his successors to follow his example. Court officials, in turn, gener-ally identified with the dynasty and supported strengthening central control. Many were outstanding men, committed to good government and willing to stand up for what they believed. Fan Zhongyan, a scholar–official who during 1043 and 1044 attempted to institute a reform of personnel recruitment and local adminis-tration, described the duty of the Confucian scholar–official as being 'to be first in worrying about the world's troubles and last in enjoying its pleasures'.

Despite an ample supply of worthy emperors and statesmen, the Song govern-ment still exhibited two main weaknesses: factionalism and bureaucratism. Per-haps because printing made it so easy, bureaucratic regulations came to be issued in enormous quantities. Rules about use of one imperial ritual hall filled 1,200 volumes and rules concerning reception of envoys from Korea, 1,500. Changing regulations or procedures became so cumbersome that many officials objected to any and all reform as too bothersome.

Factionalism proved just as intractable. Because there were no legitimate means to resolve political conflicts, disputes among officials seeking to influence the emperor often escalated, with each party lining up allies and focusing their energies on devising ways to oust their opponents. The most divisive episode of this sort began when Emperor Shenzong (r. 1067–1085) took the throne at the age of twenty and decided to let Wang Anshi launch a thorough reform of the government. Wang's goal was to enrich the country and bring more of the wealth into state coffers. In the course of totally restructuring the fiscal administration, he changed the basis for land tax assessments, introduced new schemes for collecting and transporting special tribute taxes, instituted interest-bearing loans to peasants to keep them from becoming dependent on landlords, converted labour

The connections between water transport, water-powered mills, and the production of grain are captured well in this anonymous early Song painting on silk.

Su Dongpo

Identifying oneself as Chinese has meant, over the centuries, taking pride in association with symbolically charged figures from the past. Of the great figures from the Song, perhaps none has inspired greater admiration than Su Shi (1037–1101), better known by the name he chose for himself, Su Dongpo. Ranked among the greatest of poets and essayists in the Chinese tradition, Su was also deeply enmeshed in the politics of his day. From shortly after his death up to our own day, people have sought out pieces of Su's calligraphy, paintings depicting him, inscriptions on stone marking his visits, and shrines dedicated to his memory.

From Sichuan in western China, Su passed the civil service examinations in 1056/57 and quickly entered leading literary circles. During his lengthy career in the bureaucracy, he was an outspoken policy critic and became a leader of the opposition to Wang Anshi and other reformists. He was once arrested and thrown into prison on the grounds that his poems slandered the emperor and his appointed officials. Su expected execution, but instead was banished to Hubei, an area he came to love and where he wrote some of his best poetry. Years later, after returning to office, he was banished once more, ending up at Hainan island, the southernmost extremity of the realm. He died on his way back from this second period of exile.

Su Dongpo wrote prodigiously. Some 800 of his letters survive along with over 2,700 poems. His poetry is characterized by a remarkable variety of subject matter and minute attention to detail. Some poems have a playful tone, other exude warmth and tenderness. During his exile, for instance, he wrote a playful but biting poem to celebrate the first bath of his month-old son, in which he claimed, 'All I want is a son who is doltish and dumb. No setbacks or hardships will obstruct his path to the highest court posts.' The visual quality of Su Dongpo's poetic descriptions may owe something to his mastery of both calligraphy and painting. In his writings on the theory of painting, he explicitly argued that the purpose of painting was not to depict the appearance of things but to express the painter's own feelings, making it much more like poetry.

In his writings Su upheld Confucian ideas of public service but he was drawn to Daoist and Buddhist philosophical ideas as well. Two of his best-loved poetic essays were occasioned by his visits to Red Cliff, the spot on the Yangzi River where a famous battle took place in AD 208. In the first he and his friend discuss the shortness of life and the joys to be had from enjoying the breeze along the river. In the second he described hiking along the rocks with friends, then drifting in the river on a boat, letting the current determine their direction.

For twenty-five years after his death, Su's writings were proscribed because of his association with the anti-reform faction. Once the ban was lifted, however, commercial publishers, private patrons, and Buddhist monasteries began publishing his works, at least nine separate editions appearing in Song times.

Su Dongpo at Red Cliff, by Li Song (c.1190–1225).

service obligations to money taxes, reformed the local clerical service, set up government pawnshops, and introduced a local militia to aid in national defence.

Eager to do everything at once, Wang Anshi quickly antagonized much of the bureaucracy. Because leading officials such as the historian Sima Guang and poet Su Shi denounced his programs as un-Confucian, Wang had to bring in his own men. To do this he revised the examinations for entry to office and increased the number of government schools, which only incensed his critics. Personal antagonism, differences of regional and class interest, and opposing philosophies of government all contributed to the mounting hostility between those for and against Wang's policies. Wang Anshi ousted from office many of those who opposed him, and when they got their turn they acted in like fashion. Factional hostility persisted long after Wang and his original supporters and opponents had died, marring relations among scholar–officials for half a century.

THE BURGEONING ECONOMY

As mentioned in the last chapter, the late Tang political fragmentation so lamented by political thinkers seems, if anything, to have stimulated economic growth. One of the clearest signs of this is the doubling of the population between 750 and 1100. In 742 China's population was still approximately fifty million, the same as it had been in AD 2. Over the next three centuries, with the expansion of rice cultivation in central and southern China, China's food supply steadily increased and so did its population, which reached 100 million by 1100. Agricultural prosperity and denser settlement patterns both aided commercialization. Peasants in more densely populated regions were drawn more deeply into commercial networks, selling their surpluses and buying charcoal, tea, oil, and wine. Farming families whose main crops were grain frequently could also engage in small-scale sideline production of products like wine, charcoal, paper, and textiles, which they could sell through brokers. Some farmers were even finding specialization profitable. Local farmers near Suzhou, for instance, often devoted themselves to raising silkworms and producing silk thread. In Fujian, Sichuan, and Guangdong many farmers devoted their land to sugar cane. Other commercial crops included tea, vegetables, oranges, timber, bamboo, oil seeds, hemp and ramie for cloth, and, by the late Song, cotton.

The need to transport the products of interregional trade stimulated the inland and coastal shipping industries, providing employment for ship builders and

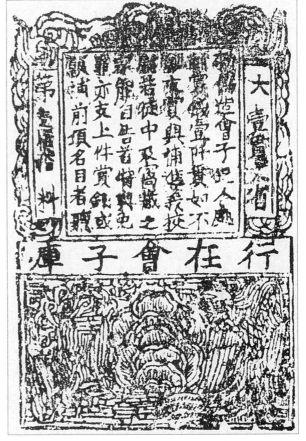

Carrying this piece of paper money, issued in Hangzhou during the Southern Song, would certainly have been less burdonesome than carrying the 'string' of a thousand cash that it represented.

The finest porcelain and stoneware were not produced in the capital, but in regional pottery centres, where techniques of mass production were perfected. Merchants then transported the pots all over the country and through much of Asia. This late-tenth-century ewer, made at the famous kiln at Dingzhou in Hebei, is 10 inches tall, and has lotus-leaf patterns carved on its body.

sailors and business opportunities for enterprising families with enough capital to purchase a boat. Marco Polo, the Venetian merchant who wrote of his visit to China in the late thirteenth century, was astounded at the boat traffic on the Yangzi River: 'I tell you that this river goes so far and through so many regions and there are so many cities on its banks that, truth to tell, in the total volume and value of the traffic on it, it exceeds all the rivers of the Christians put together plus their seas.'

As trade increased, demand for money grew enormously. The late Tang government had abandoned the use of bolts of silk as currency, which created increased demand for coins. By 997 the Song government was minting 800 million coins a year, two and a half times the largest output of the Tang. By 1085, less than a century later, the output of coins had increased almost another eightfold to over six billion coins a year. The use of silver was increasing concurrently; in 1120 the government collected eighteen million ounces of silver as taxes.

Indeed, the demand for currency was so great that paper money came into existence. The initial step was a byproduct of the peculiar coinage situation in Sichuan, where coins were made of iron rather than bronze. To avoid the weight and bulk of iron coins for large transactions, local merchants in late Tang times started trading receipts from deposit shops where they had left money or goods. The early Song authorities awarded a small set of shops a monopoly on the issuing of these certificates of deposit, and in the 1120s took over the system, issuing the world's first government paper money. The Song government proved capable of controlling this currency, on the whole avoiding the sorts of over-issuing that result in rapid inflation.

As interregional trade intensified, merchants became progressively more specialized and organized. Partnerships were common, and commercial ventures were sometimes organized as stock companies, with a separation of owners (shareholders) and managers. Credit was widely available, not only through money-lenders, but also through brokers, wholesalers, and warehousemen. In the large cities merchants were organized into guilds, such as the rice guild which arranged sales from wholesalers to shop owners and periodically set prices. Guild heads represented all the merchants when dealing with the government in matters of taxation or requisitions.

Trade was not confined to the domestic market. From the beginning of the dynasty the government encouraged foreign trade, especially maritime trade. Court officials were sent on missions to southeast Asian countries to encourage their traders to come to China. Chinese traders took the initiative as well, and in Song times Chinese merchants sailing Chinese ships displaced south and southwest Asian merchants in the south seas. Maritime trade was aided by the development of huge ships powered by both oars and sails and capable of holding several hundred men. Also important to ocean-going travel was the invention of the compass, first reported in Chinese sources in 1119. The expansion of maritime trade

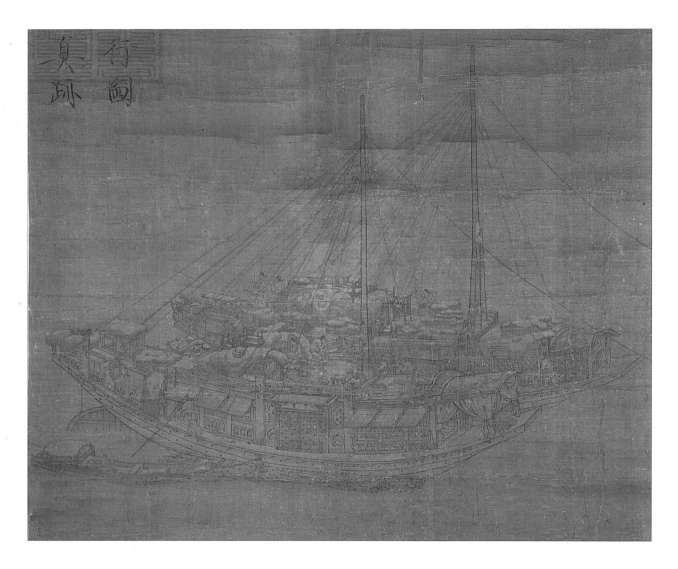

helped fill government coffers, especially in the Southern Song, as the Song government had learned effective ways to tax commerce. Just as important, this new orientation toward the sea contributed to the unprecedented creation of a powerful ocean-going navy.

Industrial development was no less impressive in Song times. Traditional industries such as silk, lacquer, and ceramics reached their highest levels of technical perfection. Many of the finest silks continued to be made in government workshops, but small-scale family-based enterprises were not uncommon. Rural families might grow mulberry trees and raise silkworms, selling reeled silk to weaving households in the cities. Ceramics also prospered under workshop conditions, with a few major regional centres acquiring reputations for high-quality wares. With the rise in demand for books, documents, money, and wrapping paper, paper-makers flourished as well. Heavy industry, especially iron production, also grew astoundingly. With advances in metallurgy, iron production grew

The commercial revolution depended on a well-developed transportation system. Cargo boats like this, a detail from a Song period painting on silk, carried goods on the extensive river and canal network.

to around 125,000 tons per year in 1078, a sixfold increase over the figure for 800. At first charcoal was used in the production process, leading to deforestation of parts of north China. By the end of the eleventh century, however, bituminous coke had largely taken the place of charcoal. Other important technical advances allowing the expansion of the iron industry were the use of hydraulic machinery to drive bellows and explosives to excavate mines. The iron produced was used in industrial processes (the production of salt and copper, for instance) as well as for tools, weapons, nails for ships, chains for suspension bridges, and even for Buddhist statues.

All of this commercial and industrial expansion fuelled the growth of cities. The population of many cities grew so rapidly that more than half the people had to live outside the city walls. Kaifeng, the capital of the Song until 1126, was as populous as the Tang capital at Chang'an, but it was much more a commercial city, dominated more by markets – open all hours – than by palaces and government offices. Multi-storey houses, situated directly on the streets rather than behind walls, became common and were often let out for rent. After the north was lost, the new capital at Hangzhou quickly grew to match or even surpass Kaifeng in population and economic development. Marco Polo described it as without doubt the finest and most splendid city in the world. 'Anyone seeing such a multitude would believe it impossible that food could be found to feed them all, and yet on every market day all the market squares are filled with people and with merchants who bring food on carts and boats.'

Cities in the provinces also grew at an unprecedented pace, dozens attaining populations of 50,000 or more. Jiankang, an inland city in north Fujian, had perhaps 200,000 residents; Quanzhou, a coastal city in southern Fujian, was even larger – its governor in 1120 claimed 500,000 residents for the city and its hinterland. In addition, market towns began springing up everywhere. Many of these towns began as periodic markets where trading occurred on a regular schedule, such as every fifth or tenth day. These markets soon attracted tea houses, then shops that sold daily necessities, and in time new residents. Eventually the government would notice these emerging towns and establish tax collection offices in them.

Economic opportunities and a growing population led to the gradual 'filling up' of much of south China. Fujian provides a good example of this process. In the early Tang an official had claimed that half the people in Zhangzhou were not Chinese but 'barbarians who button their coats on the left and have unkempt hair', and in the late Tang an observer commented on the presence in Fujian of indigenous people unable to speak Chinese who lived in caves or on rafts. Yet by mid Song population pressure in Fujian had resulted in the terracing of hills for cultivation and migration to less developed areas such as Guangdong. One observer claimed that nine out of ten pawnbrokers in one prefecture in Guangdong came from Fujian.

THE SCHOLARLY ELITE

Concurrent with these economic and political changes was the emergence of one of the most distinctive features of Chinese civilization, the scholar–official class certified through competitive literary examinations, an elite unlike that of any other major civilization. Although members of this elite called themselves *shi* or *shidafu*, terms used since classical times to mean 'scholar–gentleman' and 'scholar–official', they differed from their predecessors in several key regards. The decline of aristocratic habits and ideals, the increase in wealth, the intellectual excitement caused by the revival of Confucian teachings, and the great growth in the importance of the examination system for recruitment to office all resulted in an elite both broader and more schooled than any of its predecessors.

The examination system, used only on a small scale in Sui and Tang times, played a central role in the fashioning of this new elite. The early Song emperors,

Spring Festival along the River depicts life in and near the Northern Song capital of Kaifeng. Among the many figures in the section shown here are draymen and porters, pedlars and shopkeepers, a professional storyteller, a fortune-teller, a public scribe, a woman in a sedan chair, and scholars and monks conversing. Painted by Zhang Zeduan in the twelfth century, the full work is 9¾ inches tall and over seventeen feet long.

Producing silk involved many steps. In this detail from a thirteenth century handscroll on silk, people are shown picking mulberry leaves, sorting leaves to feed the silk worms, moving the frames on which the worms will spin their cocoons, and packing cocoons into baskets and weighing them.

concerned above all to avoid domination of the government by military men, greatly expanded the civil service examination system and the government school system. The number of those passing the highest examinations soon averaged four to five times the number in Tang times. Great efforts were put into perfecting the examinations as a tool for discovering the most qualified candidates. To assure that examiners were not influenced by their personal knowledge of the candidates (something not considered objectionable in Tang times), the papers were recopied by clerks and identified only by number. Through this system, for the first time in Chinese history, a large proportion of officialdom was recruited from families living in central and southern China, ending the dominance of the north. The prestige of success in the exams was very high. Even men who could enter the government through the privileges extended to the sons and grandsons of higher officials often chose to take the exams because success there gave one a much better chance of rising to a policy-making post at court. Men who entered government service without passing the most prestigious examinations were usually forced to start their careers as sheriffs in remote places and might well

spend their entire careers in county-level positions, never managing to rise above the post of magistrate.

Given these incentives, more and more men attempted the civil service examinations. In the early eleventh century less than 30,000 candidates took the prefectural examinations each year. This rose to nearly 80,000 by the end of the century and perhaps 400,000 before the dynasty's end. Because the number of available posts did not change, each candidate's chances of passing plummeted, reaching as low as one out of 333 in some prefectures. To prepare to take such competitive exams, candidates needed to memorize the classics so that they could recognize even the most obscure passages. They also needed to master specific forms of composition, including poetic genres. Fortunately for them, with the spread of printing, books became much more widely available. Scholarly families and aspirants for office could much more easily buy or borrow the Confucian classics, the dynastic histories, collections of poetry and prose, and reference books of many sorts. Wealthy families were now in a position to amass thousands of books for their private libraries.

Men of wealth and taste would often hold banquets in their homes, sometimes even hiring female entertainers from the courtesan quarters to help. Elegant furnishings with painted screens and fine porcelain wine ewers added to the feeling of luxury. Note the use of chairs with backs. Detail from a Song copy of the tenth-century handscroll by Gu Hongzhong.

Leading members of this new scholar–official elite were often men of remarkable intellectual breadth. Ouyang Xiu, besides serving in some of the highest offices in the land, composed excellent poetry and essays, edited two major histories, and compiled an analytical catalogue of rubbings on stone and bronze, a pioneering work in the fields of epigraphy and archaeology. Su Shi had similarly broad interests, with more emphasis on the arts. Sima Guang, besides serving as prime minister and leading the opposition to Wang Anshi, undertook to write a narrative history of China covering over 1,300 years from the late Zhou to the founding of the Song in 960. Perhaps the most broadly accomplished of them all was Shen Gua. During his official career, Shen designed drainage and embankment systems that reclaimed vast tracts of land for agriculture; he served as a financial expert skilled at calculating the effects of currency policies; he headed the Bureau of Astronomy; he supervised military defence preparations; and he even travelled to the Liao state as an envoy to negotiate a treaty. Over the course of his life he wrote on geography, history, archaeology, ritual, music, mathematics, military strategy, painting, medicine, geology, poetry, printing, and agricultural technology. Although often labelled a scientist, he wrote commentaries to Confucian classics and had deep interests in divination and Buddhist meditation.

As a class, the scholarly elite was composed of families, only some of whose men entered national political and social life. Families able to educate their sons were generally landholders, established as members of the local elite in their home area. Once a family got one member into government service, it was easier to get others to follow, not only because office holding generally helped a family's economic standing, but also because the sons, grandsons, and sometimes more distant relatives of mid-rank or higher officials had a variety of privileges and advantages, ranging from access to examinations with better success ratios to direct entry into the lowest posts. Therefore when the elite is looked at from the local, rather than the national, level, established families are more striking than new men. In a county with a population of perhaps a hundred thousand, a dozen or so families might produce virtually all the prominent figures over the course of a century or two. Not that these families had any guarantees; indeed, they were all too aware of the possibility of downward mobility as family property was divided among complacent sons. Family heads who hoped to preserve their families' economic base, one writer warned, had to know how to manage tenants and agents, buy and sell land, lend money, and invest in business, otherwise their family might well lose its property and decline into poverty.

By the end of the Song dynasty, the scholar–official elite had attained remarkable social, political, and cultural importance and marked China as different from other major societies of Eurasia. Looked at from the perspective of the central government, a much higher proportion of the most powerful posts was going to men selected for their literary abilities. Looked at from the perspective of class and the local power structure, the ruling class was becoming more closely identified with education and the examination process, even if its chief economic resource remained landholding. Looked at in terms of larger cultural symbols, the identification of Chinese civilization with the literati ideal was strengthened, thanks in part to the rivalry between the Song and the militarily stronger nomadic and semi-nomadic peoples to the north.

LOSS OF THE NORTH

The most cultivated Song emperor was Huizong (r. 1100–26). A talented painter and calligrapher, Huizong not only used the resources of the throne to build up the imperial painting collection (his catalogue lists over 6,000 paintings), but he personally developed new styles of calligraphy and bird and flower painting, often instructing the painters employed at the court how to paint. Huizong was also deeply interested in Daoist religion and had grand ritual pageants performed at court. In the popular imagination, it was because Huizong was so absorbed in aesthetic and religious matters that not only did he lose the throne but the dynasty lost north China.

In 1115 the Jurchens, an agricultural, herding, and hunting people based in eastern Manchuria, rose up in the region north of the Khitans' Liao state, declared themselves the Jin dynasty, and began a war against the Khitans

Printing could be done in a small workshop with only a few workers. After the carver had copied the text on to wood blocks, a worker brushed ink over the block, then placed a piece of paper on it, then brushed over it with the dry side of the brush. Using this method one person could print up to 1,000 pages in a day. Since blocks could be saved and used to make on average 20,000 copies, the cost of each copy could be kept low. This illustration of a printing workshop, from a Qing period book, depicts the father of the Cheng brothers printing a morality book as a charitable act.

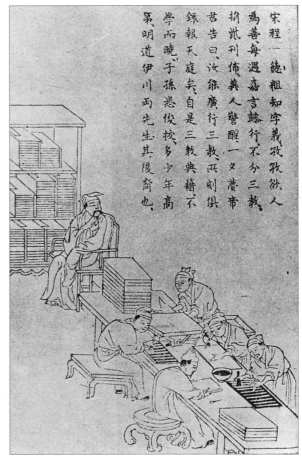

(see Chapter 7). The Song thought they had found a new ally and soon concluded an alliance with the Jin that called for a division of Khitan territory. Within three years this alliance collapsed and in 1126 the Jurchens attacked Kaifeng. The city fell after a siege lasting less than two months and was sacked. By that time Huizong had abdicated in favour of a son; he and this successor were captured and taken to the far northeast along with 3,000 members of the imperial family. Negotiations to ransom Huizong were not successful and he died in captivity in North China in 1135. The period before the loss of the north is commonly called the Northern Song, the period after it the Southern Song, north and south referring to the location of the capitals.

Chinese loyalists regrouped in the south and proclaimed a younger son of Huizong as emperor. This court now found itself in the humiliating position of having to request peace talks with invaders who were holding the emperor's parents, wife, brother, and numerous other relatives. Yet by 1138 the situation had stabilized, with the Song court at Hangzhou controlling most of the area south of the Huai River.

For the rest of the twelfth century the overriding concern of Song officials and intellectuals was regaining what they still saw as the heartland of China, the land where all major dynasties had had their capital and where the tombs of all prior Song emperors were located. Later historians have nearly uniformly condemned the various peace parties as appeasers and found a hero in Yue Fei, a general who tried to regain the north and who in fact reached the Luoyang area before being recalled and executed. After a treaty of 1142 the Song government appeased the Jin with annual tributary payments, much as it had earlier bought off the Liao. From time to time one or the other side would launch military efforts to conquer the other, but there was not much change until the rise of the Mongols in the early thirteenth century (see Chapter 7).

The loss of the north did not destroy the Song economy; in fact, having the capital in the south seems to have further stimulated the development of the region. The transport of goods to the capital had always formed a large share of total trade, and could be accomplished more cost-effectively with the capital in the south. Goods could be brought to Hangzhou economically by boat, through the many streams and canals criss-crossing the region. Moreover, the political border between the Song and Jin proved no obstacle to trade, as the north continued to import vast quantities of tea, rice, sugar, and books from the south.

A TURN INWARD

The inability of the otherwise impressive Song government to achieve the sort of military dominance the Han and Tang had attained at their heights was profoundly disturbing to Song writers, thinkers, and officials. Those who felt acutely the threat posed by northern neighbours were less open to borrowing foreign styles and more sensitive to issues of Chinese cultural identity. Writers more read-

Emperor Huizong (r. 1100–1126) was greatly interested in Daoism as well as painting and calligraphy. On this silk painting he recorded that in 1112 a flock of cranes arrived at one of the palace buildings, and that to commemorate the auspicious omen, he wrote a poem. Huizong has traditionally been credited with executing the painting as well, but it is just as likely he had one of his court artists do it for him.

ily rejected things foreign on the grounds of their origins. Like Han Yu in the late Tang, they sometimes rejected Buddhism – on Chinese soil nearly a millennium – on the sole ground that it was not indigenous. Sun Fu declared that allowing a 'teaching of the barbarians' to bring disorder to 'the teachings of our sages' was a great humiliation to Chinese scholars. Shi Jie wrote that it was perverse for Chinese 'to forget their ancestors and abandon sacrifices to them, serving instead barbarian ghosts'. In Tang times the widespread popularity of Buddhism throughout Asia had added to its appeal. In the Song, however, as international politics changed, so too did perceptions of cultural integrity. That the Tanguts, Khitans, and Jurchens were all zealous Buddhists seemed only to underline Buddhism's foreignness, rather than confirm it as the universal religion.

The complexity of issues of loyalty to Chinese culture was explored by Song painters and poets through depictions or evocations of well-known stories of Chinese women forced to live among the barbarians. One story concerned Wang Zhaojun, a Han palace woman sent as a bride to a Xiongnu chief. In a poem about her, Ouyang Xiu referred to the unfeeling winds and sands of the barbarians' homeland, and the irony that palace ladies in later centuries were eager to master the barbarian musical instruments that Wang Zhaojun had used to sing about her homesickness. Another story concerned Cai Wenji, the daughter of a well-known Han scholar, who was abducted by a band of Xiongnu and forced to marry one of their chiefs. Because she bore him children, deciding to return to China when ransomed years later was not an easy choice for her. Huizong's son, enthroned as the first emperor of the Southern Song, commissioned paintings of Cai Wenji's saga while negotiating his own mother's ransom.

Paintings of Cai Wenji's story commissioned by the Southern Song court accentuate the differences between the material culture of the barbarians and the Chinese: the tents in the wilderness contrasted to the elegant buildings of Wenji's hometown. Detail from a fifteenth-century copy of a twelfth-century handscroll.

Revitalizing Confucianism was seen by many Song thinkers as the best way to strengthen the core of Chinese culture. Even though most of the students of the leading Confucian teachers were studying to prepare for the civil service examinations, the most inspiring teachers regularly urged their students to set their sights on personal moral and intellectual growth. Teachers and their disciples debated the merits of the examination system and the ways Confucian ideas could be applied to current problems. Some Confucian thinkers concentrated on developing philosophical frameworks for understanding the world that could stand up to the challenges of Buddhism. Two brothers, Cheng Yi and Cheng Hao, developed metaphysical theories about the workings of the cosmos in terms of *li* (prin-

ciple, pattern) and *qi* (vital energies, material force, psychophysical stuff). The *li* for something could be moral or physical; thus, for example, the *li* for fatherhood is essentially moral in nature, that for mountains, physical. For either to exist, however, there must also be *qi*, the energy and substance that makes up things. The theory of *li* and *qi* allowed Song philosophers to accept Mencius' theory of the goodness of human nature and still explain the evidence of human waywardness; people had good *li* but their more or less impure *qi* accounted for their selfish desires. The sages had perfectly clear *qi*, but ordinary people have turgid *qi* and have to work to improve themselves.

In the Southern Song Confucian scholars gave more and more attention to what people could do themselves at the local level. These scholars were frustrated with the failure of the government to regain the north and aware of the drawbacks of the large-scale reform programmes of the Northern Song. Thus they proposed ways to build a more ideal society by starting from the bottom, reforming families and local communities, establishing academies, and spreading their message through publishing. The greatest of these Southern Song masters was Zhu Xi. Immensely learned in the classics, commentaries, histories, and the teachings of his predecessors, Zhu Xi managed to serve several turns in office and still write, compile, or edit almost a hundred books, all the while corresponding with dozens of other scholars and regularly teaching groups of disciples, many of whom stayed with him for years at a time. Zhu Xi considered himself a follower of the Cheng brothers and elaborated on their metaphysical theories. He gave particular weight to the 'investigation of things', intensive study that would allow the learner to discover the *li* of any matter at hand. Zhu Xi's own interests were very broad, and his recorded conversations with his disciples range widely over subjects such as how to analyse and evaluate what they read, what to make of ghost stories, how to engage in quiet sitting, and how to rid themselves of selfish thoughts. Zhu Xi played an active role in developing the institutional basis of a revived Confucianism, helping establish academies as private gathering places for teachers and their disciples. These academies were sometimes located in cities, but also often in quiet mountain settings, much like monasteries. When he taught at the White Deer Grotto Academy, Zhu Xi offered the students there both moral exhortation and scholarly exegesis, hoping they would become both virtuous and erudite.

Zhu Xi's insistence on the correctness of his own interpretations offended many as pretentious, and for a few years near the end of his life his teachings were condemned by the government as 'spurious learning'. Candidates for office were barred from the examinations unless they denied any faith in Zhu Xi's teachings. Still, within a few decades of his death, his learning received unprecedented political support. In 1241 the emperor credited Zhu Xi with 'illuminating the Way' and government students were ordered to study his commentaries on the Four Books (the *Analects*, *Mencius*, *Doctrine of the Mean*, and the *Great Learning*). This shift in the government's position probably reflected its political needs. By this time the Mongols had conquered north China and the survival of the Song dynasty was in jeopardy. To bolster support, the Song government had to demonstrate that even though it did not occupy the Central Plains, it was still the guardian of Chinese culture and the greatest patron of Confucian scholars. In subsequent dynasties as well, rulers found it to their advantage to recognize this school of Confucian learning as the correct or orthodox teaching.

Consumer goods were not to be found only in the great cities, as shown in this silk painting by Li Song (c. 1190–after 1225). This woman nursing a baby and surrounded by four small children, one too young yet to wear trousers, has stopped to look at the wares offered by a pedlar making his rounds through the countryside.

LOCAL SOCIETY

The basic realities of peasant life did not change much from century to century; ploughing and planting, paying rents and taxes, caring for the young and the elderly, arranging and celebrating marriages, defending against bandits and bullies, worshipping at local temples and buying and selling at local periodic markets, all gave rhythm to peasant life throughout the imperial period. Yet the economic expansion of the Song period was of such magnitude that even ordinary peasants found their lives changed in major ways.

Peasants were certainly affected by the emergence of widely varied forms of land tenure and landlord–tenant relations. In frontier regions like Hunan and southern Sichuan, to which large numbers of people had migrated, new lands were being opened, and the wealthy often established large manors tilled by serfs given little freedom. By contrast, in the most advanced areas where rice had long been grown, wealthy people invested in land but did not try to create consolidated, centrally managed great estates. There were no economies of scale to be had in wet-rice cultivation, nor were there advantages to centralized management. Landlords thus usually let tenants manage on their own, setting fixed rents in kind or cash and thus offering the tenants an incentive to improve their productivity. In the advanced areas, in addition to such tenants, there were small owners and owners who rented land as well to supplement what they held outright. Then there were economically peripheral areas, such as hilly areas far from trade routes and not suited to rice, where large landowners were nearly absent, and most farming was done by owner-cultivators.

Even in the most advanced areas, village life seems to have been far from serene. Local officials regularly complain of the difficulty of suppressing banditry. Legal casebooks show law courts clogged with neighbours and relatives suing each other over rights to land and other property. Yuan Cai, author of a book of advice to family heads, bluntly warned the well-to-do not to let their children out unaccompanied for fear that they would be kidnapped and held for ransom. He also urged families to have servants patrol their property at night to prevent theft and repeatedly warned of the possibility of being sued.

Economic development may have accentuated differentiation between core and peripheral areas, but other trends were tending to tie distant regions of China more closely together. Because of improvements in transportation and communication, customs, ideas, and practices spread more quickly in the Song than they had earlier. By the end of the Song, for instance, cities all over the country had temples dedicated to the god of the city wall. Many also had temples to Wenchang, a deity who began as a fearsome serpent spirit in Sichuan, but by Song times had taken on the identity of patron of the examinations. Stronger forms of local descent group organization were also spreading across broad regions of the country. Leading literati helped to publicize some key elements of these lineages: Ouyang Xiu was one of the first to show how to compile a suitable genealogy, Fan

Rice

Rice did not become a central element in the Chinese diet until Song times. In its wild form a swamp plant, rice grows most easily in standing water. It had been cultivated in the Yangzi regions since neolithic times, in some sites as early as 5000 BC. As the settlement and development of the south progressed, rice occupied a larger and larger place in Chinese life.

Rice production steadily expanded because it is a nearly ideal food crop. It tastes good, is highly digestible, and when eaten along with soy products offers good nutrition. When milled, it stores well. It is easy and economical to cook, the only cereal that can simply be boiled and eaten without disintegrating into mush. But probably most important, rice almost always yields more calories per unit of land than other crops. In the most suitable climates, two or even three crops can be grown in the same field, or rice can be alternated with other crops.

South China had the temperature and rainfall needed for wet-field rice, but much of the terrain was either too hilly or too marshy to be immediately exploited. In Song times the discovery and selection of new seed strains, including early-ripening, drought-resistant rice from Southeast Asia, made it possible to grow rice in previously unsuitable places. Technical improvements in damming methods and water pumps facilitated reconstructing the environment, allowing reclamation of land at the edge of lakes, marshes, and seas and the terracing of mountain slopes, an activity the Song government encouraged through tax incentives. In southern Fujian, for instance, until late Tang the coastal plain could not be effectively exploited for agriculture because it was too marshy. From late Tang on, however, settlers began to rebuild the

曠故或忘
晴秧卻步復伸
手整其襄紉服
水土氣趣候插
暖麥欲凉來輕
芒種時已屆緩

To allow double cropping and maximize yield per seed, rice seedlings were normally first grown in a seedbed, then transplanted into the paddy fields: a tedious and muddy job. This scene and the one opposite are from one of the many copies made during the next century or two.

Opposite
Foot-powered water pumps were an efficient way to bring up water from a ditch to flood a field of standing rice. Because the Song government wanted to promote up-to-date agricultural technology, in the twelfth century it commissioned a set of twelve illustrations of the steps to be followed.

environment, constructing drainage systems, embankments, and reservoirs. By the thirteenth century, hillsides were being terraced and supplied with irrigation systems so that they too could be planted in rice.

The spread of rice cultivation had an impact not merely on the Chinese diet and food supply but also on rhythms of labour. Even after the fields were levelled and water under control, growing rice took a lot of labour. The fields had to be ploughed and harrowed, preferably with the help of a water buffalo. Manure, properly aged and mixed with compost, had to be applied to maintain the fertility of fields in near continuous use. All hands would come out to help

with the transplanting of the rice seedlings that had been growing for a month in seedbeds. Rows of planters, their feet in the mud, would bend at the waist as they moved backwards through the field. Then, of course, there was the labour of weeding, maintaining the water levels, and finally draining the fields and harvesting them.

Zhongyan was credited with inventing the idea of the corporate lineage estate, and Zhu Xi was associated with the idea of halls for ancestral rites. By the end of the Song, lineages had become major forces in local social and political life in Fujian, Zhejiang, Anhui, Jiangxi, and other provinces.

The expansion of printing must have contributed to the spread and standardization of ideas and practices, but its impact on local social order went beyond that. By late Song, the books being printed were not confined to the histories, classics, and *belles-lettres* traditionally associated with the scholar–official class, but included handbooks on agriculture, childbirth, pharmacy, divination, and Daoist rituals. Thus traditions of knowledge that had previously been transmitted primarily through oral means came to be fixed in print, a change that opened them up to both criticism and appropriation. The well-educated could now point to inconsistencies, or identify unverifiable 'superstitions', in order to undermine the authority of these traditions. At the same time ordinary people gained access to bodies of knowledge formerly restricted to experts. They could thus organize their own funeral services, dabble in geomancy, or prescribe medicines for their family members, all with more confidence.

WOMEN'S LIVES

Due to the development of printing, many more books survive from Song times than from earlier periods, and this increase in documentation makes it possible to discern more clearly than before the roles women played in Chinese society. In Song sources one encounters widows who ran inns, maids who ran away from abusive masters, midwives still delivering babies into their seventies, nuns who called on upper-class families to preach to their women, singing girls and courtesans who entertained in cities, female mediums adept at communicating with spirits, farmers' daughters skilled at weaving mats, daughters of literati who loved to write poetry, elderly widows who accused their nephews of stealing their property, to provide a far from complete list.

These women were certainly not all confined to the home, but neither were they very powerful outside it. In descriptions of village and town life, commerce and government, and the social and cultural life of the elite, references to men vastly outnumber those to women. Inside the family, however, women were without doubt very important. They did much of the child rearing, usually played a role in selecting spouses for their children (often trying to find one of their own relatives), and continued to have strong ties to their sons after they were grown and married, since their sons stayed at home.

The great social and economic changes of Song times had a substantial impact on women's lives. With printing and the expansion of the educated class, more women were taught to read and write. It was not at all uncommon in the educated class for wives to be able to write letters and tutor their young children. One woman, Li Qingzhao, even attained great fame as a poet. Increased prosperity

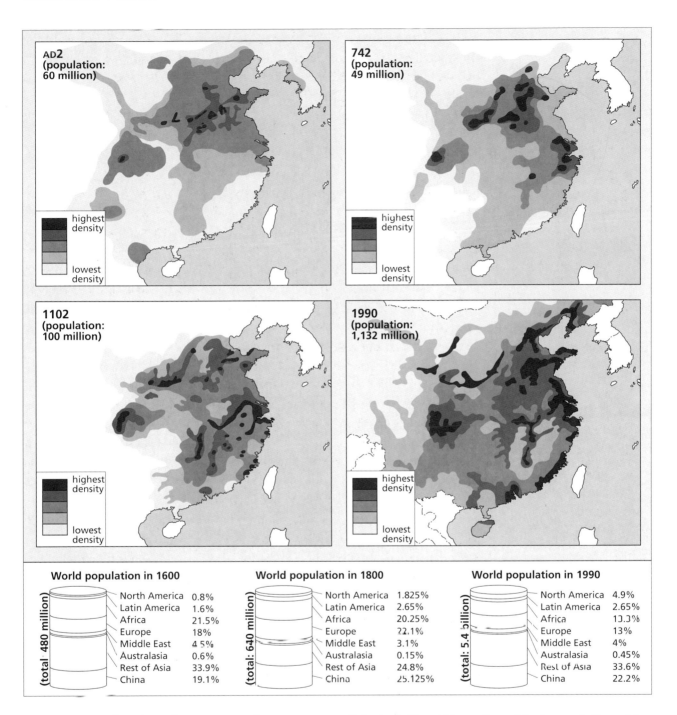

AD2
(population:
60 million)

highest
density

lowest
density

742
(population:
49 million)

highest
density

lowest
density

1102
(population:
100 million)

highest
density

lowest
density

1990
(population:
1,132 million)

highest
density

lowest
density

World population in 1600		World population in 1800		World population in 1990	
(total 480 million)	North America 0.8%	(total 640 million)	North America 1.825%	(total 5.4 billion)	North America 4.9%
	Latin America 1.6%		Latin America 2.65%		Latin America 2.65%
	Africa 21.5%		Africa 20.25%		Africa 13.3%
	Europe 18%		Europe 22.1%		Europe 13%
	Middle East 4.5%		Middle East 3.1%		Middle East 4%
	Australasia 0.6%		Australasia 0.15%		Australasia 0.45%
	Rest of Asia 33.9%		Rest of Asia 24.8%		Rest of Asia 33.6%
	China 19.1%		China 25.125%		China 22.2%

Shifting patterns of population density. Because of extensive migration and acculturation, settlement patterns in China shifted over the centuries. The Yellow River regions were nearly as dominant in 742 as they had been in AD 2, but by Song times something much closer to the modern distribution had already been attained, with a large share of the population living in the Yangzi River valley and further south. Even with major movements of population within the country, China has always had a large share of world population; if figures were available, China's share in 1100 would probably be even higher than in modern times.

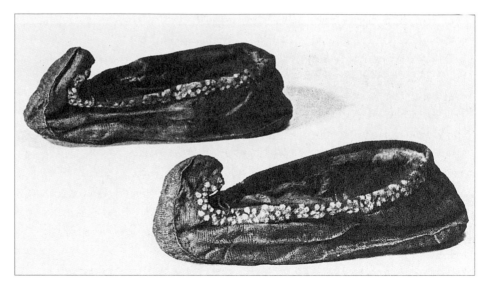

Shoes for bound feet excavated from the tomb of Huang Sheng (1227–1243), the young wife of an imperial clansman. This tomb contained several pairs of shoes for bound feet, each measuring 5 to 5½ inches in length. Unearthed at Fuzhou, Fujian province.

resulted in both dowry inflation and in an expanding market for women to be purchased as servants, concubines, courtesans, and prostitutes. In the upper class, families gave their daughters large dowries to attract sons-in-law with good prospects for official advancement. Families that had channelled significant property through their daughters wanted to see it used to their benefit, and probably as a consequence in the Song period women's legal claims to property were improved. Judges assigned orphaned daughters shares of family property for their dowries, even landed property. Moreover, wives' and widows' control over the use of their dowries was widely recognized.

These changes can all be classed as favourable for women, opening new possibilities to them and offering them more avenues for influence both within the family and outside it. But there were concurrent changes in Song times that are generally classed as detrimental to women, particularly footbinding and more rigid notions of ethically acceptable female demeanour. In the Tang, court life was occasionally dominated by powerful women like Empress Wu and Yang Guifei, and physical activity was fashionable enough that palace women played polo. In Song times, standards of beauty shifted to favour the delicate and restrained woman. Notions of female modesty became more rigid; women veiled their faces more often and rode in curtained sedan chairs when travelling through the streets. By the twelfth century medical authorities were reporting that doctors who called on women in elite households could neither view the woman nor question her; all they could do was take the pulse of a hand extended through the bed curtains.

These shifts in notions of what was attractive and becoming in a woman must have had something to do with the spread of footbinding during the course of the Song. This practice apparently began among dancers in the tenth or eleventh centuries, but in time it spread to upper-class homes. By the Southern Song, mothers were binding the feet of their five- or six-year-old daughters painfully tight to prevent them from growing normally. Tiny narrow feet were considered to enhance a woman's beauty and to make her movements more dainty.

Developments in Confucian thought also reinforced these trends toward a more restricted sphere for women. All of the leading Neo-Confucian teachers were moralists, firm in the conviction that social harmony depended on individual moral actions. When discussing family ethics, they stressed the need for men and women alike to identify with the interests of the family. In women's case, this meant identifying with the family of their husbands and sons. Women should have no desire to have their own property, feel no jealousy if their husband took a concubine, show no bias against the children of concubines, and remain to care for their parents-in-law and children if their husbands died. Learning to read and write was fine, but they should not indulge in frivolous pastimes like writing poetry. Confucian scholars found nothing objectionable about the growing tendency toward stricter seclusion of women, and encouraged clear separation of the men's and women's quarters in the house. And they reiterated in the clearest possible terms the impropriety of widows remarrying, Cheng Yi even arguing that starving to death was a lesser evil.

In the eleventh, twelfth, and thirteenth centuries China was the leading society in the world. By the eleventh century, Europe was certainly out of the shadows of the Dark Ages, but improvements in its economy were not occurring at anywhere near the rate they were in China. At the end of the thirteenth century, when Marco Polo crossed Asia, neither Venice where he came from nor any of the countries of Europe or Asia that he passed through could compare to China in agricultural productivity, industrial technology, sophistication of commercial organization, urbanization, or standard of living.

The rapid development of commerce and appearance of commercial cities did not play the same political or intellectual role in China as it did in Europe slightly later. Chinese cities did not become places identified with personal freedom. They were not communities of merchants at odds with the lords in the countryside. Merchants penetrated rural areas, and both cities and rural areas were under the political control of representatives of the central government.

Other societies in Asia had cities not unlike China's, but no other society had an elite comparable to the scholar–official elite of the Song and later. Key features of this elite can be traced back to the Han dynasty and even earlier, especially its Confucian ideology and government service, but the elements came together in a new and stronger way in the Song period. Unlike the elites of most other pre-modern societies, China's late empirical elite was not military in character, nor was it a hereditary aristocracy, nor a priestly caste. Its stature was buttressed by its ideology of duty and service, and by the ostensibly fair and objective ways in which its members gained access to ranks and honours.

hinese painting falls into two large divisions: painting on walls and painting on the portable media of paper and silk. Paintings discovered on the walls of excavated tombs and the rare surviving temple give us hints of how magnificent the interior of palaces and temples must have been, but painting on paper and silk have survived in much larger quantities. These portable paintings include vertical scrolls that could be hung against a wall, horizontal scrolls that could be unrolled little by little on a table, and small round or square pictures that could be used as the face of a fan or collected in albums. Whatever the format, the painting was done with brushes and ink much like those used for writing, supplemented often, but not always, with water-based coloured washes applied with the same sorts of brushes.

Many paintings depicting people have been reproduced in this book because they help convey a sense of Chinese social life. In the estimation of Chinese art critics, however, the greatest glory of the Chinese art of painting was not figure but landscape painting. Centuries before western artists began to see natural scenery as anything more than background, Chinese artists had developed the depiction of landscape into a great art. Mountains had long been seen as sacred places – the homes of immortals, close to the heavens. Philosophical interest in nature could also have contributed to the rise of landscape painting, including both Daoist stress on how minor the human presence is in the vastness of the cosmos and neo-Confucian interest in the patterns or principles that underlie all phenomena, natural and social.

Three masterpieces of Song landscape painting are illustrated here. Majestic mountains are the focus of the earliest of these, a hanging scroll nearly seven feet tall by Fan Kuan (active c.990–c.1020). The foreground, presented at eye level, is executed in crisp, well-defined brush strokes. Jutting boulders, tough scrub trees, a mule train on the road, and a temple in the forest on the cliff are all vividly depicted. There is a subtle break between the foreground and the towering central peak behind, which is treated as if it were a backdrop, suspended and fitted

Fan Kuan's *Travellers amid Mountains and Streams* was monumental in size as well as subject matter (around 6¾ by 2½ feet).

into a slot behind the foreground. There are human figures in this scene, but it is easy to imagine them overpowered by the magnitude and mystery of their surroundings.

Little is known of Fan Kuan other than that he loved the mountains of his native region in north China. By the late Northern Song, prominent literati like Mi Fei (1051–1107) sometimes achieved fame as both calligraphers and painters. Mi Fei and his son Mi Youren (1086–1165) had successful official careers and mixed with eminent men, who often gathered to appreciate each others' art objects. As painters, the Mis developed a distinct style of brushwork and composition; they made extensive use of washes and overlaid horizontal dabs and represented depth by showing mists between layers of mountains.

These two Northern Song works can be contrasted to a Southern Song one on a smaller and more intimate scale. Much as leading scholar–officials of the Northern Song set out to 'order the world', tackling the largest questions of the organization of state and society, Northern Song painters often painted huge scenes. In the Southern Song, Confucian scholars preferred working from what was close at hand – improvement of oneself and small units like the family and village where one could have significant hope of success – and artists often painted small, intimate scenes that suggest contemplation of what was close to the viewer. This was true even of the painters at the imperial academy, where many of the most influential painters worked in this period. The album leaf by the court painter Xia Gui is in the evocative 'one-corner' format popular in this period. The gaze of the viewer is drawn from the vividly sketched material world in the foreground to the empty space beyond, a realm without substance. Small paintings like this one were often collected into albums and paired with poems or poetic couplets, both poets and painters seeing commonalities in the ways they depicted the juxtaposition of scene, season, and human activity.

The signature of Xia Gui (active c. 1180–1224) is hidden in the lower right corner of this intimate album leaf on silk.

This silk handscroll, painted by Mi Youren in 1130, may well represent the landscape of the south, with rolling, low-lying hills seen behind rivers.

CHAPTER 7

Alien Rule:
The Liao, Jin, and Yuan Dynasties 907–1368

Over the course of four centuries, progressively greater parts of China proper were conquered by Inner Asian tribal peoples, culminating in 1276 with the Song surrender to the Mongols who incorporated all of China into their empire. Each of the three dynasties of conquest – Liao (907–1125), Jin (1125–1234), and Yuan (1215/1276–1368) – built on the achievements of its predecessors to gain greater dominance in China. The Khitans' Liao dynasty did not merely extort material benefits (as the Uighurs had in late Tang) but also occupied a strip along the northern edge of China proper, populated primarily by Chinese. The Jurchens' Jin dynasty, once it defeated the Liao, expanded the occupied zone to include all of north China. The Mongols' Yuan dynasty, after defeating the Jin, built up the machinery needed to conquer all of China. Just as the foreign conquerors gradually learned more effective ways to control and exploit China, the opportunities for the Chinese living under them became progressively more restricted. By the time the Mongols had defeated the Song, chances to serve, resist, or flee were severely limited at all social levels. And yet Chinese civilization not only survived but responded creatively, developing means of expression and modes of coping that added to the richness of the Chinese heritage.

STEPPE NOMADISM AND THE INNER ASIAN STATES

Ever since Qin and Han times, when the Xiongnu became a major threat to the Chinese empire, geography had dictated the basic contours of the relations between China proper and Inner Asia. Although as large as China proper, Inner Asia was always much more sparsely settled because it was unsuited to crop agriculture. China proper at the beginning of the Song had a population of perhaps eighty million people, but only about five million lived in all the Inner Asia regions from Tibet through modern Mongolia and Manchuria. Even fewer would have been able to survive in Inner Asia if tribes had not had access to the settled agricultural society of China. Herders could trade animals and animal products for grain, textiles, and ceramic and metal utensils from China. When drought or disease among their animals reduced their resources, or when the Chinese refused to trade on acceptable terms, the herders had the mobility and military skills to make raids to get what they wanted. This hardly promoted friendly relations or sympathy between herders and farmers. Agriculturalists saw the nomads as bullies who preferred taking from others to working for their living; the nomads looked on Chinese farmers as weaklings.

Despite diverse and shifting tribal identification among the various peoples of the steppe, the basic tribal form of social organization remained remarkably constant. All men learned to ride and shoot and were potential warriors. Families were patrilineal and camped in clan units. Clans would coalesce into tribes, with tribal chiefs selected for their military prowess. Predatory activities were taken as normal; clans and tribes were regularly at odds with each other, seizing cattle, horses, and women, thus setting off cycles of revenge. Captives would be incorporated into the victors' clans as slaves or serfs. The alternative to fighting was to form alliances, and at times a tribal leader would build up a large coalition or confederation through a combination of military victories and alliances. Personal loyalty of warrior to chief, of chief to lord, and lord to overlord tied such structures together. But lords and overlords were not autocrats; major decisions were typically reached at deliberative assemblies of military leaders. Great leaders who had defeated or won over other tribes could aggregate huge armies and keep them happy with the spoils of expansion. Expansion could not be sustained indefinitely, however, and squabbles among heirs or successors might conceivably

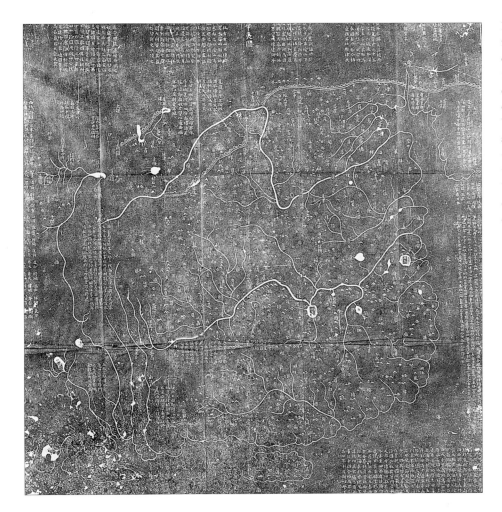

Rubbing of a 'Map of the Chinese and the Barbarians' carved on a stone about $2\frac{1}{2}$ feet square in 1137. The map depicts the major rivers and cities of China and the Great Wall, and gives historical accounts of the various non-Chinese people settled along the borders, including the Khitans, Tanguts, and numerous smaller tribes and city-states.

The material culture of Inner Asia was often in striking contrast to China's. Metalwork was more central to Inner Asian art, perhaps because treasures of gold and silver were easy to transport. The dragons on this 8-inch-tall gilded silver Khitan crown reveal Chinese influence, but the form is not borrowed from China.

lead to the break up of the confederation within a generation or two.

Between the pure nomad of the steppe and the Chinese farmer who encountered non-Chinese only when they raided his settlement, there was a large fluid frontier zone where distinctions of ethnicity and way of life were not so clear-cut. From Later Han times on there was always a broad region settled both by Chinese and non-Chinese. Some of the non-Chinese became farmers, others remained herdsmen or served in military units. Some non-Chinese were still very much members of a tribe, responding to the orders of tribal leaders, while others identified themselves as subjects of the Chinese government or were even assimilated into the Chinese population. Chinese in the frontier zone often made their living rendering services to non-Chinese, whether as farmers, traders, craftsmen, or government advisers, and some of them intermarried with and were assimilated into the non-Chinese groups.

In contrast to the non-Chinese regimes of the Sixteen Kingdoms and Northern Dynasties, who were able to rise to power above all because the Chinese state tore itself apart through civil war, the Khitan, Jurchen, and Mongol states wrested power from a strong dynasty willing and able to devote vast resources to its defence. These alien dynasties erupted into Chinese history because of the dynamics of the border zone. The first to succeed in this way were the Khitans, a proto-Mongol people from the fringes of the steppe in Manchuria, where they practised agriculture along with animal husbandry and hunting. The Khitans had participated in the Tang tributary system, sending envoys to Chang'an, but they also fought and raided as circumstances allowed. As the Tang dynasty disintegrated and north China was vulnerable to attack, Abaoji, of the Yelü clan, united some eight to ten Khitan tribes into a federation, secured control of the steppe, and proclaimed the Liao dynasty as a way of announcing his intention to compete for north China. Abaoji set aside the traditional Khitan practice of electing chiefs for limited terms. Not only did he rule until his death in 926, but he set up hereditary succession on the Chinese model to ensure that his son would succeed him. The ruling line he established married exclusively with the Xiao clan, and the Yelü and Xiao clans dominated government affairs throughout the Liao dynasty.

At the peak of their power, the Khitan probably numbered about 750,000 and ruled over two or three million Chinese. They created a dual state, with distinct Khitan and Chinese areas. The southern section encompassed sixteen prefectures in north China (compared to 300 under Song control). These were nominally governed through the institutions of the civil bureaucracy inherited from the Tang, but counties and sometimes even prefectures were granted to Khitan imperial relatives and high-ranking officials who had absolute jurisdiction in their fiefs and did not have to pay taxes to the government. The main city of this region was their southern capital at modern Beijing, which until then had been little more than a border garrison city. In the huge but sparsely settled northern part of their domain, Khitan institutions were employed. The government in the north was a mobile organization with the emperor and his important officials moving from one place to another in different seasons. A script was created so that documents could be kept in the Khitan language. Even though the Liao ruled over a population tiny by Song standards, its armies had such striking power that the Song found it easier to buy them off than try to defeat them in battle. The Liao state intimidated other neighbours as well, including at times the Korean state of Koryŏ and the Tangut state of Xia, located in modern Gansu province. Probably because they retained the northern sector as a Khitan preserve, the Khitan effectively resisted sinification. The ruling elite became culturally dual – adept in both Khitan and Chinese ways – but the bulk of the Khitans preserved their ancient customs.

It was not Chinese forces that destroyed the Khitan state but the rise of another northern confederation, this one led by the Jurchens. The Jurchens originated further east than the Khitans, in the mountains of eastern Manchuria. In the early twelfth century, Aguda, of the Wanyan clan, formed a confederation of Jurchen tribes, proclaimed it the Jin dynasty, and began attacking the Liao, soon allying with the Song for this purpose. After he died in 1123, Aguda's successor not only defeated Liao in 1125 but turned on the Song.

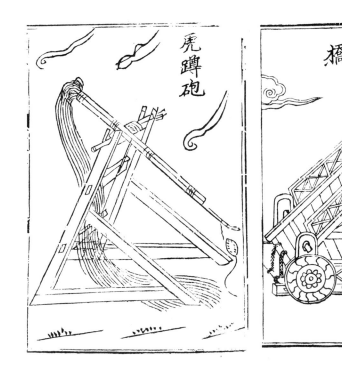

Siege warfare required up-to-date military technology, such as the portable scaling ladder and catapult illustrated here from an early Song manual, the *Comprehensive Essentials of the Military Classics* (*Wujing zongyao*), commissioned in 1040. The Khitan and Jurchen quickly mastered this technology, adding expertise in siegecraft to their previous mastery of cavalry warfare.

Jurchen military successes against Chinese-fortified cities owed much to Jurchen willingness to incorporate Chinese experts in siegecraft into their army. To take the medium-sized city of Taiyuan they brought in thirty catapults to throw a barrage of stones, and built over fifty carts protected by rawhide and iron sheeting to bring in troops to fill the moat. Kaifeng, defended by 48,000 troops, many equipped with powerful crossbows and flame throwers, posed an even greater challenge. The Jurchens brought in siege engines, including mobile towers higher than the city walls, in order to fire incendiary bombs into the city. They succeeded: Kaifeng fell, the Song imperial family was captured and held for ransom, and the remnants of the Song government and army fled south across the Yangzi.

Thus, in less than a generation, the Jurchen went from being a group of tribes concentrated in the far eastern edges of Inner Asia to being the masters of north China, the lords of a densely settled land with over forty million residents, in possession of the treasures of both the Liao and Song capitals. Having gained power so quickly, the Jurchens initially continued the Khitans' dual government and employed former Liao officials, both Chinese and Khitan. The Jin dynasty moved its capital from central Manchuria to Beijing in 1153 and to Kaifeng in 1161, all the while steadily adopting more Chinese political institutions and employing more Chinese officials. As the Liao rulers had before them (and the rulers of the Northern Dynasties still earlier), the Jin rulers found that Chinese political institutions provided them with a potent weapon in their competition with their own nobles. Hereditary monarchy and a bureaucracy of officials willing to do the ruler's bidding enhanced the power of the ruler. The Jurchen emperors, however, did not copy all aspects of Tang and Song government practice, and in particular did not treat civil officials with the respect traditionally accorded them in China. Jin emperors instituted the practice of flogging high officials in open court, a brutal violation of the Confucian dictum that corporal punishment should not extend to the educated elite. Such humiliating punishment was never imposed by the Song and only rarely by earlier dynasties.

The Jin government settled the bulk of the Jurchen in North China so that they could aid in maintaining control over the Chinese population. Immersed in Chinese society in this way, the Jurchens, unlike the Khitans, rapidly adopted Chinese customs, including language, dress, and rituals. Jurchen commanders who objected to the trend toward assimilation assassinated the Jin emperor in 1161, and the succeeding emperor sought to revitalize the Jurchen heritage. He promoted the use of Jurchen as a written language, commissioned translations of the Confucian classics into Jurchen, ordered Jurchen to study at specially established Jurchen schools, set up civil service examinations for Jurchen candidates that would test their mastery of Jurchen, and issued terrible threats against those who adopted Chinese customs. Still the process of sinification continued apace, and later emperors shifted their policies. In 1191 an emperor even forbade referring to Jurchen as people 'of the border areas', not wanting them to be seen as outsiders.

By the end of the dynasty most Jurchen spoke Chinese, wore Chinese clothes, used Chinese-style surnames, and married with the local population. A century later hardly anyone claiming to be Jurchen could be found in China proper, though there still were some in the original homelands in Manchuria.

CHINGGIS KHAN AND THE MONGOLS

Neither the Khitan nor Jurchen empires ever fully controlled the Mongolian steppe, though they sometimes got the various Turkic- and Mongol-speaking clans and tribes that occupied the area to recognize their overlordship. In the late twelfth century this region was facing a subsistence crisis because a drop in the mean annual temperature had reduced the supply of grass for grazing animals. The man who saved the situation by gaining access to the bounty of the agricultural world for them was Chinggis (Ghengis, c.1162–1227).

A brilliant and utterly ruthless military genius, Chinggis proudly asserted that there was no greater joy than massacring one's enemies, seizing their horses and cattle, and ravishing their women. His career as a military leader began when he avenged the death of his father, a tribal chieftain who had been murdered when Chinggis was still a boy. As he subdued the Tartars, Kereyid, Naiman, Merkid, and other Mongol and Turkic tribes, Chinggis built up an army of loyal followers. In 1206 the most prominent Mongol nobles gathered at an assembly to name him their overlord, or great khan. He then fully militarized Mongol society, ignoring traditional tribal affiliations to form an army based on a decimal hierarchy, 1,000 horsemen in the basic unit. A new military nobility was thus created of commanders loyal to Chinggis. They could pass their posts to their sons, but the great khan could remove any commander at will. Chinggis also created an elite bodyguard of 10,000 sons and brothers of commanders, which served directly under him. To reduce internal disorder, he issued simple but draconian laws; the penalty for robbery and adultery, for instance, was death. He ordered the Uighur script to be adopted for writing Mongol, seeing the utility of written records even though he was illiterate himself.

His organization in place, Chinggis initiated one of world history's most astonishing campaigns of conquest. He began by subjugating nearby states. First he would send envoys to demand submission and threaten destruction. Those who submitted without fighting were treated as allies and left in power, but those who put up a fight faced the prospect of total destruction. City-dwellers in particular evoked his wrath and were often slaughtered *en masse* or used as human shields in the next battle. In the Mongol armies' first sweep across the north China plain in 1212–13, they left ninety-odd cities in rubble. When they sacked the Jurchen's northern capital at Beijing in 1215, it burned for more than a month.

Chinggis's battle-hardened troops were capable of enduring great privation and crossing vast distances at amazing speed. In 1219 he led 200,000 troops into Central Asia, where the following year they sacked Bukara and Samarkand. Before his death in 1227, Chinggis had conquered Mongolia and Manchuria, brought Korea into submission, driven the Jurchen south of the Yellow River, destroyed the Tangut state in northwest China, overrun Central Asia, and plundered the Grand Duchy of Kiev in the Ukraine. He ruled from the Pacific Ocean on the east to the Caspian Sea on the west.

Chinggis's death created a crisis due to the Mongol tradition of succession by election rather than descent. In the end the empire was divided into four sections, each to be governed by one of the lines of his descendants. Ogödei, Chinggis's third son, got control of Mongolia. In 1234 he crushed the Jin and became ruler of north China. By 1236 he had taken all but four of the fifty-eight districts in Sichuan, previously held by the Song, and had ordered the total slaughter of the one million plus residents of the city of Chengdu, a city the Mongols had taken easily with little fighting. Even where people were not slaughtered, they were frequently seized as booty along with their grain stores and livestock. Ogödei's

Chinggis Khan's conquests had as much impact on west Asia as they did on China. This Persian illustration of Chinggis pursuing his enemies is from a manuscript copy of the history of the Mongols written by Rashīd al-Dīn (1247–1318), a Persian administrator in the employ of the Mongol Ilkhans in Iran.

The Mongol Empire

main Mongol campaigns 1211-40

borders of successor states after 1259

later campaigns

route described by Marco Polo

troops also participated in the western campaigns begun in 1237. Representatives of all four lines, with some 150,000 Mongol, Turkic, and Persian troops, campaigned into Europe in 1237, taking Moscow and Kiev in 1238 and striking into Poland and Hungary in 1241 and 1242. Although they looted cities in central Europe on these campaigns, the Mongols soon retreated to Russia, which they dominated for over a century.

The Mongols could not have numbered more than 1.5 million. Their success, thus, was due in large part to their willingness to incorporate other ethnic groups into their armies and government. In their campaigns against the Jurchen, they recruited both Khitan and Chinese who felt no great loyalty to their Jurchen lords.

The Mongol conquests expanded contacts across Eurasia, which led to the spread of deadly plagues but also the transfer of technical and scientific knowledge. Visitors like Marco Polo brought back to Europe reports of the wealth and splendour of Chinese cities and information on Chinese inventions such as gunpowder and printing.

Chinese catapult experts enabled the Mongols to storm walled cities, and Chinese shipbuilders enabled them to engage the Song in naval battles. Whatever their nationality, those who served the Mongols loyally were rewarded and given important posts. Uighurs, Tibetans, Persians, and even Russians came to hold powerful positions in the Mongol government.

The Mongols conquered in order to enrich themselves, but their perception of how best to do this changed over time. Looting and pillaging were a standard feature of the first phase of takeover. Lands and those living on them were appropriated and assigned to military commanders, nobles, and army units, to be exploited as the recipients wished. Skilled workers were brought back to Mongolia to provide the Mongols with the material goods of civilized life and to help populate the new capital city of Karakorum. After Bukara and Samarkand were captured, some 30,000 artisans were seized and transported to Mongolia to work as slaves, and many Chinese craftsmen suffered the same fate. More sophisticated methods of extracting revenue took longer to master. After Ogödei conquered the Jin, some Mongols suggested that he turn all of north China into pasture land. An alternative was proposed by a sinified Khitan, Yelü Qucai, who had taken up service with the Mongols after they took Beijing in 1215. Yelü convinced Ogödei that greater wealth could be gained by taxing farmers, calculating a revenue of 500,000 ounces of silver, 80,000 bolts of silk, and over 20,000 tons of grain. But his institutional arrangements did not last long. Soon Yelü's rivals convinced Ogödei that Yelü's method of direct taxation was less lucrative than their plan to let Central Asian Muslim merchants bid against each other for licences to collect taxes. These Central Asian tax farmers quickly gained a reputation for rapaciousness and came to be as hated by the conquered Chinese as the Mongol soldiers.

THE MONGOL CONQUEST OF THE SONG

It was not until Chinggis's grandson Khubilai (r.1260–94) came to power that the conquest of the Song began in earnest. Before succeeding to the title of great khan, Khubilai had ruled a prefecture in Hebei as an appanage and thus knew something of Chinese ways. He had Chinese as well as Uighur and Central Asian advisors, and even knew a little spoken Chinese. In 1264 he transferred the capital from Karakorum in Mongolia to Beijing, known then as Dadu, and in 1271 he adopted a Chinese name for his dynasty, Yuan, and instituted Chinese court rituals.

China south of the Yangzi had never been captured by non-Chinese from the steppe, in large part because the rivers, canals, and streams of the region posed an effective barrier to cavalry forces. But on the advice of a surrendered Song commander, the Mongols began the construction of a river fleet. In 1268 they set siege to Xiangyang, a city on the Han river in Hubei recognized by both sides as the key to control of the Yangzi valley. Both sides were equally determined to win, and the siege lasted five years. Thousands of boats and tens of thousands of troops were involved on both sides. The Mongols employed Chinese, Korean, Jurchen,

Uighur, and Persian experts in naval and siege warfare. Muslim engineers designed artillery that sent a barrage of rocks weighing up to a hundred pounds each. The Chinese started with substantial food stores, but had to run the blockade to get in supplies of salt and other essentials, leading to many naval engagements on the river.

The Song did not lack officials and generals devoted to the cause of stemming the Mongol onslaught, but co-ordination of their efforts was poor. The emperor at this time was a child, and the highest officials got caught up in opposing each other's plans. In 1275, after the Mongol armies crossed the Yangzi, Empress Dowager Xie issued an appeal to the populace to rise up and fight the barbarians, and within a couple of months 200,000 soldiers had been recruited. But even this force could not counter the Mongols' scare tactics; during their advance towards Hangzhou they ordered the total slaughter of the population of the major city of Changzhou. Empress Dowager Xie surrendered in hopes of sparing the people of the capital of a similar fate. Three years later, in 1279, the Mongols were able to defeat the last of the loyalists in a naval battle off the coast of Guangdong during which the last of the Song princes drowned.

By the time the Mongols had conquered the Song, there was no longer a pan-Asian Mongol empire. Much of Asia was in the hands of Mongol successor states, but these were generally hostile to each other. Khubilai was often at war with the Khanate of Central Asia, then held by his cousin Khaidu, and he had little contact with the Khanate of the Golden Horde in south Russia. In these other areas the Mongols tended to merge with the Turkish nomads already there and, like them, to convert to Islam. Thus, from Khubilai's time on China proper was united with Mongolia, Manchuria, and Tibet, but not with Persia, Iraq, or Russia.

Like the Khitans, the Mongols resisted assimilation. Although the Mongol rulers developed a taste for the material fruits of Chinese civilization, they purposely avoided many Chinese social and political practices. The rulers conducted their business in the Mongol language and spent their summers in Mongolia. Khubilai discouraged Mongols from marrying Chinese and took only Mongol women into the palace. Some Mongol princes preferred to live in tents erected in the palace grounds rather than in the grand palaces constructed at Beijing. Mongols continued to choose their rulers through competition, often bloody. As recorded in the Chinese history of the Yuan dynasty, succession after Khubilai is a sordid tale of assassinations, *coups d'état*, enthronements of youthful incompetents, fratricide, and domination by nobles.

LIFE IN CHINA UNDER ALIEN RULE

Under these alien rulers, the Chinese were not forced to adopt the customs of their conquerors. Chinese cultural life continued, much as it had under the Northern Dynasties, with members of the Chinese elite continuing to read and write books and ordinary Chinese continuing to worship gods of their choice in

In 1280 Khubilai had the Chinese court painter Liu Guandao depict him on horseback in a hunting party. In this detail from the silk handscroll, he is clothed in the brightly coloured Chinese brocades underneath the more distinctly Mongol furs.

their own ways. To Song literati, the culture of the Chinese living under the Liao, Jin, or early Yuan was rather provincial, but that did not make it non-Chinese.

Still, it would be difficult to argue that ordinary Chinese fared as well under these alien rulers as under earlier native dynasties. Large numbers had their lands expropriated or were forced into serfdom or slavery, sometimes transported far from home. Taxation, especially under the Mongols, was often ruinous. The economy of north China seems to have taken a downward turn that took centuries to reverse. Added to this was the indignity of being treated as a legally inferior caste. The Venetian merchant Marco Polo, who spent twenty years in Mongol-ruled China (1275–95), found ethnic animosity intense. 'All the Cathaians detested the rule of the great khan because he set over them Tartars [i.e. Mongols], or still more frequently Saracens [i.e. Muslims], whom they could not endure, for they treated them just like slaves.'

Since all three sets of conquerors were interested in maximizing their revenues, they did not purposely damage the economy. All three encouraged trade beyond their borders, the Jin managing extensive officially sanctioned trade with the Southern Song, and the Mongols encouraging trade throughout Eurasia. The Jurchen allowed the circulation of Khitan and Song money and issued their own currency, including paper money, which, however, suffered from serious inflation after 1190. The Mongols similarly tried to maintain the existing paper currency system and even allowed conversion of Song paper money into Yuan currency. They were no more expert than the Jurchen in its management, however, and inflation became ruinous by the fourteenth century. The Mongols, of course, fos-

Built in 1212 in the early Yuan period, the Yongle ('Permanent Joy') Temple in Shanxi province is one of the oldest surviving Daoist temples in China. The walls of its main hall, shown here, are decorated with paintings of gods in the Daoist pantheon.

tered north–south trade within China by reunifying the country. Added to this, they rebuilt the northern section of the Grand Canal, inoperative since Northern Song times, and extended it to the capital they had built at Beijing.

None of the three conquest dynasties aimed at as open or mobile a society as the Song, preferring to place people in hereditary occupational and ethnic categories. Ethnic divisions were codified to preserve the conquerors' privileges. At times the rulers' greatest concern was to prevent their own people from being assimilated into Chinese culture, at other times, to prevent Chinese from learning their language and adopting their identity. Intermarriage was usually discouraged but certainly occurred. Chinese were sometimes encouraged to learn the conqueror's language (as it demonstrated the conqueror's dominance), and sometimes discouraged (as it might undermine their privileges). During the Yuan period, the ethnic hierarchy was particularly complex, with the Mongols the most privileged, then allies of the Mongols from areas outside China (Uighurs, Turks, Tibetans, Tanguts, Persians, Central Asians, called collectively *semu*), then former subjects of the Jin (Chinese and sinified Khitans and Jurchens, called Hanren), with the bottom occupied by former subjects of Song (called 'southerners'). This system of classification affected methods of taxation, judicial process, and appointment to office. Chinese in north China, for instance, were taxed by household in ways that reflected Jin practice, whereas Chinese in south China were taxed by land owned, following Song precedents. Each ethnic group was judged and sentenced according to its own legal traditions, so that, for instance, the Chinese, but no other ethnic groups, were tattooed if convicted of theft.

Other ethnic distinctions were clearly based on the fear that the Chinese were the most likely of all the Mongols' subjects to rebel. Chinese, for instance, were forbidden to congregate in public or to own weapons. Khubilai even prohibited Chinese from dealing in bamboo since it could be used for the manufacture of bows and arrows. Chinese were subject to severe penalties if they fought back when attacked by a Mongol; by contrast, Mongols who murdered Chinese could get off by paying a fine. Probably because Chinese so outnumbered them, the Mongols were particularly vigilant in their efforts to keep the Chinese from trying to pass as Mongols and prohibited the taking of Mongol names.

Hereditary rank and station were a normal part of the social structure of these nomadic peoples, so they fostered it to make society more stable, but for China it was a regressive step. The Mongols went the furthest in this regard, registering the population into hereditary statuses by occupation, such as ordinary farmers, scholars, physicians, astrologers, soldiers, military agricultural workers, artisans, salt producers, and miners. Specialized occupational groups were required to provide unpaid services needed by the state according to rotational quotas and to earn their living during the rest of the year. The rigidity of the system led to widespread absconding by families unable to provide the required services.

The Chinese may not have welcomed alien rule but at all social levels they found ways to adapt creatively to their new situations. The Khitan, Jurchen, and Mongol rulers all needed men capable of handling the paperwork that made centralized bureaucratic government possible, and for this purpose functionaries, whom the Chinese literati dismissed as 'clerks', could be just as useful as men who had studied the classics. But scholars also found employment, if somewhat more slowly, and at lower levels than they would have liked. During the Yuan period, Chinese scholars in the north took to serving the Mongols more readily than those in the south. They were already accustomed to rule by non-Han conquerors, and saw that Mongol rule would be more palatable if Chinese scholars were the administrators. Moreover, they anticipated that the Mongols would gradually become more sinified as the Jurchens had, and could view themselves as shielding Chinese society from the most brutal effects of Mongol rule. Scholars like Xu Heng devoted their lives to teaching the Mongol rulers Chinese principles of the moral basis of politics. In the south, where the literati had identified so strongly with resistance to the Mongols, accommodation

This crate of ceramic bowls is evidence of the continuation of sea-borne commerce under the Mongols. It was excavated in 1976 from a ship that sunk off the coast of Sinan in Korea in 1323 while en route from Ningbo to Japan. The 17,000-odd ceramic pieces found on the ship came predominantly from major kilns in Zhejiang, Jiangxi, and Fujian provinces.

was slower. Still, as southern Chinese literati came to realize that Mongol dominance was not to be an ephemeral event, more and more accepted posts where they could put their learning to use, particularly by serving as instructors at government-sponsored academies.

To the literati, the best way for the alien rulers to show their commitment to good government was to hold civil service examinations and employ the best-educated in positions of authority. The Khitans maintained a limited examination system, modelled on the Tang system, which the Jurchen perpetuated and then greatly expanded. The Mongols were more hesitant. They did not reinstitute the civil service recruitment examinations until 1315, and then had quotas that ensured that Mongols and other non-Chinese candidates (such as Central Asians) would get half the degrees awarded, another quarter going to former subjects of the Jin, and only a quarter to former subjects of the Song (who accounted for well over half the total population). There were, moreover, regional quotas, restricting the number of candidates from each province, which worked to limit the influence of the educationally-advanced lower Yangzi regions. Perhaps most important, only about 2 per cent of the ranked bureaucracy was recruited through the examinations anyway. Instead, the majority entered by promotion through the clerical ranks.

Those southern literati who could not or would not work for the Mongols often supported themselves as doctors, fortune-tellers, Daoist priests, teachers of children, or playwrights. This abundant supply of talented and educated men seems to have proved beneficial to the literary art of drama, which flourished in this period. The presence of an alien elite controlling the government did not diminish the prestige of the literati within Chinese society, and they continued to

The scholar who did not find government employment under the Mongols might still hope to lead a comfortable life, attended by elegant maid-servants and surrounded by objects that evoked the cultivated life. Using the conceit of paintings within paintings to draw attention to the role of art in such a lifestyle, Liu Guandao (active 1279–1300) depicted a scholar reclining before a painted screen that itself depicts a scholar sitting by his books and antiques in front of a screen painted with a landscape.

Demons and demon quellers

The Chinese religious imagination had room for all sorts of beings, good and bad. Among the dangerous beings were vengeful ghosts, extortionate gods who could be merciless toward those who did not serve them properly, and demons who carried out the orders of gods. More benevolent spiritual beings, such as ancestors and Buddhist and Daoist gods, could protect people from the more baleful beings. There were also human exorcists who could subdue or expel them.

Although there was without doubt a genuinely fearful aspect to Chinese demon lore, there was a more playful dimension as well, as seen in the great popularity of the legend of Zhong Kui, the most famous demon queller. It is even said that in Hangzhou merchants would give their customers pictures of Zhong Kui as New Year's gifts. Such pictures were probably pasted by their doors, a custom common in later periods.

The legend of Zhong Kui goes back to a Tang story of Emperor Xuanzong encountering first a small demon who stole his favourite concubine's embroidered perfume bag and his own jade flute and then a large demon who came to the emperor's aid by not only catching the small demon but gouging out his eyes and eating him. When Xuanzong questioned this helpful demon, the demon introduced himself as Zhong Kui, a man who had committed suicide by dashing his head against the palace steps decades earlier on learning that he had failed the palace examination. In gratitude for the posthumous honours the Tang emperor had then bestowed on him, Zhong Kui had vowed to rid the world of mischievous demons.

As time went on, a variety of other stories grew up around the cult of Zhong Kui, and in paintings Zhong Kui was depicted sometimes as a solitary menacing figure, sometimes in the company of demons he had subjugated, sometimes with his sister, but almost always with a beard and a dark, ugly face, and dressed in a scholar's robe and hat and boots.

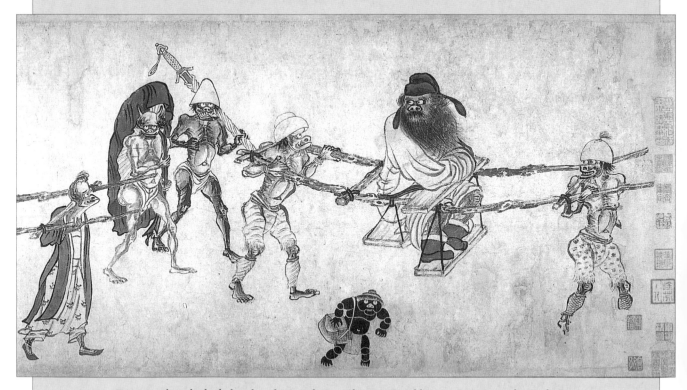

Demons whom he had already subjugated carry Zhong Kui and his sister on a new demon hunt in this detail from a painting by Gong Kai (1222–c. 1304).

be accepted by ordinary Chinese as the natural leaders of local society, active in local defence and kinship organization. Educated men could also concentrate on their cultural responsibilities, looking on themselves as trustees of the Confucian tradition. In Yuan times, in particular, academies flourished as alternative centres of cultural life, beyond the scope of state domination. These were places where scholars could attempt to assert the importance of civil as opposed to military values, and to sustain confidence in their own moral and intellectual autonomy.

ETHNICITY, LOYALTY, AND CONFUCIAN UNIVERSALISM

Confucianism had always made universal claims: the ruler was the Son of Heaven and he ruled over All-Under-Heaven. True, there were 'barbarians' at the fringes of the civilized world who did not obey the Son of Heaven, but this was the result of their not yet having received the transformative influence of Chinese culture, not the consequence of anything inherent in them as a race. To put this another way, China was superior to all its neighbours, but that was because Chinese culture was superior, not because the Chinese, as a race, were physically or biologically better. Barbarians could in time be transformed into Chinese if they adopted Chinese ways – clothes, manners, family system, ethics, and so on. At the same time, Chinese culture was not lacking in ethnic or particularistic sentiments. Deeply ingrained habits of ancestor worship required recognizing obligations to forebears – it would be a violation of filial piety for someone descended from a sinified Xiongnu, Turk, or Khitan to falsify a genealogy to claim descent from an ancient Chinese line. The importance of loyalty to one's ruler also tended to foster a sense of ethnic identity. When one's ruler was threatened by alien enemies, as they were repeatedly in Song times, it was difficult not to blur hostility to them as enemies with hostility to them as culturally alien.

Confucian theory of the transformative power of Chinese culture worked well in situations where China was the dominant force. Throughout the south, local populations that were at one period considered non-Chinese came to merge with the Chinese. Even in the north there were plenty of examples of originally non-Chinese groups that eventually were assimilated into the Chinese – the Xianbei of the Northern Dynasties offer a good example. But the conquest dynasties of the tenth to fourteenth centuries put these Confucian ideas of transformation to much more severe tests. Exposure to Chinese culture and Confucian values did not lead to full-scale sinification of the Khitans or Mongols, even if many individuals became sinified. This exposure did, however, lead to the Jurchens and the Mongols using Chinese universalistic political ideology to their own advantage. By the thirteenth century the Jin emperors presented themselves as supporting an order in which Chinese subjects and non-Chinese conquerors would live together in peace and prosperity under a universal empire. One of the last Jin emperors has come down in history as a model Confucian ruler, the patron of a cultural revival led by Chinese Confucian scholars. Khubilai similarly played up the universal dimensions of his rule. When he announced that his dynasty would be called Yuan, he cited a passage in the *Book of Changes* and pointed out that his grandfather, Chinggis, had expanded the realm to dimensions never before equalled.

Alien emperors could not both preserve their own ethnic identify and perform all of the Chinese rituals traditionally associated with the Son of Heaven and Chinese culture. Alien rulers erected ancestral temples, long identified with the dynastic principle and imperial legitimacy, but this step did not involve symbolic identification with the Han Chinese since the ancestors to be worshipped were their own non-Chinese ancestors. Chinese advisors to alien rulers convinced them to imitate or adopt some features of Chinese imperial funeral and wedding rituals, explaining to them the moral interpretations Chinese scholars traditionally put on such acts. But given the need to preserve their own ethnic identity, none of these alien rulers ever fully adopted such Chinese rituals.

Even though these alien rulers came to act out the role of ritual centre for Chinese culture, many Chinese intellectuals could not accept them as legitimate rulers of China, developing a proto-nationalistic conception of loyalty not just to ruler but to nation and culture. As discussed in Chapter 6, in the early Southern Song period regaining the north was seen as tantamount to preserving China. In the thirteenth century many of those who participated in the resistance to the Mongol invasion saw themselves as engaged in a desperate struggle to save Chinese civilization. Wen Tianxiang, the most famous of the literati-turned-generals, gave everything he had to the cause. Long after there was any real chance of driving out the Mongols, he continued to fight, withdrawing further and further south, hoping to keep the Mongols from the two Song princes the loyalists had rallied behind. Even after he was captured, for three years in captivity he resisted all inducements to serve in the Yuan government, right up to his execution by Khubilai three years later.

The Mongols' policies of favouring other ethnic groups over the Chinese further aroused Chinese ethnic consciousness. Former subjects of the Song were particularly incensed when the Tibetan cleric, Yang Lianjianjia, was given so much power he was able to convert the former Song palaces in Hangzhou into Buddhist temples and excavate the Song emperors' tombs to extract the treasures in them to pay for the building of more Buddhist temples. Defeated Song loyalists gave meaning to their survival by secretly searching out the bones of the Song emperors and burying them elsewhere..

It is true that in each of these dynasties the conquerors and their subjects reached a workable accommodation within a couple of generations as military rule yielded to civilian rule. But persisting tensions should not be underestimated. Although the Jurchen were by far the most sinified of the conquerors, Chinese and Khitan subjects of the Jin readily defected to the Mongols out of hatred for the Jurchen, and after the collapse of the Jin, Chinese common people reportedly massacred large groups of Jurchen. In the case of the Mongols, even in the four-

Zhao Mengfu

The decision to take up service under the Mongols was not an easy one for subjects of the Song. The conflicting pressures they experienced can be illustrated by the career of Zhao Mengfu (1254–1322), a member of the Song imperial clan (an eleventh-generation descendant of the founding emperor). Too young to have served in office under the Song, he had, however, enrolled in the Imperial Academy in Hangzhou. For ten years after the fall of Hangzhou, Zhao kept to himself and his circle of talented friends interested in poetry, paintings, and calligraphy, known as the 'Eight Talents' of Wuxing. Several of them had lost their property in the wars and relied on patrons, donations, or teaching to subsist. They saw painting in archaic styles as a way to express longing for the past and disapproval of the present.

In 1286, in an attempt to win over the southern literati, Khubilai sent a southerner in his employ to recruit eminent scholars in the south. Zhao was among some two dozen who agreed to travel north. After his decision became known, there were friends who refused to speak to him and members of the Song imperial clan who no longer recognized him as a relative.

Zhao quickly gained favour with Khubilai, which enabled him to speak up for Confucian values at court. He made bold proposals on currency reform, did all he could to help bring about the downfall of the notoriously corrupt Tibetan chief minister, Sangha, and argued that literati should be exempt from corporal punishment. By 1316 he had risen to the high post of president of the Hanlin Academy.

For men like Zhao, getting to see north China – to them the 'central plains', the heartland of Chinese culture – compensated a little for the humiliation of serving conquerors. During his first decade in office Zhao travelled over much of north China on various official business and gathered a large collection of paintings by Tang and Northern Song masters, paintings no one in the south had ever had a chance to see. This experience made it possible for him to break with Southern Song painting styles and gain fresh inspiration from earlier masterpieces. When he returned to Hangzhou to visit his old friends, he described for them what he had seen in the north and even painted a picture of one man's ancestral home in Shandong for him.

On a side note, Zhao's second wife, Guan Daosheng, was the first woman in China to attain fame as a painter. She was noted for her paintings of bamboo, orchids, plum blossoms, and Buddhist figures. In the epitaph Zhao Mengfu wrote for her, he reported that the Mongol emperor once asked for a piece of her calligraphy.

Much like other paintings by Zhao Mengfu (1254–1322), this one shows the influence of Tang dynasty models. Still the Mongols could easily have appreciated this rendering of a horse and groom buffeted by the wind without knowing anything of its art historical background.

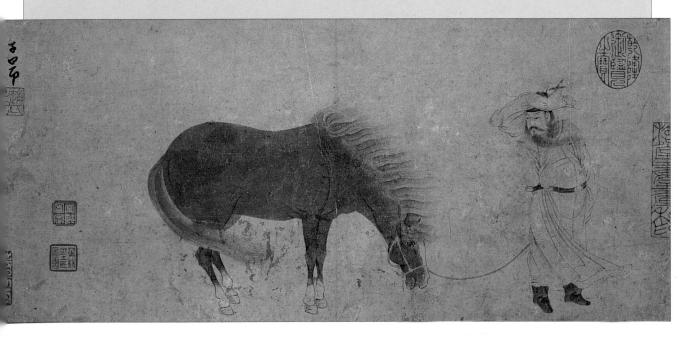

teenth century they and their Chinese subjects had considerable suspicion of each other. Bayan, the Mongol chief minister dominant at court from 1328 to 1340, made efforts to ensure that no Chinese gained leading positions in the central, provincial, or local government. Fearing that he would be assassinated by a Chinese, he reiterated rules against Chinese owning weapons or retaliating if struck by Mongols or Central Asians. The Chinese for their part were just as frightened of him, especially when rumours spread that the government was going to seize all unmarried young people in the country, and that Bayan intended to have everyone with the common surnames Zhang, Wang, Liu, Li, and Zhao slaughtered. Bayan's fears of Chinese conspiracy were thus balanced by Chinese fears of Mongol political brutality. When widespread rebellion in south China brought the Yuan dynasty to the point of collapse (see Chapter 8), the Mongols in China did not simply melt into the Chinese population the way the Xianbei and Jurchen had. Rather, those who could escape fled northward back to the steppe. The post-Yuan Mongols resumed their nomadic, tribal life, looking back on their period of hegemony over China with pride.

Chinese notions of ethnic identity were undoubtedly sharpened by defeat and occupation by the Mongols, but these sentiments should not be taken as equivalent to modern nationalism. Loyalty to one's ruler remained to many a higher virtue. Many conscientious Confucian scholars did everything in their power to make the Yuan government work well, at both the central and local level. And when the Yuan fell to a native Chinese dynasty, a not inconsiderable number of such scholars remained loyal to the Yuan and refused to serve the Ming.

During the four and a half centuries separating the fall of the Tang and the beginning of the Ming, north and south China experienced markedly different fates. The north was at peace and part of a unified China under Chinese rulers for only about a century and a half during the Northern Song (and even then a strip at the northern edge was under the control of the Khitans). For most of the rest of the time it was under the domination of states formed beyond its frontiers by non-Chinese tribesmen. Social and economic dislocation were thus greater in the north, which had hardly had time to recuperate fully from the destruction caused by the Jurchen invasion and subsequent Jin–Song wars before it was devastated by the waves of Mongol campaigns and the militarization of society that came in their wake. Confiscation of land, warlord domination, and frequently changing civil service recruitment policies upset the old power structure, so that relatively few of the families that were eminent in the Northern Song maintained elite status into the Ming.

In the south, by contrast, alien rule lasted for a little less than one century, and even then was not so thoroughly militarist or so disruptive of the old social and economic order. Alien rule did not last long enough to seem inevitable, and it was never accommodated to the degree it was in the north. To the Mongol rulers, the

Chinese of the north and the south were so different that they put them in different ethnic categories and administered them differently.

The history of the conquest dynasties has usually been told from the point of view of the conquerors and how successful they were in consolidating and extending their rule. Western historians have been fascinated with the Mongols' extraordinary war machine and have focused on Chinggis and Khubilai as conquerors of world-historical proportions. Traditional Chinese historians, with their focus on political history and reliance on the dynastic histories, have for their own reasons concentrated on the rulers. Moreover, the dictates of modern politics have required recent Chinese historians to treat the Jurchens and Mongols as minority peoples of China, rather than as alien conquerors. This allows contemporary Chinese to take pride in the geographical sweep of the Mongol empire but in the process distorts history.

When the central concern is the history of Chinese civilization and the Chinese people, the conquest dynasties look rather different. Just as Chinese culture would have to respond to the threat of the west in the nineteenth and twentieth centuries, so Chinese culture had to respond to the threat of conquest by horse-riding nomads in this period. Its response had profound effects on many aspects of Chinese culture.

Even though all three alien dynasties patronized Buddhism, China did not become a more Buddhist society under their tutelage. Buddhism probably had special appeal to the conquerors since it was a universalistic religion with no greater ties to China than to anywhere else. Still, the patronage of alien rulers did not stimulate an intellectual renaissance among Buddhists in China, nor did increased contact with Buddhists from other lands. Chinese Buddhist monks, for instance, seem to have found little to celebrate in the increased prominence of Tibetan lamas in court circles. It would be going too far to say that the patronage of alien rulers undermined the appeal of Buddhism to the Chinese at large, but it did not enhance it.

During the Mongol occupation, China was tied into a Eurasian empire, and foreigners from west Asia and Europe visited China in unprecedented numbers. These cross-cultural contacts whetted the appetite of Europeans for increased contact with distant lands but had the opposite effect on the Chinese. Chinese inventions – such as printing and gunpowder – spread westward, and the demand for Asian goods eventually culminated in the great age of European exploration and expansion. By comparison, in China protecting what was distinctly Chinese became a higher priority than drawing from the outside to enrich or enlarge Chinese civilization. Much more in the way of foreign music and foreign styles in clothing, art, and furnishings were integrated into Chinese civilization in Tang times than in Song or Yuan times. In this regard, China was more like the Islamic world, where the Mongol conquests and military threats provoked conservative reactions, not enhanced interest in distant regions.

For the Chinese, bamboo is a symbol of survival in adversity: it is strong but flexible; because it bends, it can withstand storms and winds without breaking. Perhaps for this reason bamboo was a popular subject among Chinese literati painters during the Mongol period. This 17-inch-tall album leaf was painted in ink on paper in 1350 by Wu Zhen (1280–1354), a scholar who supported himself as a fortune-teller.

The impact of Jurchen and Mongol conquests was certainly detrimental to the economy. The iron industry that had been central to the Northern Song economic expansion never regained its former vitality. Population growth was replaced by population decline. By 1100 the population of Northern Song was in the vicinity of 100 million. The Jurchen invasion led to population loss in the north, but by 1207 the Jurchens had fifty-three million people in the north, which combined with perhaps sixty-five million in lands held by the Southern Song gives a combined population of nearly 120 million. In 1290 the registered population of China was down to 60 million, and was still at that level a century later. Indiscriminate slaughter by Mongol armies undoubtedly accounts for some of this drop. Certainly some large areas, like Sichuan and Hebei, were devastated and took several centuries to recover economically and demographically from the Mongol conquest. The increased communications across Asia may also have led to the spread of deadly plagues. Shortly after the lifting of the first siege of Kaifeng in 1232 an epidemic spread, killing nearly a million people over the next three months. The turmoil of the final years of the Yuan, when civil war raged, undoubtedly contributed as well to population loss.

The Jurchens and the Mongols have also been blamed for introducing more authoritarian forms of government, forms that their Chinese successors maintained or even perfected. The alien rulers and officials often had little patience for following written regulations, and accomplished their goals more easily through violence and terror. Their governments were not necessarily stronger or more centralized than the Song; indeed, in many ways they was more decentralized, the residue of a more feudal-patrimonial mode of governance. But under foreign dynasties the imperial exercise of power was less constrained by precedent and more given to overt use of force.

Despite all these negatives – or perhaps because of them – Chinese civilization also gained something during these centuries of alien domination: a confidence in its ability to survive, to bend just enough to ward off the worst blows, and to defeat aggressors through simple staying power. Chinese civilization survived not by transforming the Mongols, but by strengthening those facets of cultural identity independent of the Son of Heaven. More important to the survival of Chinese culture than Khubilai's gestures of playing patron was what was going on far from the court – in academies where Confucian teachings were being transmitted, in circles of artists and writers who found ways to maintain confidence in their cultural traditions, in local lineages where self-defence and distinctly Chinese rituals were both promoted. The association of the conquerors with military values may well have strengthened the identification of China with the opposite – with the arts of peace and order.

Theatrical performances were so popular in Jin times that representations of actors and musicians were used to decorate tomb walls. This carved brick from a twelfth-century tomb at Jishan, Shanxi province, depicts actors in stock roles in the front row, with the musicians who accompany their performances behind them. Each figure is 12 to 15 inches tall.

Chinese performing arts have a long history. Acrobats and dancers entertained in the palaces of the Warring States period. Cities in Song times were enlivened by comedians, puppeteers, singers, and storytellers who drew on a substantial repertory of farces, moral tales, love stories, and historical legends.

Drama as a literary art was established during the Jin and Yuan periods. The titles of more than 600 Jin dramas have been preserved, but only one full script remains. From Yuan times, however, the scripts of about 160 plays have survived. Most plays were in four acts, with the scripts consisting of alternating sung lyrics and spoken passages. The Mongol rulers were patrons of the theatre, which could be appreciated by those unable to read Chinese. But the development of the literary art of drama probably owes as much to the changed career prospects of the literati. Talented writers, unwilling or unable to serve the conquerors, earned money by writing scripts for impresarios, an activity previously looked on as too vulgar for men well-educated in the literary tradition.

One of the most accomplished of these playwrights was Guan Hanqing, author of sixty-odd plays. In *The Injustice to Dou E*, a young widow, Dou E, falsely confesses to a murder to spare her mother-in-law from torture. Before her execution, which takes place on a summer day, she announces that heaven will prove her innocent by sending a fall of snow and initiating a three-year drought. As it turns out, the judicial intendant who reviews the case is none other than her father, who, years before, had sold her to raise money to travel to take the examinations. He cannot return her to life but he does bring the true miscreants to justice.

Dramas like this one were loved as much for the poetic qualities of the arias as for the plots. On her way to the execution grounds Dou E sang of her plight:

This illustration of the *Injustice to Dou E*, included in a Ming edition of the play, captures something of the erotic dimensions of the tale of Dou E's suffering.

> The virtuous suffer poverty and early deaths
> But the wicked enjoy long lives of wealth
>   and honour.
> Even heaven and earth now fear the mighty and
>   bully the weak,
> Simply letting evil take its course.
> O earth! You have not distinguished between
>   the good and the bad!
> O heaven! You have confused the worthy and
>   the unworthy!
> My tears stream down endlessly!

Some see in dramas like *The Injustice to Dou E* subtle protest of Mongol rule, but tales of injustice were common under native dynasties as well.

Even if the Chinese people loved drama and opera, the performers did not command high social status. Singers and actors were classed with prostitutes as a demeaned category of people, forbidden to marry ordinary commoners. Nor could their sons or grandsons take the civil service examinations. Women who performed in public were seen as little better than prostitutes, an attitude that led to the widespread practice of female impersonation by male actors. But men impersonating women were generally assumed to be homosexuals, adding to the association between the theatre and sexual laxity. Some people entered the theatre through birth into families of actors; others were trained from childhood by impresarios who purchased them from their parents for the purpose.

Above. Characters in theatrical performances wore elaborate costumes and stereotyped facial make-up, shown here in a large Yuan dynasty mural in a hall of the Guangsheng temple in Hongtong, Shanxi province.

Right. Story-tellers and puppeteers entertained city-dwellers with much the same stories that play-wrights worked into their polished dramatic texts. Detail from a fourteenth-century handscroll in ink and colour on paper.

CHAPTER 8

The Limits of Autocracy:
The Ming Dynasty 1368–1644

With the disintegration of the Mongol empire and collapse of the Yuan dynasty, China got a respite from alien rule. The Ming dynasty (1368–1644), founded by a poor peasant turned rebel general, managed to secure all of China proper and even to expand into areas in the southwest. The early Ming emperors, struggling to gain personal control over a huge, complex empire, used terror to keep officials in line. Despite the despotism of the rulers, however, competition to join official-dom quickly reached and exceeded Song levels. Literati culture was especially vibrant in the Lower Yangzi region, where levels of urbanization were very high and the publishing industry grew rapidly. One reason for the prosperity of this region was a burgeoning of trade, including international maritime trade. Even though the Ming rulers had little sympathy for commerce and tried to force all for-eign trade into the structure of the tribute system, the Ming government could not keep high foreign demand for Chinese silk and porcelain from drawing China into the rapidly expanding international trading system. The resulting influx of silver speeded the monetization of the Chinese economy and had pervasive social and cultural effects, some of which contributed to the unravelling of social order in the seventeenth century.

MING TAIZU AND DESPOTISM

Seldom has the course of Chinese history been as influenced by a single personal-ity as much as it was by the founder of the Ming dynasty, Zhu Yuanzhang (1328–1398), better known by his imperial temple name, Taizu, and the name of his reign period, Hongwu. The first commoner to become emperor in 1,500 years, Taizu proved shrewd, hardworking, and ruthless. He knew poverty first-hand. His destitute parents frequently had to move to look for work or escape rent-collectors; they even had to give away several of their children because they could not afford to rear them. When Zhu Yuanzhang was sixteen, a shift in the route of the Yellow River brought floods, famine, and epidemic to his region, and took the lives of both his parents. Taizu, without even the resources for coffins to bury them in, presented himself to a Buddhist monastery; but the monastery, hard-pressed itself, soon sent out the novices to beg. After several years wandering across east-central China, Taizu returned to the monastery for three or four years until it was burned to the ground by the Yuan militia attempting to suppress local rebellions. Homeless again, in 1352 Taizu joined one of the many rebel groups affiliated with the Red Turbans, a branch of the millenarian White Lotus Society whose teachings drew on Manicheism and the Maitreya cult of popular Bud-dhism, as well as Confucian and Daoist values and symbols. Taizu rose quickly in this rebel group, especially after he married the foster daughter of the commander. In 1355, on the latter's death, he took over command of the troops and the following year captured the major city of Nanjing. In these early years he attracted to his service a small band of able soldiers of peasant origins as well as a few learned men who served as advisors.

Using Nanjing as a base for campaigns against other local strongmen, Taizu gradually became supreme in the southeast, even though he still nominally recognized the dynastic claims of the head of the Red Turbans. After the latter died in 1367 (somewhat suspiciously while Taizu's guest), Taizu made clear his own imperial intentions, sending his army north toward the Yuan capital at modern Beijing. The Mongol ruler was not captured and did not abdicate; rather he and his court fled, retreating into Mongolia. Subsequent Ming efforts to defeat the Mongols there were unsuccessful, so the Ming domain never extended into Inner Asia. In 1368, after gaining control of Beijing, Taizu razed the palaces and declared the establishment of the Ming dynasty. He retained Nanjing as his capital, making the Ming the first dynasty to rule a united China from a city south of the Yangzi River. Nanjing's population rapidly swelled from about 100,000 to perhaps one million. Taizu built huge walls around the city, nearly thirty miles long, as well as palaces and other government buildings.

Influenced, it would seem, by Daoist notions of heavenly autocrats, Taizu made every effort to exalt the position of emperor. He saw his task as bringing into being a world where people obeyed their superiors and where those who did evil were promptly punished, in other words, a world quite unlike the violent, amoral one he knew. He required his officials to kneel when addressing him and did not hesitate to have them beaten. In order to lighten the weight of government on the poor, he ordered a full-scale registration of both population and cultivated land as the first step toward reallocating service and tax liabilities more fairly. For the same reasons he cut government expenses wherever he could. The army, over two million strong, was made largely self-supporting by allotting land to soldiers' families to farm. The cost of the civil bureaucracy was kept under control by retaining the Yuan system of hereditary artisan households who would provide for the needs of the palace and government. Similar principles were applied to local government; better-off village families were assigned the obligation to perform low-level judicial, police, and tax-collecting services without

Emperor Taizu's detractors described him as ugly and pockmarked, with a protruding lower jaw. Although some of the portraits preserved in the palace collection show him to have been as handsome as any other emperor, several survive that match the most negative descriptions.

pay. This village service policy also appealed to Taizu because it allowed local communities to protect themselves from rapacious tax collectors: they themselves would be responsible for assessing, collecting, and transporting taxes. Taizu also thought government intrusion could be cut back if people would observe traditional moral standards and social hierarchies and live together harmoniously. Towards this end he issued hortatory admonitions for village heads to read aloud to their neighbours, urging them to behave with filial piety towards their parents, live in harmony with their neighbours, work contentedly at their occupations, and refrain from evil.

Taizu's sympathies did not extend to the commercial and scholarly elites. Inordinately high tax rates were imposed on the rich and cultured southeastern area around Suzhou in Jiangsu province, and thousands of wealthy families from the southeast were forced to settle elsewhere, especially in the new capital Nanjing. Taizu complained about the 120 *jinshi* chosen in the civil service examination of 1371, declaring, 'We sincerely searched for worthy men, but the empire responded by sending empty phrase-makers.' Not only did he cease holding examinations for over a decade, but he even had the *Mencius* edited to remove eighty-five sections that implied curbing the authority of the ruler. Once, after the examinations were reinstated, Taizu had the chief examiner executed when it turned out that only candidates from the south had been selected as *jinshi*.

When overwhelmed by the magnitude of the problems he tackled, Taizu began to suspect that others were plotting against him or secretly ridiculing him. He turned his palace guard into a secret police force to spy on officials and ferret out political crimes. In 1380 he had his chief minister executed, and almost anyone remotely connected with him was soon arrested and executed as possible accomplices; after fourteen years of investigation over 30,000 had lost their lives. Two other major purges took another 70,000 or so lives. The return of native rule to China had become a nightmare for the literati.

These purges were not directed only at the mighty; Taizu waged repeated campaigns against the activities of the assorted underlings, runners, guards, and servants who did the bidding of officials and controlled ordinary people's access to them. As he reported in one of his proclamations, he felt driven to rid the world of evil people:

> In the morning I punish a few; by evening others commit the same crime. I punish these in the evening and by the next morning again there are violations. Although the corpses of the first have not been removed, already others follow in their path. The harsher the punishment, the more the violations. Day and night I cannot rest. This is a situation which cannot be helped. If I enact lenient punishments, these persons will engage in still more evil practices. Then how could the people outside the government lead peaceful lives? What a difficult situation this is! If I punish these persons, I am regarded as a tyrant. If I am

lenient toward them, the law becomes ineffective, order deteriorates, and people deem me an incapable ruler.

Unable to put his trust in a prime minister, Taizu acted as his own chief executive, dealing directly with officials on matters large or small. Like the First Emperor of the Qin, Taizu went through huge piles of paper work himself, exhausting himself in his determination to manage all matters.

MANAGEMENT PROBLEMS

Taizu had instructed his descendants to preserve intact the institutions he had created, a wish they did not always honour. Nanjing, for instance, did not remain the capital for even a century. Taizu was succeeded by his legitimate heir (his deceased eldest son's fifteen-year-old son), but within three years this emperor's uncle, Taizu's fourth son Chengzu, waged a civil war to usurp the throne. Chengzu moved the main capital to his power base at Beijing and demoted Nanjing to the rank of secondary capital. Thereafter Beijing was the residence of the court and seat of military power while Nanjing had supervision of fiscal matters

The layout and design of the Ming palace complex in Beijing were largely retained by the subsequent Qing rulers. Visitors to Beijing today can wander through the orderly sequence of courtyards and halls where twenty-four emperors both lived and conducted the affairs of state.

and of supplying the poorer north with tax revenues collected in the wealthier south. To build up Beijing hundreds of thousands of workmen were set to constructing walls and palaces. The city was arranged like a set of nested boxes: the main hall of the palace was the centre of the palace compound (called the Forbidden City), itself the centre of the government district (called the Imperial City), which in turn was the centre of Beijing, with movement in and out of these boxes limited to the gates that pierced the walls. By 1553 an Outer City had been added to the south, with its own walls and gates, bringing the overall size of Beijing to 4 by 4 1/2 miles. To supply Beijing with grain, the Grand Canal was brought up over western Shandong through a chain of fifteen locks, a major feat of engineering. The 15,000 boats and 160,000 soldiers of the transport army – who pulled loaded barges with ropes where needed – thus became the lifeline of the capital.

Taizu's efforts to organize his government around unpaid service created many headaches for later Ming administrators. Local officials found that legal sources of revenue were so limited that they had had no choice but to levy extra-legal ones to keep basic services going, leading to just the sort of abuses Taizu had wanted to prevent. Ordinary households, for their part, were often devastated by the burden of uncompensated responsibility for delivering taxes or maintaining local hostels for government travellers. Reforms eventually had to be introduced, which converted most obligations into a monetary tax. As in previous dynasties, the army of hereditary farmer-soldiers came nowhere near paying for itself or maintaining itself as an effective military force. Soldiers who were not paid deserted or sold their lands, and mercenary armies had to be created in their stead. The Ming monetary system never was managed very effectively; for instance, the government failed to meet the need for coinage, to control counterfeiting of coins, or to enforce the use of its poorly backed paper currency. In the end paper money was abandoned and the government acquiesced to the circulation of silver ingots.

Taizu's solution to the perennial problem of palace eunuchs also did not work as planned. Taizu had stipulated that eunuchs should not be allowed to learn to read or to interfere in politics. Within decades, however, palace eunuchs were not merely managing huge imperial workshops, but also playing major roles in military affairs and even such civil service matters as the appointment and promotion of officials. During the last century of the Ming 70,000 eunuchs were in service throughout the country, 10,000 in the capital. They had their own bureaucracy, parallel to that of the civil service bureaucracy but not controlled by it. A school was set up to educate them, and many became expert in bureaucratic procedures and documentary forms. Eunuchs staffed such palace offices as the Bureau of Ceremonial, whose chief was the undisputed manager of the palace quarters and the emperor's schedule, and when the emperor allowed it, a kind of chief of staff who could impose his will on the civil bureaucracy. Eunuch control over vital governmental processes was particularly detrimental during the long reign of Guangzong (also called Wanli, r. 1573–1620), who, weary of the bickering among his top officials and their resistance to his desire to command troops in person, simply stopped attending to the affairs of government, neither reading papers submitted to him nor filling vacancies in key posts. He let eunuchs collect taxes in the provinces, unconcerned with how they might tyrannize wealthy families.

While conscientious Ming bureaucrats were preoccupied with trying to make a flawed system work, the society and economy were continuing to grow. China's population more than doubled over the course of the dynasty, from between sixty and eighty million to between 150 and 200 million. Small market towns appeared all over the country. Regional specialization increased as communities took advantage of the availability of cheap water transport to take up cash-cropping. By the seventeenth century the Yangzi river delta area had become a centre of cotton and silk production, coastal Fujian became known for tobacco and sugar cane, and porcelain manufacture at Jingdezhen in Jiangxi had achieved unprecedented levels of output. All of this occurred despite continued government suspicion of those who pursued profit and of economic growth beyond the state's plan.

THE SOUTHWESTERN FRONTIER

It was not until Ming times that the southwestern provinces of Yunnan and Guizhou became fully incorporated into the Chinese realm. The Mongols had destroyed the kingdom of Dali in 1253 and incorporated it into their empire, settling over 50,000 soldiers and their families there, including many Muslims from the northwest. This pattern of furloughing soldiers after campaigns was repeated by the Ming after it conquered the region in 1381. By the end of the century some 200,000 military colonists had cleared at least two million *mu* (about 350,000 acres) in Yunnan and Guizhou. Subsequent settlements of military households during the fifteenth and sixteenth centuries brought at least another half million government-sponsored settlers, coming from as far away as Shanxi, Shandong, Jiangsu, and Fujian. These migrations had a major impact on the ethnic mix in the area, as Yunnan and Guizhou probably had only around three million people at the beginning of the Ming, well over half of whom were non-Han. Colonists generally opened uncultivated lands near non-Han settlements, leading to friction but also to assimilation in both directions.

In frontier areas like the southwest the Ming government followed earlier dynasties' policies of dual administration. Places with extensive Chinese populations were ruled through prefectures and counties whose regular civil servants enforced nationwide law codes and tax regulations. In other places where native tribes were clearly in control, the Ming recognized tribal rulers as hereditary chieftains and ruled 'with a loose reign,' obligating the chief to maintain order, help the Ming if other nearby tribes caused trouble, and send tribute in return for which he received ample goods in exchange. The Ming central government played the role of distant overlord, not able to control much of what occurred, but not having to expend many resources either.

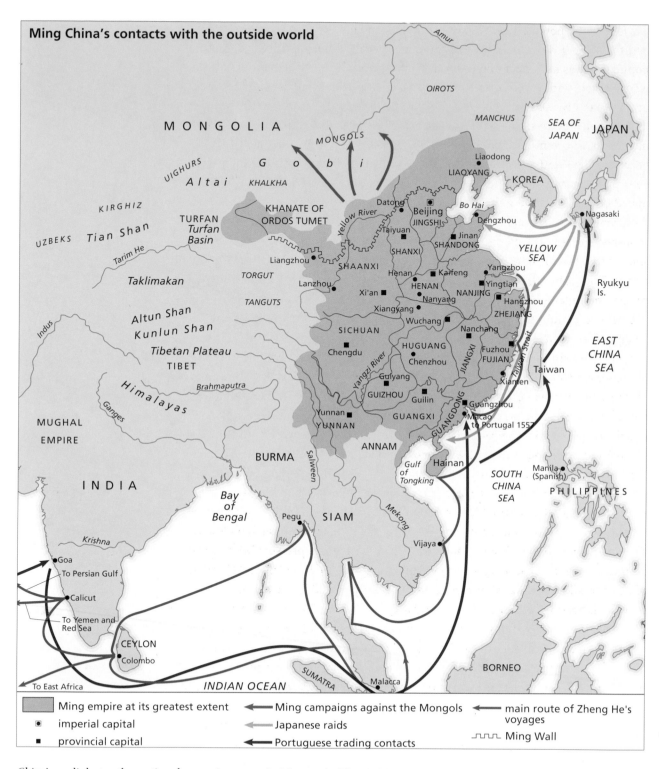

Ming China's contacts with the outside world

Ming empire at its greatest extent — Ming campaigns against the Mongols — main route of Zheng He's voyages

imperial capital — Japanese raids

provincial capital — Portuguese trading contacts — Ming Wall

China's sea links to other nations became important in Ming times. Early in the dynasty, China was sending out sea-borne missions to distant lands; late in the dynasty merchants and adventurers from distant lands were coming to China by sea.

Thus in Ming times it was not enough to defend the northern borders against horse-riding nomads; the government also had to worry about defending its southern coastal borders from pirates and smugglers.

Despite the potential benefits of this quasi-feudal system to both local chiefs and the Ming government, violent conflict between settlers and the indigenous population was not uncommon. In ways reminiscent of conflicts in the American west, provocations could come from either side: individual Chinese would exploit or reduce to near slavery local tribal people, and tribal people, where they had the military means, would rob, enslave, or otherwise terrorize Chinese settlers and merchants who ventured into their enclaves. The largest-scale uprisings occurred between 1464 and 1466 when Miao and Yao tribes in Guangxi, Guangdong, Sichuan, Hunan, and Guizhou left their remote border areas to attack heavily populated cities. Concluding that the previous conciliatory policies had exacerbated the problem, the minister of war decided to pursue a military solution. Thirty thousand soldiers, including 1,000 Mongol horsemen, were assembled in Nanjing and marched from there into Guangxi, where they were joined by 160,000 local troops. The main Yao stronghold, located in a deep gorge surrounded by jungle-covered mountains, was attacked, and the leader and 800 followers were captured and sent to Beijing to be beheaded. Armies were then dispatched to pacify the neighbouring provinces.

Some Chinese officials argued against pursuing military supremacy over the non-Chinese tribes. In 1479 an official argued that conflict with the aborigines in southern Sichuan was due largely to the Ming government's decision to assign regular civil service officials to the area, men unfamiliar with the local people and unable to speak their languages. The recent campaigns, resulting in the deaths of 270 native leaders, he reported, had provoked such hatred for the Chinese that the local people saw no alternative but to pillage and plunder. 'When they capture a Chinese, they bind him to a tree and shoot arrows at him, saying: "You have been a plague on us all too long."' Other officials sought a middle ground between granting tribal people autonomy and trying to force them into total submission. The philosopher-official Wang Yangming, experienced in suppressing Miao rebellions in Guangxi, advocated joint administration by both local chiefs and Chinese officials to allow gradual sinification. In the case of unsinified tribal people, he remarked, 'instituting direct civil administration by Han Chinese magistrates is like herding deer into the hall of a house and trying to tame them. In the end, they merely butt over your sacrificial altars, kick over your tables, and dash about in frantic fright.' On the other hand, leaving them to their own devices was likewise no solution since it was like releasing deer into the wilderness without putting up fences to keep them from trampling on young crops.

The creation of a trans-local Chinese identity not merely among the educated but also among ordinary farmers owes much to the sort of long-distance migration that filled the southwest with Chinese settlers. Migrants came from widely separated parts of China; they could not fail to notice the differences in dialects and customs that divided them, but they also came to recognize what they had in common, what distinguished them as Han Chinese from the local tribal people. In the case of the southwest, as Chinese immigrants and native people lived in closer contact, there was enough cultural interchange for new provincial dialects and identities to emerge, with Han Chinese identity and culture dominant, but incorporating many particular practices of local indigenous origins.

LITERATI LIFE

The Ming government may have been seriously flawed and careers in it full of risks, but the supply of educated men eager to enter government service never diminished. The civil service examination system thus continued to play a major role in literati life.

In terms of intellectual and literary content, the Ming examinations are notable for their narrowness. They tested above all knowledge of the Four Books (*Analects*, *Mencius*, *Doctrine of the Mean*, and *Great Learning*) as interpreted by the Song scholar Zhu Xi. This emphasis on a single scholar's interpretations made study and grading more straightforward but served to separate preparation for the examinations from intellectual life to an even greater degree than in the Song period. Preparing for the examinations became divorced from literary trends as well, especially after 1487 when it was ruled that essays had to be written in a fixed formal eight-part style dubbed the 'eight-legged' essay style. In terms of the opportunity for advancement they offered, however, the Ming examinations are notable for their geographical and social breadth. To prevent the most prosperous parts of the country, where education was most advanced, from monopolizing the civil service, and to guarantee representation to even the most backward regions,

One way to try to improve one's chance of passing the civil service examinations was to cheat, for instance by wearing undergarments on which the classics were written in small characters. This 'cheat shirt' probably dates from the nineteenth century, but the practice began much earlier.

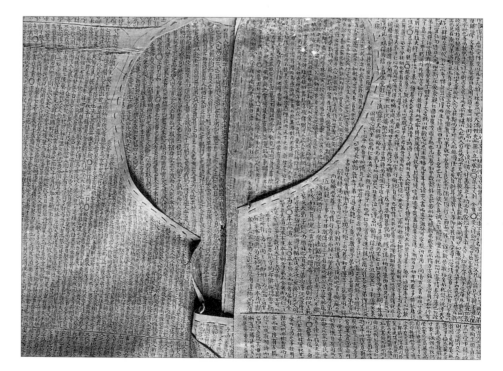

provincial quotas were instituted. Just as significant, the Ming added a new lower tier to the degree system, the government students (*shengyuan*) who qualified by passing a local examination, thus greatly expanding the numbers of degree-holders. By the sixteenth century there were generally over 100,000 government students (about one out of every three or four hundred adult males). These men could wear distinctive caps and sashes, were exempt from labour service, and were sometimes given stipends. At least as important, their titles gave them standing as community leaders and entry into educated circles; if in reduced circumstances, they could probably use their titles to secure a job as a tutor in a wealthy family. The 10 per cent or fewer who were successful at the provincial level (*juren*) were entitled to greater privileges, including eligibility for appointment to lower-level government posts, even without passing the next, and most prestigious examination, the *jinshi*, offered in the capital. There would only have been two to four thousand *jinshi* at any given time, on the order of one out of 10,000 adult males.

The key role of the civil service examination system in elite life did not make wealth no longer of significance. Since office could be used to enhance family property and property could be passed from one generation to the next, families of officials still did better than other families. As in Song times, when the class system was viewed from the county or prefectural level, a relatively small number of landholding families in a locality could well garner a disproportionately large share of the higher degrees generation after generation. In one county in Anhui, for instance, nineteen of the eight-five *jinshi* awarded in Ming times came from just three family lines.

At age eighty, the scholar–official Wen Zhengming (1470–1559) depicted an old gnarled cypress and a solid rock using only ink and paper, giving a fresh interpretation to these long-established symbols of endurance. In the upper left he conveyed the idea in a poetic couplet: 'Weighed down by snow, oppressed by frost, with the passing of years and months its branches become twisted and its crown bent down, yet its strength remains majestic.'

Hopeful candidates who had taken the civil service examinations would crowd around the wall where the results were posted. Detail from a handscroll in ink and colour on silk attributed to Qiu Ying (active 1530–1552).

The wealthy, moreover, had the resources to pursue a rather idyllic version of the literati life, combining the practice and connoisseurship of art and literature with study and occasional office holding. In 1570 the 'Four Great Families' of Suzhou invited the local literati to view their ancient bronzes and other antiquities. Wealthy Suzhou families like these often lived in elegant walled garden homes. Quite unlike the rural and urban mansions of their European counterparts, these urban retreats provided no external visual interest. Only those invited within the high walls could discover the imaginary worlds created within small courtyards, reached after zigzagging along covered galleries, pierced in places by decorative windows offering glimpses of further worlds. In the tiny gardens within these complexes could be found bamboo or plum trees as well as rocks that evoke mountains.

In this milieu the amateur ideal – already present in Tang and Song art circles – blossomed. Great literati painters like Shen Zhou, Wen Zhengming, and Dong Qichang were scholars thoroughly familiar with the classics, the works of the great poets, and the styles of former poets and calligraphers; and they tried to imbue with meaning the landscapes, gardens, trees, rocks, or other scenes they depicted. They attracted many students and followers, both amateurs who painted for self-expression while pursuing other careers, and men who decided to devote their full energies to painting. Making a living as a painter had become feasible because works of art by well-known painters commanded high prices. One wealthy man, planning the celebration of his mother's eightieth birthday, paid the prominent painter Qiu Ying 100 ounces of silver to paint a long handscroll for the occasion. Older paintings were also highly valued; one man acquired a landed estate in exchange for a set of four scrolls by Shen Zhou, a famous painter of a prior generation.

POPULAR CULTURE

The efforts literati took to perfect the cultivated life may reflect an attempt to buttress the boundaries between literati and popular culture, which were being breached bit by bit by urban culture, the explosion of the publishing industry, and the rise of vernacular literature. In the early seventeenth century, the Italian missionary Matteo Ricci commented on 'the exceedingly large numbers of books in circulation here and the ridiculously low prices at which they are sold'. The printer Mao Jin employed up to twenty craftsmen and published no less than 600 titles, using over 100,000 wooden printing blocks. More and more books were

The elegance of the hardwood furniture crafted in Ming times was never surpassed. This 'official's' chair was constructed from slender, gently curved pieces of Huanghuali wood, a beautifully grained hardwood grown primarily in tropical Hainan Island, south of mainland Guangdong province. The apron and the splat are embellished with low-relief carving of dragon and cloud motifs. Fine hardwood furniture like this chair was fashioned without the use of metal nails, the pieces being held together through elaborately fitted joints.

being published for the lower end of the market. Profusely illustrated home reference books provided everything from multiplication tables and rules for performing funerals to what to specify in a contract for buying a water buffalo. Popular religious tracts included ledgers for calculating moral worth, in which people determined their fortunes by measuring good deeds against bad ones. For school children there were primers introducing elementary vocabulary. For candidates for the examinations, there were inexpensive editions of the Confucian classics as well as collections of successful examination answers.

In the sixteenth and seventeenth centuries more and more books were being published in the vernacular. Only those able to devote years to study could comfortably read books written in the terse and allusive literary language used in the classics and employed by the literati and the government ever since. There was a much larger potential audience for fiction and plays written with the grammar and vocabulary people used in everyday speech, for this audience included women in educated families, merchants, shop clerks, and anyone else with at least a rudimentary education. The enterprising writer and editor Feng Menglong, for instance, found a ready audience for collections of vernacular short stories, often humorous, populated by a cast of clerks and brigands, kings and monks, courtesans and ghosts.

The scripts of plays also found a ready market. Tang Xianzu's love stories and social satires were particularly popular. The *Dream of Han Tan* concerns a young man who falls asleep while his meal of millet is cooking. He then sees his whole life in a dream: he comes first in the examinations, performs great deeds as an official, is slandered and condemned to death, then cleared and promoted. As he is about to die he wakes up to see his millet almost done and realizes that life passes as quickly as a dream. *Peony Pavilion*, Tang's most popular play, tells the story of Du Liniang, the daughter of a high official who dreamed of a young scholar she had met. Consumed by her longing for him, she finally pined away. But before she died she buried a portrait of herself in the garden. The young scholar later visited her family again, discovered the painting, and fell in love with her. She appeared to him in a dream, renewing their dream-time love affair, and told him to open her coffin. There she lay alive, as beautiful as ever, his ardour having brought her back to life. After some tribulations, the play ends happily, with the scholar coming first in the examinations and her family welcoming him.

Full-length novels also began to be written in Ming times. The plots of these early novels were heavily indebted to the story cycles developed by oral storytellers who had been performing in urban centres for centuries. Among the greatest Ming novels, all of uncertain authorship, are *The Water Margin* (*Shuihu zhuan*), the story of a band of outlaws in the Song; *The Romance of the Three Kingdoms* (*Sanguo zhi yanyi*), the story of the martial exploits of the rivals for power at the end of the Han; *The Journey to the West* (*Xiyuji*), the fantastic account of a Buddhist pilgrim to India in Tang times, accompanied by a monkey with magical powers; and *Plum in the Golden Vase* (*Jin Ping Mei*), an erotic tale of a lustful merchant and his wife and concubines.

The popularity of vernacular literature in late Ming times had a broad impact on cultural sensibilities. Educated men and women alike seem often to have imitated the actions of fictional characters and judged themselves and others on the standards of purity of feelings they had come to expect in literary characters. Quite a few men and women idealized headstrong romantic attachments to people, things, or causes. Zhang Dai went so far as to claim, 'One cannot befriend a man who has no obsessions, for such a man lacks deep emotion.' Courtesan culture flourished in this environment and a great many poems written by late Ming courtesans have been preserved. Late Ming writers romanticized liaisons between famous courtesans and prominent literati like Chen Zilong, Wu Weiye, Hou Fangyu, and Qian Qianyi. Writers associated courtesans with high aspirations and disappointed hopes, seeing parallels between their own predicaments and those of talented but powerless women waiting for a lover able both to appreciate them and to remove them from their demeaned circumstances.

PHILOSOPHICAL CURRENTS

The affirmation of passion evident in the *Peony Pavilion* and in the romanticization of courtesans was not unconnected to important trends in Ming Confucian thought. During the first half of the Ming, Zhu Xi's synthesis of Confucianism was treated as orthodox by both the state and most scholars. In mid Ming, however, Wang Yangming (Wang Shouren, 1472-1529) challenged Zhu Xi's understandings of metaphysics and the process of self-cultivation and inaugurated a period of wide-ranging intellectual debate.

Wang was an official of some distinction. He had earned a *jinshi* degree at the early age of eighteen and gone on to hold many posts. At one point he courageously submitted a memorial to the throne, protesting against the corrupt behaviour of a powerful eunuch. As a result, he was publicly flogged and banished to remote Guizhou. His most significant challenge to orthodox Confucianism, namely his idea of intuitive moral knowledge, came to him suddenly during this period of exile.

What Wang objected to in Zhu Xi's teachings was his understanding of moral principles as something that could be understood and realized only through careful and rational investigation of events and things, a process which generally required devoting many years to the study of the classics and other books. To Wang Yangming's way of thinking, universal principles existed in every person's mind. People could discover them by clearing their minds of obstructions such as material desires and allowing their inborn knowledge of the good to surface. He also argued that moral action results spontaneously from the extension or realization of knowledge. True knowing, he held, is not abstract intellectualization but is inseparable from experience; one does not understand filial piety if one does

Book illustration

The art of book illustration benefited from the rapid expansion of the publishing industry in Ming times. With nothing like copyright protection, no publisher could be sure another printer would not try to sell the same book. To make their version attractive in this competitive market, publishers more and more frequently hired artists to draw illustrations to be carved on wooden blocks and printed along with the rest of the book. The artistry of these illustrations advanced rapidly as publishers devoted more space to illustrations. By the seventeenth century publishers occasionally even issued books with multi-coloured illustrations. Such colour printing was expensive because it required carving separate blocks for each colour and carefully positioning the blocks and sheets of paper during the separate printing of each colour.

The illustration from a 1640 edition of the *Romance of the Western Chamber* (*Xixiang ji*) (*below*) shows Cui Yingying preparing a letter she will have her maid carry to the young scholar Zhang Gong in response to his many efforts to win her affection.

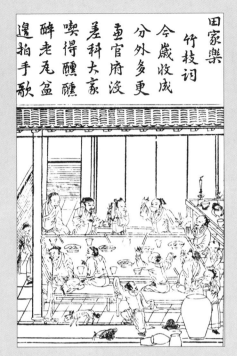

田家樂
竹枝詞

今歲收成
分外多更
重官府沒
差科大家
喫得醺醺
醉老尾盆
邊拍手歌

Illustrations were used to attract readers to many sorts of books. The depiction of farmers celebrating a harvest enlivened the *Pictorial Reference Compendium*, a 1593 manual full of information on agriculture, medicine, cooking, and other practical affairs (*left*). The depiction of the technology of coal mining is from the 1637 *Explications of the Works of Nature* (*Tiangong kaiwu*) (*right*). The scene of mayhem is from a late Ming edition of the popular novel about a gang of bandits/rebels, *Water Margin* (*Shuihu zhuan*) (*lower left*). The illustrated vocabulary lesson comes from a sixteen-page primer, the *Newly Compiled Four Character Glossary* of 1436 (*lower right*).

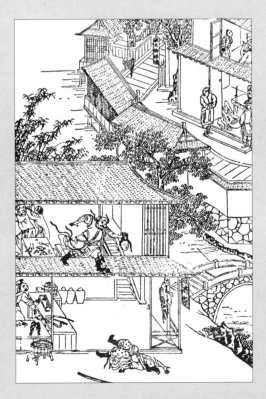

not practise it, any more than one understands pain without experiencing it. Knowing right from wrong leads to taking right action, as one is compelled to act upon what one truly knows.

Because he believed moral knowledge was innate in the mind, it followed for Wang Yangming that sagehood existed inside everyone and that the learned had no special claims to it. Self-cultivation, moreover, could be practised in the midst of everyday affairs. When an official told him that his official duties left him no time to study, Wang said there was no need to abandon his work because 'Real learning can be found in every aspect of record-keeping and legal cases. What is empty is study that is detached from things.' Wang wanted people to concentrate on the fundamental moral truths that even ordinary uneducated people could understand, once asserting that what was truly heterodox was not Buddhism or Daoism but ideas incomprehensible to average people.

Wang Yangming's ideas attracted a lot of notice, and in the century after his death, Wang's followers took Confucian thought in many new directions. Some turned with interest to Buddhism and Daoism. Others questioned the traditional hierarchical arrangement of society, such as the elevation of the scholar–official above the commoner. One of Wang's most enthusiastic followers, Wang Gen, vigorously asserted that social standing did not limit one's possibilities for moral perfection. He gave public lectures to crowds of ordinary people whom he taught to sing that happiness comes from the elimination of selfish desires. Another iconoclast, He Xinyin, proposed that merchants should rank higher than peasants on the social scale and criticized the family as a restrictive, selfish, and exclusive institution. What he exalted instead was friendship which he considered non-hierarchical and unselfish. Li Zhi, a generation later, undertook to rethink the philosophical basis of feelings, passions, and the self, a trend clearly tied to developments in literature. A fierce critic of hypocrisy, Li Zhi saw little if any value in conforming to conventional patterns of behaviour. Both He and Li made many enemies and both died in prison, having been arrested on charges of spreading dangerous ideas.

LOCAL SOCIETY

Continuing trends already apparent in Song times, local society in the Ming period steadily became less isolated. Not only were men like Wang Gen preaching to common people, but the distance between market towns was shrinking, tying villages more tightly into nationwide marketing systems. Moreover, local voluntary organizations, such as schools, descent groups, religious associations, and 'community compacts', were increasing in number and providing more and more opportunities for contact between educated men and local villagers.

Descent groups had been organized or revived sporadically and unevenly since Song times. Patrilineal principles, Confucian esteem for kinship solidarity, the economics of land ownership, and the political value of local allies all offered inducements for kinsmen to join forces. Periods of disorder often stimulated these activities, since strong descent groups could provide local defence. So did the presence of educated men, who often compiled genealogies or built halls for group ancestral rites. Still, descent groups also easily fell apart, for they required continuous leadership to maintain solidarity and joint assets. Broadly speaking, lineages were more common in south China where centuries earlier migrants had often settled in places with enough uncultivated land for many descendants to remain in the vicinity, making for a critical mass of nearby kinsmen. In Fujian, substantial descent groups were quite evident by the twelfth century, as they were in some places in Zhejiang by the next century. In Huizhou in Anhui province, lineages were flourishing in the mid Ming, undoubtedly benefiting from the willingness of the many wealthy local merchant families to make donations. In Tongcheng, as well as in Anhui but north of the Yangzi, lineages were being formed by the late Ming, but merchants played less of a significant role than successful officials who used lineage property and lineage schools as part of their family survival strategies.

By the mid Ming, lineages in some areas of the country were introducing elaborate systems to control and discipline members. In one area of Jiangxi province, for instance, lineages wrote up sets of rules, giving the lineage leaders considerable authority to settle disputes and enforce compliance. The timing of this trend suggests that it was inspired by the concurrent renewal of interest in 'community compacts', a form of local association that had been promoted by scholars in the Song period for the purposes of moral renewal. Members had to agree to correct each other's faults and offer assistance in times of difficulty, with expulsion the sanction for anyone who failed to co-operate. In the mid Ming, Wang Yangming revived the term 'compact' to refer to the organizations he set up as parts of a rebel pacification programme. His followers made even broader use of it as a basis for public preaching to assembled villagers, whom they would urge, in folksy terms, to make a commitment to doing good.

There were sound philosophical reasons for Confucian scholars to undertake these efforts at moral education: if sagehood existed in everyone, everyone could potentially gain a less clouded understanding of right and wrong, and it was worth making the effort to reach them. Self-interest played a part as well. Many people thought that the moral fabric of society was deteriorating, with enmity replacing mutual respect between rich and poor. In the mid sixteenth century the grand secretary Xu Jie reported that landlords and tenants looked on each other as enemies, the peasants refusing to pay their rents, landlords refusing to assist them when harvests failed. Lü Kun, a few decades later, observed that 'when tenants ask for help, the landlords ask for higher interest'. Besides lecturing, literati turned to charitable works as a way to alleviate social tension. At the end of the sixteenth century, for instance, one man set up a Society for Sharing Goodness whose members paid monthly dues into a fund used to support community projects like

The Great Wall

No relic of China's past is more imposing than the Great Wall. Faced with brick and stone and averaging twenty-five feet high and wide, this wall extends about 1,500 miles from its westernmost point at Jiayuguan in modern Gansu province to its easternmost point at Shanhaiguan, near Beijing. Built to keep out invaders, it is dotted with a series of large watch towers. Europeans who first saw the wall wrote home and greatly praised its immense size. The seventeenth century observer Ferdinand Verbiest recorded that 'the seven wonders of the world put together are not comparable to this work; and all Fame hath published concerning it among the Europeans, comes far short of what I myself have seen.' Chinese in the twentieth century have picked up on these ideas, making the Great Wall into a symbol of China's indomitable will.

Closer reading of history reveals that it was the Ming government's siege mentality that led to the wall we see today. Governments from pre-Han times on engaged in the construction of defensive walls. Most famous was the First Emperor of Qin whose costly wall-building was classed as one of his crimes against the Chinese people. But subsequent dynasties did not keep a solid wall in constant repair because walls, even massive ones, did not keep out raiders or invaders and other defence strategies were usually more cost-effective. The Ming rebuilt the wall because it had found no other way to protect against the Mongols. The preferred policy during the first century of Ming rule was to control the Mongols through a combination of offensive attacks and controlled trade carried out under the guise of tribute. This strategy was of limited success, and in 1449 the Mongols won a decisive battle at Tumu, capturing the Ming emperor Yingzong. The Ming chose to instal a new emperor rather than bargain with the Mongols over ransom, but could not agree on how to deal with the Mongol threat. A deadlock between officials who rejected any contact with the Mongols and those who saw increased trade with them as the best solution prevented effective decision-making for decades, allowing the Mongols to grow stronger. No longer financially able to undertake offensive actions, the government resorted to reconstructing the Great Wall instead.

The towers in this heavily fortified section of the Great Wall were intended as signalling stations, to allow rapid warning of the approach of such mobile opponents as the Mongols.

repair of roads and bridges or to provide assistance to families facing heavy expenses for weddings and funerals.

By bringing together the educated and commoners, both community compacts and lineages added to the sharing of ideas, values, assumptions, and frames of reference across class lines. To some extent, the common people were being indoctrinated, but that does not mean that they were necessarily being exploited or pushed into situations detrimental to their interests. Lineages, in particular, were often of genuine benefit to ordinary members who did much to keep them going. An ordinary poor farmer had much to gain from belonging to a group with clout; a neighbour might not make such a fuss about your water buffalo wandering into his field if your kinsmen were known to stick up for you. Even community compacts may have served the practical interests of local residents by expanding their contacts with members of the elite.

RELATIONS WITH THE OUTER WORLD

The second half of the Ming dynasty coincided with the great age of European exploration and the first phase of its expansion. At the beginning of the Ming, however, Europe was not yet a force in Asia, and China could continue to look on the outer world in traditional terms. The early Ming emperors had no desire to return to the multi-state system of the Song; their goal was to reassert Chinese centrality in East Asia on the model of the Han or Tang dynasties. They re-established the tribute system, posited on the moral centrality of the Chinese emperor who received tribute and conferred largesse. Taizu forbade private foreign trade, wanting all exchange to occur through the framework of this tribute system. The third emperor, Chengzu, sent out a series of emissaries to visit potential tributary states. The grandest of these were the overseas voyages of 1405 to 1433, led by one of his most trusted servants, the Muslim eunuch Zheng He. The huge flotilla assembled for the first expedition carried 27,000 men on sixty-two large and 225 small ships, the largest of which was 440 feet long. The first three voyages stopped at places as distant as India. The fourth went further, to Hormuz on the Persian Gulf, and the last three as far as the east coast of Africa. Unlike the European oceanic expeditions later in the fifteenth century, trade and exploration were not the primary motive behind these voyages; their purpose instead was to enroll far-flung states into the Ming tributary system. They were abandoned when court officials persuaded later emperors that they were not cost-efficient.

The tribute system tended to work best for the conduct of relations with small or remote states. The northern frontier zone was harder to confine within its framework. The northern border was porous, with Chinese settled in Mongol territory, Mongols (many of them soldiers in the Ming army) settled inside China, and Chinese garrison troops carrying on surreptitious trade and smuggling with the enemy. Nor did China militarily dominate this border zone. In 1449 an emperor foolishly led an army into Mongol territory, allowing himself to be cap-

Residents of coastal areas often had to take to boats themselves to battle the pirates who attacked their settlements.

tured and many of his courtiers slaughtered. A century later the Ming was no more successful in defending itself against the raids of Altan Khan. In 1542, for instance, in a single month Altan Khan captured or killed 200,000 people, seized a million head of cattle and horses, and reduced several thousand houses to ashes. Because of events like these, in the fifteenth and sixteenth centuries the Ming court invested heavily in reconstruction of the Great Wall.

The tributary system implied paternalistic obligations for China to come to the aid of loyal vassal states, which the Ming government accepted, sometimes at considerable cost. In 1407 the Ming sent troops to Vietnam to support the collapsing Tran dynasty. The situation rapidly deteriorated and the Ming attempted an outright annexation, giving up only in the face of widespread armed resistance. Near the end of the Ming dynasty, China similarly undertook a massive campaign into Korea (1592–98) to defend it against a Japanese invasion led by Hideyoshi. These battles were the first China fought in which muskets played a major role, the Japanese using matchlocks they had copied from the Portuguese.

Despite the naval strength displayed by Zheng He's expeditions, China's maritime frontier came, in Ming times, to cause almost as many defence problems as the northern frontier. By the sixteenth century, official prohibitions against foreign trade ran up against the emergence of an international East Asian maritime community made up of Japanese, Portuguese, Spanish, Dutch, and Chinese merchants and adventurers. In theory, for instance, official relations with Japan were

supposed to be conducted only through the port of Ningbo on the Zhejiang coast, those with the Philippines only through Fuzhou, and those with Indonesia only through Guangzhou. There were in addition limits on the frequency and size of tribute missions; Japanese embassies, for instance, were not to call more than once every ten years and to bring no more than 300 men on two ships. In fact, however, both open and clandestine trade took place all along the Chinese coast. Merchants often turned into smugglers, especially when official obstacles hindered their pursuit of profit. Boats laden with goods attracted pirates, and Japanese and Chinese pirates became a scourge along the coast in the mid sixteenth century, raiding at will anywhere along the coast from northern Shandong to western Guangdong. Ming anti-pirate efforts did not achieve much success until forceful military measures were accompanied by a relaxation of the maritime trade restrictions. Under the new policies, Portugal was allowed to establish a trading base at Macao in 1577, beginning the era of European penetration (discussed more fully in Chapter 9).

In the burgeoning maritime trade, China exported mainly silk and porcelain. Silks included gauzes, crepes, velvets, taffetas, damasks, and brocades, both bolts of cloth and finished garments. In one case a galleon to the Spanish territories in the New World carried over 50,000 pairs of silk stockings. In return China imported mostly silver from Peruvian and Mexican mines, transported via Manila. Chinese merchants were active in these trading ventures, and many emigrated to such places as the Philippines and Borneo to take advantage of the new commercial opportunities.

Besides stimulating the Chinese economy, the expanding maritime trade brought with it new goods and new ideas. New-world plants entered China, including sweet potatoes, maize, and peanuts, foods which facilitated population growth because they could be grown in land previously left uncultivated, such as hilly or sandy soil. European ideas, including scientific ones, began to filter in through Christian missionaries. The first missionary to have much of an impact on China was the Italian Jesuit

A giraffe acquired in Africa during one of Zheng He's voyages of 1405 to 1433 aroused considerable interest at court and lived for several years on the palace grounds. The court painter Shen Du depicted it in this painting dated 1414. The inscription associates this animal with the unicorn (*jilin*), whose appearance was interpreted in ancient texts as a sign of heaven's favour.

Matteo Ricci, who arrived in Macao in 1583. Of the opinion that European missionaries would do best by presenting themselves as men of education rather than as monks, Ricci concentrated his initial efforts on acquiring command of written and spoken Chinese. These skills enabled him to win many influential friends in Beijing, where he lived from 1601 to his death in 1610. Ricci and other Jesuits were accepted in late Ming court circles as foreign literati, regarded as impressive especially for their knowledge of astronomy, calendar-making, mathematics, hydraulics, and geography.

By the end of the Ming, there were Jesuit, Dominican, or Franciscan missions in most of the coastal provinces and even some inland areas. Although quite a few late Ming intellectuals showed an interest in western ideas and knowledge, the obstacles to quick understanding of western philosophy, science, and religion were just as great as the obstacles encountered over a millennium earlier to full understanding of Indian Buddhism. Many educated Chinese were entirely hostile to Christianity, disturbed especially by the missionaries' efforts to convert common people, filling their heads, they thought, with wild, impossible ideas. Even relatively open-minded Chinese found some ideas hard to swallow, such as the dogma that the universe came into being because of the actions of a creator. Christian social teachings also aroused resistance; many scholars could not accept the requirement that they get rid of their concubines in order to convert to Christianity, viewing such an action as callous to both the woman and their children by her.

FACTIONALISM AND POLITICAL PROTEST

Confucianism in the Ming is usually discussed in terms of the ideas of philosophers like Wang Yangming and his followers. This story is generally told as one of increasing openness to ideas of non-Confucian origin, to people of non-literati background, and to people with eccentric tastes or unconventional preferences.

There was another historically important strain of Ming Confucianism, which was, however, much more political and judgmental. Throughout the Ming many officials, imbued with Confucian notions of loyalty to the throne and the responsibility of officials to speak out on matters of principle, courageously protested against bad officials and harmful policies. In 1376 when Taizu asked for criticism of his rule, Ye Boju submitted a memorial that criticized the harsh punishment of officials for minor lapses, noting that many literati considered themselves fortunate not to be summoned to serve. Taizu was so incensed he had Ye brought to the capital in chains where he died of starvation in prison. A few decades later some officials were willing to protest against Chengzu's usurpation of the throne. Among those who suffered the consequences was the leading scholar Fang Xiaoru, executed along with hundreds of relatives, students, neighbours, and friends. In 1519, when Emperor Wuzong announced plans to tour the southern provinces, officials submitted a flood of negative memorials and over a hundred officials staged a protest by kneeling in front of the palace. Outraged, the emperor ordered that as punishment they kneel there for five days, after which he also had them flogged. Eleven eventually died of the beatings. Only a few years later in 1524 hundreds of officials again gathered at the palace gate, this time to protest against the new emperor's refusal to treat the previous emperor as his adoptive father and his plan to reserve the title father for his own deceased father. Unable to bend them to his interpretation of Confucian family ritual, the emperor had 134 imprisoned; sixteen died of the floggings they received.

The last great protest movement of the Ming was as much a factional struggle as an expression of conviction. It had an institutional base in the Donglin Academy, near Wuxi in Jiangsu province, and in the censorate, an organ of the government whose officials had the right and responsibility to speak out against malfeasance and abuse of power. After the Academy was rebuilt in 1604 it became a centre for frustrated ex-officials to discuss the evils besetting the empire. They called for a revival of orthodox Confucian ethics, rejecting the more liberal views of Wang Yangming and Li Zhi. Gu Xiancheng, for instance, claimed that the idea of following naturally the dictates of innate moral knowledge was used by unscrupulous literati as a justification for the greedy pursuit of personal gain. These teachers' zeal inspired younger activist officials in the censorate who labelled themselves men of integrity, the 'good sort', the 'pure current', and called their opponents 'small men', 'deviant officials', and 'cliques'. Officials from both sides impeached each other, accusations and counter-accusations crossing so frequently it is no wonder that emperors wearied of the in-fighting of their officials.

The most dramatic phase of the struggle occurred when the censor Yang Lian submitted a long memorial accusing the eunuch Wei Zhongxian of twenty-four 'great crimes'. The central thrust of Yang's argument was that the young emperor, only eighteen, had ceded his rightful prerogatives to the cruel and power-hungry eunuch. Even though the emperor flatly denied the charge, other censors sent up a flood of memorials supporting Yang Lian, defying the court's warning against such action. Eventually Yang and five others were arrested in highly public ways, crowds gathering along the way to see them carted off to Beijing. All were eventually tortured to death. Other rounds of arrests, tortures, deaths, and protests soon followed.

In protests of these sorts, Confucian officials diagnosed the problems of the dynasty in moral terms. The Confucian tradition celebrated these acts of political protest as heroic – the morally committed individual taking a stand against the abuse of power. There is a negative side to these acts as well, however. The line between heroism and factionalism was not always clear, because so much of the struggle consisted in officials condemning the character or motives of their adversaries. Judging by results rather than motives, the penchant of Ming officials for risking their lives to assert the purity of their cause and the moral turpitude of their opponents may have made it more difficult to find political solutions to the problems of the Ming government.

FISCAL COLLAPSE

Some of the most destructive warfare in Chinese history occurred in the early and mid seventeenth century when the Ming government lacked the capacity either to come to the aid of the indigent or to mount effective campaigns against insurgents and invaders. Despite the expansion in the Chinese economy during the course of the sixteenth century, the government became progressively less solvent, and by the early seventeenth century was nearly bankrupt. The cost of maintaining the imperial clan had got out of hand. In the Wanli reign (1573–1619), there were 23,000 clansmen receiving stipends, and more than half the revenue of the provinces of Shanxi and Henan went to pay these allowances. Military campaigns were also a huge drain; those in Korea against the Japanese, for instance, had cost the treasury twenty-six million ounces of silver.

The decline of Ming finances can be explained in part by reference to the traditional dynastic cycle. Government expenses inevitably increase as the population grows and the bureaucracy becomes less efficient; revenue does not keep up because of long-standing tendencies for peasants to lose their land and rich landlords to find ways to minimize their tax payments. Short of revenue, the government cannot respond effectively to natural disasters, such as those brought on the the early seventeenth century by the 'little ice age', a drop in average temperatures that led to lakes freezing over that had never frozen before in recorded history and a shortening of the growing season, leading to poor harvests. In 1627–8 famine became serious in northern Shaanxi, and soon army deserters and laid-off soldiers were forming gangs and ravaging the countryside. In 1632 they moved east into Shanxi and Hebei and south into Henan and Anhui. The government armies proved unable to destroy these gangs, which kept gaining new adherents. By 1636 two main leaders had emerged, Li Zicheng, a former shepherd and postal relay station worker who was paramount in the north, and Zhang Xianzhong, a former soldier who became paramount in the area between the Yellow and Yangzi rivers. Neither Li nor Zhang gained control of the lower Yangzi, but conditions there were not much better. Tax increases in 1639, followed by floods, drought, locusts, and epidemics took such a toll that hordes of beggars became a common sight. Tenants rose up against landlords, and urban workers rioted. A folk song of the period accused the Lord of Heaven of failing to perform his duties:

> Old Skymaster,
> You're getting on, your ears are deaf, your eyes are gone.
> Can't see people, can't hear words.
> Glory for those who kill and burn;
> For those who fast and read the scriptures,
> Starvation.
> Fall down, old master sky, how can you be so high?
> How can you be so high? Come down to earth.

The fiscal problems at the end of the Ming were in part unprecedented, due to a sudden shutdown in the flow of silver rather than the dynastic cycle. In 1639 the Japanese authorities refused to let traders from Macao into Nagasaki, ending trade that had brought huge quantities of silver into China. A few months later, Sino-Spanish trade in the Philippines came to a virtual standstill when tensions between the Chinese and Spanish in Manila turned bloody, leaving over 20,000 Chinese dead. This cut off China from another major source of silver. The effect on the Chinese domestic economy was rapid deflation, hoarding of the silver that remained, then hoarding of grain, which created artificial famines. Tax defaults became widespread, as did rent riots. In these conditions it became impossible for the government to collect even its usual taxes, much less what it needed to conduct military campaigns.

With rebellion spreading and the Ming government facing bankruptcy, the death toll mounted steadily. In 1642 a group of rebels cut the dykes of the Yellow River, thereby killing several hundred thousand people in the flood and subsequent famine. Epidemics, especially of smallpox, also contributed to a demographic disaster of huge proportions – China's population dropped by several tens of millions during these decades. As the social fabric unravelled, Li Zicheng took hold of Hubei, Henan, and Shaanxi; in 1644 he moved through Shanxi and Hebei into Beijing, where the last Ming emperor, in despair, took his own life. Meanwhile Zhang had moved into Sichuan, where he caused great loss of life in his attacks on Chongqing and Chengdu. Both Li and Zhang announced the establishment of dynasties, setting up governments complete with civil service examinations and coinage, but neither inspired much confidence that orderly life would be soon restored. Looting and violence of all sorts remained pervasive. In the end it took an army from beyond the Great Wall to restore order.

The Ming period is generally judged rather harshly. Since it was the only extended period of native rule over all of China proper from the fall of the Northern Song in 1126 to the fall of the Manchus in 1911, historians wish they could assign more accomplishments or advances to it or at least discover a few heroes.

From the perspective of traditional Confucian statecraft, the Ming government failed to do what a Chinese state should do, namely to manage through a minimum of force the affairs of All-Under-Heaven. The Mongols, the Japanese, the eunuchs, and the flows of revenue were all beyond the government's control. Worse yet, tensions inherent in the Chinese bureaucratic monarchy between arbitrary power and orderly rules, between absolute monarchs and their advisors and surrogates, recurrently reached the point where the government was immobilized. Over the course of Chinese history a few exceptional emperors managed the imperial system with consummate skill, getting officials to perform to the standard set by the throne, neither antagonizing nor demoralizing them, nor letting them take over and serve their own interests. But the Ming offers no such exemplary emperors. Taizu, frustrated by his inability to make the system work as he wanted, fell back on full use of his arbitrary powers. Other Ming emperors delegated these management chores to officials or eunuchs, with highly variable results. A few simply opted out, refusing to let officialdom control them, but not really controlling the situation themselves either.

From a modernist perspective, where the implicit standard is Europe, the Ming does not come off any better. Here the implied charge is not that the Ming state was too weak, but that it was a dead weight, slowing down innovation and entrepreneurship just when some real competition was about to emerge. Precisely when western maritime nations were sending ships into Asia, China was withdrawing from the sea. Just when Europeans were learning to put to good use Chinese technological advances like printing, gunpowder, and the compass, China was letting its scientific and technological leadership slip and forgoing opportunities to take part in the scientific advances beginning to transform European intellectual life.

Probably the only way to view the Ming more positively is to view it from the bottom up. The arbitrary actions of the emperors undoubtedly demeaned the status of high officials and jeopardized their welfare, but they had less impact on villagers and townspeople who were left to run many of their affairs on their own. The Chinese population was growing. Increased commercialization, a growing publishing industry, and increased elite leadership and intervention in local community life were all strengthening ties among this population, giving them a stronger sense of common history and identity. The southwestern region of modern Yunnan and Guizhou was absorbed into the Chinese sphere to a degree never true before. The inability of the government to control everything was not entirely bad, after all. Indeed, if judged in comparative terms, the Ming government's success in managing problems of scale is truly impressive. For over two centuries it maintained a high level of peace among a huge population spread across a subcontinent, using inexpensive forms of motivation like the examination system and imperial exhortations to keep the cost of government down. The magnitude of this accomplishment does not seem insignificant when it is measured against the lawlessness that resulted when it collapsed.

Of the material artefacts surviving from the Ming dynasty, none is appreciated more than the fine porcelains produced in the town of Jingdezhen in northern Jiangxi province. During the Ming dynasty these kilns produced enough porcelain to supply not only the whole country but also much of the rest of the world as well.

Porcelain is distinguished from other types of ceramics by its whiteness, smoothness, and translucence. Producing it requires special clays and high temperature firing (1280–1400°C, 2336–2552°F). The clays were found in particularly pure form near Jingdezhen, which also was favoured with access to forest-covered mountains for fuel and rivers for inexpensive transport.

Imperial patronage led to a rapid increase in the production of high-quality porcelain at Jingdezhen. The palace placed orders for specific wares – in 1551 for 8,400 small pieces and 2,300 large ones; in 1577, the peak year, for 96,500 small pieces, 56,600 large ones, and 21,600 items for use in sacrificial ceremonies. Many of these pieces were destined for use in the palace, others for gifts, including gifts to vassal states in return for their 'tribute gifts'. Imperial quality controls were exacting; archaeologists have discovered huge piles of shards of imperial porcelain that was deliberately broken because they did not meet standards of colour, form, or design, but could not be put on the open market because of their imperial markings.

In the early Ming much of the labour required for these imperial orders was supplied on an unpaid basis by hereditary artisan households who owed no other taxes. Later, labour at imperial kilns and workshops was paid. When large orders came in, however, much of the work would be sub-contracted out to the numerous private workshops and kilns. Mass production techniques were employed at both private and imperial workshops. In other words, potters did not see an object through from the mixing of the clay to the firing and packing; rather there were separate workshops involved in each process, with workers speedily and repetitively performing a single task on a large number of objects. Those who painted on the underglaze designs, for instance, needed to work in very clean quarters, far from those who handled wet clay or chiselled partially dry clay. A French missionary, visiting the kilns in the early eighteenth century, reported watching a cup pass through more than a dozen hands, one worker giving it an initial shaping on a wheel in a matter of seconds, another setting it on a base, another pressing it into a mould to make sure its size was uniform, another polishing it with a chisel, and so on. Altogether, he reported, as many as seventy people could be involved in the production of a single item. Besides high-skilled workers, there were thousands of low-skilled workers employed during the busy summer season who came into town from nearby counties. In 1601 10,000 workers rioted to protest against the demands for increased production of the eunuch director of the imperial works; in 1604 rioters demanded higher wages from the merchants who controlled much of the business.

Jingdezhen produced porcelain in many shapes and designs but became particularly noted for its pieces decorated in blue underglaze and polychrome enamels. These highly decorative pieces were in immense demand outside China, in Japan, Southeast Asia, West Asia, and eventually Europe. Thus when imperial orders declined in the early seventeenth century when the court had to devote all its revenues to defence and other urgent matters, the ceramic industry was able to survive by responding to the preferences of foreign markets. The cult of tea in Japan led to a huge market for all sorts of small dishes, cups, and bowls. Europeans sought dinner services, especially after 1604 when two Portuguese ships were captured by the Dutch and their cargoes of 200,000-odd pieces of Chinese porcelain were put up

In 1743 Tang Ying, the director of the imperial kilns, wrote explanations of a set of paintings illustrating the steps in producing porcelain. The paintings have not survived, but his descriptions largely match a somewhat later set of wood block illustrations. He described the division of labour employed in the application of the decoration to large sets of dishes as follows: 'If the painted decoration on each piece is not exactly alike, the set will be irregular and spoiled. For this reason the men who sketch the outlines learn sketching but not painting; those who paint study only painting, no sketching; by this means their hands acquire skill in their own speciality and their minds are not distracted. In order to secure a certain uniformity in their work, the sketchers and painters, although kept distinct, occupy the same house.'

for sale, attracting bidders from all over Europe, including agents for Henri IV of France, James I of England, and the Grand Duke of Tuscany. Over the next two centuries exports to Europe were huge. Between 1602 and 1682 the Dutch East India Company imported about twelve million pieces of polychrome Chinese porcelain (not including the more common blue-and-white wares). By the eighteenth century European traders often commissioned specific designs, sending samples to China for potters to copy.

In Europe, Chinese porcelain was used for both table service and decoration. Depicted here is the ceiling of the 'porcelain room' in the Santos Palace in Lisbon, which in the late seventeenth century was covered with 260 Chinese plates and bowls dating from 1500 on, the time the kings of Portugal had begun collecting Chinese porcelain.

Opposite
The decoration of the fine porcelains produced at Jingdezhen shows extraordinary inventiveness in pattern and motif. These pieces, ranging from the fourteenth to the seventeenth centuries in date, include pictures of dragons, birds, fish, and children at play.

Narrative scenes were not uncommon on Jingdezhen porcelains. Depicted on this one is the widow Li, recorded in history for her remarkable commitment to chastity: she cut off her hand after it was grabbed by an innkeeper who did not want her and her son, both in deep mourning, inside his inn.

CHAPTER 9

Manchus and Imperialism:
The Qing Dynasty 1644–1900

After the Ming collapsed, a new dynasty was founded not by a warlord or rebel leader but by the chieftains of the Manchus, a non-Chinese people living in the hilly forests and plains to the northeast of China proper. Although Chinese elites and commoners in many parts of the country put up a determined resistance to Manchu rule, within a generation Chinese were co-operating with the new rulers. The three Manchus who ruled in the course of the eighteenth century – Kangxi, Yongzheng, and Qianlong – proved excellent managers, and by many measures that century was the high point of traditional Chinese civilization. Over the course of the nineteenth century, however, China's place in the world plummeted. By the end of the century, China was derided abroad as pathetic; its size seemed a burden and its form of government seemed woefully inadequate to the needs of the time. Although China did not suffer outright colonization or dismemberment, after its defeat by the British in the Opium War of 1840 to 1842, western nations posed more and more of a threat to China as a polity and a civilization. Western merchants sold manufactured goods that competed with Chinese industries; their missionaries competed with the Chinese literati for moral and religious leadership in the countryside; and their armies and navies repeatedly proved themselves superior to China's, raising fundamental questions about what, if anything, China should copy from these aggressive foreigners.

MANCHU RULE

The Manchus were not nomadic horsemen like the Mongols, living on the open steppe and engaging in near constant warfare to defend and augment their herds. Rather they were a hunting, fishing, and farming people of central Manchuria (Heilongjiang and Jilin provinces), east of Mongolia and northeast of the eastern end of the Great Wall. They believed themselves to be descended from the Jurchen who had ruled north China as the Jin dynasty, contemporaneous with the Southern Song. In Ming times several different Manchu tribal groups had participated in the Ming tribute system. Many Manchus had settled to the south in the Liaodong peninsula, where they lived among Chinese villagers and townsmen; some served as soldiers of the Ming, others as farmers or traders in furs, horses, and other goods.

The creation of a Manchu state was accomplished by Nurhaci (1559–1616) over a period of thirty years. The entire population under his control was enrolled in four military units, each identified by a coloured banner. Eventually the number of Manchu 'banners' was increased to eight, and eight Mongol and eight Chinese banners were established as well. This shift from tribal toward bureaucratic organization was aided by the creation of a script for writing in Manchu (based on the Mongolian alphabet); translations of the Ming law code and other basic Chinese books into this script further aided the adoption of administrative practices modelled on Chinese experience. In 1616, as conditions in Ming China were deteriorating, Nurhaci renounced fealty to the Ming, and two years later he attacked Ming territory in the Liaodong area. He promised opportunities to serve in his government to officials and officers who surrendered. He did not make service optional for the craftsmen needed by his army – especially ones with knowledge of artillery – or for the farmers he forced to produce food for the troops. All men in the areas he subjugated were ordered to adopt the Manchu hairstyle, which involved shaving the fronts of their foreheads and braiding the rest of their hair into a long plait or queue. When the Chinese in Liaodong rebelled in 1622 and again in 1625, the Manchus responded by executing many of the educated, who were suspected of having fomented dissatisfaction, and by instituting stricter separation of Chinese and Manchus. Manchus were henceforth required to stay in their own sections of the towns and to carry arms at all times, while possession of weapons by Chinese was declared illegal.

Nurhaci's successor, his eighth son Hong Taiji (r. 1626–1643), went further in adapting Chinese institutions and made increasing use of Chinese subordinates. Ming generals began to defect with their armies, and Mongols also joined in large numbers. After ten years of successful expansion of his domain, Hong Taiji declared the establishment of the Qing ('pure') dynasty, implicitly staking a claim to sovereignty over China.

The key advantage the Manchus had over Chinese rebels like Li Zicheng was that they were able to build up a state structure outside the Great Wall, largely beyond the reach of the Ming government and army. By the time the Manchus crossed the wall and competed for the throne of China, they had a much stronger military and administrative machinery than any contender in China. In 1644, after the Ming emperor in Beijing committed suicide and the armies of the rebel Li Zicheng sacked the city, prospects for reattaining order seemed better with the Manchus than with the rebels – at least to the general Wu Sangui, who was charged with guarding the easternmost pass of the Great Wall. Working with Wu and other Ming generals, the Manchus crossed the wall, defeated the rebels, and rid north China of bandits.

Ming generals had wanted the Manchus to play the time-honoured role of barbarian auxiliaries, but the Manchus quickly showed they intended to rule the country themselves. In Beijing they forced all Chinese to move into the southern part of the city. They got rid of most of the eunuchs, assigning many of the tasks eunuchs had performed instead to Chinese they had enslaved years earlier in Liaodong. Like the Mongols before them, the Manchus confiscated hundreds of thousands of acres of farmland in north China to support their huge armies, some of which had been Ming imperial land, but much of which had been in private

Maintaining the dykes on the Yellow River required periodically calling up large levies of labourers. Inspecting dyke work also provided an excuse for the emperor Kangxi to make several tours of the provinces.

hands. Some of this land was assigned to Manchu noblemen and imperial clans-men, while the rest was divided up among the banners for their support. All men, of whatever rank and station, had to show their submission through their hair: in 1645 it was decreed that any man who did not cut his hair and start a queue within ten days would be executed. This tonsure decree allowed the conquerors to tell at a glance who had acquiesced to their rule and who persisted in resisting. Chinese felt humiliated by the order, but most saw no alternative to obeying.

Opposition soon concentrated on keeping the Manchus from penetrating south of the Yangzi, but none of the Ming loyalist courts proved any more com-petent than the court in Beijing. The Manchus offered the southern gentry peace and stability, and threatened them with awful destruction – like the massacre at Yangzhou, where the Manchus slaughtered thousands. Even with the assistance of

The Qing dynasty expanded the territorial reach of the Chi-nese state to its maximal dimensions. Areas not settled primarily by Chinese, how-ever, were given considerable autonomy to manage their own affairs. Suppressing uprisings in such a far-flung empire proved very taxing for the Qing government, espe-cially in the nineteenth century when they occurred with increasing frequency.

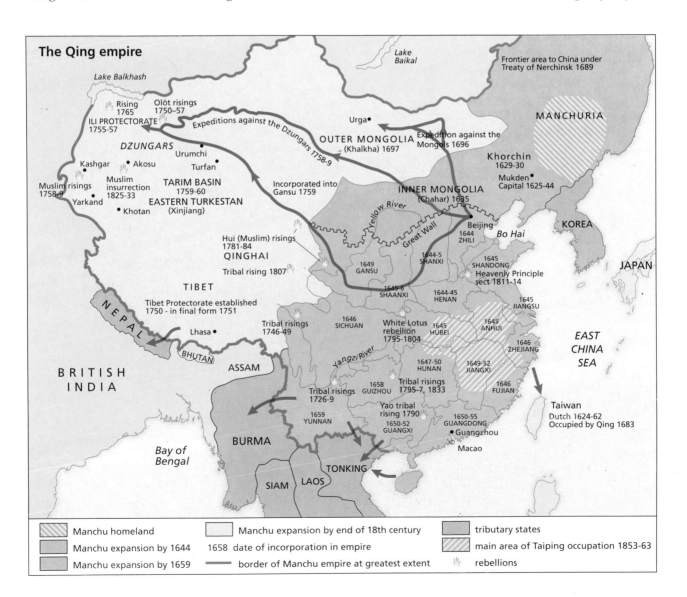

former Ming generals like Wu Sangui, it took fifteen years to subdue the south. In 1662, finally, Wu hunted down the last Ming pretender in Burma. There was one major attempt to throw off Qing rule – led by Wu Sangui himself in 1673. Wu's past as a collaborator made it difficult for him to rally the full support of Ming loyalists, and after several years of bloody fighting, the rebellion was suppressed and the Manchus were in firm control of all of China proper.

KANGXI, YONGZHENG, AND QIANLONG

From 1669, when Kangxi (r. 1662–1722) reached the age of fifteen and assumed rule himself, until 1799, when Qianlong died (r. 1736–95), China was ruled by only three emperors. The stability Europeans saw in China in this period is probably due to the exceptional longevity of Kangxi and his grandson Qianlong, each of whom ruled no less than sixty years. By the standards of the Ming, all three of these rulers were outstanding managers, willing to work hard at the art of governing, to temper the exercise of arbitrary power and concentrate on developing routine, institutional ways to solve the daily problems of raising revenue, keeping officials in line, and maintaining peace. During their reigns the Manchus won over the Chinese gentry by restoring social order and reconfirming the gentry's place in Chinese society. Looking at these emperors' accomplishments one could almost argue that Chinese political institutions survived the Ming crisis only because new leadership was brought in, leadership committed to the Chinese form of government but capable of instituting tighter discipline and doing away with much of what did not work. The fact that these rulers were not Chinese made it easier for them to break with longstanding but often paralysing patterns of court politics.

All three of these Manchu rulers presented themselves as both protectors of China's cultural heritage and at the same time Manchu military leaders. Kangxi was an active man who loved to go on hunting expeditions and take tours of the provinces (ostensibly to inspect rivers and water control projects). The extension of the Manchu's military positions along the borders with Russia, Mongolia, and Tibet were a source of great pleasure for him. He patronized the Chinese literati and made efforts to induce prominent scholars to join the government, but also saw to it that bannermen dominated the government; each of the six boards was to have both a Chinese and a Manchu minister, and half the grand secretaries were to be Manchus. Regular provincial posts went mostly to Chinese, but the higher supervisory level, the governor-general positions, were filled by Manchus.

Kangxi not only gained familiarity with Chinese literati culture, but also became intrigued by Western mathematics, science, and mechanical devices. He was hospitable to the Jesuit missionaries at court, and appointed Jesuits to direct the Imperial board of Astronomy when their predictions proved more accurate than calculations made by their Chinese counterparts. In 1692 he issued an edict tolerating Christianity so long as converts continued to perform ancestral rites, a position that matched Matteo Ricci's view that ancestral rites were commemoration, not worship. He reversed his position, however, after the Vatican sent a legate, Maillard de Tournon, who after several meetings with Kangxi, ruled against permitting ancestral rites, siding with other Catholic orders against the Jesuits. De Tournon moreover insisted on papal authority over missionaries and their converts in China, to be exercised by a papal nuncio resident in Beijing. Kangxi responded by ordering the expulsion of missionaries who would not support his stance.

Kangxi's heir Yongzheng (r. 1722–36), already forty-five when he ascended the throne, proved a hardworking emperor, able to curb the military power of the Manchu aristocracy and tighten central control over the civil bureaucracy. He put particular effort into trying to set state finances on a sound footing, substituting new public levies for the patchwork of taxes and fees inherited from the Ming. Another step toward uniformity and rationalization was his decree forbidding any sort of hereditary servile status, which legally emancipated members of various local demeaned castes.

Qianlong, Yongzheng's fourth son, benefited from his father's fiscal reforms, and during his long reign the government regularly ran a large surplus. Much of Qianlong's own energies were put into making sure he went down in history as a sage emperor, exemplifying both Chinese and Manchu ideals. From dawn until afternoon he tended to affairs of the state, after which he would read, paint, or write. He made many displays of his filial devotion to his mother, visiting her daily and attending to her every comfort. Far from an outstanding poet, Qianlong nevertheless published over 42,000 poems under his name and freely inscribed his own poetry on hundreds of masterpieces of painting and calligraphy in the palace collection he had amassed. His concern with preserving Manchu identity led him similarly to patronize projects that glorified Manchu history and culture, such as the compilation of dictionaries, histories, and genealogies.

There was, however, a darker side to the Qianlong emperor. Any hint of anti-Manchu activity brought quick and forceful action. When rumours reached him in 1768 that sorcerers were 'stealing souls' by clipping the tips of queues, he was quick to suspect seditious conspiracy and pushed his officials so hard that their interrogations under torture turned up more and more evidence implicating people in several provinces of complicity in a non-existent plot. A few years later Qianlong orchestrated a huge literary inquisition. Thousands of books collected for a worthy bibliographic project (the *Complete Books of the Four Treasuries*) were scrutinized for slighting references to the Manchus or previous alien conquerors and all copies of offending books were ordered destroyed. So thoroughly was this proscription carried out that no copies have been recovered of over 2,000 titles.

After he reached the age of sixty-five, Qianlong's political judgment began to falter. He was taken with a handsome and intelligent twenty-five-year-old imperial bodyguard named Heshen. Before long he promoted Heshen to posts normally

The Manchus cultivated an image of themselves as tough warriors. One hundred portraits of the emperor Qianlong's bodyguards, including this silk hanging scroll painted in 1760, decorated the palace hall where state banquets were held.

held by the most experienced officials, including ones controlling revenue and civil service appointments. Officials began to suspect Qianlong was senile, as he did nothing to curb Heshen's blatant corruption. The extent of Heshen's abuse of power was corroborated after Qianlong's death, when his successor had Heshen executed and confiscated his property, assessed at 800 million ounces of silver.

TERRITORIAL EXPANSION

It was during the century and a half of Kangxi, Yongzheng, and Qianlong that Greater China – the multi-ethnic territory controlled by the Chinese state today – was staked out. Taiwan, Chinese Central Asia, Mongolia, and Tibet were all attached to China proper to form a single polity.

The large island of Taiwan was acquired in 1683. Populated by indigenous peoples who spoke a language related to languages spoken much further south in Indonesia, Taiwan had attracted Portuguese and then Dutch traders since early in the century, as well as Ming loyalists in the 1640s and 1650s. In 1662 Zheng Chenggong (known in the west as Koxinga), a pirate and trader who had taken on the Ming cause, attacked Taiwan and drove out the Dutch. For the next two decades, while Taiwan was under the control of his sons and grandsons, over 100,000 Chinese emigrated there, creating a booming frontier community. Finally the Qing sent a naval expedition to defeat these forces and made Taiwan a prefecture of Fujian province.

More territory was added in the interior as the Manchus worked at subduing the Mongols. The Qing forces were equipped with cannons and other modern weapons, giving them military superiority over nomads armed only with bows and arrows, allowing them to dominate the steppe cheaply, effectively ending 2,000 years of defence problems. The Manchus conquered the Eastern Mongols in the 1630s and subdued the Western (Dzungar) Mongols in 1696. These Dzungar Mongols still held the Islamic cities in modern Xinjiang province, and tried to expand their territory into Tibet, invading it in 1717. The Qing responded by invading Tibet themselves, taking Lhasa in 1720. Tibet was made a protectorate and a permanent Manchu garrison was established there. Previously Tibet (like Korea and other neighbouring states) had acquiesced to tributary status but had not had troops or governors from China proper stationed in its territory. Still, the Qing interfered relatively little in Tibetan affairs, allowing local leaders to do most of the actual governing.

Chinese Central Asia (modern Xinjiang province) had had Chinese troops stationed there in the Han and Tang dynasties, but not during the Song or Ming dynasties. The Qing acquired the region in the 1750s when their armies defeated the Dzungar Mongols and Uighurs in a series of campaigns. Like Tibet, these largely Muslim areas were ruled rather lightly. The local population was allowed to keep their own religious leaders, follow their own dietary rules, and not wear the queue. Qing expansion into Central Asia brought China into contact with the

Opposite
Not one to do things in a small way, the Qianlong emperor spent over twenty million ounces of silver on his six tours of the south (1751, 1757, 1762, 1765, 1780, 1784). For many of his subjects it was their one opportunity to gain a glimmer of the pomp surrounding the imperial institution. This detail is from a set of twenty-six handscrolls in colour on paper, altogether 500 feet long, painted by the court artist Xu Yang to commemorate the nearly four-month tour in 1751 through Hebei, Shandong, Jiangsu, and Zhejiang provinces.

海晏堂西面十

The emperor Qianlong, an admirer of European painting and clocks, decided to test out European architecture as well and had the Italian missionary painter Castiglione (1688–1768) design for him a new Summer Palace. Qianlong used the new palace mostly as a storehouse for his growing collection of European objects, and in 1783 commissioned a set of copperplate engravings of its buildings and grounds, one of which is shown here. In 1860 the palace was burned by British and French troops, but the ruins remain open to visitors today.

Russians, also expanding into the same territory. To the Chinese, the Russians were another Central Asian confederation, to be treated circumspectly, since so many powerful states had been founded to China's north and west. Treaties with them were signed in 1689 and 1728 that ignored the conventions of the tribute system, discussed in Chapter 8.

In the nineteenth century Russia steadily acquired more and more territory in Central Asia, taking Samarkand, Tashkent, and Bokhara in 1865–68, arousing fears in the British that Russia might threaten its interests in India. For a while it seemed that China was in danger of losing its claims in the area. The British supported the local leader Yakub Beg when he declared the establishment of an independent state in Kashgar 1870. The Russians seized the Ili valley in 1871. Yet the Chinese were eventually able to reassert military supremacy in the region, in large part because Russia and Britain felt more threatened by each other's expansion than by China. In 1884 the region was made a regular province of China with the name 'New Territory' (Xinjiang).

CULTURE AND SOCIETY

Chinese culture took a conservative turn during the Qing period. This complex phenomenon had philosophical, political, social, and probably even economic roots. The collapse of social order in the late Ming and the Manchu conquest seemed to many irrefutable evidence that the more open and fluid society emerging in late Ming was profoundly dangerous. As population increase outpaced the growth of resources (not only at the level of the farmer but also at the level of the educated elite, since the number of examination degrees was fixed) and society became more competitive, those who felt their position jeopardized favoured the imposition of rules and norms supportive of traditional social hierarchy. The impulse for this conservative turn came from within Chinese society, but the Manchu rulers had nothing against it, since they themselves were inclined toward a more disciplined social style and were content to see the Ming condemned as a degenerate dynasty the world was better off without.

This conservative reaction was manifested in many ways. Laws against behaviour deemed deviant, such as homosexuality, became much harsher. Many literati turned against drama and fiction as socially subversive or licentious. Official injunctions were issued with some frequency banning novels and plays or ordering theatres closed. The highly learned Qian Daxin went so far as to condemn vernacular novels as the main threat to Confucian orthodoxy. Concern for the purity of women reached an all-time high. There was a staggering increase in the number of recorded cases of faithful widows who refused to remarry, and engaged teenagers who spent their lives as celibate 'widows' of men who died before they had even met. The local history of one Jiangnan prefecture, for example, records four faithful widows in the Song, ninety-five in the Ming, and 203 by the mid Qing. Construction of memorial arches to honour faithful widows got so out of hand that in 1827 the government decreed that only collective arches could be built and in 1843 that only widows who had gone to the extreme of committing suicide should be honoured by arches. Literati competed among themselves to bring attention to the virtues of the women in their families or communities; they also took practical measures to encourage widow chastity, such as the establishment of group homes for impoverished widows where visits by men would be strictly limited.

These stern and strict views of socially acceptable behaviour were not unrelated to intellectual trends. Many Confucian scholars concluded that the Ming fell as the result of moral laxness: they thought Wang Yangming and his followers, by lauding spontaneity and emotion, had undermined commitment to duty; then because the educated abandoned their obligation to provide ethical leadership, the common people understandably lost their respect for authority. These scholars saw a solution to laxness in the reassertion of Zhu Xi's teachings, with their emphasis on objective standards outside the individual.

As the Qing progressed, the search for norms and certainty led some scholars to turn their attention to earlier and earlier texts. Many Confucians turned to the Han commentaries in the hope that they could free their understandings of the classics from the contamination of Buddhist and Daoist ideas. Some became absorbed in close textual analysis of the earliest texts, trying to sort out genuine ancient texts from later accretions. Yan Ruoju, for instance, compiled a guide to the placenames in the Four Books and proved conclusively that the 'old text' ver-

Memorial arches honouring chaste widows were erected throughout the country during the Qing period. Shown here are some still standing in She county, Anhui province.

sion of the *Book of Documents* could not be genuine. Such 'evidential' research required access to large libraries, making it the speciality of scholars in the wealthy lower Yangzi region, with its concentration of academies and private libraries. Even in the world of art, recovering and re-embodying the best of the past became a central concern of most painters and calligraphers. Collecting rubbings of old inscribed stones became a passion, as Qing scholars assiduously modelled their calligraphy on rubbings of Han dynasty inscriptions.

The overall conservative direction of Qing cultural change did not prevent creative innovations on the part of many exceptional individuals. During the Ming–Qing transition some of the most probing minds looked for the institutional roots of China's crisis. Huang Zongxi, a committed Ming loyalist, reconsidered many basic tenets of Chinese political order, coming to the conclusion that the problems were not minor ones, like inadequate supervision of eunuchs, but much more major ones, such as the emperor having too much power. Equally probing were the political and historical analyses written by Gu Yanwu, who travelled across north China to gain a better grasp of such economic issues as banking, mining, and farming. Moreover, even those who participated in fairly conservative literati circles could be personally open to unconventional ideas. The eighteenth-century poet Yuan Mei, for instance, was on familiar terms with the great classicists and philologists of his day but was willing to risk their censure by taking on women as poetry students. Even more powerful evidence that Chinese civilization had not grown too rigid for creative growth is the appearance near the end of the eighteenth century of one of the masterpieces of world literature, the novel *Dream of Red Mansions* (*Honglou meng*).

It is perhaps in the world of painting that departure from convention – even cultivation of eccentricity – was given the most room to flourish. During the Ming–Qing transition Zhu Da and Shi Tao, both members of the vast Ming imperial clan, ended up taking on the persona of Buddhist monks to avoid having to get involved with the new government. Zhu Da resolved to stop talking after the Manchus took the throne. His paintings of birds, fish, rocks, and mountains evoke the sense of crazy, creative energy that he apparently also conveyed to those who

The painter Zhu Da (also known as Bada Shanren, 1616–1705), a Ming imperial clansman who refused to co-operate with the Qing, developed a highly expressionistic style, making the most of sparse, wet strokes. The inscription on this page from a 22-leaf album painted in 1694 for a friend says, 'After spending all day chatting we feel like two birds – Yellow Gold and White Sun – kept in captivity for imperial hunts.'

Dream of Red Mansions

The greatest masterpiece of traditional Chinese fiction is the *Dream of Red Mansions*, a 120-chapter novel conceived and substantially written by Cao Xueqin (1715–64). As a work of literature, the novel can be read on many levels: as a mythic story on the Buddhist themes of attachment and enlightenment, as a psychologically realistic autobiographical novel, or as a novel of manners chronicling the mores of the upper reaches of Chinese and Manchu society in the eighteenth century.

Cao Xueqin came from a Chinese family that had risen to great power and wealth as bondservants of the Manchus in

the seventeenth century but lost favour and went bankrupt in the eighteenth century. The *Dream of Red Mansions* portrays in magnificent detail the affairs of the comparably wealthy, imperially favoured Jia family. The central characters are three adolescent relatives: Jia Baoyu and his two female cousins, the sickly, difficult Lin Daiyu, and the capable, cheerful Xue Baochai, both of whom come to live with his family. An idyllic period in which the three get to live in a splendid garden and amuse themselves with literature is brought to an end when Baoyu is tricked into marrying Baochai and Daiyu dies after learning of the deceit. The

novel ends with Baoyu passing the highest level of the civil service exams as his father wanted, then leaving his new wife and crumbling family to seek religious goals.

Since it was first published in 1791, the *Dream of Red Mansions* has entranced readers with its numerous subplots and a host of minor characters from all walks of life. The seamier side of political life is portrayed through memorable cases of miscarriage of justice. The machinations of family politics are just as vividly captured through numerous incidents in which family members compete for advantage. The *Dream of Red Mansions* is especially celebrated for its sensi-

tive depictions of female characters, not merely the two main heroines, but also Baoyu's grandmother, mother, sister, sisters-in-law, and the dozens of maids with whom they reside.

In the scene given below, the well-educated and sensitive Lin Daiyu is alone in the garden:

> With Baoyu gone and the girls evidently all out, Daiyu began to feel lonely and depressed. She was on her way back to her own room and was just passing by the corner of Pear Tree Court when she heard the languorous mean-

derings of a flute and the sweet modulations of a girlish voice coming from the other side of the wall, and knew that the twelve little actresses were at their rehearsal inside. Although she was paying no particular attention to the singing, a snatch of it suddenly chanced to fall with very great clarity on her ear, so that she was able to make out quite distinctly the words of two whole lines of the aria being sung:

'Here multiflorate splendour blooms forlorn
Midst broken fountains, mouldering walls–'

They moved her strangely, and she stopped to listen. The voice went on.

'and the bright air, the brilliant morn

Above and opposite The *Dream of Red Mansions* shaped notions of the ideal young woman as sensitive, elegant, and delicate. These paintings of characters in the *Dream* were done by the woman painter Xu Bao (b. 1810).

Feed my despair.
Joy and gladness have withdrawn
To other gardens, other halls –'

At this point the listener unconsciously nodded her head and sighed.

'It's true,' she thought, 'there is good poetry even in plays. What a pity most people think of them only as entertainment. A lot of the real beauty in them must go unappreciated.'

She suddenly became aware that her mind was wandering and regretted that her inattention had caused her to miss some of the singing. She listened again. This time it was another voice:

'Because for you, my flowerlike fair,
The swift years like the waters flow –'

The words moved her to the depth of her being.

'I have sought you everywhere,
And at last I find you here,
In a dark room full of woe –'

It was like intoxication, a sort of delirium. Her legs would no longer support her. She collapsed on to a nearby rockery and crouched there, the words turning over and over in her mind:

'Because for you, my flowerlike fair,
The swift years like the waters flow ...'

Suddenly she thought of a line from an old poem she had read quite recently:

'Relentlessly the waters flow, the flowers fade.'

From that her mind turned to those famous lines written in his captivity by the tragic poet-emperor of later Tang:

'The blossoms fall, the waters flow,
The glory of the spring is done
In nature's world as in the human one –'

and to some lines from *The Western Chamber*, which she had just been reading:

'As flowers fall and the flowing stream runs red,
A thousand sickly fancies crowd the mind.'

As these different lines and verses combined into a single overpowering impression, riving her soul with a pang of such keen anguish that the tears started from her eyes, she might have remained there indefinitely, weeping and comfortless, had not someone just at that moment come up behind her and tapped her on the shoulder.

European-style buildings began to appear in Guangzhou in the eighteenth century in the restricted district where the foreign merchants were allowed to arrange for the loading and unloading of their ships.

met him as he wandered across China. Shi Tao was more sociable but no less expressive in his paintings. In the eighteenth century Shi Tao's style inspired much of the best of the individualist painters conventionally labelled the Yangzhou Eccentrics.

MARITIME TRADE AND RELATIONS WITH EUROPEAN NATIONS

The balance of world power slowly shifted in the eighteenth century without anyone in China taking much notice. Until 1700 China's material culture had been unrivalled; its standard of living was among the best in the world, and inventions flowed more commonly from east to west than vice versa. Yet by the nineteenth century, China found itself outmatched in material and technological resources by western nations.

Europeans had been coming to trade at south Chinese ports since the late Ming. Spain and Portugal had been the main European traders in the sixteenth century, their place taken by the Dutch in the seventeenth century and the English in the eighteenth. During the eighteenth century the trade between China and England was handled mostly by government-recognized monopolies, on the English side the British East India Company, a joint-stock company, and on the Chinese side the Co-hong, the official merchant guild in Guangzhou (Canton), after

1759 the only city in which Europeans were allowed to trade. To keep the foreigners from disrupting Chinese society in this city, they were obligated to reside in a special quarter and stay only as long as business required. After a few weeks in their 'factories' (office and warehouse buildings) the Europeans would go to the Portuguese colony of Macao, some residing there permanently, others waiting only until the winds changed so that they could return to India or Europe.

The demand for Chinese silk and porcelain remained strong, and a new taste for tea developed. Over the course of the eighteenth century British demand for tea increased exponentially. From five chests in 1684, English imports of tea rose to 400,000 pounds by 1720, then grew over fiftyfold to reach twenty-three million pounds in 1800. By this point the British were purchasing about a seventh of the tea sold in China and deriving a tenth of their state revenue from the import tax on tea. The flow of silver into China rose from about three million ounces of silver per year in the 1760s to sixteen million in the 1780s.

In this same period European estimation of China and Chinese culture gradually grew less rosy. The seventeenth-century Jesuit missionaries had sent back admiring accounts of the laws and customs of China, undoubtedly putting their emphasis on the positive to encourage financial support for their endeavours. Voltaire later drew on their writings to portray China as a remarkable civilization based on ethics instead of religion and thus free from the domination of a church. It was not long, however, before other Europeans, including the philosophers Montesquieu, Rousseau, and Hegel, were describing China as inferior to Europe because neither liberty nor progress was valued there. They contrasted China's antiquity with the modernity of Europe.

This shift in attitudes and the concurrent emergence of Britain as a major military power led British merchants and the British government to begin demanding change in the way they traded with China. To improve their profits and their balance of payments, the British wanted to create a market for their goods in China and get tea cheaper by trading closer to its source in the Yangzi river provinces. They also wanted China to abandon the tributary system and deal with other nations through envoys, ambassadors, commercial treaties, and published tariffs, in the way that European nations dealt with each other. In 1793 the distinguished Lord George Macartney, a cousin of the king and former ambassador to Russia as well as governor of Madras, was sent as an envoy to Qianlong, charged with making headway on these goals. He brought a retinue of eighty-four, including scientists, musicians, artists, and Chinese-language teachers, and 600 cases packed with scientific instruments, carpets, woollens, knives, plate glass and other gifts intended to attract Chinese interest in British manufactured goods. Macartney had trouble getting received since he refused to perform the kowtow (a formal bow that involved kneeling and touching the forehead to the floor), but in the end was allowed to see Qianlong at his summer retreat in Rehe. Macartney sized up the Chinese more accurately than Qianlong sized up the British. Macartney reported that the Chinese were ill-prepared for war with European powers as poverty was widespread, the literati were not interested in material progress, and soldiers still used bows and arrows. Qianlong, for his part, could see no merit in the British request for a permanent envoy in Beijing, remarking that there were too many nations in Europe to allow each an envoy. Moreover, even though the government derived important revenue from taxes on maritime commerce, Qianlong saw no real use to trade. 'We possess all things,' he wrote in a letter to the king of England. 'I set no value on objects strange or ingenious, and have no use for your country's manufactures.'

OPIUM AND THE OPIUM WAR

It would be tedious to relate all of the military encounters between China and Western powers over the course of the nineteenth century and the penalties China suffered in consequence. The first of these encounters, the Opium War of 1840–42, is, however, worth recounting because it set the tone for those to follow and came to carry great symbolic weight in China. In Chinese eyes there could not have been a more blatant case of international bullying, of the morally repugnant imposing their will on those trying to do the right thing. This moral dimension in turn made it that much more difficult for Chinese to discern in western civilization anything worth adopting.

The rise of Britain as a great naval power dependent on foreign trade probably made conflict with China inevitable, since China had no desire to organize trade on the European model and Britain had the power to force acceptance of its terms. The specific circumstances of the conflict, however, were tied up with trade in the narcotic opium. Opium, a derivative of the poppy, had long been used in China for medicinal purposes, such as control of diarrhoea. In the seventeenth century the practice of smoking opium in combination with tobacco spread from southeast Asia. In the eighteenth century a way was found to smoke pure opium sap in a pipe. Soon people were smoking opium simply for its narcotic effects: it relieved both physical and emotional pain and made tedious or physically taxing work seem less onerous. But opium was addictive; withdrawal symptoms included severe cramps, muscle twitching, chills, and nausea.

Following the British conquest of large parts of India, the British invested massively in the manufacture and distribution of opium, seeing its sale as a way to solve the problem of their balance of payments with China. The East India Company controlled the sale of opium in India and licensed private traders to ship it to China. Beginning with only 200 chests of opium in 1729, imports had passed 1,000 chests in 1767 and 4,500 by 1800. During the next quarter century imports more than doubled to 10,000 chests, then quadrupled to 40,000 in 1838.

The Chinese authorities were well aware of the evils caused by opium smoking. By the early nineteenth century addicts included government clerks and runners as well as imperial clansmen and eunuchs at court. To fight the spread of addiction, in 1800 both importation and domestic production were banned. In 1813 smoking opium was outlawed, made punishable by 100 blows and wearing the 'cangue' (a heavy wooden collar) for a month. Open trading then disappeared but the British and other traders managed to stay clear of the Chinese authorities by docking their boats off the coast of Guangdong and selling the drug to Chinese smugglers who would distribute it through a series of middlemen, making it very difficult for the Qing government to trace the major dealers. Suppression was also hampered by the huge profitability of the trade; criminal gangs stepped in and found ways to buy off police and officials, in ways the modern world is all too familiar with.

Soon the outflow of silver caused by the opium trade gave additional urgency to the need to solve the opium problem. By the 1820s two million taels of silver were flowing out of China a year, which rose to nine million by the early 1830s. In 1839, after proposals to legalize opium were rejected in favour of tougher anti-smuggling measures, the experienced and high-minded official Lin Zexu was dispatched to Guangzhou to compel the foreign traders to stop bringing opium into China and the Chinese to stop smoking. He confiscated pipes, seized opium stores, and arrested some 1,600 Chinese. The foreigners proved harder to manage. Lin Zexu used threats and bribes to get the foreign merchants to turn over their

The English proudly commemorated their victory in the Opium War. In this lithograph Chinese wooden ships are destroyed by the *Nemesis*, a paddle-wheel iron ship that could operate by sail or steam.

Crime and punishment

One of the main functions of the Chinese government, like any government, was to maintain order by deterring and punishing crime. Peaceable, hardworking people had to be protected from bullies and thieves; rapists and murderers had to be caught and punished. Thus, despite the disrepute law fell into because of its association with Legalism and the Qin dynasty, every major dynasty issued a law code, drawing on the models of its predecessors.

By Qing dynasty times the legal code listed 436 main statutes and about 1,900 supplementary or substatutes. Penalties were tailored to circumstances; penalties for killing or injuring varied depending on whether the action was by intent, by accident, in the course of robbery, and so forth. In line with Confucian, rather than Legalist, principles, punishments were also graded according to the social relationship between the parties. Contributing to the death of a parent was a capital offence even if it was clearly accidental and unintended, whereas beating a son to death was considered a relatively minor crime if the son had done something to warrant punishment, such as curse the parent.

The code was interpreted and applied by regular civil servants beginning with magistrates and prefects, who were charged with investigating crimes, arresting criminals, holding trials, and punishing the guilty. Officials themselves were liable to punishment if they failed in any of these matters. In more serious cases local officials compiled a dossier to be passed up the administrative hierarchy for approval before punishment was carried out. Confessions were considered essential to the disposition of most cases, and trials would typically take place after the confession had been secured. To militate against the impression that the government was unduly harsh, emperors periodically issued amnesties, thereby sparing many of those awaiting punishment and demonstrating imperial mercy and benevolence.

Western observers in the seventeenth century had much good to say about the Chinese legal system, but by the end of the eighteenth century, standards had changed in western Europe, and Europeans in China worried about being subjected to what they saw as lack of due process or concern for the rights of the accused, since the Chinese legal system had no independent judiciary, no lawyers for the defence, and no presumption of innocence. The potential for conflict between Chinese and western notions of due process was already apparent in late eighteenth-century Guangzhou, where Europeans were already trading. In 1773 the Portuguese authorities in Macao arrested an Englishman accused of killing a Chinese but after finding him innocent, they released him. The Chinese officials, insisting that since the victim was a fellow national they should have jurisdiction, arrested him again, found him guilty, and executed him. Eleven years after this incident a British ship firing a salute near Guangzhou accidently killed two Chinese bystanders. When the captain claimed not to know who was responsible for the error, the ship's business manager was arrested and the local authorities threatened to cut off all trade with foreign ships. The captain eventually capitulated and turned over a gunner who was soon executed. Because of conflicts like these, when Britain and other western nations gained the upper hand in the nineteenth century, they demanded the right to try their nationals according to their own laws and procedures.

To aid in extracting confessions, interrogators could apply legally prescribed instruments of judicial torture, such as finger, leg, or ankle presses. In this scene from a Ming short story, finger presses have been used to force a woman to confess.

stores of opium. He offered to trade the opium for tea at a ratio of one to five and threatened to execute the heads of the Co-hong. He wrote a letter to Queen Victoria with the following appeal: 'Suppose there were people from another country who carried opium for sale to England and seduced your people into buying and smoking it; certainly your honourable ruler would deeply hate it and be bitterly aroused.' He even barricaded the foreigners in their factories to pressure them to turn over their stocks.

By this point the British had abolished the East India Company and a superintendent of trade had been appointed to represent British interests in Guangzhou. To end this impasse, the British superintendent, Charles Elliot, collected the opium from the merchants and turned it over to Lin, who promptly destroyed it in the presence of the British. Lin ruled that only traders who put up bonds and promised not to deal in opium would thereafter be allowed to trade at Guangzhou. Lin also pressured the Portuguese to expel the British from Macao, as a consequence of which they moved to the barren island of Hong Kong. Meanwhile, in England, commercial interests were pushing for war with China. William Jardine, of the major opium trading firm of Jardine, Matheson, and Company, sailed to London to lobby for war. Once the decision went his way, he supplied assistance, leasing vessels to the British fleet and lending pilots and translators. A British expeditionary force left India in 1840 with sixteen warships and thirty-one other ships.

In preparation for a military confrontation, Lin bought new cannons for the forts and laid great chains across the estuary leading into Guangzhou. This caused no problem for the British expeditionary force, since they simply bypassed Guangzhou and made for the major ports of Ningbo and Tianjin, which they shut down in short order. The Chinese could no longer refuse to negotiate. The agreement worked out in Guangzhou called for ceding Hong Kong, repaying the British the cost of their expedition (an indemnity of six million Mexican silver dollars), and allowing direct intercourse between officials of each country.

Upon learning the terms of the settlement, the public in both countries was outraged. Lin Zexu had already been exiled for having allowed the war to start; now the official who negotiated the treaty was brought to the capital in chains. In England a new expeditionary force was ordered, this time with 10,000 men, more than twice the previous number, and in 1841 the British occupied several strategic coastal cities, including Shanghai. Dozens of Qing officers committed suicide when defeat was certain. Finally, when the British took up positions outside the walls of Nanjing, the Chinese were forced to sue for peace. The Treaty of Nanjing, concluded at gunpoint, raised the indemnity to twenty-one million ounces of silver, abolished the Co-hong, opened five treaty ports (Guangzhou, Xiamen, Fuzhou, Ningbo, and Shanghai), and fixed the tariff at 5 per cent. Through the provision of 'extraterritoriality', British subjects in China were answerable only to British law, even in disputes with Chinese. The 'most-favoured nation' clause provided that if another nation extracted a new privilege from China, that same privilege would be extended automatically to Britain.

During the course of the nineteenth century China signed many more 'unequal' treaties with imperialist powers, but the basic terms had been set. China could not set its own tariffs and eventually even had to appoint European officers to collect them. When Chinese did not buy the Europeans' woollens, knives, and pianos in the hoped-for numbers, European merchants did not fault their own expectations but the obstructionism of Chinese officials; they demanded more treaty ports and fewer restrictions on trade. In 1860, an Anglo-French expedition occupied Beijing for a month to force the acceptance of new treaties, which brought the number of treaty ports to fourteen. By the end of the century more treaty ports were added and large areas within some treaty ports were leased in perpetuity to foreign powers. These concessions, where foreigners did not have to obey Chinese laws, came to resemble international cities attached to the Chinese mainland. Foreign countries won the right to establish legations and consulates in China, with their diplomats treated according to European definitions of international protocol. Also as a result of gunboat diplomacy, Christian missionaries obtained rights to preach throughout China. By the end of the century foreign businessmen had even gained the right to open factories on Chinese soil.

Another consequence of the Opium War was the continued increase in opium addiction. Trade in opium was legalized by treaty in 1860, and opium remained a major item of trade until the end of the century, though the proportion imported declined after 1880 with the expansion of domestic production. By the end of the century, western observers estimated that about 10 per cent of the population of China smoked opium, with a third to a half of them addicted. This would mean on the order of fifteen million opium addicts and about another thirty million occasional users. The highest rates of addiction were probably found among imperial clansmen and bannerman, living on meagre stipends without much to do.

INTERNAL ADVERSARIES

Until 1860, no high-ranking official viewed the foreign adversaries along the coasts as a major threat to the survival of the Qing dynasty. The trouble they caused could not be compared to the danger posed by internal adversaries.

Suppressing insurgencies could be enormously difficult. It took eight years, from 1796 to 1804, to defeat a rebellion of the millenarian White Lotus sect, well entrenched in the hilly frontier areas of Hubei, Sichuan, and Shaanxi provinces. Several hundred forts had to be constructed, the local people recruited into militia, and the equivalent of five years' revenue expended. In 1813, 100,000 followers of the millenarian Eight Trigrams sect rose not far from the capital itself, seizing several cities in the north China plain and even penetrating the Forbidden City in Beijing. Some seventy thousand people died before the rebellion was quashed. Most difficult of all to suppress was the massive Taiping rebellion

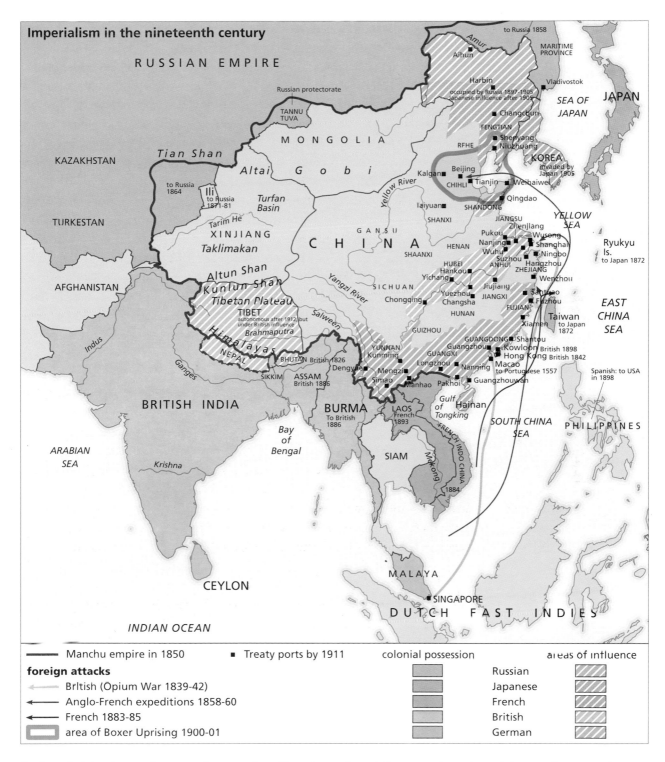

Imperialism in the nineteenth century

RUSSIAN EMPIRE

Russian protectorate

to Russia 1858

MARITIME PROVINCE

Amur

Aihun

Harbin
occupied by Russia 1897-1905
Japanese influence after 1905

Vladivostok

SEA OF JAPAN

JAPAN

Changchun

FENGTIAN

RFHE

Shenyang
Niuzhuang

KOREA
invaded by
Japan 1905

TANNU TUVA

Tian Shan

MONGOLIA

Altai

G o b i

KAZAKHSTAN

to Russia
1864

Ili
to Russia
1871-81

*Turfan
Basin*

Tarim He

XINJIANG

Taklimakan

GANSU

Yellow River

Kalgan

Beijing

CHIHLI

Tianjin

Weihaiwei

Qingdao

Taiyuan

SHANDONG

*YELLOW
SEA*

Ryukyu
Is.
to Japan 1872

TURKESTAN

TANNU TUVA

SHANXI

C H I N A

SHAANXI

HENAN

JIANGSU

Zhenjiang

Pukou
Nanjing
Wuhu

Wusong
Shanghai
Ningbo

AFGHANISTAN

Altun Shan

Kunlun Shan

Tibetan Plateau

TIBET
autonomous after 1912, but
under British influence

Brahmaputra

Himalayas

NEPAL

Yangzi River

SICHUAN

Chongqing

HUBEI

Yichang

Hankou

Yuezhou
Changsha

HUNAN

ANHUI

Suzhou
Hangzhou

ZHEJIANG

Wenzhou

Jiujiang

JIANGXI

FUJIAN

Santuao
Fuzhou

Taiwan
to Japan
1872

*EAST
CHINA
SEA*

Indus

Salween

GUIZHOU

GUANGDONG

Shantou

Ganges

BHUTAN British 1826

SIKKIM

ASSAM
British 1886

YUNNAN

Kunming

Dengyue

Mengzi

Simao

Manhao

GUANGXI

Longzhou

Guangzhou

Nanning

Pakhoi

Kowloon British 1898
Hong Kong British 1842

Macao
to Portuguese 1557

Guangzhouwan

Spanish: to USA
in 1898

BRITISH INDIA

*Bay
of
Bengal*

BURMA
To British
1886

LAOS
French
1893

*Gulf of
Tongking*

Hainan

*SOUTH CHINA
SEA*

PHILIPPINES

ARABIAN
SEA

Krishna

SIAM

Mekong

FRENCH INDO CHINA

1884

CEYLON

MALAYA

SINGAPORE

D U T C H   E A S T   I N D I E S

INDIAN OCEAN

—— Manchu empire in 1850	■ Treaty ports by 1911	colonial possession	areas of influence

foreign attacks

⟵ British (Opium War 1839-42)
⟵ Anglo-French expeditions 1858-60
⟵ French 1883-85
▭ area of Boxer Uprising 1900-01

colonial possession		areas of influence
	Russian	
	Japanese	
	French	
	British	
	German	

By the end of the nineteenth century, the expansion of imperialist powers in Asia raised fears that China might soon be dismembered. Ironically the lands being developed by the imperialist powers in southeast Asia were also among the favourite destinations of Chinese emigrants, especially Singapore, Malaysia, and the Dutch East Indies.

(1850–64), which eventually spread over sixteen provinces and led to the destruction of six hundred cities and the deaths of twenty million people.

The Taiping Rebellion is the best documented of any of the great peasant uprisings in Chinese history. It got its start in south China, an area of secret societies, lineage feuds, and conflict between the locals and the Hakka or 'guest people', later migrants to the area with a distinct dialect and distinct customs (their women did not bind their feet, for instance, and were active in farm work). This region, in addition, had suffered the most disruption from the Opium War. Opium addiction was particularly pervasive in the area, as was resistance to allowing foreigners to reside in Guangzhou. Added to that, huge numbers of porters were put out of work after new ports were open, obviating the need to transport tea across the hills of south China to the port at Guangzhou.

The charismatic religious leader who mobilized the discontented of south China was a Hakka who had failed the civil service examinations, Hong Xiuquan. His career as a religious leader began with visions in which a golden-bearded old man and a middle-aged man who addressed him as younger brother told him to annihilate demons. After reading a Christian tract, Hong interpreted his visions to mean that he was Jesus' younger brother. He turned to a Christian missionary to learn how to baptize, pray, and sing hymns. Attracted especially to the monotheism of the Old Testament, and austerely puritanical, he instructed his followers to destroy idols and ancestral temples, give up opium and alcohol, and end footbinding and prostitution. There was a virulent anti-Manchu strain to his teachings as well: these wicked oppressors were the devil incarnate whom God had commanded him to destroy.

By 1850 Hong had 20,000 ardent followers at his base in Guangxi, armed to protect themselves against banditry, but sometimes coming into clashes with imperial forces. That year he instructed them to sell their property and pool the proceeds in a common treasury. Early the next year he raised the standard of anti-dynastic revolt and declared himself king of the Heavenly Kingdom of Great Peace (Taiping). Inspired by a militant commitment to throw off oppressors, Taiping soldiers proved brave warriors. Other discontents, including secret-society members, joined forces with the Taipings as they moved east and north, and large stores of government weapons and cash fell into their hands as they captured cities. By early 1853 they had reached Wuchang on the Yangzi River. They proceeded to Nanjing, where they defeated a major Manchu banner force of about 5,000 combat soldiers and 35,000 dependants. All Manchus who did not die in battle, even the children, were rounded up by the victorious rebels and slaughtered by burning, stabbing, or drowning.

In Nanjing the Taipings set up a government and issued utopian calls for a new type of society based on the equalization of land holdings and the equality of men and women. Civil service examinations – open to women as well as men – were to be based on mastery of Hong's teachings and Chinese translations of the Bible.

The Taipings held on in Nanjing for a decade even though they never gained many gentry followers. Nor, despite their overtures, did they get aid from Christian missionaries, who quickly concluded that the Christian elements in Taiping doctrines were heretical. When the Taipings tried to take Shanghai in 1860 and 1862, the westerners there organized a vigorous counterattack. Leadership problems plagued the Taipings as well; Hong remained the religious leader, but he let other men run much of the government and army, and they sometimes manipulated him. Dissension eventually led to assassination of several top leaders. Still, whatever the Taipings' weaknesses, the Qing court did not find them easy to suppress. Only after the Chinese scholar–official Zeng Guofan built an army from his home base in Hunan did the situation begin to turn around. Zeng, personally appalled by the threat the Taipings posed to the Confucian order, recruited scholars to serve as officers, and these officers recruited peasants from their communities to serve under them. It took Zeng and the 120,000 troops of his Hunan army ten years to destroy the Taipings. When Nanjing was finally captured, the death toll was enormous – Zeng claimed that the Taipings were so fanatical that they all took their lives, though systematic slaughter is at least as likely an explanation for the lack of survivors.

Once the Taipings were defeated, the new armies had to be reassigned to deal with insurrections that had broken out elsewhere, since the evident weakness of the central government had invited malcontents everywhere to seize power for themselves. In the north China plain, especially along the route of the Grand Canal, villagers driven to banditry had become a scourge; these 'Nian' gangs would seize villagers' crops, rob merchants, and kidnap wealthy landlords to hold them ransom. In the southwest and northwest, Muslim and Miao rebellions flared up, revealing the potential for ethnic separatism to lead provinces on the periphery to break away from central control. It took Zeng and his protégé Li Hongzhang four more years to suppress the Nian rebels. It took until 1873 before the insurrections of Muslims in Yunnan and Gansu had been put down by other provincial generals. Not until 1879 was Zuo Zongtang able to lead troops from Gansu into Xinjiang to defeat Muslim invaders there.

The Qing dynasty's success in suppressing these rebellions can be taken as evidence that the Chinese gentry fully sided with it. Uprisings on the scale of the Taiping rebellion had toppled many dynasties: the Yellow Turbans brought down the Han, White Lotus rebels destroyed the Yuan, and Li Zicheng brought an end to the Ming. In most of these cases, those generals who proved able to defeat the rebels were soon fighting among themselves to see who would get to found the new dynasty. The Qing after the Taiping rebellion had some resemblance to the late Tang, which survived the An Lushan rebellion only by creating regional armies that in turn undermined central control. The Hunan army of Zeng Guofan and the Anhui army of Li Hongzhang, however, functioned as imperial armies, deployed outside their home provinces. The power of the central government was

To defeat the Taiping rebels, troops loyal to the Qing often had to lay siege to their strongholds.

somewhat compromised, however, since in the post-rebellion period provinces gained greater fiscal autonomy, able to keep more of the taxes collected for their own purposes. In addition, Manchu domination of the military establishment was brought to an end. The Chinese scholar–official Li Hongzhang, who outlived Zeng Guofan by nearly three decades, came to hold as much power as any of the Manchus at court.

SELF-STRENGTHENING

In 1860 the Taipings held Nanjing; the Russians were encroaching in Central Asia; and British and French troops were in Beijing, where they had destroyed and looted the Summer Palace as retaliation for Chinese refusals to meet the terms of a recent treaty. That the dynasty might collapse if it did not take urgent action was a plausible fear.

Reform-minded officials had to try to revitalize the dynasty. Their first goal was to re-establish local control and restore the economy by reducing government expenditures, repairing the transportation infrastructure, and inducing peasants to return to abandoned land. They drew on a large body of writings on tax assessment, water-control, grain transport, defence, suppression of bandits, and similar statecraft topics. But they also recognized the need to reorganize the military along western lines and to deal with western nations in accordance with western diplomatic protocol, if for no other reason than that problems with foreigners were distracting the government from its most urgent tasks.

In the 1860s and 1870s, on the advice of men like Zeng Guofan and Li Hongzhang, the court authorized setting up factories and dockyards to manufacture western-style weapons and warships. Even these measures, which turned out to be insufficient, provoked considerable resistance and became the subjects of factional struggles. One respected neo-Confucian scholar, the grand secretary Woren, objected to the establishment of an interpreters' college on the grounds that 'from ancient down to modern times' there had never been 'anyone who could use mathematics to raise a nation from a state of decline or to strengthen it in times of weakness'. At all social levels from peasants to Chinese and Manchu officials, a majority probably kept hoping the west would just go away and thought that copying western social or political practices was compounding defeat. Nor was the pay-off for these modernizing ventures quick in coming. In 1884–85 when China was drawn into a conflict with France over Vietnam, it took only an hour for the French to destroy the warships built at the Fuzhou dockyard. Few Chinese yet understood the speed with which western science was producing improved technology, nor that modern weapons by themselves would not be enough without modernized training and leadership.

Knowledge of the west did, however, gradually improve. Books were translated and foreign language study introduced. Modern newspapers, with up-to-date coverage of world affairs, began to appear in Shanghai and Hong Kong. Information was also acquired through visits abroad. In 1868, the retiring American minister Anson Burlingame was sent along with a Manchu and a Chinese envoy to represent China on a visit to major foreign capitals. By 1880 China had legations in London, Paris, Berlin, Madrid, Washington, Tokyo, and St Petersburg. Guo Songdao, the minister to England, already in 1877 wrote home of the importance of railroads to economic development. Even though Guo had to withdraw from public life on his return – so savage was the attack on him from reactionary 'purist' critics – those in power did begin to shift their attention from strictly diplomatic and military issues to economic development.

Li Hongzhang, in particular, became convinced that guns and ships were merely the surface manifestation of the western powers' economic strength and therefore in order to compete China had to modernize its economy. Li played an active role in starting the China Merchants' Steam Navigation Company (1872), the Kaiping coal mines (1877), a telegraph network (1879), a cotton spinning factory (1882), and a cotton weaving mill (1890). He had the first railroad track laid to connect the Kaiping mines to the docks at Tianjin (1880), aiding the development of Tianjin into a manufacturing city. A few other provincial officials undertook comparable projects; Zhang Zhidong, for instance, opened the Hanyang Iron Works at Wuhan in 1890. In these joint government-merchant ventures, merchants provided the capital, officials the initiative and political connections. The first steps of technology transfer were thus underway, but not industrial take-off, as bureaucratic control prevented the sort of reinvestment of profits that would have allowed self-sustaining growth.

There are many other reasons as well that China did not transform itself into a modern industrial power in the rapid way Japan did in these decades. The unequal treaties, with their low tariffs, kept China from protecting its fledgling industries from competition with better-established foreign manufacturers. A modern communications infrastructure was difficult to establish because of resistance from people who thought railroads and telegraph lines would create unemployment or disturb graves (by 1894, only 195 miles of track had been laid). Local resistance to new projects also grew from poor people's suspicion that they were being taxed to pay for projects whose benefits would go not to them but to a small reformist elite.

POPULATION GROWTH AND PEOPLES' LIVELIHOOD

From the time when the Roman Empire broke up, China was never seriously rivalled as the world's most populous country. Indeed, China regularly had a greater population than all of the countries of Europe put together. Until 1700 population growth was slow everywhere in the world, never exceeding half a per cent per year for any lengthy period. Thereafter, populations through much of Eurasia began growing at more rapid rates, increasing 50 per cent or more during the course of the eighteenth century, probably as a result of a combination of such developments as global warming that lengthened the growing season, new crops increasing food supply, a reduction of disease after a period when increased global traffic had spread new diseases, and advances in state organization improving the delivery of relief in times of famine. In a small part of the world – western Europe – increased rates of growth were soon moderated by changed family practices, primarily later marriage and increased rates of celibacy. In even more limited regions of England and the Netherlands the eighteenth century upswing in population coincided with the industrial revolution, allowing standards of living to rise as the population grew. Elsewhere population growth was less of a boon. In 1800 China had about 300 million people, Russia 40 million, Japan 30 million, and England 11 million. From 1800 to 1850 China added at least another 100 million people, reaching over 400 million.

In China the population explosion had enormous consequences for every aspect of Chinese life. For every Chinese person living in 1650, there were three in 1850. Villages and towns grew closer, farms grew smaller, forests were hewn down and ploughed up, labour was in surplus everywhere, suppressing wages and intensifying the competitiveness of everyday life. Until the end of the eighteenth century these processes had as many positive consequences as negative ones, as they fostered regional development and commercialization, but by the beginning

恰斯送行

城黑方那樣文進科拜必認此拜色
古報其文使州鎮國和衾其是講儀文
怪乎此振由起腮而文攻其是脫膚傳
此相親尤謂情文之心不稱儀之華之文
尚儀文不同中至理而之其二人起非心國成其要程
此尚儀久理令父行於起近殷搖深
娘起向何公體世家理令須蒲自家
然起其魂觀嘴之親與民此習
而不發親送邊青院女想與須禮敬
禮也團觀嘆之恰世貯世有喪程
謂其奢如惠之吃則誤矣

As the west came to loom larger in Chinese affairs, Chinese began to show curiosity about western customs, not unlike the curiosity Europeans had felt about Chinese customs a couple of centuries earlier. The caption to this illustration in a popular 1890s magazine begins 'Different places have different customs', and notes that western conventions like shaking hands and kissing cheeks should be likened to Chinese kneeling and bowing. Thus in France, as depicted here, a daughter-in-law kisses her father-in-law and brother-in-law goodbye, something required by good manners among high-ranking families there. To the Chinese, it goes without saying, such behaviour was considered quite indecent.

of the nineteenth century the negative consequences were becoming pronounced. Both the massive rebellions of the mid-nineteenth century and the difficulties reformers and entrepreneurs encountered in developing modern industry owe much to the economic consequences of these demographic trends.

As population pressure mounted, farmers intensified their efforts; they expanded use of irrigation and fertilizer and opened lands previously considered too marginal (sometimes growing new-world crops like sweet potatoes and maize). But once all of the land that could profitably be exploited using traditional methods was under cultivation, any increase in food supply had to come from less and less rewarding additions of labour or marginal land. Not only did this reduce agricultural productivity, but it had long-term effects on local ecology. Cutting forests on hills to grow new crops hurt those further downstream, since deforestation worsened soil erosion and silting of rivers, leading to flooding. When arable land was extended by building polders or dykes along the edge of lakes, lakes disappeared or shrunk, their catchment basins so reduced that they could no longer contain flood waters.

The steady increase in population also complicated the introduction of industrial manufacturing. As farms grew smaller, there was a surplus of labour available in farming households. Peasant households with unprofitable farms made ends meet by sending men out to work or engaging in sideline production at home,

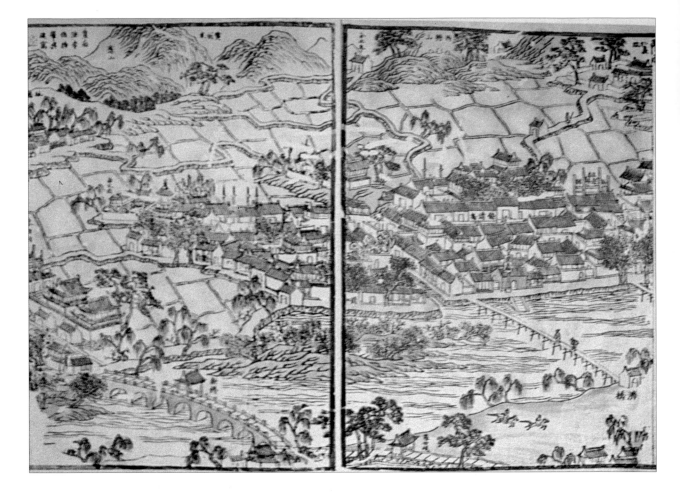

With the doubling of the population in the first half of the Qing period, villages often became densely packed towns. This depiction of a village in Shexian in southern Anhui province was included in the 1757 book, *Scenes of Old She*.

mostly spinning and weaving performed by women and girls. These sidelines posed an obstacle to the establishment of textile factories. Because farmers' wives and daughters would work at spinning and weaving for a return that would not be sufficient to maintain a full-time worker, urban factories could not compete.

Too many people trying to make a living on too few resources naturally also exacerbated social tensions. As an area filled up and the choicest lands were occupied, the potential for conflict over rights to water or rights to tenancy naturally increased. Feuds between ethnic groups, lineages, or villages became all too common. Hard times also led to a rise in the rate of female infanticide, as families felt they could not afford to raise more than two or three children, but saw sons as necessities. The inescapable consequence was a shortage of marriageable women, reducing the incentive for young men to stay near home and do as their elders told them. Those who did not join bandit gangs or emigrate tended to drift into cities where they might find work as boatmen, carters, sedan-chair carriers, and, by the end of the century, as rickshaw pullers.

The new international order China was forced to join during the nineteenth century did little to ease these economic strains. Some merchants and entrepreneurs in the treaty ports amassed fortunes, but no region really boomed. As the importation of opium skyrocketed, China's balance of payments suffered, and this in turn resulted in a long period of deflation and recession. Prices dropped by half from 1815 to 1850. Yet because of changing copper–silver ratios a tax obligation that had required handing over 100 copper cash in 1800 required 200 cash by 1850.

The slow introduction of machine-powered manufacturing also caused dislocations. As late as 1875 almost all cotton yarn used in China was hand-spun there, but by 1905 only half. Machine-spinning, which is certainly much more efficient than hand-spinning, helped the Chinese economy in the long run, but until the machine-spinning was done in China (which was largely the case by 1925), and until those who had depended on hand-spinning for extra income found other employment (such as knitting or weaving with machine-spun yarn), tens of thousands of village families suffered financially from its introduction.

THE CHINESE DIASPORA

During the nineteenth century, when millions of Europeans emigrated to the

Lineage organization remained strong through the nineteenth century, especially in south China. In some areas, descendants had paintings made of their ancestors for use during the group sacrifices performed at New Year. In this detail from a large painting owned by the Wu family of Liancheng county in Fujian, the ancestor of the eighteenth generation is shown flanked by his two wives and above his three sons. Although these individuals were ordinary commoners in life, they are depicted in officials' garments, a reflection of the ranks it was hoped they had attained in heaven.

Americas and Australia, millions of Chinese emigrated as well, mostly to Southeast Asia, but some travelling much further from home. As in the case of Europe, both push and pull factors prompted emigration. As population swelled, opportunities for internal migration to thinly populated regions all but disappeared. Then, after 1842, the economic decline around Guangzhou brought on by the local collapse of the tea trade increased the supply there of young men in need of a way to make a living.

On the pull side were new opportunities abroad. Since Ming times, Chinese from the southern coastal regions of Fujian and Guangdong had formed mercantile communities throughout Southeast Asia. In Buddhist countries like Thailand and Vietnam, Chinese often assimilated, intermarrying with the local population and adopting their language and customs. They rarely assimilated in Muslim areas (such as Java), Catholic areas (such as the Philippines), or primitive tribal areas (such as northern Borneo). In these places, Chinese communities remained separate and distinct, many of them consisting primarily of speakers of one dialect. Voluntary associations, such as the Triads, were frequently the main organizational force in these Chinese communities, as local authorities preferred to let them govern themselves.

With the expansion of European imperialism into Southeast Asia, new opportunities were created for enterprising Chinese. After Singapore was founded on a nearly barren island in 1819, Chinese poured in. The region around Guangzhou was soon sending thousands of men to work in the tin mines in nearby spots in Malaysia. By 1850 there were about 10,000 Chinese in the city of Malacca, and the Chinese had become the dominant ethnic group in the nearby cities of Kuala Lumpur and Singapore. Further away, in Sarawak and Sabah, on the north side of the island of Borneo, Hakkas from Guangdong were arriving in large numbers, encouraged by British authorities who perceived a local shortage of labour.

Chinese fared better in some places than in others. Great fortunes were made from the tin business in British-dominated Malaysia, where the Chinese community included both old overseas families long settled in Malacca, who spoke Malay, and a much larger number of more recent immigrants, mostly Cantonese speakers. In the Spanish-controlled Philippines and Dutch-controlled Indonesia, however, the Chinese had to put up with repeated persecutions. Early in the nineteenth century, the Dutch seized the mines in Borneo that Chinese had worked for generations, and hostilities between the Chinese settlers and the Dutch lasted until 1854, after which Chinese emigration to the region essentially ceased. Yet the Dutch conquest of southern Sumatra led to a massive immigration of Chinese to work in the sugar and tobacco plantations there, beginning in 1864. In Java, where Chinese merchant communities were well established, the Dutch used Chinese merchants as tax farmers, and some Chinese became very rich in this way. By 1900 there were more than 500,000 Chinese living in the Dutch East Indies (now Indonesia).

Starting in the 1840s, because the world-wide anti-slavery movement had largely ended the trade in African slaves, labour contractors began coming to China to recruit cheap workers. Unscrupulous foreign contractors and equally unsavoury Chinese middlemen signed up hundreds of thousands of Chinese to work for plantations and mines in Cuba, Peru, Hawaii, Sumatra, and elsewhere. These 'coolies' (from the Chinese *kuli*, for 'bitter labourers') were often treated little better than slaves during transit and at the plantations and mines. Some of the worst abuses were in Peru, where nearly 100,000 Chinese had arrived by 1875, lured by promoters who had promised them easy riches only to find themselves forced to work in chains if they tried to flee. In Hawaii, sugar planters brought over the first Chinese labourers in 1852 on three- or five-year contracts, giving them $3 per month plus room and board for a twelve-hour day, six days a week. Yet many of those who finished their contracts chose to stay in Hawaii, where they set up small businesses, eventually forming an important part of the Hawaiian business community. By 1900 there were about 25,000 Chinese in Hawaii.

Discovery of gold in California in 1848, Australia in 1851, and British Columbia in 1858 led to a large voluntary migration to these still thinly settled areas. In California few arrived soon enough to make lucrative strikes, and they drifted into other lines of work. Thousands found employment laying railways and others took up mining in Wyoming and Idaho. In 1880 more than 100,000 Chinese men were living in the western part of the United States, but only 3,000 women. Friction between Chinese and white settlers erupted periodically, spurred by racist rhetoric that depicted Chinese as depraved, lawless opium smokers. In 1882

The Chinese who settled in Singapore or nearby regions of the Malaysian Straits adopted a style of dress that incorporated diverse features, as seen in this 1918 family gathering.

Because the US government made it difficult for Chinese women to enter the country, during the first years of the twentieth century Chinatown in San Francisco was a peculiarly male place.

Chinese labourers were banned from obtaining American citizenship and immigration of Chinese labourers was suspended. In 1888 President Cleveland declared the Chinese 'impossible of assimilation with our people, and dangerous to our peace and welfare'. It became nearly impossible for Chinese men to bring over wives, and even to bring sons Chinese labourers usually had to engage in deception, such as getting a merchant to claim the boy was his son.

Chinese in these scattered communities retained an interest in what was going on in China, where most had relatives. Although a majority of those who left China were probably illiterate, as they prospered they saw to it that their children learned to read Chinese, and Chinese-language newspapers circulated in all areas of significant Chinese settlement. Even though few Mandarin speakers were to be found among the immigrants, and spoken language could not tie them together, the written language and common ties to China made it possible for scattered communities of overseas Chinese to identify with each other. By the end of the nineteenth century they were playing a role in Chinese politics (see Chapter 10).

TOTAL HUMILIATION, 1894–1900

Nothing seemed to go right for China in the last years of the nineteenth century. First came the humiliating discovery that Japan had succeeded where China had failed and now posed a threat to China. From about the time the Taiping Rebellion began, Japan had embarked on a determined effort to make itself into a modern country, capable of defending itself against any of the western powers. By the 1890s Japan had achieved a great deal: it had a constitutional monarchy; the privileges of the old ruling class had largely been eliminated; new industries had been founded; and a universal school system was turning out young men ready to take positions in a modern army and navy. Japan thus felt ready to become an imperialist itself.

In the 1870s Japan laid claim to the Ryukyus, islands that had long had tributary relations with China. Next Japan turned its attention to Korea, which had been one of Qing China's most loyal vassals, sending four tribute missions a year. Japan had forced Korea to 'open' itself in 1876, much as the United States had forced Japan to 'open' two decades earlier. When a rebellion broke out in Korea in 1894 both China and Japan rushed to send troops. The Japanese were looking to provoke a war with China and so sank a steamer carrying Chinese troops. In the ensuing war, the Chinese navy fared poorly, its worst losses coming when the Japanese went overland to take the Chinese port city of Weihaiwei from the rear,

Japanese efforts to strengthen the country in the late nineteenth century had verged on wholesale westernization, as is evident in the differences in dress of the Chinese and Japanese officials assigned to negotiate a treaty after China's disastrous defeat in 1894/95. The elderly Li Hongzhang is depicted seated in the front. After a Japanese fanatic shot and wounded him in the face, the Japanese had to temper their demands.

turning the Chinese guns on the Chinese fleet in the bay. This then was a defeat not of Chinese-produced weapons (most were actually foreign-bought) but of Chinese leadership and strategy.

China sued for peace and sent its most distinguished elder statesman, Li Hongzhang, to negotiate. China agreed to the cession of Liaodong and Taiwan, an indemnity of 200 million ounces of silver, and Japan's right to open factories in China, which by the terms of the most-favoured national clause then was extended to all of the other powers. Much to the indignation of the Japanese, the European powers were not pleased with this outcome, and pressured Japan to give back Liaodong for an additional fifty million ounce indemnity.

This was the era when Africa and Southeast Asia were being carved up by the powers, who each feared the others would get the best pickings. Seeing how easily China was defeated by Japan, the western powers began scrambling for concessions in China. Germany seized Jiaozhou in Shandong; Russia got Liaodong; Britain leased Weihaiwei in Shandong and the New Territories next to Hong Kong; France leased Guangzhou bay near Hainan island. Only the Italian demand for territory was successfully refused.

At this juncture, when China seemed about to be dismembered, a group of young scholars in Beijing to take the *jinshi* examination presented a long memorial to the throne urging thorough-going reforms. China needed to raise taxes, develop a state bank, build a railway network and a commercial fleet, and set up a modern postal system, they argued. The government should call on Chinese

Even the modern urge to find positive role models among women of the past cannot make a heroine of Empress Dowager Cixi, the power behind the throne during the reigns of two young emperors from 1861 to 1908. When her son the Tongzhi emperor died at the age of eighteen in 1875, she appointed her three-year-old nephew as heir, assuring herself continued tenure as regent. Selfish and ignorant, at a time when China needed bold, risk-taking leadership, she played reactionaries off against reformers, seeming to support modernization projects while encouraging critics to attack them.

who had emigrated abroad for technical help in these and other modernizing endeavours. The leaders of this group were Kang Youwei, thirty-seven, and Liang Qichao, twenty-two, both from Guangdong. Of all the Confucian scholars then struggling to find justification for modernization from within China's tradition, Kang was perhaps the most brilliant, presenting Confucius in a new light, as an institutional innovator and proponent of change. In 1898 when the empress dowager allowed her nephew, the 23-year-old Guangxu emperor, to rule on his own, he called on Kang to help him step up reform. Kang submitted several essays, including one on the fate of Poland (divided by the European powers in the eighteenth century) and one on the triumphs of the Meiji reformers in Japan. The emperor was soon issuing edict after edict ordering reforms in education, commerce, government and the military. After three months of this, Empress Dowager Cixi had had enough. Afraid that the reforms would undermine the position of the Manchus, she locked up Guangxu and captured and executed those of the reformers she could find. Kang and Liang, safely out of Beijing at the time, managed to flee to Japan. But hopes for reform from the top were dashed.

Further humiliation for the Qing dynasty came just two years later with the Boxer Rebellion. The secret society at the centre of this uprising called itself the 'Harmonious Fists'. Like many earlier secret societies, the Boxers combined traditional martial arts with shamanistic belief in special powers; to this they added the explosive ingredient of xenophobia, blaming China's ills on the evil of foreigners, especially the missionaries who had ventured out of the treaty ports into the Chinese interior to tell Chinese that their beliefs and practices were wrong and backward. In 1898 the Boxers emerged in impoverished northwest Shandong. As they seized and destroyed the property of foreign missionaries and the Christian converts whose privileges they decried, they attracted more and more young men trying to survive on the margins of local soci-

In 1896, at the age of seventy-four, Li Hongzhang went on a world tour, representing China at the coronation of the Russian czar and visiting the German, Dutch, Belgian, French, British, and American heads of state. Here he is shown sitting with the retired British prime minister William Gladstone.

ety, including peasants, discharged soldiers, canal boat trackers, and salt smugglers. When the government in Shandong took action against them, the Boxers moved elsewhere. Small groups of Boxers began to appear in Beijing and Tianjin in June 1900, harassing and sometimes killing both foreigners and converts. Western powers protested and prepared for war. Empress Dowager Cixi wavered but finally decided to support the Boxers, deluding herself into thinking they might solve the foreign problem for her, since nothing else had worked. When the Boxers laid siege to the foreign legation quarters, the empress dowager issued a declaration of war: 'The foreigners have been aggressive toward us, infringed on our territorial integrity, trampled our people under their feet… . The common people suffer greatly at their hands, and each one of them is vengeful.' Boxers spread also to other provinces where they attacked mission compounds. In August, 20,000 troops drawn from over a dozen nations marched from Tianjin to Beijing, where they lifted the siege and looted the city. Meanwhile the empress, with the emperor in tow, had fled. Li Hongzhang was again called on to negotiate, and he had to accept a whole series of penalties, including cancelling the examinations for five years in areas where anti-foreign violence occurred (punishment for gentry collaboration), and a staggering indemnity of 450 million ounces of silver, almost twice the government's annual revenues, to be paid over forty years, with interest. Ordinary people had risen up, thinking they could rid China of its enemies, only to find that their efforts left China in an even worse predicament.

China as a polity was expanded during the Qing dynasty, but China as a civilization suffered a series of blows. First was the alien conquest by the Manchus. That

Above. The Boxers – mostly poor peasants from Shandong and Hebei provinces – placed the blame for hard times on foreign encroachment and Christian missionaries. When the Boxers appeared in Tianjin, depicted here, they alarmed foreign residents, who had already heard many rumours of the viciousness of their attacks.

Right. On 14 August 1900, 20,000 foreign troops – mainly from Japan, Russia, Britain and its colonies, the United States, France, and Germany – entered Beijing through this great gate on its wall. After lifting the siege on the legation quarter, they set about capturing and punishing Boxers in and near the capital and looting the city.

China had once again succumbed to the military might of a northern neighbour and that Chinese men had to alter their hairstyle as a sign of submission raised questions about China's greatness. Committed Confucians could take comfort in notions of Confucian universalism and maintain belief in China's moral centrality by focusing on the Chinese side of Manchu rule, such as the ways the Manchus adopted Chinese institutions and fulfilled the role of Son of Heaven, ruling All-Under-Heaven through their moral virtue. After all, Kangxi, Yongzheng, and Qianlong proved their ability to manage the Chinese state as well or better than any Ming emperor. Still, ethnic tensions erupted from time to time, and even after two centuries of Manchu rule ordinary people retained an awareness that the rulers were alien conquerors – witness the use made of anti-Manchu slogans by the Taiping rebels.

The failure of China to come off well in its nineteenth-century encounters with the western imperialist powers was at least as heavy a blow to Chinese self-confidence. Western Europe had undergone dramatic change between the mid Ming and the mid Qing – moving from the Renaissance and age of Columbus through the Reformation, the rise and fall of the Spanish empire, to the Enlightenment, the French Revolution and the Industrial Revolution. Both in technology and in political organization China found itself at a disadvantage. It had become enmeshed in an international economic order stacked against late comers, an order whose rules China had no ability to shape.

But even if we recognize that China's precipitous drop in world standing had as much to do with the rise of Europe as the decline of China, it remains difficult to be upbeat about the history of China in the nineteenth century. It is much easier to find people to criticize than people to celebrate. Chinese and Manchu officials who resisted every effort to copy from the west seem irresponsibly obscurantist, blind to the damage delay was inflicting. Chinese officials who promoted limited measures to learn western science or military technology without any other aspects of western culture can be dismissed as short-sighted and inept, wasting time with half measures that would not work. Similarly, officials who thought they could attain industrial growth through projects designed and sponsored by the government can be charged with failing to appreciate the key dynamic elements of capitalist expansion and thus wasting scarce resources. Outside the scholar–official class it is just as difficult to find heroes. None of the leaders of the mid-century rebellions showed the kind of visionary leadership that would have been needed to unite China and lead it forward. The Boxers' solution to the foreign menace can hardly be seen as helpful. Chinese merchants in the treaty ports, it is true, often found ways to build great fortunes, but rarely did they develop ways to extend the benefits they were gaining to a broader segment of the population.

Could things have turned out differently? Would China have fared better if culture had not taken a conservative turn in the early Qing? Did this turn keep scholars from following up on their initial interest in the Jesuits' scientific knowledge? Would China have modernized as quickly as Japan if Qianlong had been entranced by Macartney and taken up his offers and suggestions? Or if its leaders had not been preoccupied by internal adversaries in the 1850s and 1860s? Would China have done better if the Taipings had succeeded in overthrowing the Qing, and someone like Zeng Guofan or Li Hongzhang had founded a new dynasty and provided vigorous leadership? What if the dynasty in power had not been an alien one? Would that have made mobilization for modernization any easier? This list could be extended indefinitely. There is nothing inevitable, I think, about the results of the confrontation between China and the imperialist powers: a whole concatenation of contingent events contributed to the outcome.

The exact twist one puts on China's decline during the nineteenth century depends on one's assessment of China in the twentieth century. Those who celebrate how thoroughly China broke with the past in the twentieth century to become a modern, forward-looking society can view China's steady decline in standing during the nineteenth century as a blessing in disguise: the centralized bureaucratic monarchy, the patriarchal family, and the scholar–official elite were all so deeply embedded in Chinese culture and society that it took a century of bad news to undermine people's belief in them and force them to recognize that change was both possible and necessary. On the other hand, those who look on the twentieth century as just as tragic as the nineteenth have reason to feel that the Chinese people might have been spared much suffering if China had managed to muddle through this stage of its encounter with the west without suffering so much humiliation, for then revolutionary change might not have come to seem absolutely necessary to so many thinking Chinese.

Through the nineteenth century, industrialization had very little impact on how most people in China made their living. The new technology of photography, however, gives us a new perspective on the lives of ordinary Chinese. Glimpses of men, women, and children at work were captured by western visitors from 1860 on, especially after 1880 when cameras became easier to carry and use. Impressions of what Chinese life was like in earlier periods owes much to the images created by artists who usually tended, consciously or unconsciously, to prettify much of what they depicted. No such filter keeps us from seeing the harsher side of daily toil in more recent times.

Left
A common fate of those trained in the classics but unsuccessful in the examinations was teaching in village schools. Even at the end of the nineteenth century, most schoolchildren were taught to read the traditional way, learning passages by rote then reciting them with their backs to the teacher.

Below
Farmers who could not afford to keep a draft animal had to pull their ploughs themselves.

Transport in many parts of the country remained largely a matter of human muscle power well into the twentieth century. These porters, photographed in 1908, are carrying about 300 pounds of brick tea through the mountains from Sichuan to Tibet.

Left
Even women with bound feet could find employment in Shanghai with its many workshops. These women (grouped for the photographer's convenience) are sorting tea leaves.

Below
When only hand tools were available, sawing logs for construction required both skill and strength.

CHAPTER 10

Taking Action:
The Early Twentieth Century 1900–1949

The half century from 1900 to 1949 was a period of intense effort on the part of an increasingly diverse elite to refashion China into a powerful, modern state. Centre stage was taken by energetic men and women who felt compelled to act: to promote new ideas, start new enterprises, build new institutions, organize the oppressed, fight corruption, and defeat aggressors. Patriots wanted to reconstitute China as a nation of the Chinese people and make it strong enough to stand up to foreign threats. Intellectuals and artists wanted to create a new culture that would be Chinese but modern.

Revolutionaries succeeded in toppling the Qing dynasty in 1911, but their initial efforts to replace it with a republican government foundered. From 1916 to 1927 China was politically fragmented as local warlords competed for supremacy and imperialist powers extended their domination. Even after political division was largely overcome by the Nationalists, bitter strife between the Communists and the Nationalists and Japan's progressive aggression kept the Nationalists in a state of war, deflecting them from their goals of modernization. During the war with Japan, the Communist Party successfully mobilized poor peasants into a well-disciplined fighting force, an army that eventually defeated the much better-equipped Nationalist army in civil war.

UNDERMINING THE QING DYNASTY

During the first decade of the twentieth century, the Qing dynasty was undermined simultaneously on nearly every front. Its moral authority had been greatly weakened by the final events of the nineteenth century, the defeat by Japan, the Empress Dowager's coup against the emperor, and the imperialists' intervention into the Boxer Rebellion. In localities across the country, a more activist local elite was emerging, eager to take part in the refashioning of the political order, out of both idealistic and self-interested motives.

The story of the overthrow of China's 2,000-year tradition of monarchical rule has generally been told as a story of revolutionaries inspired by ideas from abroad. In the last decades of the Qing the educated were gaining a better grasp of how wealth and power had been secured by the European powers and Japan. Yan Fu, one of the first to study in England, published translations of Huxley's *Evolution and Ethics* (1898), Adam Smith's *Wealth of Nations* (1900), J.S. Mill's *On Liberty* (1903) and *Logic* (1905), Herbert Spencer's *A Study of Sociology* (1903), and Montesquieu's *The Spirit of Laws* (1909). Yan Fu argued that the western form of government freed the energy of the individual, which could then be channelled toward collective goals, in contrast to the Chinese 'Way of the Sages' which dis-

China, 1935–1945

Communist strongholds to 1935
route of the Long March Oct 1934–Oct 1935
Communist base 1935-45
area occupied by Japan by 1944
areas controlled by Communist groups by 1945
main urban/industrial centres

occupied by Japan 1933
Japanese sponsored puppet state 1935
under effective control of Nationalist government at Nanjing 1928
Nanjing control 1929-34
Nanjing control 1935-37

Nationalist China

The Nationalist Party and government were preoccupied with military matters from the start. Even after the Northern Expedition of 1926/7, large parts of China were under the domination of warlords, the Japanese, or the Communists. The Nationalist army succeeded in driving out the Communist Party from central China in 1934 (beginning the famed Long March, which eventually took them to Yan'an in Shaanxi), but had little success in stemming the Japanese invasion of 1937.

couraged the development of the people's capabilities. Yan Fu once commented that only 30 per cent of China's troubles were caused by foreigners; the rest were her own fault and could be remedied by her own actions.

During the decade 1900 to 1910 probably the best-known reformers were Kang Youwei and Liang Qichao. After fleeing the wrath of the Empress Dowager, Kang travelled widely, visiting overseas Chinese communities, while Liang settled in Japan where by 1906 over ten thousand Chinese students were studying. The experience of living in a foreign country, where they felt humiliated by China's weakness and backwardness, aroused ardent nationalistic feelings in these students. Liang published magazines for them in which he analysed China's deteriorating condition and introduced western ideas. He promoted the idea that China could become strong through 'democracy', which to him meant a government that drew its strength from the people, not necessarily a representative government or one that defended individual rights. Having travelled in the United States for five months in 1903, Liang was not enthusiastic about the American form of republican, populist democracy, but he found much to admire in the statist ideas and constitutional monarchies of Japan and Germany.

Back in China, the Qing court was itself edging in the direction of constitutionalism and parliamentary government. In 1905 the civil service examinations were abolished and steps were taken to set up both a modern school system and a modern government bureaucracy. A modern police force, for instance, was introduced. After collecting advice from abroad, in 1908 Empress Dowager Cixi announced a plan to phase in constitutional principles over a nine-year period of tutelage.

With the mysterious death of the 33-year-old Guangxu emperor, reported to have occurred the day before the empress dowager died at age seventy-three, China once again had an infant on the throne, and hope for a Japanese-style constitutional monarchy looked less and less promising. Still, in 1909 consultative provincial assemblies met in each province and sent representatives to Beijing. Although only a tiny portion of the population had been allowed to vote in the elections, the impact of the assemblies was magnified by the excitement that the idea of participatory government generated.

Such top-down reforms were not change enough for the growing reformist segment of the elite, not to mention real revolutionaries. In 1903 the nineteen-year-old Zou Rong had published an inflammatory tract, calling for the creation of a 'revolutionary army' to 'wipe out the five million barbarian Manchus, wash away the shame of 260 years of cruelty and oppression, and make China clean once again'. He described the 'sacred Han race, descendants of the Yellow Emperor' as the slaves of the Manchus and in danger of extermination. The language of Social Darwinism and the struggle for survival in an international arena of predatory states was borrowed from European rhetoric of the period, but seemed to many Chinese an accurate analysis of their current crisis.

The anti-Manchu revolutionary who would eventually be mythologized as the founding figure of the movement was Sun Zhongshan (Sun Yatsen, 1866–1925). Like Hong Xiuquan, Kang Youwei, and Liang Qichao, Sun came from Guangdong, but unlike them, he was neither from a literati family nor trained in the Confucian classics. Two of his uncles had emigrated to the United States in the gold rush days, and another uncle and brother went to Hawaii, where Sun was sent in 1879. After Sun became interested in Christianity, his brother sent him back to China. No longer fitting into his village, he went to Hong Kong, where he was baptized and studied western medicine. It was in Hong Kong that Sun and his friends began discussing the advantages of a republic, the kind of government they had learned about in their westernized schools. They thought the best way to overthrow the Manchus would be to ally with the secret societies so pervasive in the south. The Triads were not only anti-Manchu, but they had large mass followings and an organizational base reaching from one province to another.

In 1894 Sun went to Beijing in the hope of seeing the leading reformist official Li Hongzhang, but when that failed he returned to Hawaii where he founded a hundred member chapter of the Revive China Society. The next year he set up a similar group in Hong Kong. The society's efforts to instigate an uprising with secret society members as the muscle never got very far, however. Meanwhile Sun continued to look for support outside China. In 1896 he cut off his queue and began wearing western clothes. He spent time in England where he discovered that many westerners saw flaws in their own institutions and were advocating a variety of socialist solutions. As others would after him, Sun began to try to devise ways for China to skip ahead of the west by going directly to a more progressive form of government. He also spent time in Japan, where he found Japanese eager to participate in the regeneration and modernization of China. In 1905 they helped Sun join forces with the more radical of the student revolutionaries to form the Revolutionary Alliance. Despite the difference in social background, the students from gentry families were attracted to Sun's promise of quick solutions to China's problems. This Alliance sponsored seven or eight attempts at uprisings over the next few years. Sun himself continued to spend most of his time travelling in search of funds and foreign backers.

Sun was in Denver when a plot finally triggered the collapse of China's imperial system. A bomb that accidentally exploded in the headquarters of the revolutionary group in Wuchang led to a coup by the army officers fearful that their connections to the revolutionaries would be exposed. After taking over the city in less than a day, they telegraphed all the provinces asking them to declare their independence. Within six weeks fifteen provinces had seceded. The court in desperation turned to its top general, Yuan Shikai (1859–1916). Rather than mount a military campaign, Yuan negotiated with the revolutionaries, who, out of fear of foreign intervention, were willing to compromise. In the end agreement was reached to establish a republic with Yuan as president; the emperor would abdi-

Sun Zhongshan spent much of his time abroad, trying to gain financial support for his cause. He is shown here, centre front, in Japan in 1916.

Yuan Shikai, a leading general under the Qing, became president of the new republic in 1912 and promptly began acting like a dictator.

cate but he and his entourage would be treated well and allowed to keep much of their property. In February 1912, the last Qing emperor abdicated, and in March Sun Zhongshan, back in China, issued a provisional constitution.

The speed with which the Qing was ousted is evidence of how much Chinese society had changed since the Taiping rebellion when the educated class had rallied behind the throne. Forced to look after their own interests, local elites increasingly found themselves in opposition to the state. Merchants, now frequently organized into chambers of commerce, were more actively engaged in running the cities in which they lived. By the beginning of the century, both rural and urban elites shared the revolutionaries' zeal for modernization and reform, even if for different reasons; to the local elite they appeared to offer the best means of achieving local order.

The new republican government never really got off the ground. The attempt to co-opt Yuan Shikai and his army proved a total failure. Parliamentary elections were held, but when in 1913 the Nationalist Party (the successor to the Revolutionary Alliance) succeeded in winning more than half the seats, Yuan showed he had never become a constitutionalist by ordering the assassination of the key Nationalist organizer, Song Jiaoren. Local elites had never approved Yuan's concentration of power at the centre, and six provinces promptly declared their independence. Yuan successfully used military force against them, thus establishing himself as a military dictator. In late 1915 he even announced that he would become emperor on 1 January, 1916. This action aroused enormous protest, which ended only when Yuan died unexpectedly in June 1916.

DISLODGING AUTHORITY

The twelve years from Yuan Shikai's death until the establishment of the Nationalist government in 1928 are usually referred to as China's warlord period. In the absence of a strong central power, commanders in Yuan's old army, governors of provinces, local strongmen, and gangsters busied themselves building up power bases. Territories conquered by the Qing but never fully integrated into China proper, like Tibet and Mongolia, declared their independence. While Sun Zhongshan and his allies tried to build a power base for the nationalist revolutionaries at Guangzhou in the far south, a government of sorts was maintained in Beijing, with six different presidents and twenty-five successive cabinets. For a while the key struggle seemed to be for control of the north, as the strongest warlords waged highly destructive wars across north China. With no one in charge, bandit gangs appeared everywhere, often causing more disruption to everyday life even than the warlord armies, and forcing villages to form local defence forces.

While all this was going on, young intellectuals were waging their own wars against old and outmoded ideas. Those who received modern educations felt that they had inherited the obligation of the literati to advise those in power; they moreover believed themselves uniquely qualified by their modern educations to 'save' China. This was particularly true at the newly reorganized Beijing University, where Chen Duxiu, the founder of the periodical *New Youth*, had been appointed Dean of Letters. Chen, who had studied in Japan and France, was a zealous advocate of individual freedom. In the first issue of *New Youth* in 1915 he

Political cartoons began appearing in newspapers and magazines early in the century. In this 1918 cartoon, the warlords of the north and south are shown trampling on the people as they battle each other.

Lu Xun on Chinese characteristics

One of the most appealing personalities of the early twentieth century was the author and commentator Lu Xun (1881–1936). As he explained in the preface to one of his collections of stories, 'Those who come down in the world learn in the process what society is really like.' Thus his uncharitable view of both the old Chinese literati and ordinary Chinese peasants and townsmen probably owes something to his childhood in a family on the way down – his grandfather, an official, was imprisoned for bribery, his father was an opium addict, and Lu Xun himself as a boy made many a visit to pawn shops to keep the family from going under.

Through his writing career, Lu Xun responded with merciless sarcasm to calls to preserve China's 'national essence'. Not only were there a great many traits he would have been happy to see the Chinese discard, but he thought it folly to try to distinguish between what was Chinese and what was not – Did his moustache, which some thought looked Japanese, make him less Chinese? What if the Japanese moustache style was itself copied from the Germans? Or if Chinese men in Tang and Song times had had moustaches that like his turned up at the tips? If fountain pens worked better than old-fashioned Chinese brushes and inkstones for students taking notes in class, wouldn't it be better to manufacture them, as the Japanese did, than denounce their use as un-Chinese? Would anyone benefit from making China into some huge antique, other than foreign tourists in search of the quaint or literati who had nothing to be proud of other than their knowledge of old books and curios?

Lu Xun's commentary took on more of a political edge starting in 1926 when some of his students were among forty-seven protestors killed in an unarmed demonstration in Beijing. The next year, when the Nationalist Party turned on the Communists, the slaughter that ensued shook him further. The following item, published in April 1928, contains both indictments of Chinese character, which were typical of his earlier essays, and expression of leftist leanings found in his later writing.

WIPING OUT THE REDS – A GREAT SPECTACLE

The [Shanghai newspaper] *Shen Bao* of 6 April carried a 'Letter from Changsha' describing the seizure of the provincial committee of the Communist Party by the Hunan authorities, who sentenced over thirty of them to death and executed eight of them on 29 March. This article is so well written that I am quoting it:

'After the execution that day, because three of the prisoners were female – Ma Shuchun, aged sixteen, Ma Zhichun, aged fourteen, and Fu Fengjun, aged twenty-four – the whole city turned out to have a look. You could hardly move for the crowd. The fact that the head of the Communist ringleader Guo Liang was on display at Court Gate increased the number of spectators. Between Court Gate and the Octagonal Pavilion there was a traffic jam. After the citizens near the South Gate had seen Guo Liang's head, they went on to the Teachers' Association to see the female corpses. Once the citizens near the North Gate had seen the female corpses at the Teachers' Association, they went on to see Guo Liang's head at Court Gate. The whole city was in a ferment, and fresh impetus was given to the urge to wipe out the Communists. Not till dusk did the spectators begin to disperse.'

Having copied this out, I realize I have blundered. I simply meant to make a few observations, but I see now that I shall probably be suspected of sneering (some say I do nothing but sneer). Others will denounce me for spreading darkness, and call down destruction upon me so that I can carry all the darkness with me into the grave. Still, though I cannot keep quiet, I will confine my observations to 'art for art's sake'. How powerful that short report is! As I read it, I felt I could see the head impaled at Court Gate and the three headless female corpses at the Teachers' Association. They must have been stripped to the waist at least, too – or perhaps I am guessing wrongly because I am so depraved. And then all those 'citizens,' one contingent heading south, another north, jostling and shouting ... I could fill in the details too, the

Above. As perhaps the best-known writer of his generation, Lu Xun was frequently asked to take stands on the issues of his day. He is shown here addressing a crowd at Beijing Normal University in November 1932.

Right. The modernity of Lu Xun's ideas and rhetorical style were subtly advertised by the striking designs of his book covers. Lu Xun admired European graphic art and promoted Western printmaking techniques. Shown here is the cover for *Wandering*, a collection of his short stories published in 1926.

rapt anticipation on some faces, the satisfaction on others. I have never come across such powerful writing in all the 'revolutionary' or 'realist' literature I have read....

Let me conclude by exposing a little more darkness: Our present-day (present-day, not transcendental!) Chinese actually do not care about political parties – all they want to see are 'heads' and 'female corpses'. If these are available, no matter whose they are, our citizens will go to have a look. I have seen or heard of a good many cases of this in the short space of the last twenty years: the Boxer Uprising, the suppression of revolts at the end of the Qing dynasty, the 1913 events [when Yuan Shikai suppressed the republicans], last year, and this year.

challenged the long-standing Confucian deference toward elders by celebrating youth: 'Youth is like early spring, like the rising sun, like the trees and grass in bud, like a newly sharpened blade.' He urged his readers not to waste their 'fleeting time in arguing with the older generation on this and that, hoping for them to be reborn and remodelled.' They should think for themselves and not let the old contaminate them. In other articles he wrote that Confucianism had to be rejected before China could attain equality and human rights: 'We must be thoroughly aware of the incompatibility between Confucianism and the new belief, the new society, and the new state.'

One of the first faculty members appointed to Beijing University by Chen Duxiu was Hu Shi, just back from seven years' study of philosophy in the United States at Cornell and Columbia. Hu Shi was not as all-encompassing in his rejection of tradition as Chen. The aim of the new thought, he wrote in *New Youth*, was not to replace old beliefs with ones imported from the west but to develop the habit of critical thought: ancient wisdom had to be re-evaluated on the basis of whether its tenets were still suitable to the needs of the day.

While still in the United States, Hu Shi began a campaign to get people to abandon writing in the classical literary language that had been the mark of the educated person for so many centuries. 'A dead language', Hu declared, 'cannot produce a living literature.' Since Chinese civilization had been so closely tied to this language, his assertions came dangerously close to declaring Chinese civilization dead. Hu Shi did recognize that the old written language had allowed communication between speakers of mutually unintelligible dialects and thus had been a source of unity, but he argued that once a national literature was produced in vernacular Chinese, a standard dialect would establish itself, much as such standard vernaculars had gained hold in Europe. Chen Duxiu supported Hu's literary reform, and soon *New Youth* was written entirely in colloquial Chinese. To Chen, the liberating effects of language reform were its strongest drawing points; its use would open literature to 'the people' and free thought from the stultifying effect of old mindsets.

One of the first to write well in the vernacular was Lu Xun (1881–1936), educated in Japan and well read in European literature, especially Russian. The May 1918 issue of *New Youth* contained his first vernacular short story, 'Diary of a Madman', a powerful condemnation of traditional Chinese civilization. In it the main character goes mad (or is taken to be mad) after he discovers that what his seniors saw as lofty values was nothing more than cannibalism. The humour of Lu Xun's longest story, 'The True Story of Ah Q', was also black. The protagonist is a man of low social standing. Always on the lookout for a way to get ahead, he is too cowardly and self-deceiving ever to succeed. No matter how he is humiliated he claims moral superiority. His ears prick up in 1911 when he hears talk of a revolution, but soon he discovers that the old, classically educated elite and the new, foreign-educated elite are collaborating in taking over the revolution for themselves and want no interference from him. He comes to a sorry end, executed by representatives of the revolution for a robbery he would have liked to have committed but actually had not managed to pull off. In stories like these, Lu Xun gave voice to those troubled by China's prospects and weary of China's old order but reluctant to set their hopes on easy solutions.

In 1919, four years after *New Youth* had set the 'New Culture' movement in motion, young people determined to arrest China's decline took to the streets, their anger triggered by news of how the Versailles Peace Conference was handling the disposition of German rights in Shandong. In 1914 Japan as an ally of Britain and France had seized German territories in China. In 1917 the Chinese joined the allies as well, and even though they sent no combatants, they did send some 140,000 labourers to France, where they unloaded cargo ships, dug trenches, and otherwise provided manpower of direct use to the war effort. China was, thus, expecting some gain from the allies' victory, particularly in light of Wilson's stress on national self-determination. Unfortunately for China, Japan had reached a secret agreement with Britain, France, and Italy to support Japan's claim to German rights in Shandong. Japanese diplomats had also won the consent of the warlord government that held Beijing at the time.

On 4 May 1919, when word reached them that the decision had gone in favour of Japan, some 3,000 Beijing students assembled at Tiananmen Square in front of the old palace, where they shouted patriotic slogans and tried to arouse spectators to action. After some students broke through police lines to beat up a pro-Japanese official and set fire to the home of a cabinet minister, the governor suppressed the demonstrators and arrested their leaders. These actions in turn set off a wave of protests around the country in support of the students and their cause. Everyone, it seemed, was on the students' side – teachers and workers, the press and the merchants, Sun Zhongshan and the warlords. Soon strikes closed schools in more than 200 cities. The Beijing warlord government finally arrested 1,150 student protestors, turning parts of Beijing University into a jail, but patriotic sympathy strikes, especially in Shanghai, soon forced the government to release them. The cabinet fell and China refused to sign the Treaty of Versailles.

The protestors' moral victory set the tone for cultural politics through the 1920s and into the 1930s. The personal and intellectual goals of the New Culture Movement were pursued along with and sometimes in competition with the national power goals of the May Fourth Movement. Nationalism, patriotism, progress, science, democracy, and freedom were the goals; imperialism, feudalism, warlordism, autocracy, patriarchy, and blind adherence to tradition were the enemies. Intellectuals struggled with how to be strong and modern and yet Chinese, how to preserve China as a political entity in the world of competing nations. Many concentrated on the creation of a new literature in the vernacular, others on the study of western science, philosophy, and social and political thought. Prominent intellectuals from the west were invited to visit China and lecture. When the

The outside world learned of the plight of China's starving peasants when an international relief effort was mounted to aid the twenty million people devastated by the north China drought of 1920/21.

educational reformer John Dewey visited in 1919 to 1921, he was impressed by the openness of Chinese young people, commenting, 'There seems to be no country in the world where students are so unanimously and eagerly interested in what is modern and new in thought, especially about social and economic matters, nor where the arguments which can be brought in favour of the established order and the status quo have so little weight – indeed are so unuttered.' Others who visited include Bertrand Russell (1920–21), Albert Einstein (1922), Margaret Sanger (1922), and George Bernard Shaw (1933).

The attraction to liberal western culture was strong but it did not go unchallenged. Some who for a while had been attracted to things western came to feel western culture was too materialistic, especially after World War I. Out of fear that China was in danger of losing its 'national essence', concerned scholars turned to studies of ancient history and folklore to try to identify this essence.

With the success of the Bolshevik revolution in Russia in 1917, intellectuals also began to take an interest in Marxism–Leninism. This strain of socialism offered a blueprint for a world of abundance without exploitation and had the added appeal that it was anti-western and anti-imperialist and had just proved itself capable of bringing revolution to a backward country. The basic tenets of Marxism–Leninism were even more at odds with traditional Chinese thought than western liberal ideologies of democracy and representative government. The emphasis on class struggle and violent overthrow of those in power was diametrically opposed to Confucian emphasis on harmony and on respect for hierarchy, though descriptions of an eventual utopia of to each according to his needs had some resonance with Chinese millenarian rebel ideologies.

For the May 1919 issue of *New Youth* Li Dazhao, the librarian at Beijing University, wrote an introduction to Marxist theory, explaining such concepts as class struggle and capitalist exploitation. Soon intellectuals were looking not only into the works of Marx but also those of Lenin and Trotsky with their evocations of an imminent international revolutionary upheaval that would bring an end to imperialism. Though China did not have much of an urban proletariat to be the vanguard of its revolution, the nation as a whole, Li Dazhao pointed out, could be looked on as exploited by the capitalist imperialist countries. Li organized a Marxist study group at Beijing University that attracted progressive young intellectuals, including Mao Zedong, recently arrived from Hunan. At much the same time

Chen Duxiu was also becoming interested in Marxism. Chen had ended up in jail as a result of the May Fourth demonstrations, and had became disillusioned with the west and its talk of democracy. He resigned from his university post and went to Shanghai where he formed Marxist study groups.

The early Marxist study groups might not have amounted to much if it had not been for the Comintern, the Russian-led organization to promote communist revolution throughout the world. Soon after the Comintern learned of the existence of Marxist study groups in China, agents were sent to help them turn themselves into communist party cells. These agents taught Chinese organizations how to attain party discipline through 'democratic centralism'. Each local cell elected delegates to higher levels, up to the national party congress, with its central executive committee and the latter's standing committee. Delegates flowed up, decisions flowed down. Decisions could be debated within a cell, but once decisions were reached, all were bound to obey, decisions made by higher levels being binding on lower ones. This Leninist form of organization provided a degree of discipline and centralization beyond anything in the existing repertoire of Chinese organizational behaviour. Following Comintern advice, in July 1921, at a meeting of thirteen delegates representing fifty-seven members, the Chinese Communist Party constituted itself as a secret, exclusive, centralized party seeking power; it broke with the anarchists and guild socialists and asserted the primacy of class struggle.

BUILDING A PARTY-STATE

The central story in the politics of China from the early twenties to 1949 concerns the effort to create a new type of political centre. The ease with which Yuan Shikai had pushed the revolutionaries out of power demonstrated that they needed their own army. From the early twenties on, both the Nationalist and the Communist parties made concurrent attempts to build up Leninist party-states and party armies. Twice the two joined forces in united fronts, but at bottom they were rivals, both pursuing full control of a government governing all Chinese territory.

The similarity of their party-building endeavours owes much to Comintern influence on both of them. Until representatives of the Comintern offered assistance to Sun Zhongshan in 1921, he had had little luck in gaining the help of foreign powers, who treated whatever government held Beijing as the legitimate government of China. The newly established Soviet Union saw its interests differently; it wanted to help build a revolutionary China not only to spread world revolution but also because a weak China might invite the expansion of Japan, the USSR's main worry to the east. In Marxist–Leninist theory, socialist revolution would occur by stages, and since China had not yet gone through a bourgeois, capitalist stage, a victory by the Nationalist revolutionaries who would overthrow the imperialists seemed the next stage for China. Then, in the future, when conditions ripened, there could be a social revolution and a communist victory.

To help the Nationalists build a tight party organization, the Comintern sent advisors who introduced democratic centralism to them as well. On Borodin's encouragement, Sun Zhongshan elaborated his 'Three Principles of the People' into an ideology for the Party. The principles were nationalism (anti-imperialism), democracy (anti-monarchy), and 'people's livelihood' (now equated with socialism). Building a party army to allow seizure of power also was a Comintern priority; by 1925 there were about 1,000 Russian military advisors in China helping the Nationalists. Chinese officers were also sent to the Soviet Union, including Jiang Jieshi (Chiang Kaishek, 1888–1975), who was sent there for four months' training before being made head of a new military academy at Huangpu (Whampoa) near Guangzhou. The communist Zhou Enlai (1898–1976), recently returned from France, became deputy head of this academy's political education department.

At the same time that Comintern advisors were aiding the build-up of the Nationalists' power base, they continued to guide the development of a Chinese Communist Party. This party grew slowly, and at no time in the 1920s or 1930s had nearly as many members or supporters as the Nationalist Party. In 1922, on Comintern urging, the decision was made to ally with the Nationalists, as a consequence of which members of the Communist Party joined the Nationalist Party as individuals but continued separate Communist Party activities on the side.

The development of China's industries made labour organizing a fertile field for communists in the 1920s. During World War I, a drastic reduction in Europe's capacity to export allowed China's industries to expand rapidly; from 1914 to 1922 the number of looms in textile factories increased threefold, from 4,800 to 19,000. Conditions in China's factories in the 1920s were as bad as they had been

Child labour was common in the textile industry, not only because young children could be hired for very low wages, but also because, with their small fingers, they were good at tending spinning machines.

a century earlier in Britain, with twelve-hour days, seven-day weeks, and widespread child labour, especially in textile mills. Labour contractors often recruited in the countryside and kept workers in conditions of debt slavery, providing the most minimal housing and food. That many of the factories were foreign-owned (increasingly Japanese-owned) added to friction between the proprietors and the workers. With the support and encouragement of organizers, such workers were quite willing to strike; there were fifty major strikes in 1921 and ninety-one in 1922. Anti-union violence became common as well. In one incident in 1923 soldiers of the warlord Wu Peifu killed sixty-five striking railway workers in Henan.

Agitation against capitalist factory owners became more and more entangled with agitation against the unequal treaties and the privileges of foreigners in the treaty ports. The incident that created the greatest uproar occurred on

30 May 1925, when the British police in the International Settlement in Shanghai shot at a group of demonstrators, killing eleven. Almost immediately strikes, boycotts, and demonstrations were staged all over the country. Then in June in Guangzhou fifty-two Chinese demonstrators were killed when British troops opened fire, which led to a huge strike and a boycott of trade with Hong Kong. In these circumstances union and party recruiting by both the Communists and the Nationalists was very successful. The time seemed ripe to mobilize patriots across the country to fight the 'twin evils' of warlordism and imperialism, to reunify the country under a government strong enough and determined enough to end the unequal treaties and the semi-colonial status of the treaty ports.

In 1925, before the planned Northern Expedition to reunify the country could be mounted, Sun Zhongshan died of cancer. The recently reorganized Nationalist Party held together after his death despite the jostling of more leftist and more rightist leaders to succeed. In July 1926 the Northern Expedition was finally launched with Jiang Jieshi as military commander and with Communists aiding the military advance by organizing peasants and workers along the way. By the end of 1926 the Nationalist government was moved from Guangzhou to Wuhan, where the left wing of the party became dominant.

In 1927, Jiang Jieshi married Song Meiling, daughter of a wealthy Christian industrialist and sister of Sun Zhongshan's widow. Song Meiling had been educated in the United States, spoke perfect English, and worked hard to gain American help, especially after the outbreak of war.

The United Front between the Nationalist and Communist parties was expedient for both at the time, but covered over deep differences. Many of the supporters of the Nationalists felt rightly threatened by talk of class warfare, and the Nationalist military included many staunch anti-communists. In April 1927, with the Nationalist army approaching Shanghai, Jiang organized members of the Green Gang, a Shanghai underworld racketeering gang, to kill all labour union members and Communists in the city. Within a few days, hundreds had been slaughtered and Jiang had secured control of the Nationalist Party.

During this crisis Comintern representatives and Communist Party leaders in Wuhan still followed Moscow's instructions to try to salvage the situation by working with the left wing of the Nationalist Party. Finally in August Communist forces began fighting back. Mao Zedong's attempted 'Autumn Harvest Uprising' was quickly suppressed, as were comparable insurgent actions elsewhere. From 1927 to 1930 the hunt was on for Communist organizers all over the country – in some areas the only evidence troops needed to conclude that a young woman was a Communist was bobbed hair. What Communist leadership survived was driven underground and into the countryside.

As the anti-Communist terror continued, the military unification of the country proceeded, and in 1928 the Nationalists gained the allegiance of three key warlords to reunite the country. International recognition quickly followed, and the prospects for China looked brighter than they had for decades. With many returned students appointed to key government posts, the Nationalist government appeared increasingly progressive to foreign powers, who over the next several years consented to reductions in their special privileges. Tariff autonomy was recovered, as well as control over the Maritime Customs, Salt Administration, and Post Office. In addition the number of foreign concessions was reduced from thirty-three to thirteen, and extraterritoriality was eliminated for some of the more minor countries.

From 1928 on Jiang Jieshi was the key leader of the Nationalists. A determined patriot, Jiang was above all a military man. From a landlord-merchant family near Ningbo, he had aspired to take the civil service examinations but when they were abolished he went to Japan to study military science, joining the precursor of the Nationalist Party while there. His appointment to head the Huangpu Academy was crucial to his rise because it allowed him to form strong ties to young officers in the party's army. A skilful politician, once Jiang became fully enmeshed in party and government matters, he proved able to balance different cliques and build personal ties to key power-holders.

When the Nationalists reached Shanghai in 1927, they turned on the Communists and unleashed a 'White Terror', searching out and killing union members and party organizers.

Many of Jiang's efforts at state building focused on the army, for the new government still needed to rein in surviving warlords, suppress the Communists, and resist Japan's aggressive designs. To modernize the army, Jiang turned to Germany, attracted by the success the Nazis were having in mobilizing and militarizing their nation. German advisors helped Jiang train an elite corps and plan the campaigns against the Communist base in Jiangxi. They also arranged for the import of German arms. Besides modernizing the military, the Nationalist government made concerted efforts to revive and modernize the economy, battered by the disruption of the warlords, who, for instance, often took over railroad lines for their own purposes. For guidance on economic matters the Nationalists turned to the liberal, capitalist west. Western-trained economists and engineers undertook to modernize the banking, currency, and taxation systems, as well as to improve transportation and communication facilities.

In 1923 the Comintern sent the experienced organizer, Mikhail Borodin, to China to help the Nationalists organize themselves into a Leninist party, with strong discipline and central control. He is shown here at a rally in Wuhan in 1927 during the Northern Expedition.

During his first few years in power, Jiang had considerable success in gradually eliminating his warlord opponents. He proved less successful in state building, however, due in large part to his mistrust of institutions and his unwillingness to allow the emergence of rival centres of power. To combat the intellectual appeal of the communists and build support for his government, in 1934 Jiang launched an ideological indoctrination program, the New Life Movement, inspired by contemporary fascist movements in Europe. Its goal, he claimed, was to 'militarize the life of the people of the entire nation' and to nourish in them 'a capacity to endure hardship and especially a habit and instinct for unified behaviour', to make them 'willing to sacrifice for the nation at all times'. Also based on fascist models was the creation of an organization of graduates of the Huangpu military academy, dubbed the 'Blueshirts', who pledged themselves to an ascetic life devoted to their leader, Jiang. The Blueshirts came to play a significant role in the Nationalists' secret police.

In the early thirties China appeared to be rapidly modernizing. Despite the worldwide depression, life in the major cities was taking on more of a western look. The urban middle class frequently wore western dress for work and school. Banks, trading firms, and clubs constructed large European-style buildings on the main streets, not hidden behind walls in the traditional style. In the coastal treaty ports foreigners and their material goods were as pervasive as in the outright European colonies of the period in south and southeast Asia. Other cities remained more distinctly Chinese in appearance – Beijing, for example, still had its huge walls – but conveniences like electricity were gradually changing the way all major cities functioned. Even intellectual life acquired a more western form, with higher education and the public press emerging as the key institutions. A professional class was gaining influence, composed not simply of intellectuals (heirs to the old literati elite) but also of scientists, engineers, architects, economists, physicians, and others with technical expertise, often acquired through study abroad. Even those who remained in China for their education had become comfortable with western ways of thinking and acting; not only did they study books written by western authors, but they frequently studied under foreign teachers, especially if they attended one of the many Christian colleges active in the period. One should not imagine, of course, that everyone in the cities was middle class or prospering. With an enormous reservoir of labour, life for the urban poor seemed hardly to improve at all. In 1937 Lao She published one of the most successful novels about life at the bottom in Beijing, *Rickshaw*. But the west, after all, also had its proletariat, and those who wished to see signs of progress toward a more prosperous future could find them in 1930s China.

Much good can be said of the Nationalists' efforts to build China into a strong and modern nation, but they were focused on the cities, not the countryside. When the British economist R. H. Tawney surveyed China in the early 1930s, he found China's peasants caught in an ecological crisis of soil exhaustion, deforestation, erosion, and flooding, made worse by primitive technology, inadequate credit and transportation systems, and exploitative tenancy arrangements. 'In some districts,' he reported, 'the position of the rural population is that of a man standing permanently up to the neck in water, so that even a ripple is sufficient to drown him.' Most peasants had seen no improvement in their standard of living since Qing times. Continued population growth – by 1930 the figure was over 500 million – resulted in relentless increase in the pressure on available land. The advantages brought by modernization, such as cheaper transportation via railways and cheaper manufactured consumer goods, were yet to have a major impact on the rural economy. China's exports of silk and tea were suffering, first because Chinese producers lost ground to Japanese and Indian competitors, then because foreign demand plummeted due to the Great Depression. Villagers also suffered from local bullies, warlords, and local elites who put their own survival ahead of anything else. The Nationalist central government did little to build new political institutions in rural areas, giving provincial governments considerable autonomy. The Northern Expedition had succeeded by accepting virtually anyone willing to throw in his lot with the Nationalists, and thus all sorts of local power holders had been incorporated. The government and private philanthropic organizations did sponsor some rural reconstruction projects that tried to raise the level of rural education, create facilities for credit, encourage modern enterprises, and form peasant associations, but gains were usually limited to small areas and short periods. Moreover, after the purge of the Communists, grass-roots reforms like land redistribution were looked on with suspicion.

LIBERATING WOMEN

Of the many social changes of the early twentieth century, the most fundamental may be the changes in the family and women's roles in society. Assumptions about women's place in society that had gone unquestioned for centuries came under concerted attack in the early decades of the century, and women began to participate in society in ways never before imagined.

Political and intellectual revolutionaries of the early twentieth century – from Kang Youwei and Liang Qichao to Sun Zhongshan, Chen Duxiu, Lu Xun, and Mao Zedong – all spoke out on the need to change ways of thinking about women and their social roles. Early in the century the key issues were footbinding and women's education. In a short period of time, women's seclusion and tiny feet went from being a source of pride, a basis for asserting the superiority of Chinese culture, to a source of embarrassment. That foreigners pointed to footbinding as proof of the barbarity of Chinese civilization undoubtedly made modernizers even more determined to get Chinese to give up the practice. Opponents of footbinding described it as a gruesome custom that stood in the way of modernization by crippling a large part of the Chinese population. The earliest anti-footbinding societies, founded in the 1890s, were composed of men who would agree not only not to bind their daughters' feet, but even more crucially not to marry their sons to women with bound feet. The proportion of women with natural feet steadily increased in the early twentieth century, and after 1930 only in scattered, outlying areas did young girls still have their feet bound, though, of course, there remained many older women with bound feet, as it was difficult and painful to reverse the process once a girl had reached ten or twelve.

Female political activists even began to appear, such as Qiu Jin, a woman who became an ardent nationalist after witnessing the Boxer Rebellion and the imperialist occupation of Beijing. Unhappy in her marriage, in 1904 she left her husband and went to Japan, enrolling in a girls' vocational school but devoting most of her time in Japan to revolutionary politics, even learning to make bombs. She also took up feminist issues. In her speeches and essays she castigated female infanticide, footbinding, arranged marriages, wife-beating, and the cult of widow chastity; she called on women to stop submitting to oppression and to give up attempting to please men. In 1906 she returned to Shanghai where she founded the *Chinese Women's Journal* and taught in a girls' school. Anti-Manchu political revolution was still her principal objective, however, and in 1907 she was executed for her role in an abortive Nationalist uprising, making her a heroine to many of the young.

Schools for women, like the one Qiu Jin taught at, were growing more and more common in this period. In 1907 the Qing government approved a national system of women's education. By 1910 there were over 40,000 girls' schools in the country, with 1.6 million students; by 1919 the figures had reached 134,000 schools and 4.5 million students. Although there were still seven times as many boys in school as girls, girls' opportunities had been more fundamentally altered. After 1920 opportunities for women in higher education rapidly expanded, and by 1935 there were more than 6,000 colleges, universities, and teachers' colleges admitting women, resulting in a substantial supply of women as teachers, nurses, and civil servants in the larger cities. In the countryside, of course, change came much more slowly. A large-scale survey of rural households in the 1930s discovered that fewer than 2 per cent of the women were literate, compared to 30 per cent of the men.

Women in middle and higher schools were subjected to the same bombardment of new ideas as their male counterparts, and were just as enthusiastic about whatever was new and modern. Both men and women became caught up in enthusiasm for the new woman after a special issue of *New Youth* included a full translation of Ibsen's play, *A Doll's House*, in which the central figure, Nora,

By the 1930s and the 1940s city residents were no longer surprised to witness women students take to the streets to protest government actions. Here a group of female students are photographed protesting against the black market in 1949.

decides by the play's end to leave her husband and find her own destiny. The play was soon being performed on stages around China, with people latching on to lines such as 'don't become a man's plaything', 'recognize individuality', and 'demand freedom'. The pursuit of personal fulfilment through love came to be looked on as legitimate, obedience to the demands of elders as craven. Not that people thought achievement of these new goals was easy. Ba Jin's highly popular novel, *The Family*, published in 1931, narrates the struggle of the youngest members of an old, wealthy, scholarly family to save themselves from being crushed by the oppression of traditional morality and traditional authority structures. Sons and daughters and masters and servants are all shown to be equally trapped, but the obstacles keeping the women from extricating themselves are even more formidable than those confronting the men.

Besides attempting to change people's ways of thinking about parental authority and women's proper roles in society, activists fought for changes in women's legal status. Efforts to get the vote were generally unsuccessful. However, in the 1920s both the Nationalists and Communists organized women's departments and adopted resolutions calling for equal rights for women and freedom of marriage and divorce. Divorce proved the trickiest issue. As Song Qingling, the widow of Sun Zhongshan, reported, 'If we do not grant the appeals of the women, they lose faith in the union and in the women's freedom we are teaching. But if we grant the divorces, then we have trouble with the peasant's union, since it is very hard for a peasant to get a wife, and he has often paid much for his present unwilling one.' Once in power, the Nationalists set about drafting a new civil code, issued in 1930. Daughters were given not only the right to choose their husbands and repudiate betrothals made in their childhood by their parents, but also rights to inherit family property equally with their brothers. Wives were given rights to initiate divorce on nearly equal terms with their husbands. The new labour law issued the next year ordered that women get the same pay as men when they did the same work.

To women outside the educated class, these legal changes had a limited impact. No campaign was undertaken to spread knowledge of the provisions of the new marriage laws in the countryside, and getting them observed in rural areas was never given any priority. Surveys of rural villages in the 1930s and 1940s found not only that arranged marriage and inheritance by sons continued, but that few people even knew that the laws had changed. Changes that did alter the lives of working women had more to do with the growth of industrial capitalism than with new liberal ideas about women's equality with men. Growing industrial cities provided many employment opportunities for women, but few of them were very attractive. In Shanghai in 1930 over 170,000 women worked in industry, about half in cotton mills. There were also about 50,000 prostitutes and probably as many household servants. The typical prostitute or mill hand was a young unmarried illiterate woman recruited in the countryside by labour contractors. The con-

Opposite
Shanghai in the late 1940s was
an exciting city where the new
and the old, the rich and the
poor rubbed shoulders with
each other. Here two women
have set themselves up to take
on mending in front of a shop
selling western hats.

tractor would supply a small advance payment, often to the girl's parents, and would make arrangements in the city for employment, housing, and food. The women were often kept in conditions of debt servitude, and few found their situations in any way liberating. Some factory workers joined unions and engaged in strikes; others put their hopes on getting married and returning to the patriarchal structures that educated women were decrying as oppressive.

DEFENDING AGAINST THE JAPANESE INVASION

From the time of the May Fourth protests in 1919, Chinese patriots saw Japan as the greatest threat to China's sovereignty. In 1895 Japan had won Taiwan. In 1905, after an impressive victory over Russia, it gained a dominant position in southern Manchuria. In 1915, by applying pressure on Yuan Shikai, Japan had secured a broad range of economic privileges. The Japanese Army in Manchuria, ostensibly there to protect Japan's railroads and other economic interests, was full of militarists who kept pushing Japanese civil authorities to let the army occupy the entire area. In 1928 Japanese officers assassinated the warlord of Manchuria, Zhang Zuolin, hoping for a crisis that would allow Japan to extend its power base. In 1931 Japanese soldiers set off a bomb on the Southern Manchurian Railroad to give themselves an excuse to occupy Shenyang 'in self-defence'. China did not attempt military resistance, but did appeal to the League of Nations, which recognized China as being in the right but imposed no real sanctions on Japan. Then in January 1932 Japan attacked Shanghai to retaliate against anti-Japanese protests. Shanghai was by that point such an international city that the Japanese assault was widely witnessed and widely condemned, especially the bombing of civilian residential areas. After four months the Japanese withdrew from Shanghai, but in Manchuria they set up a puppet regime, making the last Qing emperor the nominal head of 'Manchukuo'.

Anger at Japanese aggression heightened Chinese nationalism and led to the formation of national salvation leagues and boycotts of Japanese goods. Still, Jiang Jieshi, like most military men of the day, did not see any point in putting up a fight when Japanese firepower was so clearly superior. Thinking in traditional terms that coupled unity and strength, Jiang assumed that all Chinese would have to be united under one leader in order to oppose Japan – a country with only about a fifth of China's population. His first priority, therefore, was to rid the country of internal enemies. It took a mutiny to compel him to change his policy. In 1936 troops that had been driven out of Manchuria by the Japanese kidnapped Jiang on a visit to Xi'an, and would not release him until he agreed to form a united front with the Communists to fight Japan.

In 1937 Jiang decided to fight when the Japanese staged another incident as an excuse for extending their territory. Jiang was probably hoping to inflict a quick defeat to convince Japan that the Nanjing government was a power to be reckoned with, so that they would negotiate with him rather than continue to move into

Village fairs

Despite the bombardment of new ideas and new technologies, cultural change was slow to penetrate the Chinese countryside, where 80 to 90 per cent of the population continued to live. By the end of the 1920s, most villagers had given up footbinding and were willing to let their children attend modern schools. Still, even in the 1940s rural cultural life focused more on fairs, festivals, and rituals than on the circulation of newspapers or magazines, much less radio or phonographs.

Many customs varied from one village to the next, but certain cultural patterns were widely shared across China. New Year, the Lantern Festival two weeks later, the Qingming grave-sweeping festival in the spring, and a few other seasonal festivals were celebrated all over the country, providing opportunities for amusement, socializing, and special food. Another common focus of village culture was the temple fair, scheduled on different days in different places, depending on the birthday of the god enshrined at the main local temple. These fairs were major community events. Committees had to be formed to collect funds and arrange facilities. During the days of the fair, hundreds of temporary shops and stalls would spring up and transform a backwater village into a crowded commercial centre where peasants could take care of necessary business, pay respect to the gods, and have fun at the same time. The popular culture that enlivened these fairs included lion dancing and stilt walking, martial arts, and music full of drums, cymbals, and trumpets.

In one county in Hebei surveyed in the late 1920s, there were fifty annual fairs, thirty-five of them in villages, the rest in cities. In one village of 326 families, a fair was held at the temple of a god associated with buckwheat. On the first day of the fair people went to the temple, many spending the whole night burning incense and bowing to the ground. The god was given a new robe, fanned, and feasted. The next three days were devoted to commerce and amusement. The shops and stalls occupied over twenty-five acres and attracted some 10,000 people a day. At the animal market nearly 2,400 head were sold. The stalls included about eighty cloth dealers, twenty barbers, ten fortune tellers, and thirty jewellery sellers. Peep shows, story tellers, and martial arts experts were on hand to provide additional entertainment.

Gambling was an attraction at most fairs, even though it was frowned on at other occasions. Free theatrical performances – put on as offerings to the gods – were also a popular feature of village fairs. Illiterate and semi-literate peasants were great fans of operas performed by local amateur or travelling professional groups. In the same Hebei county, amateur groups generally consisted of fifteen or sixteen men, some of whom took female roles. The better singers would take on boys as apprentices and teach them roles, which had to be memorized. The themes of the plays tended to be traditional, with stories of filial piety, wifely devotion, and martial heroes; gods regularly intervened, and plots were often leavened with a good sprinkling of broad humour.

Village women were among the most avid fair-goers, attending not only those in their own villages, but in neighbouring ones as well. Women and girls welcomed the opportunity to leave the house, be entertained, and visit friends and relatives. Some women sold their handicrafts at fairs, and most enjoyed the chance to go shopping and to watch the operas.

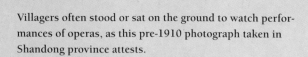

Villagers often stood or sat on the ground to watch performances of operas, as this pre-1910 photograph taken in Shandong province attests.

China as though it was unoccupied, but Japan instead launched a full-scale offensive sweeping south. Jiang was forced to abandon Beijing and Tianjin, but he used his best troops to hold off the Japanese at Shanghai for three months. He asked for an all-out stand, and his troops courageously persisted despite heavy shelling and bombing, in the process absorbing 250,000 casualties, killed or wounded. After Shanghai fell, the Nationalist troops streamed toward the Nationalist capital at Nanjing. When the Japanese conquered Nanjing in December 1937, they went on a rampage, massacring tens of thousands of civilians and fugitive soldiers, raping at least 20,000 women, and laying the city waste. The seven weeks of mayhem was widely reported in the foreign press, where it was labelled the Rape of Nanking.

During the course of the next year, the Japanese secured control of all of eastern China and set up puppet regimes headed by Chinese collaborators. When the Chinese had to retreat from Kaifeng, Jiang ordered his engineers to blow up the dykes on the Yellow River, creating a gigantic flood that engulfed more than 4,000 villages and held up the Japanese for three months. The Nationalists' capital was moved inland first to Wuhan, then to Chongqing, deep in Sichuan. After the retreat to Chongqing, the war was locked into stalemate until the Japanese offensive of 1944. Free China contained 60 per cent of China's population but only 5 per cent of its industry. Chinese engineers made heroic efforts to build a new industrial base, but constant Japanese bombing, the end of Soviet aid in 1939, and the closing of the Burma Road in 1942 made it impossible to build a modern army capable of driving the Japanese out of China. After 1941 American advisors and American aid flown over 'the Hump' from Burma enabled Jiang to build a number of modern divisions, but the bulk of China's five-million-man army consisted of ill-trained, demoralized conscripts.

During the first few years after the Japanese invasion, there was some genuine co-operation between the Communists and Nationalists. This largely ended, however, after the Communists' New Fourth Army was attacked by the Nationalists in January 1941 because it had not complied rapidly enough with an order to retreat north of the Yangzi. Not only were around 3,000 troops killed in battle, but many were shot after arrest or sent to prison camps. From this point on the Nationalists imposed an economic blockade on the Communists' base area in Yan'an, which led to serious shortages of food and weapons.

In this period international alignments were shifting rapidly. Britain proved unable to defend Hong Kong, Singapore, or Burma from Japanese invasions in 1941–42, and it became apparent that the emerging power in the Pacific was the United States. The American-educated wife of Jiang, Song Meiling, was popular with the American press and lobbied effectively for China. Roosevelt, looking ahead, wished to see China become the dominant power in East Asia after the defeat of Japan, and convinced his allies to include Jiang in major meetings of the allies at Cairo and Yalta (though Churchill referred to the idea of making China one of the Big Four as 'an absolute farce'). It was as a result of this sort of geo-politics that China, so long scorned as weak and backward, became one of the five permanent members of the United Nations' security council after the war.

THE COMMUNIST VICTORY

The rise of the Communist Party is one of the most intensively studied subjects in all of Chinese history. The more scholars uncover about life in the 1930s and 1940s, the more failings of the Nationalists they find: widespread government corruption, spiralling inflation, intractable poverty, the alienation of the educated elite, the persistence of warlordism, and so on. The accumulation of this evidence makes the victory of the Communists seem almost adventitious: they just happened to be there as the Nationalists lost popular support. On the other hand, scholars who have studied the Communists' local programmes have been impressed by the way they turned dismal rural poverty and foreign invasion into assets, using them to convince villagers that radical change was imperative and the Communist Party was best qualified to institute it. Seen in this light, the victory of the Communists seems almost foreordained, the result of superior strategy and organizational methods. Then again, research into internal Communist Party politics has revealed the importance of Mao Zedong (Mao Tse-tung, 1893–1976) as a master tactician who almost single-handedly transformed the party into a potent weapon, responsive to his will. There is probably truth to all three of these perspectives; if the Nationalists had been more successful, the Communist Party, no matter what its internal organization or external strategies, would not have been able to bring revolution to China; but the sort of revolution that came to China was powerfully shaped by the ideas, experiences, and personality of Mao Zedong and the policies for training cadres and mobilizing peasants that he succeeded in getting established.

Mao was from a farming family in Hunan; his mother was illiterate and his father, a hard worker, was slowly able to build up his holdings to the point where he could be classed as a rich peasant. Mao rose through the emerging modern school system, going to the provincial capital, Changsha, for middle school and teachers' college. On graduation, he travelled to Beijing where he worked in the library of Beijing University and participated in Li Dazhao's Marxist discussion groups. Heeding Li's call for educated youth to go to the countryside to organize peasants, he returned to Hunan. He was the Hunan delegate to the first meeting of the Communist Party in Shanghai in 1921. Through the 1920s he concentrated on rural work.

After the Nationalist purges of 1927–28, those Communists who had survived scattered, some going underground in major cities, other seeking rural bases far from Nationalist strongholds. The party had to assess its mistakes and decide what to do next. Chen Duxiu was made the scapegoat and purged from positions of authority for opportunism, though in fact he had merely been following directives from the Comintern. Mao led a few thousand men into the mountains along the Hunan–Jiangxi border where they soon joined other Communists to form the Jiangxi Soviet. They set up a government that gained the support of the peasants by redistributing land and promoting social programmes like family reform. In the autumn of 1932 they were joined by the Central Committee of the Communist Party, which had finally been forced to flee Shanghai. The very real dangers the Communists faced in these years were compounded by fears of spies and conspiracies, intensified by the presence of Soviet agents who brought with them the mentality that had resulted in Stalin's factional struggles and purges. Between 1928 and 1935 the Chinese Communist Party killed thousands of its own adherents in purges or betrayals to the Nationalists.

After several years battling the Nationalist armies sent to destroy them, the Communist Party had to give up the Jiangxi Soviet, having been thoroughly defeated in the fifth of the 'extermination campaigns'. In October 1934, 80,000 Communist soldiers, cadres, porters, and followers broke out of the Nationalists' encirclement. This was the start of the much mythologized Long March in search of a new base area. Most wives and children, as well as over 20,000 wounded troops, had to be left behind. For a year the Red Army and party command columns kept retreating, fighting almost all the time, suffering enormous casualties. By the time they had found an area where they could establish a new base, they had marched almost 6,000 miles. They had crossed south and southwest China and then turned north to reach Shaanxi. Only about 8,000 of the original Red Army made it the whole way, though some new recruits and Communists from other base areas had joined en route to bring the total to nearly 20,000. For the next decade the Communist Party made its base at Yan'an, a city in central Shaanxi where homes were often built by cutting caves into the loess soil cliffs. This group of survivors came to see themselves as men of destiny, with a near sacred mission to remake China.

When the American journalist Edgar Snow visited Yan'an in 1936, the survivors of the Long March appeared to him to be an earthy group of committed patriots and egalitarian social reformers, full of optimism and purpose. They lived in caves, ate simple food, and showed no disdain for the peasants whom they were mobilizing to fight against the Japanese. During the war, too, outside observers were impressed with the unselfish commitment to group goals of the Yan'an forces. This image of the leaders of the Yan'an soviet as a solidary group of battle-toughened but warm-hearted and idealistic revolutionaries was cultivated in China as well all through Mao's lifetime, to inspire dedication in the young.

Most of Mao's most famous writings date from the Yan'an period, adding to its lustre. During the early years at Yan'an, Mao had time to read Marxist and Leninist works and began giving lectures at party schools in which he spelled out his version of Chinese history, the party's history, and Marxist theory. Neither Marx nor Lenin had seen much revolutionary potential in peasants, viewing them as

At the soviet base in Jiangxi, Mao Zedong was active in pushing land reform. He is shown here addressing peasants at a meeting in 1933.

petty capitalist in mentality, and in Russia the party had seized power in an urban setting. Since in China the Communists had failed in the cities, Mao needed to reinterpret Marxist theory in such a way that the peasants could be seen as the vanguard of the revolution. Indeed Mao came more and more to glorify the peasants as the true masses and elaborate the theory of the 'mass line': party cadres had to go among the peasant masses and learn from them before they could become their teachers. Everyone at Yan'an had to study Mao's writings in small study groups, acquiring a vocabulary and conceptual framework that united them and strengthened their sense of purpose.

Since Mao's death in 1976, another side of this period of party history has been revealed. The 'Thought of Mao Zedong' did not win out in a free competition of ideas among the survivors of the Long March, but in a brutal power struggle in which Mao proved a master tactician, able to eliminate his rivals one after the other, getting the central committee to label them deviationists of the right or left, that is, opportunists or adventurists. Moreover, it was not just study of Mao's writings that united the growing collection of students and activists who gravitated to Yan'an, but an extraordinarily potent technique of intellectual and moral remoulding perfected during the 'rectification campaign' of 1942–43. Everyone able to read was swept up in an intense drama, starting with close discussion of assigned texts, then moving on to personal confessions and struggle sessions. Everyone watched the dramatic public humiliations of the principal targets, including the party theorist Wang Ming and the writer Wang Shiwei. People learned to interpret any deviation from Mao's line as defects in their thinking due to subjectivism and liberalism, characteristics of their petty bourgeois background. One man, for instance, who confessed to being bothered by the party elite's special privileges (such as getting to ride on horseback while others walked) was taught that liberal ideas elevating the individual over the collective lay behind his feelings. Many of those invited to overcome their errors truly developed a new collective consciousness that greatly increased their usefulness to the party. Others, by contrast, simply learned to be more circumspect when they talked.

At least as important to the Communists' victory was its success in building a base of popular support. The Japanese invasion proved a perfect opportunity in this regard. In areas of north China where the Japanese armies had penetrated, peasants were ready to be mobilized against the Japanese. They hated the Japan-

The 8,000-odd survivors of the Long March became the core of the Communist Party leadership for the following decades. Depicted here in Shaanxi in 1938 are (left to right) Peng Dehuai, Zhu De, Feng Xuefen, Xiao Ke, and Deng Xiaoping.

ese for seizing women for prostitution and men for forced labour levies and especially for their 'three all' policy of retaliating against resistance by 'killing all, burning all, looting all'.

Since the Japanese forces were stretched thin, occupying major cities and towns and guarding railway lines, there was plenty of room for resistance forces to hide and conduct guerrilla operations. These resistance forces were not exclusively communist. Patriotic urban students fled to these relatively uncontested rural areas where they helped both Nationalist and Communist resistance forces. The Communists, however, were particularly successful in gaining control of the social, political, and economic life in villages because they gave peasants what they wanted: an army of friendly troops who not only did not steal their crops but helped them bring in the harvest and who implemented popular but gradual economic reforms. Even without much confiscation of land, considerable redistribution was accomplished by imposing graduated taxes in such a way that larger landholders voluntarily sold land because it was no longer profitable. Class struggle was not emphasized in this period. Larger landowners were more than welcome to help with forming and supplying militia forces, and educated youth from better-off families were recruited as party members. Party propagandists taught villagers songs to stir patriotic passions and glorify the Soviet Union. They also

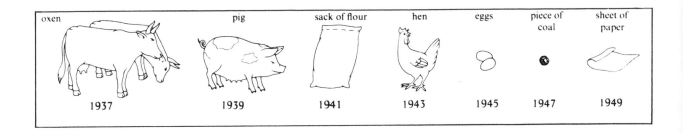

oxen	pig	sack of flour	hen	eggs	piece of coal	sheet of paper
1937	1939	1941	1943	1945	1947	1949

Urban populations became increasingly disenchanted with the Nationalist government as it failed to control inflation in the 1940s. The decline in the purchasing power of 100 Chinese dollars is represented graphically in this political cartoon.

held meetings, leading rural folk in Hebei to quip 'Under the Nationalists, too many taxes; under the Communists, too many meetings.' People were indoctrinated with the message that they could build a better, more egalitarian future by working together with each other and accepting the leadership of the party.

The end of the war with Japan laid the stage for the final confrontation. When Japan surrendered after the atomic bombing of Hiroshima and Nagasaki in August 1945, there were over a million Japanese troops in China proper and nearly another million in Manchuria, as well as about 1,750,000 Japanese civilians. Disarming and repatriating them took months, as the Nationalists, the Communists, the Americans, the Russians, and even some warlords jockeyed for position. The United States airlifted 110,000 Nationalist troops to key coastal cities like Shanghai and Guangzhou, and American troops were sent to help secure Beijing and Tianjin. The Russians entered Manchuria in early August in fulfilment of their secret promise to the United States and Britain to join the eastern front three months after victory in Europe. They dismantled as much as they could of the Japanese industrial plant to take back to the Soviet Union, but did help the Red Army by seeing to it that large stores of Japanese weapons got into their hands. For over a year, until January 1947, the United States made efforts to avert civil war by trying to convince Jiang to establish a government in which opposition parties could participate. When these efforts failed, full-scale civil war between the Communists and the Nationalists ensued. The unpopularity of the Nationalists was soon apparent. Unchecked inflation had so alienated those living in cities that they wanted the government thrown out. Moreover, Nationalist army officers and soldiers were widely seen as seizing whatever they could for themselves rather than working for the common good. As a result, to most people's surprise, the civil war was over in less than two years of actual fighting. The Nationalists were defeated militarily even though they had started with much more in the way of modern armaments and several times the number of troops. Jiang Jieshi and much of his army and government retreated to Taiwan and re-established their government there.

Little of what China experienced in the first half of the twentieth century was unique to China. In most other Asian societies, including Japan, the educated similarly struggled with the contradictions between nationalism and modernity, trying to create a new culture that could incorporate elements of modern science and western social and political ideologies while enhancing rather than undermining pride in their own national identity. There were analogies between China's experience and those of countries colonized by western powers, such as India, Vietnam, and Indonesia, in that the privileged position of the westerners aroused enormous resentment and feelings of injustice. Several other old states were torn apart by social revolutions in the early twentieth century; the comparison with Russia is undoubtedly the most striking. China even shared experiences with some of the most economically advanced countries of Europe, including those like Germany and Austria that witnessed the abolition of once powerful monarchies, and the many who lived through the destructive power of modern warfare during World War I or II.

These correspondences are not simply coincidences but evidence that Chinese history had entered a new phase, becoming integrated into global history to a degree never before true. The course of Chinese history during the nineteenth century can be analysed in terms of what was indigenous and what was external, between what was sparked by something foreign and what came entirely from within China's own culture and society. By the early twentieth century, such distinctions become increasingly meaningless. It was Chinese who were making Chinese history, but these Chinese were struggling to fashion meaningful lives in an environment where national boundaries had become increasingly porous, letting in goods, people, and ideas, all of which interacted in complex ways with what was already there. No region of China was so isolated that it totally escaped the impact of the political struggles between the Nationalists and Communists or the war with Japan, all of which had roots in events that occurred outside China. There were, it is true, people who strove to keep some domain of their lives free of anything foreign; some artists and intellectuals, for instance, did their best to preserve distinctively Chinese art forms like Beijing opera or ink painting. Paradoxically, the passion with which such cultural patriots erected barriers against foreign influence can be taken as further evidence of how overpowering the global context had become in shaping Chinese life.

At a time when most intellectuals were transforming their fields through growing contact with their western counterparts, Chinese painters were creating a highly successful modern art form that owed a great deal more to native roots than to foreign influence.

In the second half of the nineteenth century, as Shanghai grew into the largest, richest, and most vibrant city in China, the artists who congregated there perfected bold, colourful styles that appealed both to traditionally educated scholars and the emerging commercial elite. The art of this Shanghai school was modern in that it responded to the taste of the time, but it was not an art that rebelled against the past. The possibilities inherent in both the old and the new were explored; conservative landscape paintings were as popular as iconoclastic bird and flower paintings; archaic calligraphy styles were incorporated into painting at the same time as artists were experimenting with western techniques of shading to achieve more photographic facial likenesses.

In the early twentieth century opportunities in the art world expanded rapidly. New printing techniques made possible much better reproductions, which the booming publishing industry quickly exploited, issuing art books and magazines in profusion. The establishment of art schools changed the ways painters mastered their art, allowing them to study with more than just one master and even to learn western techniques. The opening of the Palace Museum in Beijing in 1925 allowed the public to view masterpieces long hidden away by the Qing emperors. Selling paintings through public exhibitions at commercial galleries became a common practice, adding both to the public's access to art and to the artists' means of earning a living.

Stylistically, however, Chinese painting continued to develop in directions laid out in the nineteenth century. The preeminent painter of the first quarter of the twentieth century was Wu Changshi (1844–1927), a man of literati background who had established a reputation as a poet, calligrapher, and seal-carver before he turned to painting. In his plum, flower, and bamboo paintings, he adopted the style of the masters of the Shanghai school, but Chinese connoisseurs also detect in his brushwork a

Below left
The influence of calligraphy is readily apparent in this depiction of a tangled mass of plum branches, painted on a hanging scroll by Wu Changshi in 1915, aged seventy, when he was living in Shanghai.

Below
Xu Peiheng had been back from Europe for four years when he painted this rooster in 1940.

strength and self-confidence derived from his years of calligraphy practice.

The next generation of painters, coming of age in the twentieth century, could not be quite as oblivious as Wu Changshi to alternatives to traditional modes of painting. Still, even those who went abroad to study art did not necessarily turn against Chinese materials, techniques, or aesthetics. Xu Peiheng (1893–1953) went to Europe to learn realistic, academic painting techniques, seeing in them an antidote to the repetition and imitation he disliked in Chinese painting. Yet, after eight years studying painting in Paris and Berlin, he came back to perfect a style that made use of Chinese media and drew heavily from Chinese painting traditions.

Nationalistic pride played a role in Fu Baoshi's (1904–1965) efforts to develop distinctively Chinese modern painting. The son of an umbrella-repairer, Fu was a struggling student when Xu Peiheng noticed him and helped him get to Japan to study at the Imperial Art College in Tokyo. There his teacher told him it was ridiculous for a Chinese to come to Japan to learn Chinese painting. 'Chinese ink painting is the greatest and highest form of art in the world. It is your enviable national treasure, handed down from your ancestors.' Fu then turned to the study of Chinese art history, and on his return to China in 1936 was appointed to the faculty of the art department of National Central University in Nanjing, then headed by Xu Peiheng. In the highly esteemed landscapes and figures he painted through the forties and fifties, Fu celebrated China's history, geography, and scholarly and artistic traditions.

Not all important painters in the early twentieth century came as close to the old scholar-painter ideal as Wu Changshi, Xu Peiheng, and Fu Baoshi. Among those who successfully painted in Shanghai-school styles close to Wu Changshi's were Pu Hua (1834–1911), a

painter of undistinguished origins who lived in the brothel district of Shanghai, Qi Baishi (1863–1957), who began as a carpenter but found an eager audience for his inventive, playful paintings of

homely subjects such as mice, shrimp, crabs, and fruit; and Wang Yiting (1866–1938), a successful Shanghai merchant and lay Buddhist who painted as a hobby.

Right
Qi Baishi's whimsical, almost folksy paintings were immensely popular in both China and Japan. The inscription on this one, painted in 1935, reports that it was painted by candlelight one night when the artist returned home to find everyone asleep except the mice who were perusing a book.

Below
In the 1940s Fu Baoshi frequently painted scenes from Chinese poems, such as this one of Tang poet Bai Juyi requesting wine.

CHAPTER 11

Radical Reunification:
China Since 1949

With the victory of the Communists in the civil war, China was once again held together by a powerful central government. Committed to a more egalitarian social and economic order, Mao Zedong and other leaders of the Communist Party set about to fashion a new China, one that would empower peasants and workers and limit the influence of landlords, capitalists, intellectuals, and foreigners. New values were heralded: people were taught that struggle, revolution, and change were good while compromise, deference, and tradition were bad. Wealth and power were redistributed on a vast scale. Massive modernization projects were begun and soon new factories, railroads, schools, hospitals, and reservoirs were transforming the landscape of China. Ordinary life was politicized in unprecedented ways; what farmers would produce, where and how their children would be educated, what they might read in books and newspapers, where they could live or travel, all came increasingly under political control.

The Communist Party's efforts at refashioning China entered a more radical phase after the launching of the Cultural Revolution in 1966, then a more moderate phase after the death of Mao in 1976. In the 1980s the intrusion of the government and party into daily life abated, leaving people more leeway to get on with their lives in their own ways. Not only did the government permit increased market activity and private enterprise, but it began courting foreign investment and sending students abroad. During the 1980s and early 1990s, the economy grew at a spectacular rate, and it became more and more difficult for the government to cut China off from global cultural trends.

IMPOSING CONTROL

The Communist Party came to power through a civil war that almost amounted to a plebiscite. Because of the support of the population in north China, where the party had been active for a decade and where key battles took place, it was able to defeat the better-equipped Nationalist armies in less than two years of actual fighting. On 1 October 1949 Mao Zedong as party leader proclaimed the establishment of the People's Republic of China.

By 1949 the Communist Party was experienced at taking control of rural areas. Cities, however, were a new challenge. As the Red Army entered cities its peasant soldiers clamped down on vice – ending looting and rounding up beggars, prostitutes, opium addicts and petty criminals to be re-educated and set to productive work. Through street committees they tried to rid the cities of what they saw as decadence – flashy clothes and provocative hairstyles, for instance. But urban institutions like factories, railways, universities, newspapers, law courts, and tax-collecting stations could not simply be shut down, nor could they easily be run by peasant soldiers. The party wanted to reorganize China on the model of the Soviet Union and needed to keep open these modern institutions so that the transition could proceed in an orderly way.

In terms of formal political organization, the Soviet Union's model was followed, though in contrast to the dictatorship of the proletariat in the Soviet Union, China had a 'people's democratic dictatorship', which included rich peasants, the national bourgeoisie, and others in a united front. Some high posts in the government were given to non-Communists in an attempt to win broad support. The people as a whole were represented by a hierarchy of irregularly scheduled People's Representative Congresses convened at each level from the village up to the National People's Congress. Real power lay with the Communist Party, however. By the end of the 1950s there were more than a million branch party com-

The People's Republic of China is organized into twenty-two provinces, five autonomous regions (for the Tibetan, Uighur, Mongolian, Muslim, and Zhuang nationalities), and three independent municipalities (Beijing, Tianjin, and Shanghai). The country's exact boundaries are still in dispute in several places.

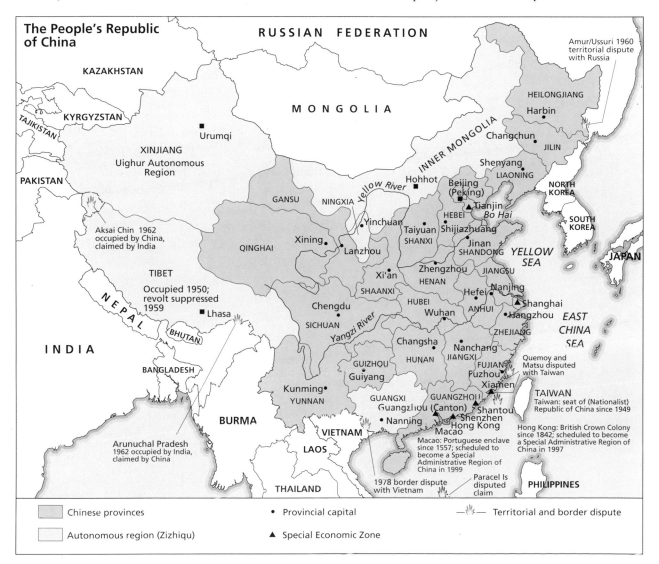

The People's Republic of China

Mao Zedong and Zhou Enlai travelled to Moscow soon after the establishment of the People's Republic. They are shown here with Stalin, concluding a treaty of friendship and economic co-operation. Although this treaty was signed, Mao felt that Stalin had not shown him proper courtesy.

mittees in villages, factories, schools, army units, and other organizations. Each party committee sent delegates up to higher units, including county and province committees, leading up to the three top tiers, the Central Committee with around a hundred members, the politburo with around a dozen members, and its standing committee, which in 1949 consisted of Mao Zedong, Liu Shaoqi, Zhou Enlai, Zhu De, and Chen Yun and was subsequently expanded to include Deng Xiaoping. Within the standing committee Mao Zedong was recognized as the paramount leader; his image adorned buildings and his pronouncements were treated almost like those of an emperor.

The Communist Party's economic goals required that the economy be both revived and restructured. The new government promptly took over the banks and got hold of money and credit. Within a year it had brought inflation under control, an impressive achievement. Building on the Nationalists' wartime industrial policies, the new government took control of key industries, including the railways and foreign trade. The Five-Antis campaign of 1951–2 was launched to weed out the least co-operative of the capitalists still controlling private enterprises. With much fanfare people were mobilized to accuse merchants and manufacturers of bribery, tax evasion, theft of state assets, cheating in labour or materials, or stealing state economic secrets. In the single month of April 1952, 70,000 Shanghai businessmen were investigated and criticized. Family members and friends were often induced to join in attacking those accused, a tactic that led to intense feelings of betrayal. Once the businessmen confessed, they had to pay restitution, which often meant turning over all their assets. The party thus secured control of more factories, often retaining the former owners as government-paid managers. Many small manufacturing plants, stores, and restaurants remained in private hands, but gradually the government came to dominate them by controlling supplies and labour.

Expanding heavy industry was seen as the key step to lifting China out of poverty. Mao spent nine weeks in Moscow in early 1950, negotiating a treaty that called for Soviet loans and technical assistance to help with industrialization. Before long over 20,000 Chinese trainees went to the USSR and some 10,000 Russian technicians came to China to help set up 156 Soviet-designed heavy industrial plants. To pay for these projects, agriculture was heavily taxed, again on the Soviet model. According to the five-year plan put into effect for the years 1953 to 1957, output of steel was to be quadrupled, output of power and cement doubled. Consumer goods, however, were to be increased at much lower rates – cotton piece goods by less than half, grain by less than a fifth.

The new government did not have even a year to get its new structures and policies in place before it was embroiled in a war in Korea. After World War II, Korea had ended up with the USSR dominant above the 38th parallel and the United States below it. In June 1950 the north attacked the south, probably on Stalin's urgings, since Kim Il Song, the north's leader, was Stalin's protégé. US forces, fighting under the UN flag, came to the south's defence and in early October crossed the 38th parallel and headed toward the Yalu River, the border between North Korea and China. With an enemy approaching its border, the Chinese government found it could not demobilize its armies as planned. 'Volunteers', under the command of Peng Dehuai, began to cross the river secretly. In late November they surprised the Americans and soon forced them to retreat south of Seoul. Altogether, more than 2,500,000 troops were sent to Korea, as well as all of China's tanks and over half its artillery and aircraft. A stalemate followed, but peace talks dragged on until 1953, largely because China wanted all prisoners repatriated but 14,000 begged not to be sent back.

This war raised the legitimacy of the Communist Party in China: China had 'stood up' and beaten back the imperialists. But the costs were huge. Not only were the casualties enormous, but the war eliminated many chances for gradual reconciliation, both internal and external. The United States, now viewing China in Cold War terms, imposed an economic embargo and sent the seventh fleet to patrol the waters between China and Taiwan. American protection effectively guaranteed that the Nationalists would be able to survive as bitter opponents of the Communist regime. China began to vilify the United States as its prime enemy and out of fear of espionage expelled most of the remaining western missionaries and businessmen.

A worse fate awaited those who had served in the Nationalist government or army, now suspected of being enemy agents. A campaign of 1951 against such 'counter-revolutionaries' resulted in the execution of tens or hundreds of thousands, and similar numbers were sent to harsh labour reform camps. This campaign was also used to disarm the population; over 500,000 rifles were collected in Guangdong province alone.

COLLECTIVIZING AGRICULTURE

In the 1940s, one out of every six people in the world was a Chinese peasant. The lives of these hundreds of millions of people were soon to be radically altered by the progressive collectivization of land and the creation of a new local elite of rural cadres. As the Communist Party took control of new areas it taught peasants a new way to look on the old order. Social and economic inequalities were not natural, but a perversion caused by the institution of private property; the old literati elite were not scholars who acted according to elevated moral principles, but the cruellest of exploiters, content to pressure their tenants to the point where they had to sell their children. To replace that antiquated 'feudal' order, the party brought a vision of a communal order where all would work together unselfishly for common goals.

For twenty years the party had been redistributing land wherever it established bases, but its methods and approaches varied depending on the political exigencies of the moment. On some occasions, hostility was minimized, on others it was stirred up as a way to generate enthusiasm on the part of the poorest. Typically, the party would send in a small team of cadres and students to a village to cultivate relations with the poor, organize a peasant association, identify potential leaders from among the poor peasants, compile lists of grievances, and organize struggles against those most resented. Eventually the team would supervise the classification of the inhabitants as landlords (those who lived off the rents of their lands), rich peasants (those who rented out some land but worked the rest themselves), middle peasants (those who worked their own land without the help of tenants or hired hands), poor peasants (tenants and owners of small plots who also rented or worked for wages), and hired hands (those with no land who worked for wages). The analysis of class was supposed to be scientific, but application of the rules was not always straightforward. Many people felt uncomfortable classifying as exploiters widows who rented out their meagre holdings because they were incapable of working them themselves and the somewhat better-off families of veterans, or, for that matter, classifying as hired hands those who had been reduced to working for others only after wasting their inheritance through gambling or opium addiction. But once a moral dimension was added to the classification process, it created room for manoeuvring, for helping friends and getting back at enemies. In some villages there really was not much of a surplus to redistribute; in others there was a reservoir of ill-will from previous conflicts unrelated to land ownership that complicated matters. At times terror tactics were employed, especially to try to get those labelled landlords or rich peasants to reveal where they had buried their gold. Landlords and rich peasants faced not only loss of their land, but also punishment for past offences. How many were executed is uncertain; estimates range from hundreds of thousands to tens of millions. Another result of the class-struggle stage of land reform was the creation of a caste-like system in the countryside. The lowest caste was composed of the descendants of those labelled landlords, while the descendants of former poor and lower-middle peasants became a privileged class.

Redistribution of land was only the first step toward reorganizing the countryside. Agricultural collectivization followed in several stages. First farmers were encouraged to join mutual-aid teams, then to set up co-operatives. The members of co-operatives pooled resources and were compensated on the basis of their inputs of land, tools, animals, and labour. In the 'old liberated areas' in north China this was accomplished in the early forties; in south China these measures were initiated during the period 1950 to 1953. From 1954 to 1956 a third stage was pushed – higher-level collectives that amalgamated co-operatives and did

away with compensation for anything other than labour. Most of these higher-level co-operatives (labelled 'production teams' from 1958 to 1978) were old villages or parts of large villages. Once higher-level co-operatives were in place, economic inequality within villages had all but been eliminated.

As collectivization progressed, the Chinese state took over control of the grain market. After taking 5 to 10 per cent of each collective's harvest as a tax, it allowed the unit to retain a meagre subsistence ration per person, then purchased a share of the 'surplus' at prices it set. In 1951–52, as a by-product of the Five-Antis campaign, interregional commerce was redefined as criminal speculation, an extreme form of capitalist exploitation. Trade was taken over by the state and rural markets withered. Many peasants lost crucial sideline income; this was especially true in many of the poorer areas where peasants had made ends meet by operating such

During the land reform campaigns of the late forties and early fifties, poor peasants, even women as depicted here, were encouraged to speak out against landlords who had exploited them. At such meetings, landlords not only had their land confiscated, but were frequently beaten, even executed.

Collectivization of agriculture and mobilization of labour led to a much greater participation of women in agricultural work. By 1965, the date of this photograph, women were performing around half the lower-skilled farm labour in many areas; by the late 1980s, by which time opportunities for men outside of farming had expanded, women were often doing considerably more than half the field labour.

small enterprises as oil presses, paper mills, or rope factories. Carpenters and craftsmen who used to travel far and wide became chained to the land, unable to practise their trades except in their own localities.

Reorganization of the countryside created a new elite of rural cadres. Policy may have been made at upper reaches of the party, by Mao's whims or through struggles between different lines and different factions, but the way policy shifts were experienced by ordinary people depended on the personal qualities of the lowest level of party leaders who now had power over almost every facet of their lives. In villages, team leaders were generally local residents who had been selected for any of a number of reasons. In some villages, middle peasants who could read and write, keep books, and knew a lot about farming rose to leadership positions. In others village, toughs from the poorest families rose because of the zeal they showed in class struggle against the former landlords or rich peasants.

To get ahead, a team leader had to be energetic in producing a substantial surplus to serve the needs of the revolution; on the other hand, to keep the members of his team motivated, he had to make sure too much was not taken away. His success depended on his skill in ingratiating himself with both sides and stretching the truth when needed. As units were urged to consolidate and enlarge, rural cadres had to spend much of their time motivating members and settling squabbles among them.

Team leaders and other local activists had opportunities to rise in the party hierarchy, creating social mobility way beyond anything that had existed in imperial China. The party grew steadily, from 2.7 million members in 1947 to 6.1 million in 1953 and 17 million in 1961. Many of these party members were poor peasants who had joined the Red Army or emerged as activists in various political campaigns.

NEW CHINA

The aspirations of Mao and the other Communist leaders were not limited to restructuring the social organization of production. Chinese culture and the Chinese state were both to be transformed as well. China's new leaders called their victory in the civil war 'the liberation'. The Chinese people had been freed from the yoke of the past and now could rebuild China as a new, modern, socialist, egalitarian, forward-looking nation. China would no longer be shunted to the margins of world history, but would regain its rightful place in the centre. It would demonstrate to the world the potential of socialism to lift the masses out of poverty and create a better form of human community.

Spreading these ideas was the mission of propaganda departments and teams, which quickly took over the publishing industry. Schools and colleges were also put under party supervision, with a Soviet-style Ministry of Education issuing directives concerning such curricular matters as the textbooks to use for Chinese history and the promotion of the 'common' language as a standard dialect.

Tiananmen Square combines some of the finest surviving architecture from the Qing period with huge buildings and spaces directly inspired by the example of the Soviet Union.

Numerous mass organizations were set up, including street committees in cities, the Youth League, Women's Federation, and Labour Union Federation. Party workers who organized meetings of these groups were simultaneously to learn from the masses, keep an eye on them, and get them on the side of new policies. They decorated meeting halls and other buildings with banners and posters proclaiming party slogans. In the early 1950s, these efforts at mobilization and propaganda met with considerable success. People began giving their children names that testified to their patriotic hopes, names like 'Build China' or 'Make the Nation Flourish'.

New China needed symbols of its rebirth. The old city of Beijing was given a new look to match its status as capital of New China. In the late 1950s the huge walls around Beijing were torn down because they impeded traffic. At the same time the area south of the old imperial palace was cleared of buildings, creating room for the world's largest square, Tiananmen Square, soon to be the site of huge May Day and National Day rallies. On either side of this square two huge Soviet-style buildings were erected, the Great Hall of the People and the Museum of Chinese History. In the very centre was placed a 100-foot-tall stone Monument to the Martyrs of the People, decorated with carved reliefs depicting heroic revolutionaries of the past century. Neither monuments nor squares had been a part of old China's cities; the 'international' socialist style, adopted to update China's look, introduced elements of western art, architecture and urban planning.

The pervasive attack on the old was extended to many features of traditional culture: much of traditional religion was labelled feudal superstition, as were social customs such as deference to superiors and women's deference to men. The state endorsed the goal of women's equality and promoted reform of family and marriage practices (as the Jiangxi and Yan'an soviets had done earlier). In 1950 the Marriage Reform Law granted young people the right to choose their marriage partners, wives the right to initiate divorce, and wives and daughters the right to inherit property. The provisions of these laws did not go a lot further than the Nationalists' Civil Code of 1930, but they had a considerably greater impact because campaigns were launched to publicize them and to assure women of party support if they refused a marriage arranged by their parents or left an unbearable husband or mother-in-law. During the first five years of the new law, several million marriages were dissolved, most at the request of the wife. This campaign should not, of course, get full credit for changes in the Chinese family system, for many other forces contributed to undermining the old family, such as the drastic shrinkage of family property as a result of collectivization of land and appropriation of business assets, the entry of more children into schools and mass organizations like the Youth League and Young Pioneers, the mobilization of women in large numbers into the workforce, and the public appearance of more women in positions of authority, ranging from street committees to university faculties and the upper echelons of the party.

CHINA AS A MULTI-NATIONAL STATE

Old China had been an empire; new China was proclaimed to be a multi-national state. Officially, at least, the old view of China as the civilizing centre, gradually attracting, acculturating, and absorbing non-Chinese peoples along its frontiers was replaced by a vision of distinct but equal ethnic groups joined in a collaborative state. 'Han' was promoted as the correct term for the ethnic group; 'Chinese' would be stretched to encompass all ethnic groups in the People's Republic.

The policy of multi-nationality can be seen as another instance of imitating the Soviet Union, which had devised it as the best way, in an age of nationalism, to justify retaining all the lands acquired by the czar in the eighteenth and nineteenth centuries. For China the model similarly provided a way to justify reasserting dominion over Tibet and Xinjiang, which had been attached to the Qing but had broken away after the collapse of the dynasty in 1911. (Mongolia had fallen away as well, but under the Soviet Unions influence it had established a communist government in the 1920s, so China did not challenge its independence.)

Identifying and labelling China's minority nationalities became a major state project in the fifties. Stalin had enunciated a nationalities policy with four criteria for establishing a group as a 'nationality': common language, common territory, a common economic life, and a common psychological make-up manifested in common cultural traits. Using these criteria, Chinese linguists and social scientists investigated over 400 groups requesting recognition, rejecting most as local sub-branches of larger ethnic groups, and ending up with more than fifty recognized minority nationalities. There were a few clear cases of distinct nationalities like the Tibetans and Uighurs who spoke distinct languages and lived in distinct territories. But there were many more ambiguous cases ranging from the Hui, Chinese-speaking Muslims scattered throughout the country, to the Zhuang of Guangxi who had long been quite sinified, to those labelled Miao, spread out over many provinces whose unity depended more on Han folk categories than their own sense of identity, to small tribal groups of a few thousand people in the hills of the southwest. In cases where a particular minority dominated a region (from county to province in size), the region could be recognized as 'autonomous', giving it the right to use its own language in schools and government offices. Tibet, Xinjiang, Ningxia, Guangxi, and Inner Mongolia were all made autonomous regions (for the Tibetan, Uighur, Hui, Zhuang and Mongol peoples, respectively) and large parts of Sichuan, Yunnan, and Guizhou were declared autonomous districts of the Zhuang, Miao, Yi, and other minorities. Officially, all of these regions are glad to be part of the grand multi-national People's Republic of China, and by 1957 400,000 members of minority groups had been recruited as party members. There is plenty of evidence, however, that satisfaction has been far from universal, especially in the case of Tibet. In Tibet, incorporation was resisted in 1950, a revolt was staged in 1959, and protests and other forms of resistance have recurred with some frequency ever since.

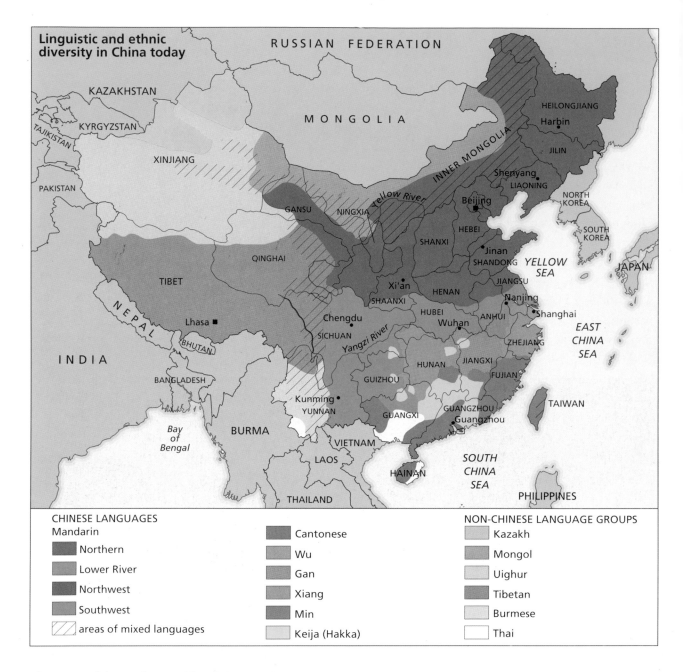

Linguistic and ethnic diversity in China today

CHINESE LANGUAGES
Mandarin

- Northern
- Lower River
- Northwest
- Southwest
- areas of mixed languages

- Cantonese
- Wu
- Gan
- Xiang
- Min
- Keija (Hakka)

NON-CHINESE LANGUAGE GROUPS

- Kazakh
- Mongol
- Uighur
- Tibetan
- Burmese
- Thai

The citizens of the People's Republic of China speak many languages. Nearly a billion, about 94 per cent of the population, speak a Chinese language. Not all of these people can understand each others' speech, however, since many of the 'dialects' of Chinese differ more than French and Spanish and could easily be considered separate languages. Over the centuries, pronunciation has diverged considerably; for instance, the word for 'difficult' is pronounced nan in Beijing, but le in Yanzhou, ne in Suzhou and lan in Changsha. All of the Chinese languages employ tones, but northern Mandarin has four tones, Cantonese has twelve. Traditionally, the major way the divergence of dialects was overcome was through the written word, since Chinese ideographs can be read using any dialect. Educated men also learned to speak 'official speech', a version of Mandarin, to communicate with people from other regions. Early in the twentieth century, proponents of the New Culture advocated making this official speech the national language. The People's Republic has promoted it as well, requiring that the 'common language' be used in schools as well as on radio and television.

SUBORDINATING INTELLECTUALS

In the 1920s and 1930s, intellectuals – like Chen Duxiu and Li Dazhao, Lu Xun and Ding Ling – were among the most enthusiastic supporters of socialism, seeing in it a way to rid China of poverty and injustice. In the late 1930s and 1940s, quite a few well-known writers made their way to Yan'an where they soon learned that their job was to serve the party, not stand at a critical distance from it.

After 1949 the party had to deal with a new category of intellectuals, individuals who had not publicly sided with it, but rather had stayed in the cities, holding jobs that linked them one way or another with the Nationalist cause. Most members of this small urban educated elite responded with enthusiasm in the early fifties to the signs that China finally had a government that could get the job done – control inflation, end corruption, spread literacy, promote equality for women, clean up the streets, and get everyone working. Many enthusiastically volunteered to serve the new government in whatever capacity they could, and thousands who were studying abroad hurried home to see how they could help. The party for its part needed experienced supervisors, administrators, teachers, journalists, scientists, writers, and functionaries. Thus even though Mao insisted that 'being red

Tibet was largely independent from the time of the collapse of the Qing dynasty in 1911 until the People's Republic reasserted military control. Here the People's Liberation Army is entering Lhasa in 1951.

China's ethnic diversity was made a part of the official representation of China through the images depicted on Chinese paper money.

was more important than being expert', most of the educated were kept in their jobs, whatever their class background.

The new state did, however, devise ways to limit the influence of the intellectuals it had inherited. Schools, universities, publishing houses, research institutes, and other organizations were all reorganized and the intellectuals employed there 're-educated'. 'Thought reform' generally entailed confessing one's former subservience to capitalist imperialism, guilt at betraying the Chinese people, and gratitude to Chairman Mao for having pointed out one's errors. Many who went through it were inspired to dedicate themselves to the socialist cause. The independence of intellectuals was also undermined by the elimination of alternative ways to make a living. There were no more independent presses or independent colleges; society no longer tolerated men of leisure who derived income from investments and spent it on art or antiques.

Some branches of intellectual work were given generous government support, none more so, perhaps, than archaeology. The Institute of Archaeology was founded in 1950 to co-ordinate archaeological excavations and research throughout the country. It soon set up permanent field stations at major sites such as Anyang, Xi'an, and Luoyang, and despatched trained teams to investigate whenever ancient graves or relics were uncovered in the course of construction of roads, factories, or reservoirs. As a way of approaching the past, archaeological research had the attraction of being scientific; it was expected that excavated materials would demonstrate the conformity of the Chinese past to the Marxist scheme of historical development from primitive clan to slave to feudal society. Archaeology also promised a less text-centred view of the past, one that would allow celebration of the contributions of the working people who crafted the objects discovered rather than the elites who wrote texts.

By 1956 Mao was confident that the combination of inducements and retraining had won over the educated. That year Mao called on the intellectuals to help him identify problems within the party, such as party members who had lost touch with the people or behaved like tyrants. Although most intellectuals were wary when they first heard Mao's call to 'Let a hundred flowers bloom', they lost their inhibitions as praise was lavished on those who came forward with criticisms. The outpouring of criticism that followed apparently took Mao by surprise; he abruptly reversed course and angrily accused the critics of harbouring rightist ideology and opposing the party.

In the massive anti-rightist campaign that followed, half or more of China's tiny educated elite were stigmatized, ostensibly because of something anti-party they said during the 'Hundred Flowers' period, but actually often for no other reason than that unit leaders felt compelled to discover their quota of rightists. Altogether almost three million people were labelled 'rightists', which assured that they would no longer have any real influence at work, even if they were allowed to continue in their previous jobs. Half a million were sent to the countryside to overcome 'separation from the masses' through manual labour among them. Victims included the young and the old, those who had taken a stand and those who had stayed on the sidelines. Thirty reporters who had written stories exposing the much resented secret shops for officials ended up in labour reform camps. There were also many cases like that of a railway engineer relegated to menial labour for twenty years because someone reported hearing him say 'how bold' when he read some of the Hundred Flowers critiques of the party. By removing so many of those with higher educations from positions of authority, the new elite of party cadres – largely from worker and peasant backgrounds and often both xenophobic and anti-intellectual – destroyed the urban, educated, western-influenced professional elite created in the 1930s and 1940s. Old China had been dominated, culturally at least, by an elite defined by lengthy education; Mao refused to let that happen to new China. Those with higher educations had been put in their place: they were employees of the state, hired to instruct the children of the labouring people or provide technical assistance; they were not to have ideas of their own separate from those of the party or a cultural life distinct from that of the masses.

Ding Ling

Chinese intellectuals have not had it easy during the twentieth century, especially those most committed to using their talents to assist in the creation of a better China. Ding Ling (1904–85), the most prominent woman writer of her generation, not atypically found herself in trouble with authorities again and again.

Ding Ling grew up in Hunan province among the pioneers of women's education. Her widowed mother entered school at thirty and later taught at girls' schools. Ding Ling in time proved just as ready to break conventions. In 1919 she entered one of the first men's high schools to turn co-educational. The next year, at sixteen, she left Hunan to escape her uncles' efforts to arrange a marriage for her and to throw herself into the exciting world of the May Fourth movement. Thus she began an emancipated life in Nanjing, Shanghai, and Beijing that mixed study, writing, frequent moves, and the never-ending pursuit of ways to make ends meet. She joined the Anarchist Party and read about the lives of liberated women in the Soviet Union. She also met and fell in love with the young poet Hu Yepin.

Ding Ling's first story was published in 1927 and her first collection, an instant success, in 1928. The heroines in her early stories were modern women; they were daring, passionate, and eager to be independent, but unable to find emotional satisfaction or to develop truly independent personalities. Miss Sophie, the title character of her best-known story, is a lonely, fretful, tubercular young woman who describes in her diary not only her dissatisfaction with life around her but also her erotic longings for an unworthy man and the confusion these feelings cause her.

In 1930 Hu and Ding Ling had to flee Shandong where Hu was teaching because he was about to be arrested for teaching proletarian literature. In Shanghai a son was born to them, Hu became a member of the Communist Party, and both became active in the League of Left-Wing Writers. The next year Hu was arrested and executed by the Nationalists. Devastated, Ding Ling committed herself to revolutionary work. She joined the party and took up writing proletarian literature. She announced to a group of students that she would no longer write about love. Abducted by Nationalist agents herself in 1933, Ding Ling was imprisoned for a time, then held in house arrest in Nanjing for three years.

After she managed to escape, Ding Ling made her way to Yan'an. There she got to know many of the top Communist leaders, taught, did political work, wrote short stories, and married another writer. Like many writers in Yan'an, Ding Ling found it difficult to write compellingly and still satisfy the party leadership. Her stories contained characters not entirely comfortable with all aspects of the revolutionary life. For instance, in one a woman party member came to feel the 'needs of the party' had become an iron collar around her neck when the party ordered her to quit studying to become a doctor because they needed her as a nurse. In 1942 Mao Zedong convened a Forum on Art and Literature to rein in writers. He reiterated the principle that the writer's job was to serve the needs of the revolution. Ding Ling was one of many targets and was forced to undergo self-criticism. After spending two years in the Central Party School studying politics, she was sent out of Yan'an to write about soldiers and peasants.

During the civil war, Ding Ling was assigned to observe land reform in north China. The novel she wrote based on her experiences there depicted the senior communist cadre as near perfect, able to survive any hardship, always shrewd and kind in his dealings with peasants and younger party members. Ding Ling had learned to write socialist realism: this novel was awarded the prestigious Stalin Prize and earned her a trip to Moscow. In political favour for several years thereafter, Ding Ling was appointed to a variety of high posts and published

THE GREAT LEAP FORWARD

By late 1957, to Mao at least, following the Soviet model no longer seemed good enough. Growth was too slow, too dependent on technical experts, too constrained by the scarcity of capital. China had to find a way to use what it was rich in – labour power – to modernize more rapidly. Mao began talking of a Great Leap Forward. Through the concerted hard work of hundreds of millions of people labouring together, China would transform itself from a poor nation into a mighty

such titles as *Impressions of a Visit to the Soviet Union* and *Songs of Praise for the Five Year Plan*. When the writer and editor Hu Feng became the target of a campaign against liberal writers in 1955, however, she too was criticized, the prominent writer Mao Dun charging that she retained the ideology of Miss Sophie. In her self-criticisms she admitted that the May Fourth era had profoundly shaped her thinking and that her characters often felt alone and helpless.

Despite having twice been made a target of criticism, Ding Ling spoke out during the Hundred Flowers Campaign, calling for freedom of literature from state control. During the Anti-Rightist campaign that followed she and her early writings became the subject of numerous struggle sessions. Professional rivalries, long-standing personal conflicts, and bureaucratic in-fighting led to considerable viciousness as Ding Ling was accused not only of political errors but 'unchaste' activities while under house arrest in Nanjing in the 1930s. When she refused to admit to any crimes against the party, she was stripped of her posts, expelled from the party, and sent to perform 'reform through labour' on a farm near the Siberian border. Her life there was not too bad; old friends and patrons could send paper and special food, and she remained in contact with her family. Later, during the Cultural Revolution, however, rival teams from two nearby communes competed to struggle with her and she was beaten, humiliated, and put in solitary confinement. From 1970 to 1975 she was incarcerated in a large state prison.

In 1978, when Deng Xiaoping arranged for the rehabilitation of victims of the Cultural Revolution, Ding Ling reappeared in Beijing. From then until her death in 1985, she enjoyed celebrity status, travelling abroad, giving interviews, and commenting on events. Many young people who had expected her to speak out on either feminist issues or party control of literary activity were disappointed, however; to the younger generation she seemed to have finally absorbed the party line.

The Yan'an soviet was a small enough place that Ding Ling got to know many of the top Communist leaders. Still she was severely criticized for the feminist tone of some of her stories.

one. The latent creative capacity of the Chinese masses, previously held in check by the domestic and foreign exploiting classes, would be unleashed and China would surpass Great Britain in industrial output within fifteen years.

Soon visions of accelerated industrialization were coupled with yet further transformation in the countryside. In 1958, in a matter of months, agricultural collectives all over the country were amalgamated into gigantic communes. These communes were expected to complete the proletarianization of the peasantry –

divorcing them totally from the ownership of the means of production and bringing them such benefits of modern urban life as schools and hospitals. China's leaders proclaimed that productivity would reach new heights as peasants ingeniously planted seeds more densely and opened small-scale factories using locally available materials.

Trusting Mao, both party cadres and ordinary working people got caught up in a wave of utopian enthusiasm. Economists and engineers, like other educated experts, had been downgraded or removed in the anti-rightist campaigns of the year before, so plans were formulated not by experts, but by local cadres eager to show their political zeal. During the late summer and autumn of 1958, communes, factories, schools, and other units set up 'backyard steel furnaces' in order to double steel production by combining small, native techniques with large, foreign ones. Peasant men were marched in military style to work on public-works projects while the women took over much of the fieldwork. Both were exhorted by slogans like 'More, faster, better, and more economical' and songs like 'Communism is heaven./ The commune is the ladder./ If we build that ladder,/ We can climb the heights.' As workers were mobilized to put in long hours on these projects, they spent little time at home or in normal farm work, and to meet their needs units were encouraged to set up mess halls where food was free. Commen-

tators hailed this as a major step in the transition from socialism to communism. Counties claimed 1,000 and even 10,000 per cent increases in agriculture production. Pictures were even published of fields where the wheat grew so thickly that children could stand on top of it without pushing it down. The Central Committee trumpeted abroad claims that national production had nearly doubled in a single year.

Some Great Leap projects were successes; bridges, railroads, canals, reservoirs, power stations, mines, and irrigation works were constructed all over the country, many of them proving of enduring value. All too often, however, projects were undertaken with such haste and with so little technical knowledge that serious mistakes were made, such as ploughing so deep that the soil became salinized. By the time the first year of the Great Leap had passed, even Mao began calling for a less frenetic pace and more realistic goals.

In the summer of 1959 the veteran revolutionary and minister of defence Peng Dehuai offered measured criticisms of the Great Leap policies at a party meeting. Mao Zedong was deeply affronted. He vehemently countered the charges and had Peng forced out of the leadership. The call for a Great Leap Forward was reintensified; problems with it were now blamed on Peng and all those like him who lacked faith in its premises.

Mobilization of labour on a grand scale during the Great Leap Forward made possible some highly valuable public works, such as flood control projects along the Yellow River, depicted here. Removing so many men from agricultural work, however, aggravated other planning errors and led to severe food shortages during the next few years, reaching famine proportions between 1960 and 1962.

Because Mao dominated party decision-making and because the party apparatus had gained power over all aspects of China's economy, Mao's faulty economics ended up creating a famine of massive proportions. The size of the 1958 harvest was wildly exaggerated and much of it was left to rot in the fields, the men deployed elsewhere. When harvests fell the next two years, the effects of shortages were magnified by cadres who continued to report gains in production to show their revolutionary zeal. Because the central government based requisitions on these reports, much too large a share of the food supply was removed from the countryside: in many places the local people were left with less than half of what they needed to survive. Rationing was widespread and soup kitchens serving weak gruel were set up to stave off starvation. Still, from later census reconstructions, it appears that during the Three Hard Years (1959–62) there were on the order of thirty million 'excess' deaths attributable to the dearth of food.

Not surprisingly, the Great Leap Forward strained the relations between China and the Soviet Union. With the death of Stalin, Mao thought he deserved to be recognized as the senior leader of the international communist movement, a view Khrushchev did not share. The Russians began to fear that China would drag them into a war with the United States because during the Great Leap period China intensified its anti-imperialist rhetoric and began shelling the islands off the coast of Fujian still held by the Nationalists on Taiwan. Khrushchev made two visits to Beijing in 1958 and 1959, and concluded that Mao was a romantic deviationist, particularly wrongheaded in his decision to create communes. (It did not help that Mao claimed that the creation of communes would allow China to achieve communism sooner than the USSR.) Khrushchev reneged on a promise to give China atomic weapons, then in the summer of 1960, when famine was hitting China, he ordered all Russian technical advisers out of China. By 1963 Mao was publicly denouncing Khrushchev as a revisionist and capitalist-roader and challenging the USSR's leadership of the international communist movement. Communist parties throughout the world soon developed pro-Soviet and pro-Chinese factions. Fearing a Soviet invasion, the Chinese built air-raid shelters on a massive scale all over the country. The government also devoted enormous resources to constructing a defence establishment in mountainous inland areas far from both the sea and the Soviet border.

The long-term impact of the Great Leap on the countryside was also largely negative. The struggle to survive led to rampant self-seeking that brought with it cynicism and loss of faith in the lower levels (at least) of the party state. People saw not only that the powerful few could impose irrational top-down policies, but also that they frequently worked for the parochial interests of their own families, cliques, or neighbours. Just as devastating was a further blow to peasants' mobility. Beginning in 1955 a system of population registration bound rural people to the villages of their birth, or in the case of married women, their husbands' villages. When the hasty expansion of the nation's industrial plant was reversed, millions of unemployed workers were sent out of the cities to the countryside. To keep them from returning, or other peasants from sneaking into the cities, a system of urban household registration was introduced, tied to grain rationing. Only those with permission to reside in that city could get the ration coupons needed to purchase grain. These residence policies had the unintended effect of locking rural communities with unfavourable man–land ratios into dismal poverty. Compared to life in the countryside, life in the cities was secure, especially for the substantial share of city-dwellers employed in the state sector who had housing at low prices, pensions, health care, and various subsidies, not to mention a reliable supply of subsidized food. Children could stay in school through middle school and the luckiest (or best-connected) could go further. In the countryside, however, only a tiny proportion of exceptionally wealthy communities could come anywhere near to providing such benefits. In the poorest regions farmers, forced by the government to concentrate on growing grain, could do little to improve their situations other than invest more labour. Weeding more frequently, levelling and terracing fields, expanding irrigation systems, and so forth, did not always bring much of a return, leading to a decline in agricultural productivity right across the country.

THE CULTURAL REVOLUTION

Mao's vision of revolution, made clear in his grand plans for the Great Leap Forward, was voluntaristic: it emphasized the potential for people, once mobilized to struggle, to transform both themselves and the world through the power of their wills. Inherent in Marxism, however, was another, quite different view of revolution and historical change. Marx was, after all, a materialist who rejected idealist interpretations of history. Ideas, he asserted, did not make history, rather they reflected the economic base, the mode of production and the relations of production. A committed Marxist could, therefore, quite reasonably concentrate on changing the economic system and expecting ideas and culture to change as a result. Many members of the Chinese Communist Party, despite the great prestige of Mao and his thought, were themselves more inclined toward the materialist interpretation of history; political mobilization, to them, could not replace party control of the economic base.

In the aftermath of the failure of the Great Leap, economic planners and party organization men came to the fore. Mao withdrew from active decision-making and Liu Shaoqi, Chen Yun, Zhou Enlai, Deng Xiaoping and other leaders set about reviving heavy industry and market activity. The need to take ideological stands was dismissed by Deng Xiaoping in language as pithy as Mao's: 'White cat, black cat – either will do as long as it catches mice.'

By this time the party had become an enormous bureaucratic organization with some 17 million members. At the upper reaches, the fate of Peng Dehuai had not been forgotten, and honest debate of party policy was no longer attempted in front

Mao Zedong encouraged the Red Guards by coming out to review them in the summer and autumn of 1966 when they converged on Tiananmen Square in Beijing by the millions from all over the country.

of Mao. This opened the door to factionalism and secret manoeuvring. Mao's sense that the party was shunting him aside probably lies behind his call for a Great Revolution to Create a Proletarian Culture – or Cultural Revolution for short – a movement that came close to destroying the party he had led for three decades. But ideology entered into Mao's thinking as well. He probably genuinely feared that China was slipping in the inegalitarian direction of the Soviet Union; he would not stand by and watch as a new elite took over the party and subverted the revolution. To Mao the revolution had to be continued to succeed; it had to be a permanent process, constantly kept alive through unending class struggle. In a manner reminiscent of Stalin, Mao was convinced that hidden enemies within the party and intellectual circles had to be identified and removed.

The Cultural Revolution was set in motion in the spring of 1966 when the mayor of Beijing was denounced for allowing the staging of a play that could be construed as critical of Mao. A Cultural Revolution Small Group was formed, with Mao's wife Jiang Qing (1914–91) as a key member. Jiang Qing had not played much of a part in politics before, and was widely seen as a stand-in for Mao, now over seventy. Soon radical students at Beijing University were agitating against party officials 'taking the capitalist road'. When Liu Shaoqi tried to control what was going on at Beijing University, Mao intervened, had him demoted by a rump

session of the Central Committee, and sanctioned the organization of students there into Red Guards.

The Cultural Revolution quickly escalated beyond the ability of Mao, Jiang Qing, or anyone else to control or direct. Young people who had grown up in new China responded with alacrity and enthusiasm to calls to make revolution, happy to help Mao oust revisionists. In June 1966 middle schools and universities throughout the country, from large cities to small towns, were closed as students devoted all their time to Red Guard activities. The initial membership of the Red Guards was limited to those with 'good class backgrounds' – the children of peasants, workers, cadres, military men, and revolutionary martyrs. The children of high-ranking cadres, who boasted of themselves as the 'natural reds', became the leaders and treated with contempt their fellow students from ordinary or bad class backgrounds – especially the children of intellectuals who tended to do well in examinations. At the same time, they completely avoided the issue of the new privileged elite in socialist China. The students from ordinary or bad class backgrounds who suffered in the first phase of the Red Guard mobilization gradually formed their own Red Guard organizations. In place of class background they emphasized personal loyalty to Mao Zedong Thought as the criterion for judging a revolutionary. From August through November 1966, eight massive Red Guard

Revolutionary films, plays, and operas were avidly promoted by Jiang Qing during the Cultural Revolution. Performers were expected to instil martial spirit, discipline, and zeal in their audiences.

rallies were held in Beijing at Tiananmen square, attracting more than eight million youths from all over the country. These Red Guards waved their little red books, *Quotations from Chairman Mao*, compiled a few years earlier by Lin Biao (1908–71) to indoctrinate soldiers, and filled with such wisdom as, 'In class society everyone lives as a member of a particular class, and every kind of thinking, without exception, is stamped with the brand of a class', or 'The people, and the people alone, are the motive force in the making of world history.'

Tensions and antagonisms that had been suppressed by tight social control broke into the open as Red Guards found opportunities to get back at people or vent their fury. Red Guards roamed the streets in their battle against things foreign and things old, breaking into the homes of teachers, cadres, those with bad class backgrounds, and those with connections to foreigners, searching for old books, genealogies, or art treasures to seize or destroy. They orchestrated countless denunciation meetings at which accused cadres, teachers, or writers were forced to stand with their heads down and their arms raised behind them in the aeroplane position while listening to erstwhile friends and colleagues jeer and curse them. In the words of a *People's Daily* editorial in 1966, 'With the tremendous and impetuous force of a raging storm,' the Red Guards had 'smashed the shackles imposed on their minds by the exploiting classes for so long in the past, routing the bourgeois "specialists", "scholars", "authorities", and "venerable masters", sweeping every bit of their prestige into the dust.'

Targets included well-known intellectual figures like Ba Jin, author of *Family*, the novel that had captured the mood of educated youth of the 1920s and 1930s. In 1966 Ba Jin was publicly 'struggled with' in Shanghai, compelled to kneel on broken glass before a huge angry crowd. His wife was forced to clean the streets and became ill; since she had been classed as an 'enemy of the people', however, she was denied medical care, and Ba Jin was left to feel grievously responsible for her death. The Red Guards, with the blessings of the Maoists, even took on the head of state, Liu Shaoqi, now labelled the 'chief capitalist-roader'. In the summer of 1967 they stormed Zhongnanhai, the well-guarded quarters where the party hierarchy lived, and seized Liu. Then they taunted and beat him before huge crowds. Liu died two years later from the abuse he received; and four other members of his family also died as a result of beatings or mistreatment in prison where interrogators made every effort to force them to reveal evidence that Liu or his wife were spies.

By November 1966 workers were also being mobilized to participate in the Cultural Revolution. Rebel students went to factories to 'learn from the workers' but actually to instigate opposition to party superiors. Party leaders tried to appease discontented workers by raising wages and handing out bonuses, but Mao responded to this 'economism' by instructing students and workers to seize power from corrupt, revisionist party leaders. Confusing power struggles were the predictable result; as soon as one group gained the upper hand, another would

challenge its takeover as a 'sham power seizure' and attempt 'counter-power seizure'.

Up to this point, the involvement of the military in the Cultural Revolution had been minimal. However, as armed conflict spread, Mao turned to the People's Liberation Army as the only organization capable of restoring order. The army was given conflicting tasks: to help leftist groups seize power and to ensure that industrial and agricultural production continued. Generally the army pursued its own interests by supporting conservative mass organizations and disbanding the rebel organizations as 'counterrevolutionary'. Maoist leaders initiated a counterattack, accusing the army of supporting the wrong side. In July 1967 a conservative faction in Wuhan kidnapped two of the radical leaders from Beijing, and the Cultural Revolution Small Group responded by calling on the Red Guards to arm themselves and to seize military power from the 'capitalist roaders' in the Army. Thus began the most violent stage of the Cultural Revolution, during which different factions of Red Guards and workers' organizations took up armed struggle against not only each other but also in opposition to regional and national military forces.

At Beijing University students had to use ladders to post new 'big character posters' in 1967. Such posters denounced by name 'revisionists' and 'capitalist roaders' among the faculty and administrators.

Chinese food

Traditionally men and women ate separately, even in the home, but in the late twentieth century it had become the custom for everyone to sit down together.

During the twentieth century, Chinese in even the most remote villages have adopted numerous features of western material culture, not merely ones that could be classed as objectively superior on technical grounds (railroads, electric fans, thermos bottles, buses, ball-point pens), but also ones of no technical advantage (such as the collars on men's shirts and printing across rather than down). Chinese cuisine, however, has managed to resist insidious westernization. The Chinese have not abandoned chopsticks for forks or soy sauce for butter. Nor do they eat western food alongside their own the way Japanese do. Even the most westernized of the urban elite usually take pride in Chinese food, firm in the conviction that no other cuisine in the world can rival it.

Precisely which vegetables, meats, and grains Chinese eat varies considerably across the country, but certain basic principles make all of it identifiably 'Chinese'. Grain is always central, with rice preferred most places and wheat, made into noodles, buns, or flat cakes, coming next. Accompanying dishes are made from combinations of vegetables, meat, or fish, the pieces cut small enough to be cooked quickly with a minimum of fuel. Ginger, garlic, vinegar, and sauces made from fermented soy beans are widely used to enhance flavour. In some areas, notably Sichuan and Hunan, red pepper is also liberally used. Meat has never supplied a large share of the calories consumed, but neither has it been intentionally avoided. Pork is the most widely available meat; sliced thin or shredded, a small amount can flavour bean curd or such vegetables as cabbage or bamboo shoots. Even routine family meals usually include a soup as well as a vegetable dish or two. Feasts and banquets can easily include ten or more different dishes, with emphasis on variety of ingredients and styles of preparation: meat, fish, poultry, and vegetables steamed, stir-fried, stewed, and deep-fried.

In the People's Republic, eating, like almost everything else, has had its political aspects. The supply of grain to the cities has been controlled by the government. Through the 1980s, only those with grain ration coupons could purchase grain or even buy a bowl of rice or noodles at a small restaurant. Other foods have also been rationed at times, including cooking oil and meat. With the loosening of state control over the economy since the early 1980s, free markets have greatly expanded the quality and variety of foods available for home cooking, and free-enterprise restaurants have flourished, ranging from street stalls selling noodles or dumplings to elegant establishments in the many new luxury hotels. Food is connected to politics also through its association with the pursuit of connections and favours. Cadres have been accused of growing fat because of all the meals they accept from favour-seekers. In the 1990s newly prosperous entrepreneurs are eager to entertain business associates at expensive restaurants.

Communications and transport came to a standstill and consumer goods became scarce in urban areas.

Faced with this deteriorating situation, Mao had no choice but to moderate the whole movement in order to prevent full-scale civil war. In July 1968 Mao disbanded the Red Guards, who were soon sent off to work in the countryside. He and other leaders called for the creation of Revolutionary Committees to take the place of the old party structure. Each committee would have representatives from the mass organizations, from revolutionary cadres, and from the army; in most places the army quickly became the dominant force. Military control did not mean an end to violence, however. The military's search for hidden enemies and traitors among intellectuals and party members plunged the Cultural Revolution into a phase of state-instigated terror. The military's investigation of the probably fictitious 'May 16 Group' conspiracy culminated in the torture and execution of thousands of people.

By this time the Cultural Revolution was also having an impact in rural areas. In a manner reminiscent of the Great Leap Forward, those with bad-class labels again became scapegoats and extreme collectivism was pushed. All sideline activities, even raising chickens and pigs, were labelled incipient capitalism and had to be dropped. Because peasants did not spontaneously support these policies, heavily coercive tactics frequently had to be employed. Thus, although ideological emphasis was placed on mass participation in the political process, in actuality the power of local cadres tended to increase much more than the power of local people.

The dominance of the military declined after the bizarre downfall in 1971 of the minister of defence, Lin Biao. To the public, Lin Biao was a paragon of devotion to Mao, and the Chinese press regularly referred to Lin as Mao's close comrade-in-arms and best student. Yet, according to the official account, Lin became afraid that Mao had turned against him and decided to assassinate him. When Lin's daughter exposed his plot, he decided to flee to the Soviet Union, but died when his plane, out of fuel, crashed over Mongolia. Whatever the truth of the matter, news of his plot was kept out of the press for a year, the leadership apparently unsure how to tell the people that Lin Biao turned out to be just like Liu Shaoqi, a secret traitor who had managed to reach the second highest position in the political hierarchy.

In the early 1980s, walking down Nanjing Road, the main shopping street in Shanghai, was enough to convince anyone that China has too many people.

The fall of Lin Biao left Jiang Qing the main leader of the radical faction. During these years she devoted much of her energies to promoting revolutionary operas and other 'proletarian' art and standing vigil against the intrusion of feudalist, capitalist, or revisionist ideas into art or culture. The leader of the more moderate faction was Zhou Enlai, still principally responsible for foreign affairs. During the Cultural Revolution, China's main external fear was of Soviet invasion. In the more fluid situation after the fall of Lin Biao, Zhou Enlai sought ways to improve relations with the United States to make it a counter-weight to the Soviet Union, and he arranged for the US President Richard Nixon to visit in 1972. By 1973 Zhou, although ill with cancer, was able to bring back many disgraced leaders, including Deng Xiaoping, and reinstate them to important posts. Zhou died in January 1976. When residents of Beijing spontaneously gathered in April to pay respects to him at Tiananmen Square, Jiang Qing's group condemned them as 'counter-revolutionary' and purged Deng again. But with Mao's death in October that year, Jiang Qing and her Gang of Four were arrested. At a show trial held in 1980–81, they were convicted of most of the excesses of the Cultural Revolution.

When Deng regained power a second time in 1978, there were nearly three million victims of the Cultural Revolution to be rehabilitated. But almost everyone who had participated in any way ended up feeling a victim, short-changed or manipulated if not actually abused. Urban young people who had been exhilarated when Mao called on them to topple those in power soon found themselves at the bottom of the heap, sent down to the countryside where hostile peasants

In April 1976, three months after the death of Zhou Enlai, a spontaneous movement to put wreaths by the Memorial to the Martyrs of the Revolution ended in violent confrontation and the arrest of hundreds of demonstrators.

could make life very harsh. Their younger siblings had their education seriously interrupted, with schools closed for long periods, then reopened with watered-down curricula. The cadres, teachers, and intellectuals who were the principal targets suffered appalling physical abuse, but the sense of betrayal often was worse. When they had to continue working with people who had beaten, humiliated, or imprisoned them, the wounds were left to fester for years. Even those who agree that elitist values and bureaucratic habits were rife in the party and educational institutions find little positive in the outcome of the Cultural Revolution's massive assault on entrenched ideas and the established order. Indeed, most inside China and out put this episode of China's history high on a list of man's inhumanity to man.

The historical verdict on Mao Zedong has not been quite so negative as that on the Cultural Revolution, but seems to have steadily declined as the years have passed since his death. In 1981 when the party rendered its judgment on Mao, it still gave him high marks for his leadership during the war and his intellectual contributions, but assigned him much of the blame for everything that went wrong from 1956 on. Since then, Mao's standing has been further eroded as doubts are raised about the impact of Mao's leadership style in the 1940s and early 1950s. Some critics go so far as to portray Mao as a megalomaniac, so absorbed in his project of remaking China to match his will that he was totally indifferent to others' suffering. Other Chinese intellectuals, however, worry that making Mao a monster relieves everyone else of responsibility and undermines the argument that structural changes are needed to prevent comparable tragedies from recurring.

PROMOTING ECONOMIC GROWTH

In the long sweep of Chinese history, periods of turmoil have been associated with population declines. The Mongol and Manchu invasions, as well as the rebellions of the fourteenth, sixteenth, and nineteenth centuries are all believed to have caused drops in population of ten million or more. Measured on this sort of scale, the disorder created by the Great Leap Forward and the Cultural Revolution does not even register. From 1957 to 1970 China's population grew from about 630 million to 880 million. Public health measures promoted in the 1950s deserve much of the credit for reducing the death rate and thus improving life expectancy, which increased dramatically from forty years in 1953 to sixty in 1968 and sixty-five in 1984. As a consequence, however, population growth accelerated, and even the terrible famine of 1959–62 could only make a temporary dent in its upward course. Mao rejected the idea that China could have too many people, but by the time Mao died, China's population was approaching the billion mark, and his successors recognized that China could not afford to continue experimenting with policies that favoured egalitarianism over economic growth.

After he gained ascendance in 1978, Deng Xiaoping placed the problem of poverty high on his agenda and let ideology and class struggle recede. Deng had

Good agricultural land is in such short supply in China that efforts must be made to use every bit of it efficiently. In this fertile region of Jiangsu, the houses are concentrated along the canal to allow full use of tillable land.

In the 1980s and 1990s, popular magazines were encouraging young women to beautify themselves and become fashion-conscious.

as impressive a revolutionary pedigree as Mao, going back to the early 1920s when he was active with Zhou Enlai in France and continuing through the Shanghai underground, the Long March, and guerrilla warfare against Japan. In 1956, at age fifty-two, he became a member of the standing committee of the politburo and general secretary of the Communist Party. Having been twice ousted from power during the Cultural Revolution, Deng Xiaoping labelled as absurd the Cultural Revolution slogan that it was 'better to be poor under socialism than rich under capitalism', insisting instead that 'poverty is not socialism'. As guiding slogans, Deng formulated the Four Modernizations (of agriculture, industry, technology, and defence) along with the Four Cardinal Principles (retaining the socialist path, the dictatorship of the proletariat, the leadership of the Communist Party, and the ideology of Marxism, Leninism, and Maoism).

Deng's policies set in motion an economic boom that led to a tripling of average incomes by the early 1990s and moved, the World Bank calculated, 170 million peasants out of extreme poverty. Poverty was most intractable in the countryside, and to battle it Deng sanctioned steps toward dismantling collective agriculture. He instituted a 'responsibility system', under which rural households were assigned land and other assets that they could treat as their own, and were given incentives to increase production. Each production team contracted with member households who agreed to provide the team with specified crops in exchange for use of particular fields; whatever the household produced above what it owed the team was its to keep or sell. Teams were, in essence, renting out their land rather than farming it directly. Families were both landlords (as members of the team) and tenants (on the land they had contracted for). Sideline enterprises like growing vegetables and raising pigs or chickens were encouraged, as were small businesses of all sorts, ranging from fish farming and equipment repair to small workshops producing consumer goods for export. Especially in the coastal provinces, where commercial opportunities were greatest, the income of farmers rapidly increased. Even the poorest areas benefited, especially when restrictions on travel and residency were eased, freeing millions of young men to move to where the jobs were and send money home.

Deng also pushed for reform of education, asserting that the influence of the Gang of Four had created 'an entire generation of mental cripples'. Party members qualified to manage and direct the modernization projects were in particularly short supply. The oldest cohort of party cadres, those recruited before 1949, had mostly minimal educations; the youngest cohort, those recruited during the Cultural Revolution, had been selected more for anti-intellectual fervour than academic achievement. As a result, in the early 1980s only 14 per cent of the forty million party members had finished the equivalent of high school and only 4 per cent had college educations. Moreover, many of those with college degrees had attended college in the 1970s when the quality of their education suffered from

Lingering resentment of Japan did not dampen Chinese enthusiasm for newly available Japanese consumer goods, ranging from tape recorders and televisions to washing machines and televisions.

the anti-elitist and anti-intellectual policies of the period. College entrance examinations were reinstituted in 1977. The new prospect of getting a chance to study abroad in Europe, the United States, or Japan provided an incentive for students to apply themselves and even soon led to a craze for studying English.

To speed up economic development, Deng also abandoned Mao's insistence on self-sufficiency and began courting foreign investors, even encouraging joint ventures between foreign firms and Chinese government agencies. Foreign manufacturers were attracted to the low labour costs in China, and both set up factories to produce goods for the Chinese market (such as vehicles) and contracted with Chinese manufacturers to produce consumer goods for western markets (such as clothing, stuffed toys, watches, and bicycles). Guangdong, with the best access to the financial giant Hong Kong, did especially well in the new environment. Between 1982 and 1992, 97 per cent of Hong Kong's 3,200 toy factories had relocated to Guangdong. Many had moved to Shenzhen, a special economic zone set up at the border with Hong Kong, which grew at a dizzying speed. By the end of 1991 some 300,000 people in southern Guangdong had acquired electronic pagers and 30,000 had already graduated to cellular phones, the talisman of Hong Kong businessmen, a remarkable change considering that only a decade earlier making phone calls between cities in China had been a major hassle.

Even in the cities, not all have benefited equally from reform. Those who worked for the state found that reform meant they could lose their jobs. Moreover, their wages did not always keep up with inflation, something they had not had to

Once stock markets were introduced into the People's Republic, the desire to get rich fast led to frequent, rather frenzied efforts to buy stock. These eager buyers were photographed in Shenzhen in 1992.

worry about during the era of tight central control over the economy. Intellectuals felt left out when they saw the new independent entrepreneurs – even street vendors – earning enough to buy all sorts of consumer goods never available before, such as motorcycles. But most galling of all were signs that the children of high officials were getting rich by using their connections to secure lucrative contracts.

The list of the negative consequences of the otherwise promising political and economic reforms can easily be expanded. Illicit trade has grown rapidly, not only in narcotics traffic, but also in art objects looted from graves. Pollution and other environmental problems have been exacerbated. Women have lost many of their advances in employment and education as parents pull girls out of school to put them to work, and employers disproportionately lay off women. Freer markets have even led to renewed buying and selling of women as wives; in 1989 and 1990 more than 65,000 people were arrested for abducting or selling women and children. The disparity between the coastal and the inland provinces has created new inequalities. When internal controls on migration collapsed, the coastal regions flooded with job seekers willing to live in shanty towns or a dozen to a room to get a chance to share in the wealth that the market economy has been bringing to the fortunate regions. In Guangdong internal migrants, especially those who cannot speak Cantonese, have become an exploited class, hired for the worst work, kept on the job for ten or twelve hours a day, seven days a week, unable to protest without losing their jobs.

Post-Mao efforts to blunt population growth have also given rise to considerable resentment. Because Mao rejected the Malthusian premise that productive capacities were limited, during his lifetime there were only sporadic attempts to curb population growth through such measures as encouraging late marriage. Since his death, however, the government has worked hard to promote the one-child family. Targets have been set for the total numbers of births in each place, and quotas then assigned to smaller units. Young people have needed permission from their work units to get married, then permission to have a child. Women who become pregnant outside the plan, if they do not manage to hide, face often unrelenting pressure from birth control workers and local cadres to have an abortion. When ultrasound screenings became available – in the late 1980s and early 1990s – many gave in and had an abortion if an ultrasound scan showed the foetus to be female. Others have apparently practised female infanticide or concealed female births, since the reported sex ratios for second and subsequent births are strongly skewed in favour of sons.

In the 1980s and 1990s censorship was relaxed and film rapidly became a major medium for exploring the meaning of China's recent history. Film makers were allowed to be critical but not too critical: the script for *The Blue Kite*, the story of a family's suffering during the political movements of the 1950s and 1960s, was approved by the authorities but seized by them after it was filmed. It was finished abroad and proved a success there, but in 1994 it was banned in China.

CULTURAL TRENDS IN THE 1980S AND 1990S

Culture did not prosper during the decade of the 'Cultural' Revolution; intellectuals learned to keep quiet and ordinary people were fed a dull and repetitious diet of highly politicized stories, plays, and films. With the downfall of the Gang of Four, people's pent-up desire for more varied and lively cultural expression quickly became apparent. A literature of the 'wounded' appeared at the end of the 1970s, as those who had suffered during the Cultural Revolution found it politically possible to express their sense of betrayal. Greater tolerance on the part of the government soon resulted in much livelier press and media – with everything from investigative reporters like Liu Binyan and Dai Qing reporting on corruption of cadres, to philosophers who tried to re-examine the premises of Marxism, to novelists, poets, and film-makers who experimented with previously taboo explorations of sexuality.

Television as a cultural force expanded enormously as TV sets became a readily available consumer good and programming became diverse enough to capture people's interest. Television brought knowledge of what was happening in the outside world. Such knowledge was also enhanced by the fact that tens of thousands of Chinese got the opportunity to go abroad and similar numbers of foreigners visited China for business, study, or tourism. Moreover, Chinese began to gain access to information outside the control of the government – from Chinese-language publications elsewhere, television broadcasts from Hong Kong, and from BBC and VOA shortwave broadcasts in English and Chinese. People came to understand how underdeveloped China was in comparison both to the old impe-

Below left
The image of this lone protestor standing in front of a line of tanks on 5 June 1989, a day after the bloody crackdown on the democracy protests, made a deep impression outside China. Millions around the world who had watched the progress of the protests on television saw this brave individual as a symbol of China's hopes.

Below right
The 1989 student democracy protests were re-energized in late May when art students at the Central Art College erected a 37-foot-tall 'goddess of democracy' statue. Placing it across from the portrait of Mao in Tiananmen Square was meant to be provocative.

Taiwan's economic miracle

When the victory of the Communist Party in the civil war seemed imminent, Jiang Jieshi and large parts of the Nationalist government and army evacuated to the island of Taiwan, a hundred miles off the coast of Fujian province. Under Japanese colonial rule from 1895 to 1945, Taiwan had only recently been returned to Chinese rule, and the initial encounter between the local population and the Nationalist government had been hostile – in 1947 the government responded to protests against the corruption of its politicians by shooting at protestors and pursuing suspected leaders, killing, it is estimated, 8,000 to 10,000 people, including many local leaders. In part because of the support the United States gave Jiang and his government as the Cold War in Asia intensified, the Nationalists soon stabilized their government and were able to concentrate on economic development.

In 1992 Taiwan's per capita income was second only to Japan in Asia and way beyond China. Several factors contributed to this extraordinary economic growth. The Nationalists started with the advantage of Japanese land reform and industrial development. They also benefited from considerable foreign investment over the next couple of decades, especially from the United States and Japan. But hard work and thoughtful planning also deserve credit for Taiwan's growth. The Taiwan government gave the technically trained real authority. Economists and engineers, including many trained abroad, became heads of ministries. Through the 1950s emphasis was placed on import substitution, especially by building up light industry to produce consumer goods. The 1960s saw a shift towards export-driven industries, especially electronics, as Taiwan began to try to follow the pattern set by Japan, moving into stereos and televisions as Japan moved into cars. In 1966 the first tax-free export processing zone was set up, attracting foreign capital and technology. By the 1980s there was adequate wealth in Taiwan to develop capital-intensive industries such as steel and petrochemicals. By the early 1990s, there was so much capital in Taiwan in search of lucrative investment possibilities that large amounts were pouring into the mainland, especially nearby Fujian where wages were less than a tenth those in Taiwan.

Anyone over forty in Taiwan today has witnessed extraordinary changes. The standard of living has improved dramatically, the cultural scene has become lively and very international, and politics have become more open. After Jiang Jieshi died in 1975 he was succeeded by his son Jiang Jingquo, who lifted martial law, allowed visits to the mainland, and opened up the political process. In the late 1980s and early 1990s Taiwan succeeded in making the transition from one party rule to parliamentary democracy, with opposition parties (legalized in 1986) proving successful in winning elections. Even though Taiwan lost its seat in the United Nations in 1971 and was no longer recognized as the government of China by very many countries (the United States abandoned its resistance and recognized the People's Republic in 1979), its economic success made it internationally important. The Nationalist government did not renounce its claims to be the legitimate government of all of China, but political and economic union with China no longer seemed a realistic or even a desirable goal to much of the population in Taiwan.

With the building boom of the 1980s and early 1990s, Taibei became a city of skyscrapers.

rialist powers but also to more recently developed places like Taiwan and South Korea.

The government tolerated the loss of its monopoly on information but did not renounce its authority to censor publications or condemn writers for expressing counter-revolutionary ideas. When college students, writers, artists, intellectuals, and urban young people became attracted to western popular culture – especially its music, eroticism, hairstyles, and apparently self-centred individualism, conservative party critics responded with periodic campaigns against 'bourgeois liberalism' and 'spiritual pollution'.

Much more threatening to the party elite was growing interest in western political ideas. Chinese intellectuals were beginning to draw on western ideas to protest not merely against abuses of the government, but some of the basic principles underlying the communist system. The first 'big character' posters were pasted on Democracy Wall in Beijing in the autumn of 1978. Soon an electrician named Wei Jingshen had courageously pasted up a call for the 'fifth modernization', namely real democracy, which he identified as the right of the people to choose their own representatives. The party state, Wei claimed elsewhere, had become an autocracy imposed on the workers and peasants of China. By April 1979 Wei had been arrested and the Democracy Wall shut down. Wei eventually served fourteen-and-a-half years in prison for these offences, with long stretches in solitary confinement during which he was forbidden even to talk to his jailers.

Wei's fate did not deter intellectuals from more measured analyses of the state of China's culture and political system. Many were fascinated by the economic success of the 'four little dragons', Taiwan, Hong Kong, Singapore, and South Korea, where authoritarian governments, suffused with Confucian values, had managed to promote rapid growth; their successes seemed to imply that China should consider reviving some elements of its old culture. A diametrically opposed view was widely publicized in the spring and summer of 1988 in a popular six-part TV documentary entitled *River Elegy* which traced many of China's problems back to its ancient traditions, especially its persistent inward orientation and lack of interest in the outside world. *River Elegy* attacked some of the country's most revered symbols, re-labelling the Yellow River, the Great Wall, and the dragon as symbols of backward passivity, not greatness.

Debate about China's culture and political form spilled out into the streets in the spring of 1989 where it was captured by the world press, present to witness the Soviet premier Mikhail Gorbachev bring a formal end to the Sino-Soviet split. The students' protest began modestly in April with a parade honouring the memory of Hu Yaobang, a recently deceased party leader who had been relatively tolerant of dissent. Buoyed by the positive reaction of the Beijing citizenry and angered at the negative reaction of the government, student leaders gradually escalated their activities and their rallying cries. They called for more democratic government: 'Make officials disclose their income and assets!' 'Renounce the use of mass political campaigns!' 'Abolish prohibitions against street protests!' 'Permit journalists to report protest activities!' Many evoked the ideas of the May Fourth Movement, claiming that China had still not achieved science and democracy.

Through much of May 1989 there were students in Tiananmen Square, their numbers ranging from a few thousand to, at the greatest rallies, perhaps a million. To testify to their sincerity and determination, a couple of thousand students staged a hunger strike. On 17 May, during Gorbachev's visit, the square was filled not merely with students from every university in Beijing, but also from other organizations, even government ones like the Foreign Ministry, the Central Television Station, the National Men's Volleyball Team, even the Public Security Bureau Academy. There were also workers in their work clothes, holding banners inscribed with the names of their factories. The formation of the Beijing Autonomous Workers Federation was announced, calling for democracy and opposed to the 'lawlessness and brutality of corrupt officials'. The next day the *Beijing Youth News* reported that 95 per cent of those surveyed considered the student movement 'patriotic' and 80 per cent thought it would ultimately 'compel the government to give in and initiate democracy'.

The public's support for the students – the farmers who bicycled in to give food, the vendors who passed out free drinks, the citizens who displayed homemade placards and banners with the words 'support' on them – were a humiliation to Deng and the other hard-line leaders, who declared martial law as soon as Gorbachev left. Yet when truckloads of troops attempted to enter the city, the citizens in Beijing took to the streets to stop them. Successful against these unarmed soldiers, they were exhilarated by this evidence of 'people power'. Only two weeks later, on the night of 3/4 June, tanks and artillery were brought in, and though many unarmed citizens still tried to halt their advance, the armoured vehicles got through the blockades after bloody clashes and successfully ended both the protest and the occupation of the square. At least several hundred people lost their lives that night, many of them ordinary citizens trying to stop the soldiers from entering central Beijing.

This bloody suppression, so damaging to China's international image, was considered essential to party hard liners who saw the entire power structure in jeopardy. In their view, allowing non-party forces to interject themselves into the decision-making process was a greater threat to stability than corruption or inflation. In Poland it was the workers' union, Solidarity, after all, that had recently undermined the Communist Party there. Soon Deng and the hard-liners, led by Li Peng, followed up the initial military seizure of the square with the arrest and sentencing of hundreds of participants along with well-known intellectuals like Dai Qing who had never gone to the square but whose writings could be interpreted as encouraging dissidence.

Economic progress did not suffer much of a setback in the aftermath of the crackdown. By the early 1990s, the collapse of communism in Eastern Europe and

Despite a considerable investment in the construction of high-rise housing in major cities, a large portion of the urban population in the 1980s still lived in cramped quarters along narrow alleys.

the Soviet Union reinforced Deng Xiaoping's determination to carry through his economic reform programme. The Soviet Union broke up and Gorbachev fell, Chinese leaders inferred, because central planning was not producing prosperity. Deng Xiaoping made his continuing support for market reforms and rapid economic growth as clear as possible in 1992 when he took a trip south to visit the Special Economic Zones. He told people not to worry if policies were capitalist or socialist, only whether they would make China more prosperous. Shortly after, the party constitution was rewritten to describe China as a 'socialist market economy' and to declare 'the essential nature of socialism' to be 'to liberate and develop productive forces'.

Young Chinese responded to Deng's call to make money with the same zeal their parents had shown in response to Mao's call to make revolution. In the early 1990s they were plunging into private enterprise in unprecedented numbers, setting themselves up in businesses ranging from food stalls in the lively night markets, to factories making down coats for the Russian market, Buddhist altars for the Japanese market, or stuffed toys for the US market. Many grew rich enough to buy imported cars, build lavish houses, and make generous gifts to all the officials they dealt with. In 1978 there had not been a single privately owned car in China, but by 1993 there were over a million and the number was increasing at a rate of 12 per cent a year.

Since the People's Republic was proclaimed in 1949, China has not only been transformed, but transformed several times. Some of the changes can be seen as modernization or development, comparable to changes in other countries, socialist and non-socialist. These include improvements in public health, health care, and the distribution of food, all leading to much longer life expectancy; the extension of elementary education and of modern communications which encouraged greater literacy and an expansion of shared culture; higher levels of industrialization, which led to greater availability of consumer goods, beginning with thermos bottles and electric fans, advancing to watches and bicycles, then to televisions and washing machines, and by the 1990s to cars and air conditioners.

In terms of political organization, change has also been marked. Reversals after the death of Mao have been so extensive that observers sometimes think China is cancelling or forgetting all the changes made in the name of New China in the 1950s and 1960s. But history is not easily rolled back, and much that was put in place during the Mao years still shapes contemporary China. The Communist Party still dominates the government and has its hands in much of what goes on in the country. The Chinese state no longer interferes in everyday affairs to the extent it used to, but it still has tremendous coercive force: witness its ability to force adherence to a very unpopular birth limitation programme and to silence most of its critics.

Culturally, China is a very different place than it was in the 1930s and 1940s. Several decades of tight government control over what was published, broadcast, or taught in schools did much to standardize Chinese culture, to enlarge the common vocabulary crossing regions and classes. The shared drama of political events over the last few decades has also strengthened a sense of shared identity. City dwellers and peasants in remote villages have all gone through the mobilizations for major campaigns, the blaring of loud-speakers, the political meetings and study sessions, the dependence on low-level cadres. Memories of these experiences came to bind Chinese all over the country in the way that the examination system used to bind members of the educated elite in imperial China.

This common identity, moreover, has been tied up with the Chinese state to an unparalleled degree. Mao did succeed in making people proud of China. China fought the United States to a standstill in Korea and survived its long embargo, successfully extricated itself from an unbalanced relationship with the Soviet Union, and proudly offered itself as a model to other developing nations, both in its most radical and most reformist stages.

The state, it is true, has not been able totally to manipulate popular consciousness. Declaring the People's Republic of China to be a multi-national state has not, in fact, succeeded in altering common understandings of the term 'Chinese' to make it encompass Tibetans, Mongols, and Uighurs. Still, the nationalities policies have had an impact on the construction of 'Chineseness' because they have made assimilation much more problematic than it had been through most of Chinese history. Even though forces fostering acculturation have been strengthened (more Chinese in-migration, more opportunities and more incentives to learn Chinese), the state now impedes full assimilation by giving everyone an official ethnic classification. In other words, what had been a more fluid situation, susceptible to negotiation and choice of self-presentation, has been turned into a matter of legal status. A Zhuang or a Yi or a Mongol can no longer present himself or herself one way to one audience and another way to another audience.

The project of creating a new modern China is still very much alive in the 1990s. In the Maoist years New China rejected both China's past and much of western culture, especially anything that could be labelled capitalist or bourgeois. To be modern was to have broken with the feudal past with its class exploitation, its suppression of women and youth, and its superstitions. But to be modern was also to be strong enough to resist domination and exploitation, the threat of which came overwhelmingly from places already modern – in the twentieth century the European imperial powers, then Japan, then the United States, then the Soviet Union. Mao was determined that China not let the outside world tell it what to do. China, he thought, had to go it alone, in its own way, at its own pace, toward its own goals.

Post-Mao China is not so absorbed in excluding the outside world or cutting itself off from all that is bourgeois and western. Even the old culture is not being so resolutely excluded; young people are willing to explore the possibilities of drawing both from western rock music and fashions and from such varied facets of traditional culture as fortune telling and martial arts. They even draw from recent history; in 1990 a cult of Mao appeared – taxi drivers nationwide were hanging plastic pictures of Mao from their mirrors and his portrait reappeared in many shops and offices. To some, Mao was simply a protective deity, a new addition to the Chinese pantheon. To others, he represented a better time when leaders were dedicated to the welfare of the common people rather than their own enrichment. Some liked to note that Mao had purged most of the current leaders at least once; to them honouring Mao constituted a mild form of political protest.

Epilogue

When history is viewed from the western edge of Eurasia, the natural pattern seems to be for civilizations and empires to rise and wane. By 2000 BC Egypt had eclipsed Sumeria; by 1000 BC Egypt was on the decline but Babylonia was an impressive power. In time, however, it would be surpassed by the Persians, then the Greeks, then the Romans. Some civilizations were totally destroyed and disappeared from history, others were simply overshadowed by new, more vigorous, more successful civilizations. Even in more recent periods, those viewing history from Eurasia's western edge speak of the rise and decline of the Italian city states, the Spanish Empire, the Hapsburg Empire, and the British Empire. Americans today take it quite for granted that their international predominance is unlikely to last for ever, and books about the coming Pacific Century sell well. Underlying this view of history is an unspoken analogy between civilizations and human lives, or perhaps the lives of competitive individual warrior-heroes. Civilizations have an early, creative, aggressive stage followed by a strong, mature age, but over time they lose vigour and become less flexible until eventually they are defeated in battle or succumb to old age. And only one can be supreme at any given time.

When history is viewed from the eastern edge of Eurasia, a very different pattern emerges as natural and normal. There is no sense that younger civilizations supplant aging ones, but that civilization progresses through a series of yin-yang-like reversals of direction from excessive disorder to excessive order and back again. Thus periods of creative but frightfully deadly disorder are followed by the imposition of stringent political order, sometimes so heavy-handed as to be oppressive. But order eventually unravels into disorder once again, renewing the pattern. The course of a civilization thus does not resemble that of a human life. It has some similarity to a line of descent, however, a series of entities linked one to another much the way fathers and sons are linked in a family, and the succession of dynasties in Chinese history was often discussed using the vocabulary of legitimate succession. These differences in metaphor shape expectations for historical change. In China, neither a period of disorder nor an episode of oppressive order is viewed as likely to last indefinitely or to bring about the total ruin of the civilization. Children get a lot from their parents, materially and culturally, so even though the family property may be nearly ruined by natural disasters or war, with hard work and commitment to the survival of the family, in time it can be rebuilt and even enhanced; in a comparable way the ruin of one dynasty does not preclude a successor from rising. Moreover, just as the future of one family line is nearly independent of the success or failure of other families, so outside powers can rise and decline without altering China's prospects. The rise of Japan does not mean China must be in decline.

Given the difference between these visions of the course of history, when Europeans first began to study Chinese history they often unconsciously tried to discover where China stood in the scheme of civilizations on the rise and decline based on western experience. Most seem to have felt that the China they encountered was on the decline, but they differed in their dating of its golden age. That there was little reason to expect a new glorious age in China was taken for granted; their age was the age of the European conquest of the world and while China might benefit from the fruits of western civilization, they assumed the creative impulses would be western, not Chinese.

This conceptual framework did not require westerners always to write negatively of China or its history. China has often served as the perfect 'other' for the west, as the other side of the world where everything is upside down and opposite. Thus those who wished to criticize the west have sometimes done so by celebrating China as a place that disproved the validity or universality of something western. Thus Voltaire found in China a land without an established church where rational philosophers ruled; in the 1950s western feminists found in China a land where women held up half the sky; in the 1960s western radicals found in China a place imbued with a communal spirit so strong that streets were magically cleaned by friction-free street committees; and in the 1980s western conservatives found in China a nearly crime-free society where everyone learned the virtue of self-restraint.

By bringing up these issues of conceptual framework in the epilogue, I am hoping to stimulate readers to stop and reflect on the task of understanding a culture different from their own. Readers of this book have not gained unmediated access to Chinese culture. This book is written in English for a western audience, using concepts and modes of analysis and presentation that will seem familiar and reasonable to such an audience. The kind of history I have tried to write is without doubt a western type of history, strongly influenced by trends in history writing in Europe and the United States over the last few decades. I bring women into the story more than once was common, for instance, and rarely devote much space to political intrigues at the top of the government. We can enrich our understanding of China's history by trying to see how Chinese were interpreting their world, but we only delude ourselves if we deny that our ideas, assumptions, and theories shape what we notice and consider significant about China's past.

In writing this book, the difficulty of coping with the east–west conceptual gap did not seem as challenging to me as bridging the modern–premodern gap. Two overlapping but slightly contradictory problems proved most unsettling: the first is the bias in sources that makes it easier to say good things about earlier periods, and the second is the difficulty in seeing any period except in terms of what came afterwards. In China, as elsewhere, the closer to the present, the more evidence survives. We know much more about the details of life during the twentieth century than we do about the Qing dynasty, and we probably know as much about the Qing as of all of earlier China put together. Added to this, the closer to the present, the less editing historians have done to the sources. From the time of Sima Qian in the first century BC, most Chinese historians were social critics of one sort of another. When they wrote of their own times, they usually found much to condemn. When they wrote about the distant past, they were still often subtly commenting on the present, but saying good things tended to be more useful. One of the best ways to criticize the present was to describe a better age in the past – if necessary a past so distant that contradictory evidence was scarce.

Taken together, the forces shaping what evidence has survived make it harder to take a rosy view of recent history than earlier history. I tend to believe that China in Song times was more impressive than China in the nineteenth century – that not only did it compare better to other contemporary states, but that the daily lives of people at all social levels were in many ways more satisfying. Yet how can I be sure that generations of historians have not discarded most of the evidence that would tend to refute my views? Long-ago cruelties are less vivid than recent ones: we may know that many emperors had malicious streaks, but we do not have vivid first-hand accounts from witnesses the way we do from Mao's victims. Even material evidence – the paintings, porcelains, and silks – are winnowed over time so that there is little from the eleventh century that is not pleasing in some way whereas much that is ordinary or unimpressive survives from the nineteenth century.

Exacerbating these source problems is the difficulty of telling history in chronological order, of putting the past before the present, the way people want to hear it told. The story one chooses to tell about one period depends very much on what one thinks of the next. In the 1960s and 1970s, when many westerners were inclined to look as positively as they could on both Mao Zedong and the People's Republic of China, accounts of the 1920s and 1930s often subordinated almost everything to the story of the rise of the Communist Party: the May Fourth Movement was the first step towards breaking with the past intellectually, important as a formative part of the experience of Mao and Zhou. Similarly, industrialization needed to be described, because without it one could not recount the urban labour organizing that played a role in the early stage of the Communist Party before it broke with the Comintern, and so on. We may feel superior to this generation of historians, but can we be sure that we have somehow found a vantage point that will not keep shifting? In recent years there have been many revelations of internal party viciousness. Should we totally rewrite our accounts of the last few decades? How then can we capture what Mao or the Long March or the Great Leap meant to people at the time ignorant of these happenings?

These problems are even more acute for earlier periods. Always concentrating on what proves to be important in later times makes history seem the working out of the inevitable. I could not omit mention of ideas about ancestors in the Shang dynasty, the ideas of Confucius in the late Zhou, or centralized government in the Qin and Han. Yet I am uncomfortable with conveying the impression that the direction of China's future course was firmly set at these early dates. Doing so seems to diminish the agency of the Chinese people, their capacity to respond to new situations creatively, to make use of what they inherited from their ancestors without being immobilized by it.

I am definitely not the only historian who has struggled with this difficulty in linking Chinese civilization – a story that can be told in an upbeat, even celebratory mode – and the story of modern China – where it is difficult to avoid the language of victimization from creeping in occasionally. Those with the darkest views of modern China sometimes cast the story of premodern China so that it leads inevitably to what happened in the twentieth century. China's history can be told, for instance, in terms of the development of state institutions that allowed arbitrary exercise of power or the development of Confucian cultural values that became too inward-looking. Those with the most positive views of premodern China can solve the problem a different way by making all of China's woes since the Opium War the fault not of Chinese civilization but of an unfair world system.

The reason I persisted in trying to link the story of China's more distant and more recent pasts despite these intractable problems is that I am convinced that it is a continuous story. Chinese people today do not simply occupy the same territory occupied by subjects of the Tang, Song, or Ming dynasties; their notions of who they are and of what their nation is are profoundly shaped by the ideas and institutions created during these centuries, even if they have been much transmuted in the intervening centuries. To minimize somehow the impression of inevitability, I have tried to cast the inheritance from the past as a resource, not a prison. In every epoch Chinese have made use of the resources they inherited – material, intellectual, and institutional – to set goals, respond to new challenges, protect themselves, and advance their interests. Because their actions have a cumulative impact on the resources the next generation inherits, change is inevitable but so are links to the past. This I believe is as true today as ever.

Reference guide to
The Cambridge
Illustrated History of
China

Chronology

100,000 BC *Homo sapiens* in China. Paleolithic cultures.

10,000 BC Early Neolithic cultures.

3000 BC Late Neolithic cultures (to 2000 BC).

1600 BC Shang dynasty (to c. 1050 BC).

1050 BC Zhou dynasty (to 256 BC), Western Zhou dynasty (to 771 BC).

770 BC Eastern Zhou dynasty (to 256 BC), Spring and Autumn period (to 481 BC).

c. 479 BC Death of Confucius.

403 BC Warring States period (to 221 BC).

286 BC Death of Zhuangzi (b. 396 BC).

221 BC Qin unifies China. First Emperor undertakes massive projects (to 210 BC).

213 BC Burning of Confucian books.

206 BC Han Dynasty (to AD 220), Former or Western Han dynasty (to AD 9).

141 BC Wudi succeeds to throne (to 87 BC).

133 BC Campaigns against Xiongu (to 119 BC).

126 BC Zhang Qian returns from western regions.

c. 85 BC Sima Qian completes *Historical Records*.

AD 9 Wang Mang usurps throne, founds Xin dynasty (to 25).

25 Later or Eastern Han dynasty (to 220).

105 First mention of paper.

184 Rebellion of Yellow Turbans.

220 Age of Division (to 589). Three Kingdoms period (to 265).

265 Western Jin dynasty (to 316). Reunifies China in 280.

304 Sixteen Kingdoms (to 439). Non-Chinese compete for control of north China.

317 Eastern Jin dynasty set up in south (to 420). Beginning of division between north and south (to 589).

404 Huiyuan writes *On Why Monks Do Not Bow Down Before Kings*.

427 Death of Tao Yuanming (b. 365).

589 Reunification of China by Sui dynasty (581–618).

609 Grand Canal completed.

618 Tang dynasty (to 907).

653 Earliest surviving law code.

690 Empress Wu usurps throne from her son, declares the Zhou dynasty (to 705).

713 Death of Huineng, Sixth Patriarch of Chan Buddhism.

755 An Lushan Rebellion (to 763).

843 Suppression of Buddhism (to 845)

868 Oldest extant printed book published.

907 Five Dynasties period (to 960). Khitans declare Liao dynasty (to 1126).

960 Song dynasty (to 1276). Northern Song dynasty (to 1126).

1069 Wang Anshi institutes New Policies (to 1085).

1126 Jurchen seize north China, extending Jin dynasty (1115–1234).

1127 Southern Song dynasty in south (to 1276).

1200 Death of Zhu Xi (b. 1130).

1215 Mongols seize most of north China.

1227 Death of Chinggis Khan.

1276 Mongol Yuan dynasty gains control of south China.

1368 Ming dynasty (to 1644).

1405 Zheng He's maritime expeditions (to 1433).

1528 Death of Wang Yangming (b. 1472).

1583 Matteo Ricci arrives in China (to 1610).

1592 Ming campaigns in Korea (to 1598).

1598 *Peony Pavilion* written by Tang Xianzu.

1624 Struggles between Donglin scholars and eunuch dictator Wei Zhongxian (to 1627).

1644 Ming emperor commits suicide after rebels take Beijing.

1644 Manchu Qing dynasty (to 1911).

1645 Chinese men required to wear Manchu hairstyle.

1673 Rebellion of the Three Feudatories (to 1681).

1720 Qing army enters Lhasa; Tibet made Qing protectorate.

1792 Novel *Dream of Red Mansions* published.

1796 White Lotus Society rebellion (to 1804).

1840 Opium War, ending with Treaty of Nanjing in 1842. Britain obtains Hong Kong.

1850 Taiping Rebellion (to 1864).

1860 Anglo-French expedition occupies Beijing. Burning of Summer Palace.

1862 Zuo Zongtang suppresses Muslim rebellions in northwest, regains central Asia (to 1878).

1884 Sino-French War (to 1885).

1894 Sino-Japanese War (to 1895).

1894 Sun Zhongshan establishes Revive China Society.

1898 Guangxu emperor's attempted reforms thwarted by Empress Dowager Cixi.

1900 Boxer Rebellion. International expedition to relieve siege of legations.

1901 Death of Li Hongzhang (b. 1823).

1905 Abolition of civil service exam system.

1911 Qing dynasty overthrown by revolutionaries.

1915 Periodical *New Youth* begins publication.

1916 Death of Yuan Shikai (b. 1859).Warlord period begins (to 1928).

1919 May Fourth protests in Tiananmen Square against Versailles Treaty.

1925 Death of Sun Zhongshan (b. 1866).

1926 Northern Expedition of combined Nationalist and Communist forces (to 1927).

1927 Nationalists turn on Communists; 'White Terror' (to 1930).

1927 Nationalist period (to 1949). Jiang Jieshi leader.

1930 Mao Zedong and other Communists form Jiangxi Soviet.

1930 New Civil Code gives women marriage and property rights.

1931 Japan seizes control of Manchuria.

1934 Red Army flees Nationalist encirclement, begins Long March (to 1935).

1936 Death of Lu Xun (b. 1881).

1937 Sino-Japanese War (to 1945). Rape of Nanjing.

1947 Civil War between Nationalists and Communists (to 1949).

1949 People's Republic of China founded. Mao Zedong leader.

1950 Korean War (to 1953).

1950 Marriage Reform Law.

1951 Redistribution and collectivization of land (to 1956).

1951 Five Antis Campaign (to 1952).

1956 Hundred Flowers and Anti-rightist campaigns (to 1957).

1957 Great Leap Forward. Agricultural communes established (to 1958).

1959 Three Hard Years (to 1962).

1959 Tibetan uprising suppressed. Dalai Lama flees.

1960 Sino-Soviet split.

1966 Cultural Revolution (to 1969).

1976 Death of Mao Zedong (b. 1893). Gang of Four arrested.

1978 Deng Xiaoping regains power. 'Big character posters' appear on Beijing's Democracy Wall.

1979 Special economic zones created.

1989 Pro-democracy movement violently suppressed.

Picture Acknowledgements

The author, the publishers, and Calmann & King Ltd would like to thank the museums, galleries, collectors, and other owners who have kindly allowed their works to be reproduced in this book. Every effort has been made to trace copyright holders and we apologize in advance for any unintentional omissions. We would be pleased to insert the appropriate acknowledgement in any subsequent edition of this publication.

The following abbreviations have been used:

BL: British Library, London
CHM: Chinese History Museum, Beijing
FGA: Freer Gallery of Art, Smithsonian Institution, Washington DC
NA: Nelson-Atkins Museum of Art, Kansas City, Missouri
NPM: National Palace Museum, Taiwan, Republic of China
PE: Peabody Essex Museum, Salem, Massachusetts
RH: Robert Harding Picture Library
XNA: Xinhua News Agency, London

Page 14 top China Tourism Photo Library. **14** bottom RH. **15** Palace Museum, Beijing. **16** bottom XNA. **17** Shanghai Museum. **19** bottom China Tourism Photo Library. **21** CHM. **22** Institute of Archeology, Beijing. **23** Academia Sinica, Taiwan. **24** Academia Sinica, Taiwan. **26** top Wang Yang (artwork). **26** bottom Institute of Archeology, Beijing. **29** Sichuan Provincial Antiquities Committee. **31** Capital Museum, Beijing. **32** Shaanxi Provincial Museum. **36** Shandong Museum. **37** left Shanghai Museum. **37** right Sen-Oku Hakko Kan (Sumitomo Collection). **39** XNA. **41** Hubei Provincial Museum. **42** American Numismatic Society. **43** Shanghai Museum. **50** Hubei Provincial Museum (XNA - Photo: Li Jilu). **54** left Jingzhou Museum. **54** right Jingzhou Museum. **55** Hubei Provincial Museum. **61** Shaanxi Provincial Museum. **62** RH. **64** BL. **66** Hebei Provincial Museum. **68** Metropolitan Museum of Art, Gift of J. Pierpont Morgan, 1917. **72** left Chinese Cultural Center, San Francisco. **72** right Metropolitan Museum of Art, Rogers Fund, 1917. **76** top Christie's Colour Images. **76** corners XNA. **78** National History Museum, Taiwan. **80** Werner Forman Archive. **82** top Gansu Provincial Museum. **82** bottom Royal Tomb Museum, Taiwan. **83** Yunan Provincial Museum. **88** bottom Hunan Provincial Museum. **88-9** Nanjing Museum. **94** CHM. **97** Museum of Fine Arts, Boston. Gift of Mrs Scott Fitz (22.407). Gift of Edward Jackson Holmes in memory of his mother, Mrs W. Scott Fitz (47.1407-12). **101** Patricia Buckley Ebrey. **105** CHM. **106** Ingrid Morejohn. **107** top left Ingrid Morejohn **109** *China Cultural Relics* magazine. **112** RH (Photo: G.P. Corrigan). **113** Kyoto National Museum. **115** Art Institute of Chicago. Gift of Mrs Pauline Palmer Wood, 1970.1073. **116** XNA. **117** David Kemp (artwork). **119** CHM. **122** Ann Paludan. **124** BL. **125** BL. **127** Shaanxi Provincial Museum. **130** British Museum, London. **134** Shōsō-in Treasure House. **139** Shanghai Museum. **140** NA (Purchase: Nelson Trust), 49-79. **142** Dingzhou Museum. **143** NPM. **145** Palace Museum, Beijing. **146-7** Cleveland Museum of Art, John L. Severance Fund, 77.5. **148** Palace Museum, Beijing. **149** Ying Chih Wen Thu Chu. **151** Liaoning Museum. **152-3** Metropolitan Museum of Art, Gift of the Dillon Fund, 1973. **154** NPM. **156** FGA. **157** FGA. **162** NPM. **163** top NPM. **162-3** bottom Cleveland Museum of Art, Purchase from the J.H. Wade Fund, 33.220. **165** Royal Geographical Society. **166** Museum of Fine Arts, Boston. William Sturgis Bigelow Collection by exchange. **170** Bibliothèque Nationale, Paris. **176** *Orientations* magazine. **177** NA (Purchase: Nelson Trust), 48-5. **178** FGA. **181** NPM. **184** NPM. **188-9** Art Institute of Chicago. **191** NPM. **193** RH. **198** Yurinkan Museum, Kyoto. **199** NA (Purchase: Nelson Trust), 46-48. **200** NPM. **204** Museum für Ostasiatische, Cologne. Inv. no. R62 1 (18) (Photo: Rheinisches Bildarchiv, Cologne). **208** Michael Nichols/Magnum Photos. **210-11** Historiographical Institute, University of Tokyo. **211** bottom Philadelphia Museum of Art. Given by John T. Dorrance. **217** BL. **218** M. Medley. **219** top Henan Provincial Museum. **219** bottom Percival David Foundation. **222** Musée Guimet, Paris (ET Archive). **225** Metropolitan Museum of Art, Purchase, the Dillon Fund Gift, 1986 (1986.206). **226** CHM. **228** Bibliothèque Nationale, Paris. **230** XNA. **231** Sen-Oku Hakko Kan (Sumitomo Collection). **234** PE (Photo: Mark Sexton). **237** National Maritime Museum (ET Archive). **244** Private collection (ET Archive). **251** Peter Wee, Katong Antique House, Singapore. **252** Library of Congress. **254** FGA. **255** Hulton Deutsch Collection Ltd. **256** top Library of Congress. **256** bottom Library of Congress. **259** top BL. **259** bottom PE. **260** Photographic Archives of the Arnold Arboretum. ©The President and Fellows of Harvard College (Photo: E.H. Wilson). **261** top PE. **261** bottom PE. **266** top XNA. **266** bottom Hulton Deutsch Collection Ltd. **267** BL. **269** top XNA. **269** bottom BL. **274** bottom Museum of Revolutionary History, Beijing. **275** Popperfoto. **276** Ringart Collection. **277** Range/Bettmann/UPI. **280** Henri Cartier-Bresson/Magnum Photos. **283** Sam Tata/Batsford Publishing. **284** BL. **288** XNA. **289** XNA. **292** left Patricia Buckley Ebrey. **292** right Christie's Colour Images. **293** top Museum of Fine Arts, Boston. Gift of Madam Fan Tchum-pi and her sons. **293** bottom Sotheby's, Hong Kong. **296** XNA. **299** XNA. **300** René Burri/Magnum Photos (Paris). **309** Lois Wheeler Snow. **310-11** XNA. **314** XNA **315** Camera Press, London. **317** Harry Redl/Black Star. **318** Sally and Richard Greenhill. **319** Kubota/Magnum Photos. **320** Camera Press, London. **322** top Dr G. Gerster, ©1995, Comstock. **322** bottom BL. **323** T.S. Lam/World & I. **324** Popperfoto. **325** British Film Institute. **326** left Popperfoto. **326** right Associated Press Photos. **327** Chris Stowers/Panos Pictures. **330** Cary Sol Wolinsky/Trillium Stock, Nowell, Mass.

Notes

Credit is given here to quotations from other scholars' works, primarily their translations from Chinese sources. When no credit is given for a translation, it is by the author, sometimes previously published in her *Chinese Civilization: A Sourcebook*, rev. ed. (New York: The Free Press, 1993).

Chapter 1
box, 'Ancestors' 'Take me as a substitute . . .' trans. by James Hart, in Patricia Buckley Ebrey, ed. *Chinese Civilization: A Sourcebook*, rev. ed. (New York: The Free Press, 1993), p. 6.

Chapter 4
'ensure that no land . . .' Mark Elvin, *The Pattern of the Chinese Past* (Stanford: Stanford University Press, 1973), p. 48, modified.

'Those who rejoice . . .' Wm. Theodore de Bary, et al., ed. *Source of Chinese Tradition* (New York: Columbia University Press, 1960), p. 321, modified.

Picture Spread, Early Buddhist Art. "The gold and the flowers . . . from W. J. F. Jenner, *Memories of Loyang: Yang Hsüan-chih and the lost capital (493-534)* (Oxford: Clarendon Press, 1981), p. 208.

Chapter 5
'for the superior . . .' Peter Bol, *'This Culture of Ours': Intellectual Transitions in T'ang and Sung China* (Stanford: Stanford University Press, 1992), p. 26.

Chapter 6
Marco Polo, 'I tell you that this river . . .' A.C. Moule and Paul Pelliot, trans., Marco Polo, *The Description of the World* (London: Routledge, 1938), I, 320, modified.

Marco Polo, 'Anyone seeing such a multitude . . .' Moule and Pelliot, I, 329, modified.

Chapter 7
Marco Polo, 'All the Cathaians detested the rule of the great khan . . .' Moule and Pelliot, I, 215, modified.

Chapter 8
Taizu, "In the morning I punish a few . . . trans. by Lily Hwa in Patricia Buckley Ebrey, ed. *Chinese Civilization: A Sourcebook*, rev. ed. (New York: The Free Press, 1993), p. 207.

'When they capture a Chinese . . .' Frederic Mote, The Cheng-hua and Hung-chih reigns, 1465-1505,' in *The Cambridge History of China*, vol 7, *The Ming Dynasty 1368-1644* (Cambridge: Cambridge University Press, 1988), p. 383-4.

Wang Yangming, 'Instituting direct civil administration . . .' Herold J. Wiens, *Han Chinese Expansion in South China* (New Haven: The Shoe String Press, 1967), p. 219, modified.

Matteo Ricci, 'the exceedingly large numbers . . .' Louis J. Gallagher, *China in the Sixteenth Century: The Journals of Matteo Ricci, 1595-1610* (New York: Random House, 1953), p. 20-21.

Lü Kun, 'when tenants ask for help,' Johanna F. Handlin, *Action in Late Ming Thought: The Reorientation of Lü Kun and Other Scholar-Officials* (Berkeley: University of California Press, 1983), p.24.

'Old Skymaster . . .' Mi Chu Wiens, 'Masters and Bondservants: Peasant Rage in the Seventeenth Century,' *Ming Studies* 8 (1979):57-64, quote 63.

Verbiest, 'the seven wonders of the world . . .' Arthur Waldron, *The Great Wall of China: From History to Myth* (Cambridge: Cambridge University Press, 1990), p. 206.

Photo Spread, caption, 'If the painted decoration . . ." Robert Tichane, *Ching-te-chen: Views of a Porcelain City*. (New York State Institute for Glaze Research, 1983), p. 142, modified.

Chapter 9
Qianlong, 'we possess all things . . .' Harley Farnsworth MacNair, *Modern Chinese History: Selected Readings* (Shanghai: Commercial Press, 1927), p. 4.

Lin Zexu, 'Suppose there were people . . .' Ssu-yu Teng and John K. Fairbank, *China's Response to the West: a Documentary Survey 1839-1923* (New York: Antheum, 1971), p. 26.

Woren, 'From ancient down to modern times, . . .' Teng and Fairbank, p. 76, modified.

'The foreigners have been aggressive . . .' Victor Purcell, *The Boxer Uprising, A Background Study* (Cambridge: Cambridge University Press, 1963), p. 225, modified.

Long passage from *The Dream of Red Mansions*, from Daniel Hawkes, *The Story of the Stone*

(Penguin Books), I, pp. 465-67.

Chapter 10
Zou Rong, 'wipe out the five million barbarian Manchus . . .' Michael Gasster, 'The Republican Revolutionary Movement,' *Cambridge History of China*, vol. 11 part 2 *Late Ch'ing* (Cambridge: Cambridge University Press, 1980), p. 482.

Chen Duxiu, 'Youth is like early spring . . .' Chow Tse-tsung, *The May Fourth Movement: Intellectual Revolution in Modern China* (Stanford: Stanford University Press, 1967), pp. 45-46.

'We must be thoroughly aware . . .' Lin Yü-sheng, *The Crisis in Chinese Consciousness: Radical Antitraditionalism in the May Fourth Era* (Madison: University of Wisconsin Press, 1979), p. 76.

John Dewey, 'There seems to be no country . . .' cited in Chow, p. 183.

'militarize the life of the people . . .' Jonathan D. Spence, *The Search for Modern China* (New York: Norton, 1990), p. 415.

Tawney, 'In some districts . . .' R.H. Tawney, *Land and Labor in China* (Boston: Beacon Press, 1932), p. 77.

Song Qingling, 'If we do not grant . . .' Anna Louise Strong, *China's Millions* (New York: Coward-McCann, 1928), p. 125.

'Under the Nationalists . . .' Edward Friedman, Paul G. Pickowics, and Mark Selden, *Chinese Village, Socialist State* (New Haven: Yale University Press, 1991), p. 41.

'Wiping Out the Reds – A Great Spectacle,' from Lu Xun, *Selected Works*, trans. Yang Xianyi and Gladys Yang (Beijing: Foreign Languages Press, 1956), III, 45-47, slightly modified.

picture spread, Modern Chinese Painting, 'Chinese ink painting . . .' Chu-tsing Li, *Trends in Modern Chinese Painting* (Ascona, Switzerland: Artibus Asiae, 1979), p. 131 modified.

Chapter 11
'Communism is heaven . . .' Friedman et al., p. 218.

'Compel the government . . .' Orville Schell, *Mandate of Heaven* (New York: Simon and Schuster, 1994), p. 103.

Further Reading

Readers who would like to learn more about the **main themes** of Chinese civilization would do well to read another general overview of Chinese history, such as Ray Huang's lively, interpretive *China: a Macro History* (Armonk, N. Y.: M. E. Sharpe, 1988), John K. Fairbank's *China: A New History* (Cambridge, Mass.: Harvard University Press, 1992), with its frequent references to recent scholarship, or Jacques Gernet's solid *A History of Chinese Civilization* (Cambridge: Cambridge University Press, 1989), which is particularly strong on the premodern period and China's connections to the outside world. Conrad Schirokaur's *A Brief History of Chinese Civilization* (New York: Harcourt Brace Jovanovich, 1991) is a popular and balanced textbook. For premodern China, Charles Hucker's *China's Imperial Past* (Stanford: Stanford University Press, 1975), provides broad coverage of arts and literature in addition to politics and institutions. For modern China, a concise interpretation is offered by John K. Fairbank, *The Great Chinese Revolution* (New York: Harper and Row, 1987); for a fuller yet still very readable narrative, see Jonathan Spence's *The Search for Modern China* (New York: Norton & Company, 1990). Political history is covered in the greatest detail in the multi-volume, multi-authored *The Cambridge History of China* (Cambridge: Cambridge University Press), 15 volumes to date, with more to come. Paul S. Ropp's edited volume, *Heritage of China: Contemporary Perspectives on Chinese Civilization* (Berkeley: University of California Press, 1990), offers readers essays on religion, thought, family, art, and other topics. For translations of Chinese writings providing insights into Chinese society and culture see Patricia Ebrey's *Chinese Civilization: A Sourcebook* (New York: The Free Press, 1993).

For the best single-volume **reference work** offering quick access to topics concerning contemporary and historical China, see Brian Hook and Denis Twitchett, eds., *The Cambridge Encyclopedia of China*, 2nd ed. (Cambridge: Cambridge University Press, 1991). Of similar value are the entries on China topics in the *Encyclopedia of Asian History*, ed. Ainslie T. Embree (New York: Scribner's, 1988). For provincial and city maps, as well as physical geography, populations, climate, and economic conditions, see *The Times Atlas of China*, P. Geelan and Denis Twitchett, eds. (London: Times Books, 1974). For historical maps and well-illustrated topical essays, see Caroline Blunden and Mark Elvin, *Cultural Atlas of China* (New York: Facts on File, 1983). For current scholarship on all aspects of Chinese history, society, and culture, consult the Association for Asian Studies' annual *Bibliography of Asian Studies*. See also the China section of the American Historical Association's *Guide to Historical Literature* (1994). For literature, see the *Indiana Companion to Traditional Chinese Literature*, William H. Nienhauser, Jr., ed. (Bloomington: Indiana University Press, 1986), which contains a wealth of information on fiction, drama, and poetry, with detailed entries on specific authors and titles.

Broad interpretations of **social and economic history** can be found in Kang Chao's *Man and Land in Chinese History: An Economic Analysis* (Stanford: Stanford University Press, 1986); Mark Elvin's *The Pattern of the Chinese Past* (Stanford: Stanford University Press, 1973), and Lloyd Eastman's *Family, Field, and Ancestors: Constancy and Change in China's Social and Economic History, 1550–1949* (New York: Oxford University Press, 1988). Food, not an insignificant facet of economic and cultural history, is dealt with in both E.N. Anderson's *The Food of China* (New Haven: Yale University Press, 1988); and K.C. Chang, ed., *Food in Chinese Culture: Anthropological and Historical Perspectives* (New Haven: Yale University Press, 1977).

Broad surveys of **institutional history** include two studies of law and penal institutions, T'ung-tsu Ch'ü's *Law and Society in Traditional China* (Paris: Mouton, 1961) and Geoffrey MacCormack's, *Traditional Chinese Penal Law* (Edinburgh: Edinburgh University Press, 1990). On **foreign relations**, see *The Chinese World Order*, ed. John K. Fairbank (Cambridge: Harvard University Press, 1968), and John K. Fairbank, *The United States and China*, 4th ed. (Cambridge: Harvard University Press, 1983). China's relations with northern neighbours is covered in Owen Lattimore's *Inner Asian Frontiers of China*, 2nd ed. (New York: American Geographical Society, 1951); now partially superseded by Sechin Jagchid and Van Jay Symons, *Peace, War and Trade along the Great Wall: Nomadic Chinese Interaction through Two Millennia* (Bloomington: Indiana University Press, 1989). For military history, see *Chinese Ways in Warfare*, eds. Frank A. Kierman, Jr. and John K. Fairbank (Cambridge: Harvard University Press, 1974).

The history of the Chinese **family and kinship** systems are dealt with in Patricia Ebrey and James Watson, eds., *Kinship Organization in Late Imperial China, 1000–1940* (Berkeley: University of California Press, 1986); and Rubie Watson and Patricia Ebrey, eds., *Marriage and Inequality in Chinese Society* (Berkeley: University of California Press, 1991). The classic study of Chinese lineages in Fujian and Guangdong provinces is Maurice Freedman's *Lineage Organization in Southeastern China* (London: Athlone Press, 1965). Two edited volumes look specifically at the lives of **women** in varied time periods: see Richard Guisso and Stanley Johannesen, eds., *Women in China: Current Directions in Historical Scholarship* (Youngstown, NY: Philo Press, 1981); and Margery Wolf and Roxanne Witke, eds., *Women in Chinese Society* (Stanford: Stanford University Press, 1975). Wolf's *Women and the Family in Rural Taiwan* (Stanford: Stanford University Press, 1972) is especially valuable for its attention to the ways women view the family differently than men. A more demographic approach to women's lives is offered by Arthur P. Wolf and Huang Chieh-shan's *Marriage and Adoption in China, 1845–1945* (Stanford: Stanford University Press, 1980).

Intellectual history is thoroughly surveyed by Fung Yu-lan's *A History of Chinese Philosophy*, Derk Bodde, trans. (Princeton: Princeton University Press, 1983). William Theodore DeBary, Wing-tsit Chan, and Burton Watson's *Sources of Chinese Tradition*, 2 vols. (New York: Columbia University Press, 1960, 1964) provides introductions to and selections from the works of the key thinkers in Chinese history. Several symposium volumes show the diversity of Confucianism; see David Nivison and Arthur Wright, eds., *Confucianism in Action* (Stanford: Stanford University Press, 1959); Arthur Wright, ed., *The Confucian Persuasion* (Stanford: Stanford University Press, 1960); and Arthur Wright and Denis Twitchett, eds., *Confucian Personalities* (Stanford: Stanford University Press, 1962). Two broad-ranging analyses of Confucianism by an influential interpreter are *The Liberal Tradition in China* (New York: Columbia University Press, 1983) and *The Trouble with Confucianism* (Cambridge: Harvard University Press, 1991), both by Wm. Theodore de Bary.

For the history of Chinese **science**, the standard work is the encyclopedic, many-volumed survey *Science and Civilization in China*, by Joseph Needham and co-workers (Cambridge: Cambridge University Press, 1954–). For Chinese **historiography and historical thought**, see W. G. Beasley and E. B. Pulleyblank, eds., *Historians of China and Japan* (Oxford: Oxford University Press, 1961). For overviews of Chinese **religion**, see Daniel Overmyer, *Religions of China: The World as a Living System* (New York: Harper and Row, 1986); or Laurence G. Thompson, *Chinese Religion: An Introduction* (Belmont, Calif.: Wadsworth, 1988).

Many fine surveys of **art and literature** are available, including Laurence Sickman and Alexander Soper, *The Art and Architecture of China* (New York: Penguin Books, 1978); and Jessica Rawson, ed., *The British Museum Book of Chinese Art* (London: British Museum Press, 1992). The best general survey of Chinese painting remains James Cahill's *Chinese Painting* (New York: Skira/Rizzoli, 1985). *The Chinese Garden: History, Art and Architecture* (New York: Rizzoli, 1978), by Maggie Keswick and Charles Jencks can also be recommended. A handy survey of Chinese **literature**, with extensive quotations, is Wu-chi Liu's *An Introduction to Chinese Literature* (Bloomington: Indiana University Press, 1966). A good selection of literature in translation can be found in Cyril Birch, ed., *Anthology of Chinese Literature*, 2 vols. (New York: Grove Press, 1965, 1972). For poetry, a good place to start is Stephen Owen's *Traditional Chinese Poetry and Poetics: Omens of the World* (Madison: University of Wisconsin Press, 1985). For an introduction to Chinese linguistics, see S. Robert Ramsey, *The Languages of China* (Princeton: Princeton University Press, 1987).

Besides these broad-ranging books covering long time spans, there are hundreds of excellent books covering limited epochs. For the **ancient period**, a good place to begin is with the writings of archaeologist K.C. Chang, most notably *The Archeology of Ancient China*, 4th ed. (New Haven: Yale University

Press, 1986); *Shang Civilization* (New Haven: Yale University Press, 1986); and *Art, Myth, and Ritual: The Path to Political Authority in Ancient China* (Cambridge: Harvard University Press, 1983). For a comparative perspective on prehistory and the ancient period, see Gina L. Barnes, *The Rise of Civilization in East Asia* (London: Thames and Hudson, 1993). For more detailed analyses, see David N. Keightley, ed., *The Origins of Chinese Civilization* (Berkeley: University of California Press, 1983); Cho-yun Hsu and Katheryn Linduff, *Western Chou Civilization* (New Haven: Yale University Press, 1988); and Xueqin Li, *Eastern Zhou and Qin Civilizations*, K.C. Chang, trans. (New Haven: Yale University Press, 1985), all of which make extensive use of archaeological discoveries. Sarah Allan examines Shang cosmology and Zhou myths in *The Shape of the Turtle: Myth, Art, and Cosmology in Early China* (Albany: State University Press of New York, 1991). For ancient art and technology, see the lavishly illustrated *Great Bronze Age of China: An Exhibition from the People's Republic of China*, Wen Fong, ed. (New York: Metropolitan Museum of Art, 1980); Jessica Rawson, *Ancient China: Art and Archeology* (London: British Museum, 1980); and William Watson, *Cultural Frontiers in Ancient East Asia* (Edinburgh: Edinburgh University Press, 1971).

The intellectual flowering of the **Warring States** period provided the foundation of Chinese thought for centuries to come. Excellent overviews can be found in A.C. Graham's *Disputers of the Tao: Philosophical Argument in Ancient China* (La Salle, IL: Open Court, 1989); Benjamin Schwartz's *The World of Thought in Ancient China* (Cambridge: Harvard University Press, 1985); and more briefly, in F. W. Mote's *Intellectual Foundations of China* (New York: McGraw Hill, 1989). James Legge did a complete translation of *The Chinese Classics*, 5 vols. (Hong Kong: Hong Kong University Press, 1960) in the nineteenth century. More recent translators include D.C. Lau and Burton Watson. Lao translated *Confucius: The Analects* (Baltimore: Penguin, 1979); the *Tao Te Ching: Chinese Classics* (Hong Kong: Chinese University Press, 1982); and *Mencius* (Baltimore: Penguin, 1970). Watson has published *The Tso Chuan: Selections from China's Oldest Narrative History* (New York: Columbia University Press, 1989); *The Complete Works of Chuang Tzu* (New York: Columbia University Press, 1968); the *Basic Writings of Mo Tzu, Hsun Tzu, and Han Fei Tzu* (New York: Columbia University Press, 1967). For military thinking, see *Sun-tzu: The Art of War*, translated by Roger T. Ames (New York: Ballantine Books, 1993).

The best study of the **Qin period** remains Derk Bodde's *China's First Unifier: A Study of the Ch'in Dynasty As Seen in the Life of Li Ssu* (Leiden: E.J. Brill, 1938). Good studies of the **Han period** include Ying-shih Yu's *Trade and Expansion in Han China: A Study in the Structure of Sino-barbarian Economic Relations* (Berkeley: University of California Press, 1967); Michael Loewe's *Everyday Life in Early Imperial China During the Han Period, 202 BC – AD 220*, rep. ed. (London: Carousel Books, 1973); Michele Perazzoli-t'Serstevens' *The Han Dynasty*, Janet Seligman, trans. (New York: Rizzoli, 1982); as well as essays in Etienne Balazs' *Chinese Civilization and Bureacracy: Variations on a Theme*, H.M. Wright, trans. (New Haven: Yale University Press, 1964). Other aspects of social and cultural life can be found in T'ung-tsu Ch'ü, *Han Social Structure* (Seattle: University of Washington Press, 1972); Cho-yun Hsu, *Han Agriculture: The Formation of the Early Chinese Agrarian Economy (206 BC – AD 220)* (Seattle: University of Washington Press, 1980); and Hung Wu, *The Wu Liang Shrine: The Ideology of Early Chinese Pictorial Art* (Stanford: Stanford University Press, 1989). For religion, see Michael Loewe's *Chinese Ideas of Life and Death: Faith, Myth, and Reason in the Han Period (202 BC – AD 220)* (London: George Allen and Unwin, Ltd., 1982).

Several biographies offer readers more personal glimpses of Chinese society during Han times, especially Burton Watson's *Ssu-ma Ch'ien: Grand Historian of China* (New York: Columbia University Press, 1958); and Nancy Lee Swann's *Pan Chao, Foremost Woman Scholar of China, First Century AD: Background, Ancestry, Life, and Writings of the Most Celebrated Chinese Woman of Letters* (New York: Century, 1932). Ronald Miao introduces the reader to the world of poetry in *Early Medieval Chinese Poetry: The Life and Verse of Wang Ts'an (AD 177–217)* (Wiesbaden: Steiner, 1982). Han view of their own history can be sampled in Burton Watson's translations *Records of the Grand Historian of China*, 2 vols. (New York: Columbia University Press, 1961) and *Courtier and Commoner in Ancient China: Selections from the "History of the Former Han"* (New York: Columbia University Press, 1974).

Current scholarship on the turbulent **Age of Division** after the fall of the Han can be sampled in Albert Dien's edited volume, *State and Society in Early*

Medieval China (Stanford: Stanford University Press, 1990). Also recommended is Arthur Wright's gracefully-written *The Sui Dynasty* (New York: Alfred A. Knopf, 1978). Ssu-yu Teng's translation of Yen Zhitui's *Family Instructions of the Yen Clan* (Leiden: E.J. Brill, 1968) provides a view of social life and cultural values in the sixth century, as does W.J.F. Jenner's *Memories of Lo Yang: Yang Hsuan-chih and the Lost Capital (493–534)* (Oxford: Oxford University Press, 1981). Biographies of literary figures offer important insights into cultural and intellectual developments of the period. See John Frodsham's *The Murmuring Stream: The Life and Works of the Chinese Poet Hsieh Ling-yün (385–433)*, *Duke of K'ang-lo* (Kuala Lumpur: University of Malay Press, 1967); Richard Mather's *The Poet Shen Yüeh (441–513): The Reticent Marquis* (Princeton: Princeton University Press, 1988); and John Marney's *Liang Chien-wen Ti* (Boston: Twayne Publishers, 1976).

The best short introduction to the topic of **Buddhism** in China remains Arthur Wright's brief *Buddhism in Chinese History* (Stanford: Stanford University Press, 1959). Much more thorough is the fascinating, highly scholarly study by Erik Zurcher, *The Buddhist Conquest of China: The Spread and Adaptation of Buddhism in Early Medieval China* (Leiden: E.J. Brill, 1959). See also Kenneth Ch'en's *The Chinese Transformation of Buddhism* (Princeton: Princeton University Press, 1973). Edwin O. Reischauer provides a glimpse into social and cultural aspects of Tang Buddhism in his translation, *Ennin's Diary: The Record of a Pilgrimage to China in Search of the Law*, and the companion volume, *Ennin's Travels in T'ang China* (both New York: Ronald Press, 1955). See also Jacques Ternet, *Buddhism in Chinese Society: An Economic History from the Fifth to the Tenth Centuries* (New York: Columbia University Press, 1995).

Diverse aspects of the **Tang period** are explored in two collections of essays, Arthur Wright and Dennis Twitchett, eds., *Perspectives on the T'ang* (New Haven: Yale University Press, 1973); and John Curtis Perry and Bardwell Smith, eds., *Essays on T'ang Society: The Interplay of Social, Political, and Economic Forces* (Leiden: E.J. Brill, 1976). On Tang rulership, see Howard J. Wechsler, *Mirror to the Son of Heaven: Wei Cheng at the Court of T'ang T'ai-tsung* (New Haven: Yale University Press, 1974). A history of public finance and economic conditions is offered by Denis Twitchett in *Financial Administration under the T'ang Dynasty* (Cambridge: Cambridge University Press, 1970). R.W.L. Guisso analyses the career of China's only empress in *Wu Tse-t'ien and the Politics of Legitimization in T'ang China* (Bellingham, Washington: Western Washington University, 1978). On the Tang State see also Edwin G. Pulleyblank's *The Background of the Rebellion of An Lu-shan* (London: Oxford University Press, 1955) and David McMullen's meticulously documented *State and Scholars in T'ang China* (Cambridge: Cambridge University Press, 1988).

For an introduction to Tang poetry, see Stephen Owen's *The Great Age of Chinese Poetry: the High T'ang* (New Haven: Yale University Press, 1981); or one of the many biographies of Tang poets, such as William Hung's *Tu Fu: China's Greatest Poet* (Cambridge: Harvard University Press, 1952); Arthur Waley's *The Life and Times of Po Chu-i, 772–846 AD* (London: George Allen & Unwin, 1949); or Charles Hartman's *Han Yü and the T'ang Search For Unity* (Princeton: Princeton University Press, 1985).

Probably the best general introduction to the **Song period** is Jacques Gernet's *Daily Life in China on the Eve of the Mongol Invasion, 1250–76*, H. M. Wright, trans. (Stanford: Stanford University Press, 1962). For biographies of prominent Song figures, see Herbert Franke, ed., *Sung Biographies* (Wiesbaden: Franz Steiner Verlag, 1976). The flourishing economy of the Song is analysed in Shiba Yoshinobu's *Commerce and Society in Sung China*, Mark Elvin, trans. (Ann Arbor: The University of Michigan Center for Chinese Studies, 1970). Song foreign relations are covered in the symposium volume edited by Morris Rossabi, *China among Equals: The Middle Kingdom and Its Neighbors* (Berkeley: University of California Press, 1983). The classic study of Song government is Edward Kracke, Jr.'s *Civil Service in Sung China: 960–1076* (Cambridge: Harvard University Press, 1953, 1968). More recently John Chaffee brilliantly analysed the expansion of the examination system in *The Thorny Gates of Learning in Sung China: A Social History of Examinations* (Cambridge: Cambridge University Press, 1985). Lin Yutang's biography of the literary figure Su Shi, *The Gay Genius: The Life and Times of Su Tungpo* (New York: John Day, 1947) remains valuable, despite its bias against Wang Anshi. For more balanced coverage see James T.C. Liu, *Reform in Sung China: Wang An-Shih (1021–1086) and His New Policies* (Cambridge: Harvard University Press, 1957); and Paul Smith's *Taxing Heaven's Storehouse: Bureaucratic Entrepreneurship and the Sichuan Tea and Horse Trade, 1074–1224* (Cambridge:

Council on East Asian Studies, Harvard University, 1991). Brian McKnight's *Law and Order in Sung China* (Cambridge: Harvard University Press, 1992) describes in detail both the police system and the penal institutions involved in catching and punishing criminals.

The intellectual shifts from Tang to Song associated with neo-Confucianism are analysed in Peter Bol's *'This Culture of Ours': Intellectual Transitions in T'ang and Sung China* (Stanford: Stanford University Press, 1992). For Song intellectual history, see also A.C. Graham, *Two Chinese Philosophers: Ch'eng Ming-tao and Ch'eng Yi-ch'uan* (London: Lund Humphries, 1958); and Hoyt Tillman, *Confucian Discourse and Chu Hsi's Ascendancy* (Honolulu: University of Hawaii Press, 1992). For translations of neo-Confucian texts, see *Reflections on Things at Hand: The Neo-Confucian Anthology Compiled by Chu Hsi and Lü Tsu-ch'ien*, Wing-tsit Chan, trans. (New York: Columbia University Press, 1967); and *Learning to Be a Sage: Selections from Conversations of Master Chu, Arranged Topically*, Daniel K. Gardner, trans. (Berkeley: University of California Press, 1990). For Song poetry see Jonathan Chaves, *Mei Yao-ch'en and the Development of Early Sung Poetry* (New York: Columbia University Press, 1976).

On the emergence of the scholar-official elite in Song times, see Robert P. Hymes, *Statesmen and Gentlemen: The Elite of Fu-chou, Chiang-hsi, in Northern and Southern Sung* (Cambridge: Cambridge University Press, 1986). For other topics in Song social history, see Valerie Hansen's study of popular religion, *Changing the Gods in Medieval China, 1127–1276* (Princeton: Princeton University Press, 1990); Richard von Glahn's study of frontier expansion, *The Country of Streams and Grottoes: Expansion and Settlement, and the Civilizing of the Sichuan Frontier in Song Times* (Cambridge: Harvard University Press, 1987), and Patricia Ebrey's studies of family and marriage, *The Inner Quarters: Marriage and the Lives of Chinese Women in the Song Period* (Berkeley: University of California Press, 1993) and *Family and Property in Sung China: Yuan Ts'ai's Precepts for Social Life* (Princeton: Princeton University Press, 1984).

Coverage of the **Conquest Dynasties** is almost as rich as for the Song. The Liao dynasty founded by the Khitans is the subject of the large and fully documented study by Karl Wittfogel and Chia-sheng Feng, *History of Chinese Society: Liao (907–1125)* (Transactions of the American Philosophical Society, n.s. 36). The major authority on the Jin period is Jing-shen Tao. See his *The Jurchen in Twelfth-Century China: A Study of Sinicization* (Seattle: University of Washington Press, 1976). Morris Rossabi provides a lively account of the life of one of the most important Yuan rulers in *Khubilai Khan: His Life and Times* (Berkeley: University of California Press, 1988). Readers can get a more personal glimpse into the times in *The Travels of an Alchemist* (London: Routledge and Keegan Paul, 1931), Arthur Waley's translation of the diary of a traveller to Ghengis Khan's camp. The authoritative translation of Marco Polo's diary is A. C. Moule and P. Pelliot, *Marco Polo: The Description of the World* (London: G. Routledge and Sons Ltd, 1938). Further information into social, cultural, as well as political aspects of Yuan history can be found in John D. Langlois Jr.'s edited volume, *China Under Mongol Rule* (Princeton: Princeton University Press, 1981).

For Chinese culture during the Yuan period, see Hok-lam Chan and Wm. Theodore deBary, eds., *Yuan Thought: Chinese Thought and Religion Under the Mongols* (New York: Columbia University Press, 1982), and J. I. Crump's *Chinese Theater In the Days of Kublai Khan* (Tucson: University of Arizona Press, 1980). Two important works covering the art of the era are Sherman Lee and Wai-kam Ho's *Chinese Art Under the Mongols: The Yüan Dynasty (1279–1368)* (Cleveland: The Cleveland Museum of Art, 1968); and James F. Cahill's *Hills Beyond a River: Chinese Painting of the Yuan Dynasty, 1279–1368* (New York: Weatherhill, 1976).

The transition from the Yuan to the **Ming** is covered through the life of one literati in Frederick W. Mote's work *The Poet Kao Ch'i, 1336–1374* (Princeton: Princeton University Press, 1962); and through those close to the throne in John Dardess's *Confucianism and Autocracy: Professional Elites in the Founding of the Ming Dynasty* (Berkeley: University of California Press, 1983). An accessible introduction to Chinese society and government in Ming times is Ray Huang's *1597, A Year of No Significance: The Ming Dynasty in Decline* (New Haven: Yale University Press, 1981). Other worthy studies of Ming politics include Charles O. Hucker's *The Censorial System of Ming China* (Stanford: Stanford University Press, 1966); and Arthur Waldron's *The Great Wall of*

China: From History to Myth (Cambridge: Cambridge University Press, 1990). Two important studies of elite mobility from Ming times through the end of the Qing are Ping-ti Ho's *The Ladder of Success in Imperial China* (New York: Columbia University Press, 1962); and Hilary Beattie's *Land and Lineage in China: A Study of T'ung-ch'eng County, Anhwei, in the Ming and Ch'ing Dynasties* (Cambridge: Cambridge University Press, 1979). For an analysis of the rural economy over the period, see Evelyn Rawski's *Agricultural Change and the Peasant Economy of South China* (Cambridge: Harvard University Press, 1972).

Important recent studies of Ming culture include Cynthia Brokaw's *The Ledgers of Merit and Demerit: Social Change and Moral Order in Late Imperial China* (Princeton: Princeton University Press, 1991); and Craig Clunas's *Superfluous Things: Material Culture and Social Status in Early Modern China* (Urbana: University of Illinois Press, 1992). See also David Johnson, Andrew Nathan, and Evelyn Rawski, eds., *Popular Culture in Late Imperial China* (Berkeley: University of California Press, 1985), for essays on both Ming and Qing culture. The diversity of Ming intellectual life is amply demonstrated in Wm. Theodore deBary's edited volume, *Self and Society in Ming Thought* (New York: Columbia University Press, 1970). Wei-ming Tu examines the early life of one of the Ming's most influential thinkers in *Neo-Confucian Thought in Action: Wang Yang-ming's Youth (1472–1509)* (Berkeley: University of California Press, 1976). See also Wing-tsit Chan's translation of Wang Yang-Ming's *Instructions for Practical Living and Other Neo-Confucian Writings* (New York: Columbia University Press, 1963).

The development of the **novel** in the Ming is masterfully analyzed by Andrew Plaks in *The Four Masterworks of the Ming Novel* (Princeton: Princeton University Press, 1987). For translations see Luo Guanzhong's *Three Kingdoms: A Historical Novel*, Moss Roberts, trans. (Berkeley: University of California Press, 1991); and *Outlaws of the Marsh*, Sidney Shapiro, trans. (Bloomington: Indiana University Press, 1981). Biographies of late Ming cultural figures include K'ang-i Sun Chang's *The Late-Ming Poet Ch'en Tzu-lung* (New Haven: Yale University Press, 1991); Willard Peterson's *Bitter Gourd: Fang I-chih and the Impetus for Intellectual Change* (New Haven: Yale University Press, 1979); and Wang Fangyu, Richard Burnhart, and Judith Smith, eds., *Master of the Garden: The Life and Art of Bada Shanren* (New Haven: Yale University Press, 1990). For biographies of other important individuals during the Ming Dynasty, including both Chinese and foreigners, see L. Carrington Goodrich and Fang Chaoying, eds., *Dictionary of Ming Biography, 1368–1644* (New York and London: Columbia University Press, 1976). The history of Ming painting is covered by James Cahill in two works, *Painting at the Shore: Chinese Painting of the Early and Middle Ming Dynasty, 1368–1580* (New York: Weatherhill, 1978); and *The Distant Mountains: Chinese Painting of the Late Ming Dynasty, 1570–1644* (New York: Weatherhill, 1982).

The fall of the Ming is the central issue in Jonathan Spence and John Wills's edited volume, *From Ming to Ch'ing: Conquest, Region, and Continuity in Seventeenth-Century China* (New Haven: Yale University Press, 1979). The efforts of the Ming princes to restore their rule is dealt with in detail by Lynn Struve in *The Southern Ming, 1644–1662* (New Haven: Yale University Press, 1984). The turbulent seventeenth century is seen from the perspective of a fascinating man of letters in Chun-shu Chang and Shelley Hsueh-lun Chang, *Crisis and Transformation in Seventeenth-Century China: Society, Culture, and Modernity in Li Yu's World* (Ann Arbor: University of Michigan Press, 1991), and Patrick Hanan, *The Invention of Li Yu* (Cambridge: Harvard University Press, 1988).

The best introductions to the **Qing period** are probably Frederic Wakeman's survey, *The Fall of Imperial China* (New York: Free Press, 1975); and *Chinese Society in the Eighteenth Century* by Susan Naquin and Evelyn Rawski (New Haven: Yale University Press, 1987). Jonathan Spence offers a glimpse of the Kangxi emperor through his own words in *Emperor of China: Self Portrait of K'ang Hsi* (New York: Knopf, 1974). Philip Kuhn examines the relationship between popular culture and the bureaucracy during the Qianlong reign in *Soulstealers: The Chinese Sorcery Scare of 1768* (Cambridge: Harvard University Press, 1990). The eighteenth century campaign to suppress anti-Manchu writings is studied by L. Carrington Goodrich in *The Literary Inquisition of Ch'ien-lung* (Baltimore: Waverly Press, 1935). Harold Kahn provides an subtle analysis of the Qianlong emperor's personal self-image in *Monarchy in the Emperor's Eyes: Image and Reality in the Ch'ien-lung Reign* (Cambridge: Harvard University Press, 1971). Arthur W. Hummel's *Eminent Chinese of the Ch'ing Period (1644–1912)*, 2 vols. (Washington, D.C.: U.S. Government Printing

Office, 1943) contains over eight hundred biographies of important Chinese, Manchus, and Mongols.

Insight into Qing society can be found from reading Jonathan Spence's *The Death of Woman Wang* (New York: Viking, 1978), Arthur Waley's biography, *Yuan Mei, Eighteenth Century Chinese Poet* (New York: Grove Press, 1956); Evelyn Rawski's *Education and Popular Literacy in Ch'ing China* (Ann Arbor: University of Michigan Press, 1978); and Djang Chu's translation of Liu-Hung Huang's *A Complete Book Concerning Happiness and Benevolence: A Manual for Local Magistrates in Seventeenth-Century China* (Tuscon: University of Arizona Press, 1984). Derk Bodde and Clarence Morris reveal much about Chinese society through their translation of legal cases in *Law in Imperial China: Exemplified by 190 Ch'ing Dynasty Cases* (Cambridge: Cambridge University Press, 1967). On cities in Qing times, see G. William Skinner, ed., *The City in Late Imperial China* (Stanford: Stanford University Press, 1977), as well as two volumes by William Rowe, *Hankow: Commerce and Society in a Chinese City, 1796–1889* and *Hankow: Conflict and Community in a Chinese City, 1796–1895* (Stanford: Stanford University Press, 1984 and 1989).

Readers interested in Qing intellectual and cultural history should see Benjamin Ellman, *From Philosophy to Philology: Intellectual and Social Aspects of Change in Late Imperial China* (Cambridge: Council of East Asian Studies, Harvard University, 1984); and Kai-wing Chow, *The Rise of Confucian Ritualism in Late Imperial China: Ethics, Classics, and Lineage Discourse* (Stanford: Stanford University Press, 1994). An excellent biography is *The Life and Thought of Chang Hsüeh-ch'eng (1738–1801)* by David S. Nivison (Stanford: Stanford University Press, 1966). Contact with European ideas and religion is sophisticatedly analyzed by Jacques Gernet in *China and the Christian Impact: A Conflict of Cultures* (Cambridge: Cambridge University Press, 1985). The place of painting in High Qing culture is analyzed in Ju-hsi Chou and Claudia Brown, eds., *The Elegant Brush: Chinese Painting Under the Qianlong Emperor, 1735–1795* (Phoenix: Phoenix Art Museum, 1985). China's greatest novel is available in an excellent translation by David Hawkes and John Minford, *The Story of the Stone (Dream of the Red Chamber)*, 5 vols. (Hardmonsworth: Penguin, 1973–1982). Another important and entertaining eighteenth century novel is *The Scholars*, Yang Hsien-yi and Gladys Yang trans. (Beijing: Foreign Languages Press, 1973).

Rebellions and their suppression are central to many studies of the **nineteenth century**. See Susan Naquin, *Millenarian Rebellion in China: The Eight Trigrams Uprising of 1813* (New Haven: Yale University Press, 1976); Philip Kuhn, *Rebellion and Its Enemies in Late Imperial China* (Cambridge: Harvard University Press, 1970); Franz Michael and Chung-li Chang, *The Taiping Rebellion*, 3 vols. (Seattle: University of Washington Press, 1966–1971); and Elizabeth Perry, *Rebels and Revolutionaries in North China, 1845–1945* (Stanford: Stanford University Press, 1980), which emphasizes the connection between environment and rebellion.

Contact with the West has been studied in at least as much detail as rebellions. For good overviews see Jerome Chen's *China and the West: Society and Culture, 1815–1937* (Bloomington: Indiana University Press, 1979); and *The Outsiders* by Rhoads Murphey (Ann Arbor: University of Michigan Press, 1977). Jonathan Spence's *To Change China: Western Advisors in China, 1620–1960* (Boston: Little, Brown; 1969), describes the experiences of some of the most prominent foreign advisors. For Chinese who went abroad, see David Arkush and leo Lee, *Land Without Ghosts* (Berkeley: University of California Press, 1989). For the beginning of the treaty port system, see Peter Fay Ward's *The Opium War, 1840–1842* (Chapel Hill: North Carolina Press, 1975); and Arthur Waley's *The Opium War through Chinese Eyes* (Stanford: Stanford University Press, 1968). The economic impact of the encounter with western imperialism is treated in Hou Chi-ming's *Foreign Investment and Economic Development in China, 1840–1937* (Cambridge, Mass: Harvard University Press, 1965), a controversial analysis which asserts that because foreign trade and investment were crucial to the modernization of the Chinese economy, they should not be regarded as imperialistic. Two works that deal specifically with the relationship between the Chinese and Christian missionaries are Paul Cohen's *China and Christianity: The Missionary Movement and Growth of Chinese Anti-Foreignism, 1860–1870* (Cambridge: Harvard University Press, 1963); and Jane Hunter's *The Gospel of Gentility: American Missionary Women in Turn of the Century China* (New Haven: Yale University Press, 1984), which deals more specifically with the nature of the missionary impact on Chinese women.

The concerns of leading intellectuals at the end of the nineteenth century and beginning of the twentieth are analyzed in Hao Chang, *Chinese Intellectuals in Crisis: Search for Order and Meaning (1890–1911)* (Berkeley: University of California Press, 1987). See also studies of particular thinkers, including Benjamin Schwartz, *In Search of Wealth and Power: Yen Fu and the West* (Cambridge: Harvard University Press, 1964); Paul Cohen, *Between Tradition and Modernity: Wang Tao and Reform in Late Ch'ing China* (Cambridge: Harvard University Press, 1974); Kung-chuan Hsiao, *A Modern China and a New World: K'ang Yu-wei, Reformer and Utopian, 1858–1927* (Seattle: University of Washington Press, 1975); and Hao Chang, *Liang Ch'i-ch'ao and Intellectual Transition in China, 1890–1907* (Cambridge: Harvard University Press, 1971).

On the boxers, see Joseph W. Esherick, *The Origins of the Boxer Uprising* (Berkeley: University of California Press, 1987). The subsequent decade and the collapse of the monarchical system is considered in Mary Wright's edited volume, *China in Revolution: The First Phase, 1900–1913* (New Haven: Yale University Press, 1968);and Joseph Esherick's *Reform and Revolution in China: The 1911 Revolution in Hunan and Hubei* (Berkeley: The University of California Press, 1976). See also Harold Schiffrin's *Sun Yat-sen: Reluctant Revolutionary* (Boston: Little, Brown, 1980). For a different perspective on the changing culture at the end of the century, see Dan J. Cohn, ed., *Vignettes From the Chinese: Lithographs from Shanghai in the Late Nineteenth Century* (Hong Kong: Research Center for Translation, Chinese University of Hong Kong, 1987), which looks at newspaper illustrations; and Colin Mackerras's *The Chinese Theatre in Modern Times: From 1840 to the Present Day* (Amherst: University of Massachusetts Press, 1975). Ida Pruitt's *A Daughter of Han: the Autobiography of a Chinese Working Woman* (Stanford: Stanford University Press, 1967), offers the reader a glimpse into a segment of Chinese society rarely depicted in books.

The **Republican period** is ably surveyed in James Sheridan's *China in Disintegration: The Republican Era in Chinese History, 1912–1949* (New York: Free Press, 1975). Andrew Nathan analyzes the skewed politics of the early Republic in *Peking Politics, 1918–1923: Factionalism and the Failure of Constitutionalism* (Berkeley: University of California Press, 1976). An analysis of the political situation of the warlord era is provided by Chi Hsi-sheng in *Warlord Politics in China, 1916–1928* (Stanford: Stanford University Press, 1976). The politics of the Nationalists and Chiang Kai-shek are given unfavorable reviews in Lloyd Eastman's influential *The Abortive Revolution: China Under Nationalist Rule, 1927–1937*, rev. ed. (Cambridge: Council on East Asian Studies, Harvard University, 1990) and *Seeds of Destruction: Nationalist China in War and Revolution, 1937–1949* (Stanford: Stanford University Press, 1984). Two works discuss the first United Front between the Nationalists and the Communists (1922–1927): Harold R. Issacs' *The Tragedy of the Chinese Revolution*, rev. ed. (Stanford: Stanford University Press, 1951); and Dan N. Jacobs' biography of the top Soviet advisor to Sun Yat-sen, *Borodin: Stalin's Man in China* (Cambridge, Mass: Harvard University Press, 1981). For the Nationalists' efforts to take control of Shanghai, see Frederic Wakeman, Jr., *Policing Shanghai 1927–1937* (Berkeley: University of California Press, 1995). For the life of Chiang Kai-shek see Brian Crozier's accessible biography, *The Man Who Lost China: The First Full Biography of Chiang Kai-shek* (New York: Schribners, 1976).

The major intellectual changes of the **May Fourth era** are ably analyzed in Tse-tsung Chow's *The May Fourth Movement: Intellectual Revolution in Modern China* (Cambridge: Harvard University Press, 1960); Leo Lee, *The romantic Generation of Chinese Writers* (Cambridge: Harvard University Press, 1973); Lin Yü-sheng, *The Crisis of Chinese Consciousness: Radical Antitraditionalism in the May Fourth Era* (Madison: University of Wisconsin Press, 1979); and Vera Schwarz, *The Chinese Enlightenment: Intellectuals and the Legacy of the May Fourth Movement of 1919* (Berkeley: University of California Press, 1986). Min-chih Chou deals with one of the foremost intellectuals of the time in *Hu Shih and Intellectual Choice in Modern China* (Ann Arbor: University of Michigan Press, 1984). Jonathan Spence's *The Gate of Heavenly Peace: The Chinese and Their Revolution, 1895–1980* (New York: The Viking Press, 1981) chronicles the life experiences of many of the key intellectuals of the twentieth century, including the May Fourth generation. Not all intellectuals of the period welcomed the new currents; for conservative reactions, see Charlotte Furth, ed., *The Limits of Change: Essays on Conservative Alternatives in Republican China* (Cambridge: Harvard University Press, 1976); Guy Alitto, *The Last Confucian: Liang Shu-ming and the Chinese Dilemma of Modernity* (Berkeley: University of California Press, 1979).

As an overview, C.T. Hsia's *A History of Modern Chinese Fiction* (New Haven: Yale University Press, 1971) has not yet been surpassed. On writers of the period, see Ou-Fan Lee, ed., *Lu Xun and His Legacy* (Berkeley: University of California Press, 1985); and Olga Lang, *Pa Chin and His Writings: Chinese Youth Between the Two Revolutions* (Cambridge: Harvard University Press, 1967). For translations, see *The Collected Works of Lu Xun* (or some other selection of stories). Pa Chin, *Family*, Sydney Shapiro, trans. (New York: Anchor Books, 1972), Lao She's *Rickshaw*, Jean James, trans. (Honolulu: University of Hawaii Press, 1979); and Tani Barlow and Gary Bjorge, eds., *I Myself Am A Woman: Selected Writings of Ding Ling* (Boston: Beacon Press, 1989).

For an interesting biography of one of the most popular Peking Opera stars, see A.C. Scott's *Mei Lan-Fang: Leader of the Pear Garden* (Hong Kong: Hong Kong University Press, 1959). Upper class life in the same period is depicted in Ida Pruitt's *Old Madame Yin: A Memoir of Peking Life, 1926–1938* (Stanford: Stanford University Press, 1979). Six hundred important individuals from the 1912–1949 era are given brief biographies in Howard L. Boorman and Richard C. Howard's *Biographical Dictionary of Republican China*, 4 vols. (New York: Columbia University Press, 1967–77). Additionally, Donald W. Klein and Anne B. Clark's *Biographic Dictionary of Chinese Communism 1921–1965*, 2 vols. (Cambridge, Mass: Harvard University Press, 1971) has entries for people prominent from the founding of the Chinese Communist Party up until the Cultural Revolution.

Transformations of the rural **economy** are analyzed by Ramon Myers *The Chinese Peasant Economy: Agricultural Development in Hopei and Shantung, 1890–1949* (Cambridge, Mass: Harvard University Press, 1970); and by Philip Huang in two books, both of which cover longer time spans, *The Peasant Economy and Social Change in North China* and *The Peasant Economy and Rural Development in the Yangzi Delta, 1350–1988* (Stanford: Stanford University Press, 1985 and 1990). The industrial and commercial economy are analyzed in Lillian Li, *China's Silk Trade: Traditional Industry in the Modern World, 1842–1937* (Cambridge: Harvard University Press, 1981); Sherman Cochran, *Big Business in China: Sino-Foreign Rivalry in the Cigarette Business, 1890–1930* (Cambridge: Harvard University Press, 1980); and Parks M. Coble, *The Shanghai Capitalists and the Nationalist Government, 1927–1937*, 2nd. ed. (Cambridge: Harvard University Press, 1986). The lives of urban factory workers are documented in Gail Hershatter's *Workers of Tianjin, 1900–1949* (Stanford: Stanford University Press, 1986); and Emily Honig's *Sisters and Strangers: Women in the Shanghai Cotton Mills, 1919–1949* (Stanford: Stanford University Press, 1986). For a more general analysis by an economist, see Thomas Rawski, *Economic Growth in Prewar China* (Berkeley: University of California Press, 1989).

The rise to power of the **Communist Party** is examined by Arif Dirlik, *The Origins of Chinese Communism* (New York: Oxford University Press, 1989), Mark Selden, *The Yenan Way in Revolutionary China* (Cambridge: Harvard University Press, 1971); and Suzanne Pepper in *Civil War in China: The Political Struggle, 1945–1949* (Berkeley: University of California Press, 1978). Two first hand accounts offer unique and exciting glimpses into the period. Edgar Snow covers the experiences of the Communists, especially of Mao Zedong, to the mid 1930s in *Red Star Over China* (New York: Random House, 1938. Reprint, New York: Grove Press, 1968) and Jack Belden reports on the civil war in *China Shakes the World* (New York: Monthly Review Press, 1970). William Hinton documents the effects of the numerous political movements on the residents of one rural village in *Fanshen: A Documentary of Revolution in a Chinese Village* (New York: Monthly Review Press, 1966).

An excellent narrative history of the **post-1949 period** is Maurice Meisner's *Mao's China and After: A History of the People's Republic*, rev. ed. (New York: Free Press, 1986). For the life of Mao, see Ross Terrill's *Mao: A Biography* (New York: Harper and Row, 1980). Ezra Vogel examines Communist policies at the local level in *Canton Under Communism: Programs and Politics in a Provincial Capital, 1949–1968* (Cambridge: Harvard University Press, 1980). Vivienne Shue looks at policies concerning rural China in *Peasant China in Transition: The Dynamics of Development Toward Socialism, 1949–1956* (Berkeley: University of California Press, 1980). On state organization during the Mao period, see Harry Harding, *Organizing China: The Problem of Bureaucracy, 1949–1976* (Stanford: Stanford University Press, 1981) and Victor Li's *Law Without Lawyers* (Boulder: Westview Press, 1978). Readers interested in economic development would do well to begin with Carl Riskin's *China's Political Economy: The Quest for Development Since 1949* (Oxford: Oxford University Press, 1987); see also

Dorothy J. Solinger, *Chinese Business under Socialism: The Politics of Domestic Commerce 1949–1980* (Berkeley: University of California Press, 1984). One of the most devastating critiques of the Maoist system is provided by Edward Friedman, Paul Pickowicz, Mark Selden, and Kay Ann Johnson in *Chinese Village, Socialist State* (New Haven: Yale University Press, 1991), which follows one village in north China from the late 1930s through the early 1960s.

First hand accounts and oral histories abound for life in recent China. Changes of the 1960s and 1970s are examined from the perspective of local leadership in Shu-min Huang's *The Spiral Road: Change in a Chinese Village Through the Eyes of a Communist Party Leader* (Boulder: Westview Press, 1989). Other personal views of Chinese life can be found in Michael Frolic's *Mao's People: Sixteen Portraits of Life in Revolutionary China* (Cambridge: Harvard University Press, 1980); Jung Chang, *Wild Swans: Three Daughters of China* (New York: Simon & Schuster, 1991); and Zhang Xinxin and Sang Ye, *Chinese Lives: An Oral History of Contemporary China* (New York: Pantheon Books, 1987). More analytical treatments of social change are presented by William Parish and Martin Whyte in *Village and Family in Contemporary China* (Chicago: University of Chicago Press, 1978) and *Urban Life in Contemporary China* (Chicago: University of Chicago Press, 1984). See also Anita Chan, Richard Madesen, and Jonathan Unger, *Chen Village: The Recent History of a Peasant Community in Mao's China*, 2nd ed. (Berkeley: University of California Press, 1984).

Good first hand accounts of the Cultural Revolution include Gao Yuan, *Born Red: A Chronicle of the Cultural Revolution* (Stanford: Stanford University Press, 1987); Yue Daiyun with Carolyn Wakeman, *To The Storm: The Odyssey of a Revolutionary Chinese Woman* (Berkeley: University of California Press, 1985); Liang Heng and Judith Shapiro, *Son of the Revolution* (New York: Vintage Press, 1983); and Nien Cheng, *Life and Death in Shanghai* (New York: Grove Press, 1986). Anne Thurston examines the negative effects of the movement in *Enemies of the People: The Ordeal of Intellectuals in China's Great Cultural Revolution* (Cambridge: Harvard University Press, 1988).

Readers interested in the **culture** of the PRC and its relation to the state can turn to Ellen Laing, *The Winking Owl: Art in the People's Republic of China* (Berkeley: University of California Press, 1988); Merle Goldman, *Literary Dissent in Communist China* (Cambridge: Harvard University Press, 1967), which looks at writers of the 40s and 50s; Bonnie McDougall, ed., *Popular Chinese Literature and Performing Arts in the People's Republic of China, 1949–1979* (Berkeley: University of California Press, 1984); Paul Clark, *Chinese Cinema: Culture and Politics Since 1949* (Cambridge: Cambridge University Press, 1987); and two books by Richard Kraus, *Pianos and Politics in China: Middle-class Ambitions and the Struggle Over Western Music* (New York: Oxford University Press, 1990) and *Brushes with Power: Modern Politics and the Chinese Art of Calligraphy* (Berkeley: University of California Press, 1991).

Post-Mao changes are considered in Ezra Vogel's *One Step Ahead in China: Guangdong Under Reform* (Cambridge: Harvard University Press, 1989); Orville Schell's *Discos and Democracy: China in the Throes of Reform* (New York: Anchor Books, 1989); and James Lull's *China Turned On: Television, Reform, and Resistance* (London: Routledge, 1991). The fate of women under the CCP is considered in Margery Wolf's *Revolution Postponed: Women in Contemporary China* (Stanford: Stanford University Press, 1985); and Gail Hershatter and Emily Honig in *Personal Voices: Chinese Women in the 1980's* (Stanford: Stanford University Press, 1988). Readers interested in the recent democracy movement can turn to Han Minzhu, ed., *Cries For Democracy: Writings and Speeches from the 1989 Chinese Democracy Movement* (Princeton: Princeton University Press, 1990); Liu Binyan in collaboration with Ruan Ming and Xu Gang, *"Tell the World": What Happened in China and Why*, Henry L. Epstein, trans. (New York: Pantheon Books, 1989); Lee Feigon, *China Rising: The Meaning of Tiananmen* (Chicago: Ivan Dee, 1990); and Jeffrey N. Wasserstrons and Elizabeth J. Perry, eds., *Popular Protest and Political Culture in Modern China: Learning from 1989* (Boulder: Westview, 1992). Two well-written journalists' accounts of China from 1989 to 1993 are Nicholas Kristof and Sheryl WuDunn, *China Wakes: The Struggle for the Soul of a Rising Power* (New York: Random House, 1994) and Orville Schell, *The Mandate of Heaven* (New York: Simon and Schuster, 1994).

Index